A Futile and Stupid Gesture

How Doug Kenney and *National Lampoon* Changed Comedy Forever

Josh Karp

T0155354

CHICAGO
REVIEW
PRESS

The Library of Congress has cataloged the hardcover edition as follows:

Karp, Josh.
    A futile and stupid gesture : how Doug Kenney and National lampoon changed comedy forever / Josh Karp.
        p.   cm.
    Includes bibliographical references and index.
    ISBN 1-55652-602-4
        1. National lampoon—History.   2. Kenney, Douglas C.   3. Period-ical editors—United States—Biography.   4. Comedians—United States—Biography.   5. American wit and humor—20th century—History and criticism.   6. United States—Intellectual life—20th century.   I. Title.

PN4900.N324K37 2006
070.5'72092—dc22   2006002981

Interior design: Pamela Juárez

All excerpts from *National Lampoon* magazine are courtesy of National Lampoon, Inc.

Judith Bruce grants permission to reprint the personal letter to her from Doug Kenney.

Quoted material that appears on p. xi reprinted with permission of Simon & Schuster Adult Publishing Group from *West of Then* by Tara Bray Smith. Copyright ©2004 by Tara Bray Smith.

Quoted material that appears on p. 22 reprinted with permission by Seven Locks Press from *Running from America: The Poems and Plays of Timothy Mayer*. Copyright ©1991 by Timothy Mayer, edited by Paul Schmidt.

Quoted material that appears on p. 41 from *Here Is New York* reprinted by permission of International Creative Management, Inc. Copyright © 1949 by E. B. White.

First edition
Published by Chicago Review Press, Incorporated
814 North Franklin Street
Chicago, Illinois 60610
ISBN 978-1-55652-762-3
Printed in the United States of America

For Douglas Clark Kenney
and Mary Jordan Karp—
two gentle souls.
May they be at peace.

Contents

Acknowledgments

The creation of this book involved the collaboration, time, talent, and patience of more people than I could ever hope to thank in a list that covers less ground than the many volumes tracking the life of Lyndon Baines Johnson. Thus, any individuals excluded from this brief list should know that their efforts are deeply appreciated.

Though over a hundred individuals were interviewed for the book, I would like to single out the following: Chris Miller, who served as my introduction to Doug Kenney and the people of *National Lampoon*; Michael Simmons, a good friend who was invaluable at several critical junctures; illustrator Rick Meyerowitz, who drew a fabulous cover and e-mailed with me about anything and everything; Sean Kelly, who made me laugh like no one else; Private Ollie Hallowell of Milton Academy and Harvard; S. Roger Cox; and Thom Mount, my resource for all things Hollywood.

Alex Garcia-Mata and Kathryn Walker for their willingness to discuss their relationships with Doug with honesty. I thank them both for their patience with my endless questions.

P. J. O'Rourke stands out for his thoughtfulness and candor in a situation where he had little to gain from his participation. With maturity and self-knowledge, he viewed the world of *National Lam-*

poon in the 1970s with as much objectivity as possible. For that I am indebted to him.

I would also like to thank: Judith Bruce; Robert Hoffman; Chris Cerf; Rusty Lemorande; Trevor Albert; Don MacDonald; Michael O'Keefe; Chevy Chase; Peter Kleinman; Laila Nabulsi; Brian McConnachie; Ellis Weiner; Jaime Wolf at Pelosi, Wolf, Effron and Spates; Dan Laikin at *National Lampoon*; Craig Lambert of *Harvard Magazine*; Kate Meyers; Danny Abelson; Meghan Snyder; and Lucy Fisher.

Dennis Perrin, who helped me in more ways than I can mention and is my brother in the Lampoon bio fraternity; Michael Wilde, whose insight and structural analysis opened new doors for me; Rebecca Little, who took my vague direction and came back with more information than I dreamed of; my agent, Leslie Breed (who sold it), and Cynthia Sherry at Chicago Review Press (who bought it), for their enthusiasm for this book and its subject—which speaks nothing of their patience with my missed deadlines and other travails.

At Chicago Review Press: Lisa Rosenthal, for her wonderful editing, sense of humor, and ability to understand both the material and my long explanations of fairly straightforward questions; managing editor Gerilee Hundt; production editor Allison Felus; copyeditor Brooke Kush; interior designer Pamela Juárez; and everyone else who made everything happen.

Thanks also to Mark Simonson (proprietor of marksverylarge. com, the definitive Lampoon Web site) and Joe Paulino—two Lampoon fans who helped me immensely, especially with unearthing difficult to find articles, tapes, and other ephemera. Scott Lax, my tour guide in Chagrin Falls; Mike Gerber, who discussed Doug Kenney, *National Lampoon*, and American humor with me at lengths and to depths for which both of us should be forced to enter a twelve-step program; David Standish, who introduced me to Chris Miller and helped me learn how to write good; and the esteemed Bill Zehme.

Finally, I must thank a group of friends and family, without whom, for various reasons, I'd either not be here, be less happy, or wouldn't have anyone to e-mail or live with. My oldest friend, Dan Stein; Pete Smith; Evan Kraus; Jimmy Carrane and the 2005 Chicago

White Sox; my in-laws, John and Ro McLaughlin, and their children Shamus, Kate (and Frank), and Clancy; my father, Jack Karp, who taught me the value of the written word, and my mother, Betsy Karp, who demonstrated how far determination can take a human being; my brother, Jeremy, with whom I share much; my three sons, Will, Leo, and Teddy, who provide joy, chaos, and love in equal parts.

And last, thank you to my wife, Susan, my muse, whose love, sense of humor, and beauty are more than I could have wished for.

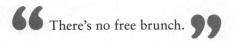 There's no free brunch.

—*Doug Kenney*

* * *

OTTER: I think that this situation absolutely requires a really futile and stupid gesture be done on somebody's part.

BLUTO: We're just the guys to do it.

* * *

[T]he sense of uncertainty plus the possibility afforded by this country, by its natural wealth, and by its growing, by the diversity of its regions and its people, made for the need of humor which would, first allow us to deal with the unexpected; and second allow us to adjust to one another in our diversity. The northerner found the southerner strange. The southerner found the northerner despicable. The blacks found the whites peculiar. The whites found the blacks ridiculous. And you know how it goes. Some agency had to be adopted which would allow us to live with one another without destroying one another, and the agency was laughter—was humor . . . if you can laugh at me, then you don't have to kill me. If I can laugh at you, I don't have to kill you.

—*Ralph Ellison*

Introduction

Midas at the Marmont

" Tourists came and went and did what they pleased. They got stuck in mountaintops and in blowholes; they fell down cliffs and waterfalls; were stung by all manner of creatures; burned preposterously; they fell on lava rocks and got lost in caves and floated off to sea. Better to pay as little attention to them as possible. "

—West of Then, *Tara Bray Smith's memoir of growing up in Hawaii*

The Chateau Marmont is where *Rebel Without a Cause* director Nick Ray simultaneously gave romantic chase to both Natalie Wood and James Dean. It is where Liz Taylor set up the penthouse as a convalescent home where Montgomery Clift could recover from a car accident. It was the Marmont where Jim Morrison injured his back one addled evening while trying to swing—via drainpipe—from the roof into the open window of his hotel room.

The Marmont is, simply put, the kind of place Doug Kenney loved, with the right combination of rock 'n' roll atmosphere and elegant Old Hollywood nostalgia that he ate up. It was symbolic of all that he adored and disdained about the particular slice of Americana that is Los Angeles. And it was the Marmont where he asked his friend Laila Nabulsi to meet him one summer day in 1978.

Eight years earlier, Doug was a twenty-three-year-old Harvard grad from the prosaically named town of Chagrin Falls, Ohio, embarking on a risky proposition with an unlikely crew: the creation of a national humor magazine. At this he succeeded beyond anyone's expectations, pulling together the angst and weirdness of 1970s America and weaving it into a wide-ranging publication that ran the gamut from fart jokes to highly literate parodies of *Finnegan's Wake*, from comic photo layouts of nude women to incisive satire about the My Lai massacre. Seemingly overnight, *National Lampoon* captured the ethos of the youth culture born after World War II, raised in Eisenhower's 1950s, and come of age in the late '60s. *National Lampoon* instinctively understood its generation's epic diversity, self-obsession, and ever-changing mores, mocking its peers, parents, and nearly everyone else. The magazine succeeded, in part, because of a genuine but difficult-to-quantify sense that the editors "got it"—and nobody "got it" better than Doug Kenney, who, by age thirty, was a millionaire three times over.

In the summer of 1978, Doug was in Los Angeles while Universal pictures prepared the release of *Animal House*—his first screenplay. Each morning Doug could rise, open the French doors of his Marmont suite, and look across Sunset Boulevard to see a gigantic billboard promoting the film's imminent appearance on movie screens. As with nearly everything he touched, it was an unprecedented success.

Doug Kenney was the golden boy of American comedy.

On that summer day in Los Angeles, Doug Kenney and Laila Nabulsi were just two young New Yorkers in the strange environs of Hollywood, meeting by a pool where gorgeous girls sunbathed without their bikini tops while someone held up a phone and screamed, "Louis Malle?! Is there a Louis Malle here?! Phone call for Louis Malle!"

Nabulsi found Doug, trim and blond in a Marmont bathrobe, sitting in a chaise longue. Open in his lap was a copy of Brooke Hayward's tragic Hollywood memoir *Haywire*, the story of life as the daughter of producer Leland Hayward and actress Margaret Sullivan, starring Pamela Churchill as the wicked stepmother and Henry Fonda as the ex-husband.

Looking up at Nabulsi, Doug reduced the aesthetic of the Marmont pool and Hollywood to one simple statement. "I'm thinking of changing my name to Charlton Hepburn," he said, smiling.

* * *

This was undoubtedly one of the happiest times in Doug Kenney's life. He was young and in love, wealthy beyond imagination, successful at nearly everything he touched, and uncorrupted creatively. Soon he would be known as the creator of Hollywood's most successful film comedy. Before long, the industry would offer him everything that it showers on bright young men who deliver financially or creatively. Doug had done both on his first try.

Two years later, Doug Kenney was found dead at the bottom of a cliff in Hawaii, broken of body and sunburned beyond recognition, identifiable only by his eyeglasses. Over the years, theories about Doug Kenney have taken diametrically opposed views of his life and death. Some believe his entire existence was a logical progression toward suicide, while others suggest that he probably enjoyed the view after falling accidentally. One magazine article concluded, metaphorically, that Doug had neither jumped nor fallen off that Hawaiian cliff. Perhaps he'd flown.

The truth, however, is not only somewhere in between, but around the margins, in the cracks, and everywhere else. Doug Kenney was a writer who fueled his life and work with colossal ambivalence, sensitivity, and a brain of untold capacities—never providing an easy answer for anything.

* * *

This is the story of Doug Kenney and *National Lampoon* during its most vibrant years. It is a story of laughter and tragedy; success and failure; love and hate; friendship and jealousy; ambivalence and clarity; exploding brains and falling off cliffs; middle America, Harvard, New York, and Hollywood; creative freedom and repression; baby boomers and the Greatest Generation; dying young and second acts; Jews, Catholics, WASPs, Brits, and Canadians; men and women; the rejection of societal institutions; and the pursuit of the American Dream.

Most of all, it is the story of a group of brilliant, overeducated skeptics and their leader, who came together by providence and changed the dialogue and content of American humor forever while paving the way for *Saturday Night Live*, the *Onion*, *The Simpsons*, and nearly everything funny that has happened since 1975—leaving a path littered with people laughing their asses off.

1

Hayley Mills in Pleasantville

66 Doug was Doris Day, a Coke and a hamburger. **99**

—National Lampoon *editor Brian McConnachie*

In the 1950s, Chagrin Falls, Ohio, was the kind of place where Americans believed that *Father Knows Best* patriarch Jim Anderson could raise Kitten, Bud, and Princess in a big fine home with total comfort and domestic bliss on an insurance agent's salary.

Chagrin Falls was a town where groceries were purchased at Greenway's or the A&P. Each fall, moms took their kids to Brewster and Church for school clothes and Brondfield's for new shoes, followed by a trip to the marble soda fountain at Standard Drug, where they washed down ten-cent burgers with the best lemon soda in the world. All the stores were closed on Wednesdays and on special occasions everyone dressed in church clothes for dinner at Crane's Canary Cottage.

1

When the blizzard of 1963 crippled Chagrin, local officials roped off one neighborhood so children could sled down Grove Hill onto Bell Street. During less extreme weather, winter meant skating on the frozen Chagrin River where adults kept a bonfire burning on the banks to warm little hands.

On Saturday mornings in the fall, the Chagrin Falls High School Tigers marching band tromped up East Washington Street to the Fairgrounds stadium, spreading school spirit through town while yards were raked and the sweet, smoky smell of burning leaves filled the air. It really was that kind of place.

"It was like Pleasantville," says Chagrin native Ginna Bourisseau. "I was four years old, walking two blocks to buy penny candy by myself. Everybody watched out for everybody's kids. That's how safe it was."

Being an adolescent in Chagrin meant worshipping the football players and hoping that someday "Firelord" would be listed among your accomplishments in the high school's Zenith yearbook. This coveted title mysteriously signified that you were one of the pranksters who burned the Tigers' winning score on an opposing team's football field in the dark of night, or anonymously painted black stripes on the Orange High School mascot. None of this was lost on Doug Kenney, who lived in Chagrin Falls from 1958 to 1964. His story neither begins nor ends in this midwestern town. Yet it is the place that defined him and by which he defined himself.

"I'm Doug Kenney from Chagrin Falls, Ohio."

It was that place in the middle of the country whose social dynamics, customs, and dreams so influenced and informed his sense of humor, self, and place in the world. It was a community that he came to remember with both great affection and profound alienation.

Despite his normal physical appearance, Doug Kenney was an outsider in Chagrin Falls—in and from the place, but not *of* it. Rather, he was a quiet observer, cloaked as a normal American kid, soaking in the rituals of prom, homecoming, and lusting aimlessly after the head cheerleader.

"We remember everybody, even if they only lived here for six months," says Jim Vittek, another Chagrin native. "We remember the way they kicked a soccer ball or threw a football. We remember where they sat in class."

Yet in Chagrin Falls, few remember Doug Kenney. It is as if he moved through town invisibly, leaving no fingerprints. They remember *The Carol Burnett Show*'s Tim Conway instead. He is Chagrin's favorite son.

* * *

Doug Kenney's story begins in Newport, Rhode Island, where in the 1920s and '30s his paternal grandfather, Daniel Kenney, was a tennis pro at the Newport Casino Club. Newport, as much as anyplace else, was home to this son of a vegetable cart operator whose parents emigrated from Ireland.

Daniel Kenney and his wife, Eleanor, had five children, the eldest being Doug's father, Daniel "Harry" Kenney, followed by Bill, Frank, Jack (who was killed in World War II), and a daughter, Margaretta. Harry was born in Massachusetts in 1915. The rest were born in Newport.

The Kenney family's existence was an itinerant one common to club pros of the time—the family usually left Newport the day after Thanksgiving for a winter of work in Palm Beach, Florida, and returned north on April 15 every year. Palm Beach was the winter home of Harold Vanderbilt, where Daniel and his sons taught tennis lessons for family and guests each day on specially built courts positioned to keep the noonday sun out of Mr. Vanderbilt's eyes, demonstrating for Harry precisely how the other half lived. In the fall, the Kenneys often found themselves at the Astor estate in Rhinebeck, New York, or Aiken, South Carolina—wherever the wealthy needed a pro to teach them the game. Arriving at either of these locations, Daniel bought the local paper, pulled out the home rental listings, and drove his family around looking for a place to live. They would never own a home.

In Newport, the Kenneys were regarded as the "first family of tennis," with each of Daniel's sons becoming pros and several uncles and cousins teaching professionally. One Kenney or another taught the game to Newport summer residents and wealthy vacationers like George Plimpton, Treasury Secretary C. D. Dillon, Jacqueline Bouvier, and her future husband, John F. Kennedy. Down in Palm Beach, it was more of the same, with Frank Kenney helping Woolworth heiress Barbara Hutton learn to serve and volley at an exclusive club, where the pair would have drinks while music wafted from the trees on warm winter afternoons and the sound of members shooting skeet on the beach could be heard in the distance.

Frank and Bill Kenney loved teaching tennis and the life it provided them. Neither man minded lower social status in a gilded world. It was all they knew and they embraced it. Their oldest brother felt differently.

Barely out of his teens, Harry taught tennis in Dark Harbor, Maine; Palm Beach; Newport; Hartford; Cleveland; Philadelphia; and elsewhere, yet he always wanted a different life, one more like the members than their servants. Harry wasn't happy-go-lucky like Frank, who was satisfied with his station in life and amused by the social fissures that placed him in the lesser economic class. By contrast, Harry was serious, ambitious, and aggressive at everything he did—on and off the court. He badly wanted an education. Brooding and quiet, he kept personal matters private. Teaching tennis was an existence Harry desperately wanted to escape.

"One day," Harry told Margaretta, "I'll never go in the back door again. Only the front."

In 1935, during a stint at the Hartford Country Club, Harry met eighteen-year-old Estelle "Stephanie" Karch, the daughter of an Eastern European immigrant iron forger from Chicopee, Massachusetts. Harry quickly learned that she was a good cook and fun to be around, with an unpretentious attitude, a great sense of humor, and an earthy manner. The pair married in Hartford on July 28, 1936, without the presence or knowledge of Harry's family. Yet when the Kenney clan met Stephanie, they loved her. It was hard not to.

Around the same time, Harry's forty-five-year-old father contracted pneumonia and died three days later with no life insurance and little money. Harry and his brother Bill were already out on their own, leaving Eleanor Kenney with three children to feed in Newport. Frank taught tennis to support the family and Harry sent his mother fifty dollars a month.

On July 21, 1939, Stephanie gave birth to a son they named Daniel Vance Kenney, known as Dan. Otherwise healthy, Dan was born with spina bifida, which required surgery and some stressful infant care. This often debilitating birth defect, however, seemed to have little impact on their firstborn, who grew into a handsome, gregarious child.

While he taught tennis all over the country, Harry was always in search of other work that would remove him from the servant class. In Hartford he joined the Governor's Guard, an elite group that protected and traveled with Connecticut's top official. In Reno he became a sheriff's deputy, and he did some personnel management for a magnesium mine in Las Vegas. While teaching in Philadelphia, Harry attended college, probably at night, and got the education he so desired.

Harry and Stephanie's second child, Douglas Clark Francis Kenney, was born in West Palm Beach, Florida, on December 10, 1946, nearly five years to the day after the Japanese bombed Pearl Harbor and America entered its defining war.

Born in a nation flush with patriotism from defeating evil, he was named for Douglas MacArthur, the legendary pipe-chomping five-star general who commanded the U.S. forces in Southeast Asia and received the formal Japanese surrender that effectively ended the war.

"I was a kind of monument to a general who brought us yellow imperialism," Doug told a reporter years later.

Doug was an uncommonly bright and sensitive child with atrocious eyesight. At the age of seven, Doug told a friend, Stephanie took him to an eye doctor for the first time. Fitted with his first pair of glasses, he recalled the drive home vividly, as every vein in every leaf seemed to be apparent from the backseat window of his mother's car; each blade of grass individual, distinct, and a rich, shimmering green. It was as if he were truly seeing the world for the first time—in Technicolor—in detail so intense that it gave him a headache.

"He was unique from birth," Victoria "Vicky" Kenney, Doug's younger sister by seven years, told *Harvard Magazine*.

In the early 1950s, the Kenneys settled in Mentor, Ohio, where Harry was a tennis pro at the Kirtland Country Club. Dan was a tall, charming boy at Riverside High School—admired by everyone who knew him. Harry and Stephanie, it seemed, couldn't get enough of their oldest child.

"Dan was really well liked by his parents," says family friend Bill Tienvieri. "I can see how Doug might have resented that a little."

If he did, however, it was hardly apparent, as Doug looked up to his all-American brother when he wasn't devouring books, radio, and comics. Filled with these images, Doug's overactive imagination kept him up late at night, unable to sleep for all the thoughts racing through his head.

Kid sister Vicky was a cute, pig-tailed blond, both very smart and very sweet. Doug adored her. The three children all filled familiar roles: Dan the family hero and golden boy; Doug the most sensitive, thoughtful, and eager-to-please child; and Vicky the mascot. They were, to all who knew them, a model midwestern, suburban family on an upward trajectory.

In the late 1950s, Harry moved the family to Chagrin Falls after a Kirtland member who sat on the board of Diamond Alkaloid in nearby Painesville recommended him for a job in the company's personnel department. Entering the corporate world, he finally left the servant class for good. Dan had just graduated from high school, Doug was twelve, and Vicky was five.

The Kenneys settled in a small ranch home on Bell Road in unincorporated South Russell (considered part of Chagrin Falls). Harry remained serious and quiet, and Stephanie was always charming, a quick-witted woman who loved a party. Their best friends in town were Don Martin, the new pro at Kirtland, and his wife, Ruth. By the time he was in high school, Doug would string rackets for Martin at Kirtland during the summer, soaking in, as Harry once had, the contrast between his life and that of the members.

In fall 1958, Dan headed to Kent State University where he became extremely popular, joined the Delta Tau Delta fraternity, and was known campus-wide as "Dan the Delt." Back in Chagrin Falls, Doug played the role of bookish, well-mannered little brother.

"Doug and I were friends during his brief stay in Chagrin Falls," says Tom Luckay. "We attended eighth grade together [at the Chagrin Falls junior high], and I remember him as a very intelligent and polite young man, which impressed my parents. I don't remember much about his sense of humor. I do remember that as suddenly as he emerged, he disappeared. . . . I may have been one of his only close friends during his stay in Chagrin Falls."

In junior high, Doug began to see that he possessed both an innate gift for humor and intellectual capabilities that exceeded those of his peers—and often his teachers. In the cafeteria, he rearranged the letters on the menu board to read "scrambled snails." In the classroom, he showed an aptitude for parroting the precise style, cadence, and expression of the writers he was asked to read. This took the form of papers about *Huckleberry Finn*, written in the manner of Twain, aping his voice and style. Teachers graded him up or down according to whether they thought he was a wiseass or a genius. Perhaps some of them didn't understand what he was doing. Nor, necessarily, did Doug, who may have simply channeled what he read into his writing without any preconceived plan.

During summer 1959, Dan Kenney's car overturned and he was rushed to the hospital, where doctors discovered serious problems with his bladder and kidneys, possibly stemming from his bout with spina bifida. Though he returned to Kent State that fall, joining the Phi Gamma Delta house and ROTC, Dan's diseased kidneys plagued him from that point forward, drawing even greater attention and affection from his parents.

Given Doug's facility with language and academic abilities, Harry and Stephanie concluded that they had "a winner" and offered him the choice for high school between the well-established and very preppy University School nearby or Gilmour Academy, a fifteen-year-old, all-boys, Catholic prep school in neighboring Gates Mill. Doug chose Gilmour.

"University School was full of WASPs and epitomized that culture," says Jim Schuerger, a Gilmour teacher who grew close to Doug and his family. "Doug would have pushed them beyond where he could indulge his wit."

Thus, on the 143-acre Gilmour campus, where the Holy Cross Brothers sought to create a disciplined environment for Catholic youth, Doug Kenney began to come out of his shell. Though neither loud nor boisterous, he was going through puberty and ready to discover his identity as a teenage boy—a smart, funny one.

* * *

Ivo Regan was known as "Mr. Gilmour." Given to wearing berets and leaning on a cane, he was the school's befrocked equivalent of Robin Williams in *Dead Poets Society*. Regan was an erudite, sophisticated, alcoholic, Holy Cross Brother from a shitty Nebraska cattle town, and likely a repressed homosexual. An extraordinary English teacher, Regan was tall, lean, intense, tortured, and explosive. Spencer Tracy's Father Flanagan he was not.

In fall 1960, Doug Kenney was a freshman assigned to Regan's English class, where the teacher frequently stood on the table to dramatically make a point and gave student assignments such as "five hundred words describing the inside of a ping-pong ball" that stopped most of them dead in their tracks.

On the first day of class, Regan asked students to write an essay from the perspective of an apple, describing life as a piece of fruit. Save Doug, it had the desired effect on the entire class, who returned with little more than some incoherent, fearful responses.

When the assignment came due, Regan went around the classroom asking each student to read his piece. Arriving at Doug, he was amazed to hear the skinny, bespectacled boy read a funny, insightful, and well-conceived essay from the perspective of a neurotic apple.

"I didn't even know what neurotic meant," recalls Doug's classmate John Mulligan.

Kenney and Regan became kindred spirits, a mentor and student who would walk across broken glass for each other. Admiring and identifying with the polite but rebellious fourteen-year-old, Regan sought to encourage, push, and protect Doug any way he could, all while exposing him to the wider world. Through Regan, Doug grew to love Graham Greene, Gerard Manley Hopkins, James Thurber, and particularly Evelyn Waugh, who would become his idol and against whose work he would one day measure his own. Moreover, Regan taught Doug how to use language economically and for maximum impact. Regan exposed Doug to the idea that the world was not as it appeared and that darkness coexisted with the light pervading the American landscape of Chagrin Falls. Though Doug had likely suspected this, it was not something that Harry or Stephanie was going to teach him. Yet it was squarely in keeping with the opposing forces that battled within his brain.

"There was a poem that Brother Ivo made a big deal out of when we were students at Gilmour," says Jerry Murphy, president of Doug's class. "It was 'Buffalo Bill's Defunct' [by e. e. cummings]. I recall the last line, 'how do you like your blueeyed boy Mister Death.'"

Beyond the academic teachings, however, Doug gained the respect, trust, and affection of an adult who could see that beneath his nerdy appearance and wiseass attitude was a kid with significant capabilities, sensitivity, and rebelliousness. Rather than destroy these qualities, Regan nurtured them, allowing Doug to see that he was a good, wise, and funny kid—and that that was enough.

Doug returned that appreciation the only way that a teenage boy can—he accepted Regan. Although Regan terrified most students with his explosive and dominating presence, in Doug he found a boy who saw through the bombast and into his tortured educator's soul.

"Doug wasn't scared of Ivo the way a limited kid might have been," says Gilmour teacher John Schubert.

Regan was not alone in realizing that Doug differed noticeably from the other kids at Gilmour.

"He was the most exceptional student I've ever taught English to," says teacher Jim Schuerger. "I may have met three or four people as smart as him during my entire life."

Doug read the encyclopedia for hours at a time and had a wide-ranging vocabulary that far exceeded those of his fellow students. Schuerger recalls that Doug sometimes mispronounced words that he'd never heard spoken at home, on the radio, or at the movies, but used them correctly in sentences and understood their meanings.

Schuerger, John Schubert, and fellow lay teacher John Gale admired Doug not only for his intellect, but also for his uncanny ability to rebel while dancing on the edge without crossing over the line. Other teachers who knew him less well saw that he was far too bright a boy to be contained within the narrow constructs of Gilmour.

"How long do you think we can keep him on our side?" a physics teacher asked Schuerger during Doug's first weeks at Gilmour.

Though he was well mannered, a subtle sense of danger emerged between Doug and the Holy Cross Brothers among the faculty.

"I think a lot of the teachers were frightened of him," says classmate Roger Cox. "He was a lot brighter than they were."

Cox's first impression of Doug was that he was "a doofus." While most students wore khakis and blue blazers to school, Doug wandered around in a green suit and porkpie hat "you'd find on Morey Amsterdam," Cox recalls. He wore his blond hair cut short and slicked across his forehead, and the thickest possible black-rimmed glasses.

"Nice green Cricketeer jumpsuit," Cox said to Doug.

From that beginning, the boys became friends. Doug, Cox soon saw, was an oddity—unlike the average, conformist fourteen-year-old, he wore strange clothes as protection. Protection from what, Cox had no idea. Soon he would realize that Doug was "the kindest, least pretentious, most brilliant guy. He got who I was right away."

Nearly everyone who encountered him throughout his life remembered Doug's ability to openly demonstrate empathy, understanding, and acceptance of others. From early on, he saw and expected the good in others and befriended almost anyone, finding something interesting in nearly everybody.

Yet Doug remained shy. Skinny and quiet in an intensely male environment and at a stage of life where pubescent posturing and sowing wild oats are rites of passage, he was not a jock and had no macho swagger. But like all teenage boys, he yearned to be one of the guys. In typical self-deprecating fashion, he was all too aware of who he was in that moment.

"I'm sort of like a male Hayley Mills," he told Jim Schuerger, who frequently drove Doug home from school.

During his freshman year, Doug began writing for the student newspaper and produced a funny and persuasive piece chiding his class for lack of school spirit. Within two weeks the freshmen responded by organizing a wide range of intramural activities and a cross-country race. When Doug didn't show, his friends tracked him down and tossed their amused and fully clothed classmate into a pool. Early on, the Gilmour class of 1964 recognized and appreciated Doug's talents.

At Gilmour, Doug made friends with all kinds of kids—the class president, the odd jock, wise guys, theater geeks, and nerds. Few grew close to him, but all admired his keen sense of humor and attitude toward authority.

Without fear, Doug pulled pranks for which he knew he'd be punished, once letting a parakeet out of its cage in a biology class run by an easily flustered Holy Cross Brother. For this offense he gladly accepted responsibility and took his paddling at the front of the classroom.

"He was a brave kid," says Gilmour classmate Jerry Murphy. "His sense of humor led him to do things that immediately landed him in hot water. Yet he persisted in doing these things."

One dour, compulsively organized Brother who taught religion wrote his lesson plan on the blackboard each day, line by line, in perfect parochial-school lettering. Walking in one afternoon, Doug saw the non-word *irregardless* in one of the ruler-straight sentences. Before the Brother entered the room, Doug calmly erased the *ir*. When the teacher noticed the correction, he became irate, demanding with a red face to know who had besmirched his tidy notes. Doug marched forward and took responsibility with a smile.

"Most of us never would have known that it wasn't a word," John Mulligan recalls.

Culturally, Doug was ahead of the curve. Beyond the latest music and pop culture, he had read the James Bond novels before they became films, was fascinated by the beatnik culture of Greenwich Village, and was perhaps the only student on campus who adored the writing of the eccentric, early twentieth-century British novelist

Ronald Firbank, whose *Concerning the Eccentricities of Cardinal Pirelli* opens with the cardinal christening a dog and ends when the cleric dies of a heart attack while chasing a choirboy around a cathedral in the buff.

During his junior year, Doug began defining himself less as an oddball and more as an outgoing, artistic young man. A member of the tennis team, he also continued to write for the school paper as well as a mimeographed humor magazine known as *The Hall Crier*. He won state championships in forensics and declamation, and starred in several school plays. As a senior he played Wagner in Marlowe's adaptation of *Dr. Faustus*, winning another state championship and performing before a crowd of six thousand at Ohio State University. His performance showed both who he had become and what he continued to hold back.

"He took his typically engaged and detached attitude toward the role," says Schubert, who directed Doug. "I always felt the detachment was something of self-protection—not committing wholeheartedly to something that may turn out to be foolish. It's pretty typical of adolescents, but it was more obvious in Doug than others."

A reasonably talented performer, Doug compensated for any deficiencies with lightning-speed adaptability and a showman's instinct, best demonstrated in a humorous declamation of Pyramus and Thisbe from *A Midsummer Night's Dream*. Doug played both roles in drag and changed voices, characters, and intention like quicksilver, even making out with himself at one point. It was the funniest, best-acted piece his classmates had ever seen. Years later, when Gilmour's class of 1964 gathered, they always asked each other, "Do you remember Kenney's Pyramus and Thisbe?"

During Doug's senior year, Schubert had the school's five top speakers prepare monologues on a topic of their choice. Doug addressed the specific time in history—1964—and the issues of the day. On the heels of the Kennedy assassination, it was a point in history where the United States was about to undergo a massive and unimaginable transition from an optimistic country working through civil rights and venturing into space into a shattered nation engaging in its most damaging war, all on the precipice of a cultural upheaval. It was a time and place where Doug would remain in his mind for the rest of his life—somewhere between boundless hope and encroaching disaster.

In the Gilmour auditorium—packed with students, teachers, Holy Cross Brothers, and middle-class, midwestern, suburban Catholic parents—Doug took the stage and talked about birth control, abortion, drug abuse, and everything he perceived was coming around the corner in America. With the presence and assurance one might impute to someone such as his brother Dan, he ran right out onto the ice without slipping.

At the conclusion of Doug's declamation there was a long, breathless pause, after which the audience rose and delivered a raucous ovation. Even some who didn't agree with him were dumbfounded by the capacities of the seventeen-year-old boy. Somewhere in that crowd, Regan, undoubtedly, was beaming.

Not beaming was Gilmour's much-feared headmaster, Alphonso Comeau, who looked to all the world as if he were about to catch fire. Comeau had been keeping an eye on Doug since his arrival at Gilmour, clearly aware that the kid was trouble and intending to put the screws to him whenever possible.

Comeau's worldview was best exemplified by his confiscation of a *Time* magazine issue that had made its way into student mailboxes. Addressing the topic of modern marriage in the early 1960s, its cover featured a demure painting of a possibly naked married couple in bed. As quickly as it arrived on campus, it was gone without a trace.

In 1963, the editor of the *Hall Crier* was Stan Jaros, a bright smart-ass who got into trouble for printing "bullshit" down the margin of one issue, after assuming that Comeau would be none the wiser. Jaros was wrong and the headmaster came down hard. Thus, Gilmour's student body eagerly waited to see what Doug Kenney would try to get away with in the *Hall Crier* during his senior year of 1964, just as they might anticipate a football game against a hated rival.

Doug wrote the *Hall Crier*'s "Pritch" column, named after a stone gargoyle that guarded the campus gates and written from the creature's knowing perspective. A typical "random musings" column, Doug turned it into high comedy each week, signing on with phrases like "Hi there Monists!," "Vale Erastians!," or "Goten Tag, Kleins

Junges!," and signing off with everything from "by for now chillun, gotta get the pinions oiled . . . " to "bye until next fishday, Papists!" The "Pritch" column allowed Doug to show off his facility with language, wide-ranging references, and his gift for the absurd.

> Is it true what this plumed aero noot has heard, that Mr. Schubert's 6th period French class has already learned to say the "Our Father" and "Hail Mary?" that's simply marvy! Quite a beginning! Now try learning it in French! Die swartz und gelb Katze donne son garcons les etuces plus faciles, vero quantum linguam cognoscent comperire difficile est. "Recta sapers per laburem," pas des mauvaises motes, ist das nicht Recht, Kinds? (You may not know it, but my mommy was frightened by James Joyce's Silver Cord and I never did quite develop right!) Well, I'm running out of ink (I write with a split claw and I waste a lot) so I'd better dix-quatre pretty soon. I've got to see that new flick, "The glory that was Grease" (it's a biography of Morton L. Penwhetter, the inventor of "Crisco").

Doug also contributed a weekly cartoon called "The Phantom" and a regular "Senior of the Week" piece where he caricatured his classmates, writing humorous thumbnails of their personalities, interests, or other defining characteristics. It was always apt, and it demonstrated an innate understanding of his subject while always seeming to get at each student's core.

"He condensed us," Cox says. "He boiled down our personalities."

That year, in response to Comeau's seizure of the *Time* issue, Doug wrote a poem about book burning at Gilmour, scribbling "fakeout" in the margins and pissing off the headmaster.

"Doug was rebellious and didn't tolerate the nonsense that others would tolerate," classmate Greg Nash says. "There were probably plenty of things in those *Hall Crier* articles that—if people had understood them—would have gotten him into trouble. He was on the edge for a conservative Catholic school. The restrictions and everything that was part of Gilmour must have seemed like nonsense to him."

No one recalls precisely what Doug Kenney did in the *Hall Crier* that sent Comeau over the top during 1964, but there is little doubt that he made reference to a nickname that he'd hung on the head-master, Brother Bonzo, which insinuated mental imbalance on the part of the school's top cleric while paying homage to the Ronald Reagan movie in which the future president costarred with a chimp. The print was barely dry when Comeau had the entire run destroyed because of Doug's piece. The lay faculty and Regan were sympathetic to Doug's plight, but their hands were tied.

"Alphonso was an exceptionally combustible man," Schubert says. "I was unhappy about it, but there wasn't anything to do."*

* * *

Socially, Doug hung out with his buddies and participated in the usual beer and burger runs. Appreciative and observant of their actions, Doug was the guy who could ape the vocabulary and speaking voice of his friends and acquaintances within moments of meeting them. It was almost an instinct or a reflex.

Girls were a different and far less satisfying matter.

"His girlfriends were really dreary. He didn't think he had it," Cox says. "He was a lot cooler than he knew, but he thought he was a nerdball."

Ginna Bourisseau, whose older sister dated Dan Kenney, went on a few dates with Doug while he was at Gilmour and she was a Chagrin Falls eighth grader.

---

*In early summer 2004, after much jumping through hoops and digging, I located Brother Alphonso Comeau (now known by his given name, Gerald—just as Ivo Regan was born as John) residing at a Holy Cross retirement home in Sherman Oaks, California. Now in his eighties, Comeau passed word through a colleague that he would gladly talk with me about Doug Kenney, whom he hadn't seen for forty years.

I asked him if he had any recollections of Douglas Kenney from the Gilmour class of 1964, who had been dead for twenty-four years.

"I did not appreciate his sophomoric sense of humor," he said dryly.

"Anything else?" I wondered.

"I did not appreciate his sophomoric sense of humor," he repeated firmly.

The conversation was over.

"He was kind of dorky," she recalls. "I can see how he would never fit in Chagrin Falls. He was way too brilliant. He was cynical. He had a very different outlook."

Bourisseau liked Doug because he was bright and well mannered. Even at thirteen, Bourisseau could see that Doug's mind was constantly going, its owner incapable of shutting it off. Doug would often call her on the phone and ramble about how he couldn't sleep and instead stayed up late every night, reading and listening to the radio.

The pair went to a dance. Doug called frequently. Then one night Doug Kenney slipped his hand down Bourisseau's blouse. It was over.

"He had way more hormones than I did," Bourisseau says.

Few people from Gilmour got to know the Kenney family. Friends were vaguely aware of Dan's hold on Doug's parents ("He was the god of the family," Cox says. "Doug was afforded second-class citizenship.") and that their classmate really loved his little sister.

"His family was never in evidence around campus," Jerry Murphy says. "I got the feeling that they were rather removed from his life."

English teacher Jim Schuerger got to know a little of Harry and Stephanie when he would drop off Doug after school. In the fashion of the times, Stephanie would invite him in for drinks most days. When Schuerger's wife would call wondering where he was, Stephanie would say, "He just left," with a smile and wink to her guest. Harry, Schuerger thought, was affable in a tried-and-true Irish way, but "you couldn't know him."

During their trips to and from school, Doug regaled Schuerger with tales of his younger sister Vicky, portraying her as a wiser-than-her-years Shirley Temple, feet up, candy cigar clenched in her teeth, watching kiddie shows and cartoons. Other times, Doug and a friend would spend the drive bedeviling the other kids Schuerger was ferrying to Gilmour with impish jokes and pranks.

Academically, Doug turned his efforts to what interested him, ignoring math and science completely in favor of English, history, and artistic pursuits. As a senior, he was the only National Merit Finalist among a class of high achievers.

During Doug's senior year, Harry took him to visit universities on the East Coast, including Princeton and Harvard. Doug's uncle Frank Kenney recalls hearing about the trips and sensing Harry's pride that a son of his might join the Ivy League. Undoubtedly, it was not a feeling that Harry shared with his middle child.

Among the Gilmour faculty, expectations for Doug ran high. Schuerger thought Doug would become another Graham Greene. Having trusted Doug for four years, he was amazed upon the boy's graduation that he'd managed to "keep a lid on it" at Gilmour.

When Doug Kenney told classmates and teachers that he would attend Harvard in the fall, few doubted that he was destined for great things; what these were, no one knew. But the seeds of who Doug Kenney was to become had already been sown in Newport, Chagrin Falls, and at Gilmour Academy.*

---

*In fall 1976, Brother John "Ivo" Regan committed suicide with a handgun in the basement of Gilmour's Tudor House.

At the same time, Doug Kenney was living in New York City and was a millionaire. He'd often spoken of Regan to close friends, though no one recalls his reaction to the news of his mentor's death.

"Glory be to God for the dappled things," Regan often said, quoting nineteenth-century English priest and poet Gerard Manley Hopkins.

2

The Most Perfect WASP

The Shroogers

RFD 1 Newbury, Ohio (the white house with the cats)

"Hello! Yes, I have been 'tensed up' lately (argh!),—so I thought I'd just say howareya and howsababy? Things all well, looking forward to Spring break—will be in to say hello, around April. Trying out for Lampoon, playing squash, cutting classes, big bad weekends. Went to Gren. Village a while back—golly! Almost as neat as Harford Sq. Will expand this at later date—keep the good faith.

Doug

P.S. How long do I hafta stay here before I get to be an intalectuel? College guys is pansies indeed.

—March 1965 postcard from Doug Kenney to Jim Schuerger. The front of the postcard is a fifteenth-century Flemish painter's depiction of "The Martyrdom of St. Hyppolytus"

*from the Boston Museum of Fine Arts. Bound at his ankles
and wrists, the Saint is being pulled in four opposite
directions by men and horses. Next to the five-cent George
Washington stamp, Doug wrote, "Come on, get serious!"*

At Harvard Doug Kenney became many things: preppy, ladies'
man, genius, humorist, savior, rebel, hippie, and friend to
many. During this time Doug began to find himself anew while
inventing a flexible persona that would serve as both saving grace
and burden.

Doug dedicated his freshman year to two things: fitting in to
a new environment and getting in to the *Harvard Lampoon*. He
achieved both tasks easily.

During his four years in Cambridge, Doug assembled an eclectic
group of friends that included: Ollie Hallowell, the closeted homo-
sexual, prep school–educated son of an old Massachusetts family;
Anil Khosla, a sophisticated Pakistani boy educated in England; Jim
Rivaldo, a working-class kid with political aspirations from upstate
New York; Chris Hart, son of the legendary Moss Hart and New
York City grande dame Kitty Carlisle; novelist Jerome (*I Can Get It
for You Wholesale*) Weidman's son John; British gent Dudley Fish-
burn; future Massachusetts governor William Weld; and Dr. Andrew
("Andy") Weil. There were many others.

"He didn't just pick cool people," says Chris Hart. "There were
hangers-on and losers. Doug enjoyed their company and found something interesting about them. He liked the people everybody else tried
to avoid."

Doug moved seamlessly among different groups and personae
with charm and grace—giving off the aura of a witty, sensitive young
man who understood each person completely. Despite being the center of much social activity, he retained a sense of reserve.

"He was the most generous and kind person. Completely wacky
in a way that offended no one," says Anil Khosla. "But he was uncat-
egorizable. Within ten minutes you knew there was something completely off-kilter about Doug. You just couldn't peg him."

Doug made his family and Chagrin Falls the stuff of legend. Both were beyond the pale: Harry, an affable, Bing Crosby–like dad who championed the little guy and laughed at the country-club snobs; Stephanie, the wacky mom who drank a little too much; and Doug, the family nerd placed between Dan and Vicky. Chagrin Falls was the idyllic midwestern small town with the unbelievable name. To Doug, everything was funny—his hometown, his family, Harvard, and, most especially, himself.

"He saw the absurd side of everything," Khosla recalls. "Everything was a joke. He couldn't let on that it wasn't a joke."

During his freshman year, Doug Kenney began relationships with three people who had an enormous influence on him: Tim Mayer, Peter Ivers, and Judith Bruce, each of whom became a lifelong friend.

"We're talking about huge, larger-than-life personalities and very complex relationships," says a Harvard friend of Doug's. "Being at dinner with Tim, Doug, and Peter, the level of conversation that went on was just so extraordinary—there's no way to re-create it. You can't do it justice."

Ivers and Mayer were as different as two men could be. A slender five-foot-five Jewish boy from Brookline, Massachusetts, Ivers possessed an open, youthful face that reflected his optimistic and experimental view of life. A classics major with a genius-level IQ, he could write Sanskrit and knew Latin and Greek. Ivers was someone on a spiritual mission from early in life. Raised by a doting mother and driven businessman stepfather (his own father died when he was three), Ivers underachieved at Boston's Roxbury Latin High School, infuriating his stepfather by claiming that he'd learned everything he'd found meaningful. By the time he was a Harvard junior, many old-time bluesmen regarded him as one of the country's finest blues harmonica players. An openly gentle soul, even gentler than Doug, Ivers was one of a generation of Harvard baby boomers who believed the world was theirs for the taking.

"I'm the little boy who sits on his knees and gets the special dessert," he told girlfriend Lucy Fisher.

"He always got special everything," Fisher says.

"He was like Peter Pan," says another friend. "A wonderful person. Warm-hearted and a supportive friend. Tim was by far the more complex relationship [with Doug]."

Ivers met Tim Mayer onstage at Cambridge's Loeb Theater.

"You're Mayer," Ivers said. "I heard you're good. Real good."

Mayer stopped.

"I'm the best technical director in town," Ivers told him.

So began a lifelong friendship and creative partnership at Harvard where Mayer directed plays for which Ivers wrote the musical score.

Mayer was the intimidating yin to Ivers's gentle yang. The product of a well-to-do Cortland, New York, family that owned a sporting goods company, Mayer was a hunchbacked only child raised by an antique snuff box–collecting mother and a father he considered the embodiment of all that America had once represented: self-sufficiency, honesty, dignity, and grace.

Mayer's favorite childhood toy was a model theater. By age ten he was acting at and working for the Oberlin Gilbert and Sullivan Players in Falmouth, Massachusetts. In love with the symbols of an America that had passed into the night by the late 1960s, he obsessed over the club cars on gleaming silver bicoastal trains and the trappings of old-time corporate boardrooms, grand success, and terrific failure. Like Doug, he viewed his America with "affection and horror," wrote his friend Paul Schmidt.

Graduating from Watertown, Connecticut's, Taft School in 1962, Mayer arrived in Cambridge with a clear vision of his purpose—to translate the American experience onstage through themes set down in the great European plays. Early on, he established himself as Harvard's artistic enfant terrible, regarded almost as a peer by many professors. As the writer and director of choice for campus productions, he reconfigured old plays to fit contemporary contexts, winning the Phyllis Anderson playwriting prize for *Prince Erie*, based on the life of railroad baron Jim Fisk and exploring the theme of American capitalism.

It was assumed that Mayer, like Ivers, would take the world by storm upon graduation from Harvard. After matriculating in 1966, he helped establish Cambridge's Aggassiz Theater, where he directed and wrote plays performed by a company that included John Lithgow, Lindsay Crouse, Tommy Lee Jones, Stockard Channing, and Kathryn Walker.

Mayer was a delicate soul, both physically and emotionally, who covered his weak spots with brains and verbal artistry, which formed a hard shell around his personality. Language was his preferred weapon, both onstage and in rambling digressive conversations. At Harvard, he was by far the most verbal in a world of exceedingly verbal people. He could be devastating in social situations, taking others apart for sport and crushing them with lethal wit.

"Tim was one of those people who would say straight out what other people would think, but never dream of saying," says one friend. Underlying all of this, however, was a lifelong quest to find a home. His friend Paul Schmidt wrote,

> Tim clung to a world defined by the porches and lawns and wicker furniture of his parents' house in Cotuit on Cape Cod and by his years at the Taft School and Harvard. Everything after that was unsatisfactory. Those places gave him a sense of a world already there, and in the New England tradition they represented, a world that had been there for a long time.
>
> What Tim never really understood was that your parents' home and your prep school and your college are by their nature places you have to leave in order to grow up. All Tim had grasped about that world was that you had to fit into it, and Tim was profoundly, genially, a misfit. He accepted the tenets of that world without question, glorified in its exclusivity, exploited its tolerance for witty eccentricity, but raged against his own physical exterior that kept him from being a natural part of it—that made him, he imagined, an outsider everywhere . . .

This yearning for home, perceived outsider status—yet retained insider credentials—and combination of cynicism and sentiment, along with verbal dexterity and an artistic mind, were the primary qualities he shared with the midwestern Doug Kenney.

***

Mayer first encountered Doug from afar, walking across Harvard Yard.

"I thought he was the most perfect WASP I had ever encountered," Mayer said. "He was flawless."

Doug Kenney no longer appeared as the geeky, green-suited debater and Chagrin Falls outsider. During his sophomore year, Dudley Fishburn won a bet with another student who swore that Doug had graduated from Groton. Doug had seemingly overnight become the embodiment of the preppy liberal values and J. Press–appearance of the early '60s Harvard student.

Doug, Mayer, and Ivers were inseparable. Ivers introduced his friends to blues music and Boston's underground nightlife. Mayer demonstrated the promise and artistic ambition of his generation. Doug absorbed both sides: gentleness, experimentation, and a love of shock value from Ivers, while seeing the world through Mayer's well-bred and sarcastic eyes.

"Peter was like the pet or mascot of the upper class at Harvard," says Lucy Fisher. "Tim was to the manner born and Doug was a wannabe."

Doug was particularly infatuated with Ivers's Jewishness and his loving mother. He made a home at the Ivers residence in Brookline, where the family had painted their piano purple to match the living room decor—a detail that couldn't have escaped his eyes. And it was in that home where Mayer recuperated after being diagnosed with cancer in the late 1960s.

***

"She was the most stunning person in all of Radcliffe," Ollie Hallowell says of Judith Bruce. "Unbelievably smart. Tall. She dressed dramatically. You'd expect her to go out with Clark Gable."

Instead, Judith Bruce wound up on Doug's arm and remained there until the early part of his senior year.

It had been Bruce, a Minneapolis blonde, who pursued Doug. The pair met at a photo shoot for a *Harvard Lampoon* parody where they'd been cast as a Tom Wolfe couple. Shortly thereafter, Doug's friend Sam White told him, "You know, Kenney, Judy Bruce has a huge crush on you. What are you going to do about it?" A dinner was arranged at Radcliffe, where the pair hit it off over bottle of wine. Doug turned on all his latent charm. Bruce, for her part, was an overwhelming force.

"He didn't have a chance," recalls Hallowell.

After dinner, there were good-byes in front of Bruce's dormitory. White gave Bruce a hug and got on his motorcycle while her dorm mates spied out their windows.

"I'd rather kiss him [Doug]!" Bruce told White.

Doug walked over, bent the nearly six-foot Bruce over backward, and gave her a Gable-worthy kiss before hopping on the back of White's motorcycle and speeding off into the night while onlookers showered them with applause.

"There's acres and acres of her," Doug said of Bruce.

Doug and Bruce were a couple from that day forward, meeting for lunch at Tony's on Harvard Yard, and engaging in long teenagery phone calls each night. They were inseparable. And it was Bruce, perhaps more than anyone at that point in his life, who saw beyond Doug's veneer. He was hilarious and undeniably attractive, but still an outsider.

"He was amused to find himself at Harvard," Bruce says. "He felt a bit of a fraud."

Bruce saw nearly all of Doug's life, including study and work habits that were uncommon for such a talented and productive young man. She sat by as Doug started work on papers in the wee hours of the mornings they were due. His thesis on Waugh was created in just a few days. Clearly, he had picked up on a common Harvard trait—never let them see you sweat—in which effortless grace was the modus operandi.

Another aspect of Doug that he'd hidden was a lack of self-confidence, at a school where everyone was insecure on some level among their sophisticated peers. Doug's response, however, was often juvenile.

"He was intimidated by the Harvard intellects," Bruce remembers. "Other students would pull out their intellects and Doug would sit on the side and make fun of them. But he became inarticulate and acted less intelligent."

Doug immersed himself in Harvard's defined social world of finals and dining clubs. The Owl was for prep-school athletes, Fly was social and stylish, Porcelain was for the true elite, and Phoenix was ill defined, best exemplified by a few artists. Doug joined Spee, a blend of creative types and preppies who didn't have the pedigree for Porcelain, nor the style and élan for Fly. Before long, the Spee Club took on Doug's personality.

"He'd show up wearing combat boots with a pinstripe suit to black-tie dinners. He could get away with it and people respected the way he was," Khosla says.

As a senior, Doug became the club's president in spite of his mocking the system and club society—particularly Spee—for its pretenses. Somehow, he did so in a way that no one bore him ill will or threatened his sense of belonging.

"It was odd," Khosla says. "He could fit in anywhere. Every time you thought he might be out of place . . . and he never was."

But of all the Harvard institutions Doug fit best at the *Harvard Lampoon*.

Established in 1876, the *Harvard Lampoon* was housed in "the Castle," its odd headquarters on Brattle Street. Built in 1909 with money from Isabella Stewart Gardner and William Randolph Hearst, the building resembles nothing so much as a laughing head with a beanie-cap roof, window eyes, and a brightly colored door mouth— all winged by heating-vent ears that pour steam in winter. Designed by legendary architect Edmund March Wheelwright, the Castle contains elements of a Flemish fisherman's cottage, gothic church, and pre-Elizabethan dining hall. Inside are strangely shaped rooms (a circular library is housed inside a trapezoid) and dark, winding hallways.

The Lampoon and its building are filled with strange rituals and myths. The third officer on the magazine's literary board is "the Narthex," an architectural term describing the passageway to the back of a church. Carved cement ibises—an Egyptian bird carrying much inexplicable symbolism in Lampoon circles—sit atop the Castle. The Lampoon vice president is "the Ibis."

"There were all sorts of ridiculous raccoon lodge names," says mid-1970s *Harvard Lampoon* editor and former *Saturday Night Live* writer Mark O'Donnell. "An officer was a 'super sir.' If they were a graduate officer they were a 'late lamented super sir.'"

Induction ceremonies involved elaborate, ritualized pranks presided over by upperclassmen and graduate editors. During his induction, Doug was asked to steal from a Cambridge convenience store run by a dour Armenian. His Lampoon brethren, however, had warned both the owner and the police about Doug's assignment. Both confronted him.

"I think he was really scared for the first time in his life," Khosla says.

The Lampoon had produced John Updike, George Santayana, *The New Yorker*'s Robert Benchley, and Fred Gwynne, with George Plimpton perhaps the foremost embodiment of its aesthetic.

At Harvard, Plimpton proclaimed, he'd majored in Lampoon and minored in everything else. As the magazine's standard-bearer, his life at the Castle is an essential part of its lore. During induction, it is said, Plimpton was so drunk that he bolted into the street and was run over by a parked car. On another occasion, Plimpton, clad in British military uniform and riding a horse, appeared out of nowhere at Governor Robert Bradford's Lexington, Massachusetts, speech commemorating Paul Revere's famous ride. Stealing the governor's microphone in stride, he led fellow Poonsters in a chant of "Disperse ye rebels."

The overall Lampoon environment had always been intensely male (girlfriends were resented), intensely secret (nonmembers were prohibited from going upstairs), and intensely Ivy League (jacket and tie at three meals a day). By the late 1950s, despite those who had passed through its doors, the magazine had become nothing but a circular for rich, preppy alumni, filled with snide inside jokes about the less affluent and cultivated students on campus. The *Harvard Lampoon* had become little more than a patrician social club that happened to publish a humor magazine.

"In 1959 the circulation was about 905—made up of former editors," says Chris Cerf. "They may not have read it, they just received it."

There were no dreams of glory for the publication, Cerf says, "only Harvard-centric dreams of glory past."

Then, in 1965, Walker Lewis became Lampoon president. Breaking with tradition, a business board member had beaten the editorial candidates for the top job. Lewis's first order of business was to examine Lampoon finances, which he soon realized were nonexistent.

"We had receivables people owed us but most were in no mood to pay," Lewis says. "Dues were not being collected from members, and they were in no mood to pay either."

Lewis quickly instituted efforts to collect debts and sell new ads with the assistance of Rob Hoffman, a student from Dallas, who had the respect of his Lampoon brethren and was instrumental in bringing order to the magazine's chaotic financial state.

With newsstand sales declining, Lewis began giving the Lampoon away on campus, while switching the publication schedule from whenever there was adequate material to a monthly format. Meeting with some initial success, Lewis soon learned that it was a backbreaking effort to put out a monthly humor magazine and began looking toward special issues that would parody specific magazines as a way to make some "real money." With *Playboy* selling at its historical peak on college campuses in the mid-1960s, he found the perfect target.

Lewis contacted a prominent attorney who sat on the Lampoon board, and inquired about the legal risks of parodying a national magazine. "What might happen if *Playboy* got upset?" he asked. "You'll get some publicity," the attorney replied. Shortly thereafter, Lewis mailed a letter to *Playboy* informing them about the parody. A response from Hefner and company indicated that a lawsuit would quickly follow if the parody hit the newsstand. Undaunted, Lewis visited Chicago and told *Playboy* face-to-face that the Lampoon looked forward to all of the press coverage such a suit would bring to its publication. Abruptly, *Playboy* offered to help out in any way possible and introduced Lewis to the specialty printer that produced their centerfolds.

Soon a Lampoon sales force headed to Madison Avenue, where they contracted for about twenty pages of four-color ads from major companies. Running at roughly one hundred pages, with real nudes, the *Harvard Lampoon* parody of *Playboy* (at $1 per copy) sold out its run of over 500,000 copies in five days on the newsstand. The Lampoon treasury, which had previously consisted of $3,000 discovered in a long-forgotten check register at the back of a desk drawer, jumped to $150,000. The Castle was soon refurbished and Lampoon subscriptions now numbered between thirty and forty thousand. It was at this unique juncture that Doug Kenney became an important player at the *Harvard Lampoon*, where he would meet Henry Beard.

* * *

Doug Kenney presented himself to Lampoon members as an ingenue, a self-described fresh-faced "hick kid" from Ohio.

"He started with the premise that being from Ohio was already a joke," says Walker Lewis, an Ohio native. "Anything he said initially was funny because he was this midwestern kid who didn't understand anything. It was a character he'd invented. It wasn't actually Doug."

Beginning in the fall of 1965, Doug Kenney was a star at the Lampoon, alternately dressing in handmade suits borrowed from Khosla and Fishburn, or clad in blue jeans and motorcycle boots with no socks, sometimes with no shirt and long lanky hair. Flamboyant and shocking, he made everyone laugh uncontrollably while writing arch satires of the finals club lifestyle and a *West Side Story* parody that pitted a preppy gang against a townie gang ("When you're a prep, you're a prep all the way"). Soon he was an integral part of the Lampoon and its social fabric.

"He was like George Kaufman was for my parents," Chris Hart says. "He had the ability to bring out the best in people. Like an electrical current, everybody wants to keep up. And he made everybody feel like his best friend."

Each Thursday there was a formal Lampoon dinner attended by overeducated, rich white males in tuxedoes. Everyone was drunk by six, ate their meal at eight, and capped dinner with a food fight. After leaving the table, they headed to the Castle fireplace for jokes and comic stories, passing joints and symbolically demonstrating the changing times yet retaining their establishment trappings. On these evenings Doug was always the star of the show, telling a shaggy dog story and singing silly songs for almost thirty minutes.

"He was absolutely brilliant," Hart recalls. "People begged for the performance on a weekly basis."

Much of Doug's often campy dinner performance was based on what he'd learned from a new mentor—George W. S. Trow, a thin, elegant, and effete Exeter-educated upperclassman who hailed from the old-line WASP world of Cos Cob, Connecticut. Growing up in a Cole Porter–tinged world defined by the New York of the first half of the twentieth century, Trow was highly cultured and possessed an often nasty sensibility. At a party years later, when a female friend commented that Trow seemed "sweet," Doug responded, "Are you kidding, he just bit my face!"

From Trow, Doug drew an understanding of the WASP universe and a new cultured personality that he could assume whenever he liked. But, more important, Doug possessed an ability—born of his middle-class, midwestern upbringing—to make connections between the rest of society and life in the hallowed halls of Harvard and the Castle.

"His imagination was electric," Hart says. "He did absurdist humor that was both light and dark. Others were funny and smart, but not astounding like Doug."

And then there was Henry Beard.

"Henry was like Bernard Baruch," said John Weidman. "The guy who sat on the park bench and told you how it was. He was the resident genius. His hero was S. J. Perelman and we thought of him like Perelman."

One year ahead of Doug at Harvard, and the great grandson of John C. Breckenridge, who'd unsuccessfully opposed Abraham Lincoln for president, Henry had grown up on Manhattan's Upper East Side at the Westbury Hotel on Sixty-ninth.

"Those were the days when the taxicabs were very large, the Pan Am Building wasn't there, the subways reeked of ozone, and the Yankees always won," Henry said of his childhood.

Henry's father was a Yale-educated Wall Street accountant and heir to Canadian woolen mills. Both parents were older when Henry was born, and his childhood seemed to lack emotional connection with either.

"I never saw my mother up close," he half-joked to a friend, implying that their relationship had taken place from opposite ends of the archetypal long dinner table favored by the wealthy in old movies.

At Taft, Henry was the driving force behind the school's humor magazine, and he decided to pursue literary humor after reading Joseph Heller's *Catch-22*. Like Doug, Henry was brilliant. But he was one thing that Doug was not: an aristocrat by birth. He cared little for appearance, wearing a crew cut and horn-rimmed glasses (Doug now favored the circular granny-style), rumpled, dandruff-covered Brooks Brothers suits, and bow ties. With a silver pipe perpetually rammed between his teeth, he seemed to both parody and embody the old Harvard man.

"Henry was a certain manner of affluent Harvard preppy who were totally oblivious to style. Tweed jackets. Oxford shirts. He paid the minimum attention to how he looked," Jim Rivaldo says.

Most days, Henry regaled friends with stories of waking up to search beneath his bed for the cleanest of his three pairs of underwear to put on for class.

"Henry," says Lewis, "was the oldest man that ever was a teen, while Doug viewed the world as a brilliant ten-year-old might."

Henry's persona was that of a professional grump. He was dry, somewhat absentminded, and—without malice—never had a good thing to say about anything. A talented student who occasionally wrote papers in parody, Henry sat for one U.S. Foreign Policy exam and wrote a letter to the professor stating that as a committed Communist, he deeply disagreed with the premise of the question and would answer from his own viewpoint, going on to essentially reprise the Communist Manifesto.

Disciplined and organized, Henry was a studious writer who relied on an unerring ability to understand the most complex subjects, which stood in direct opposition to Doug's intuitive, cultural approach. The contrast couldn't have been more stark.

A child of the '60s, Doug smoked pot and experimented with LSD for fun and as a means of mind expansion. Henry preferred getting bombed on brandy. He eschewed drugs, though never judged those who partook or the potential benefits and impacts they might offer.

Doug had a rapacious appetite for life experience, socializing, and all that comprised the popular culture. By contrast, "Henry was far too much of a professional misanthrope to love people the way Doug loved people," Fishburn says. "Henry would regard having friends as a sign of weakness. He wouldn't like to have friends."

Not that Henry wasn't well liked. He was more than that—he was deeply respected and revered. Socializing within the walls of the Castle, Henry was the Lampoon's finest pool player, meticulously cataloguing the force and angle of each shot. Mild-mannered and polite, he was not one of the boys but rather a presence who, by force of his intelligence, presided over the scene—above it all, but not haughty.

Doug learned all he could from Henry, further refining his use of language and taking on a dryness of wit. The ability to learn from others and incorporate the knowledge into his natural talent was one of Doug's gifts.

What neither Henry nor anyone else could learn from Doug was his empathic, vulnerable personality that channeled directly back into his humor. Henry was a character; Doug, a pair of X-ray eyes.

"Doug saw the humor in what others would have seen as embarrassing situations. That was at the core of his genius and he absolutely was a creative genius," Walker Lewis says. "He found humor in things others would find pathetic, sad, or politically incorrect. Doug would revel in it and find the humor. You knew that he had suffered, too, and that when you suffered, he was relating to it. He wore it on his sleeve."

Doug and Henry were a matched set, like business partners who balance each other's weaknesses or a married couple of disparate personae; they gravitated to one another, quickly recognizing the other's talent and contributions. Doug, the wild populist social commentator, was a natural leader by force of personality and talent, loving recognition but not interested in being in charge of anything. Henry, the old-school preppy humorist, was grounded and sensible, capable of harnessing the talents of others. By 1967, the *Harvard Lampoon* became Doug Kenney and Henry Beard.

* * *

Doug wrote in a letter to Judith Bruce,

Father took me to dinner tonight and announced that he was quite unhappy to see the indecision on my part as to future plans. More to the point, he detects a leaning to "purely creative" (i.e. artsy-craftsy-beatnik-pinko-faery) professions. I take it that this generic includes writing, theater, commercial art, journalism, criticism, toe dancing, anti-government demonstrations, male prostitution and non-corporation law. Specifically, he eyes an English major with the utmost suspicion and perhaps justifiably indicts me for unnecessary and financially disastrous frivolity. What am I to say? I am told that if I do not show immediate signs of "substantial thinking" and form definite career plans, my financial underwriter will find it necessary to cease writing under.

How serious the situation is, I do not know, but it is within the realm of possibility that I may not be allowed to continue at Harvard this coming year. The fact that I meet all his complaints with good-natured defiance cannot help but irritate matters to the point where a real showdown may take place within the next month.

As I have stated, the tab for my education is a relatively larger chunk of the family fortune, hence my rather careless attitude is proportionally less tolerated. The alternative to a tactical retreat on my part is a nice couple of years at some less elegant institution, such as Cowbell State. The only consolation is this eventually would be what I consider a license to completely fuck off and gravitate to a pseudo-bohemian existence replete with cycle + pad; a prospect which has a modicum of appeal in the contest of zero responsibility to rents.

What next week will bring is up in the air, but the resolution is bound to be unpleasant for both factions (poor mom is such a sucker, she's on my side). Family life is so incredibly 1) banal, 2) mundane, 3) prosaic, 4) boring, 5) enervating. Select one.

Moustache is 1/32nd of an inch longer! Excelcior! (unfortunately, it's all blonde and probably won't make it decorationwise.) . . .

I've always thought, at least for the past 2–3 years that I'm a naturally happy soul. I wonder if I should feel guilty about it? Almost everyone I know has some intriguing hang-up. . . . Perhaps I underestimate my own problems, but I think that's impossible. I love to whine.

* * *

One hundred and one years earlier, Mark Twain wrote to his brother, explaining that he was becoming a writer of humor, stating that he'd been called to "literature of a low order." This troubled the writer greatly, as such a career was "nothing to be proud of" but that he would pursue "seriously scribbling to excite the laughter of God's creatures," which he describes as a "poor pitiful business!"

It was this very same business to which Doug Kenney would dedicate his life.

* * *

Shortly after Doug entered Harvard, Harry Kenney was transferred to New Jersey and settled in South Orange, where Judith Bruce first met her boyfriend's parents during a visit that varied greatly from the vision of an all-American Chagrin Falls family.

Doug's mother, Stephanie, was energetic and warm. Both she and Doug could put an entire fist in their mouths. Stephanie was given to frequent commands of "SING!," immediately inspiring a light-hearted number from Doug and Vicky. Harry seemed very Irish, a stalwart, cardigan-wearing dad.

Then the facade began to crumble. Over heaping plates of mashed potatoes, Harry ridiculed Doug's brilliance and opportunities. Doug's father, Bruce thought, was defensive and jealous. Talk turned to politics and religion. Unimpressed with his artsy son, whose liberal girl-friend would soon be off to teach birth control to underprivileged women overseas, Harry screamed, "Just what the hell do you believe in, anyway?!" as he stalked around the dining table, unable to sit while in a rage. Doug was tongue-tied and intimidated, just as he'd been with the Harvard intellectuals.

Later, Judith learned that Stephanie took massive doses of diet pills and drank heavily. Frequently exploding at Harry, she once put her fist through a window and on another occasion pushed a television set down the stairs. Harry was a bully who derided Doug's inclinations and interests. Doug was, many thought, simply guilty of not being just like Dan.

While most of his friends liked the Kenneys, the turmoil that Doug endured at home and in Chagrin Falls—though papered-over with amusing stories—was not lost on them. Ollie Hallowell recalls that Harry and Stephanie would ask Doug, "Why can't you be more like Ollie?"

"And I was nothing," Hallowell says.

Anil Khosla found the Kenneys to be pleasant people who clearly didn't understand the first thing about their son. When Khosla met Harry and Stephanie, Doug introduced his mother as "the first member of her tribe to wear shoes." The Kenneys didn't crack a smile.

Another friend says, "He was the painted bird. They just didn't know what to make of him. They were flabbergasted. He realized that they had no sense of what he was about."

* * *

On a summer morning in 1967, Doug was watching Laurel and Hardy reruns in the living room of Bruce's parents' Minneapolis home when Amy Carlson burst through the door to tell her best friend, who'd just returned from teaching about birth control in the Middle East, that she had very bad news.

"You should have taught closer to home," Carlson said, "because I'm pregnant!"

Doug laughed and asked if he could put his head on Carlson's tummy or feel the baby move.

As it was no small matter to be a pregnant, unmarried college girl in 1967, Bruce conceived a plan to have Carlson drive with them in her Chevy convertible to Cambridge to have the baby out East, away from the hometown rumors and her family. With no better alternative, the threesome soon headed for Harvard.

In Cambridge it became apparent that there was little room in Bruce's apartment for a pregnant woman, causing Doug to offer a place that he was sharing with Khosla, Dudley Fishburn, a South American student named Ricardo Moreno, and a few others. To an Englishman, a Pakistani, a South American, and a few East Coast WASPs, Doug pitched the prospect of a new roommate as follows: "I don't believe this group has everything we need. We're not diverse enough. What we need is a pregnant, female midwesterner."

Wishing to reduce their rent, the group agreed to let Carlson sleep in the spare bedroom—which was little more than a glorified closet.

That fall and winter, Carlson was den mother, cleaning woman, and bookkeeper for the boys at 118 Kinnaird Street in Cambridge, with Doug serving as her protector, devoted friend, and primary connection to the outside world, who returned each evening from getting high and hanging out with his Lampoon friends to sit on the edge of her bed and report his daytime and nocturnal activities.

"It was like my morning newspaper at three A.M.," Carlson says.

Though rambling and stoned, Doug was trying to make sure that the vulnerable woman was OK. "He always had enormous sympathy for women as underdogs," Bruce says.

Moreno—whom Carlson says "had champagne bottles rolling from under his bed" and was cutting a swath through Harvard secretaries who "believed they were soon heading back to a hacienda in South America"—was unaware, or perhaps uninterested, in Doug's protective attitude toward their new roommate, and thus felt obliged to make a pass at the pregnant woman one evening. It was almost a duty. The peace-loving Doug, however, uncharacteristically shocked Moreno by throwing a wild punch at him upon learning of the transgression.

On rare social outings with Doug, Carlson was amazed at his ability to traverse any and all situations, charming any group—preppies, geeks, Lampoon people, and even the all-black party crowd at a lower-income apartment building in the neighborhood, where he knew no one.

"He just fit right in," Carlson says of the party. "He was passing out joints and I was backed up against the wall. He expected good out of the world."

Carlson also was privy to the Doug who wasn't on public display. As he prepared to go out, she would find him searching Khosla's drawers for a stylish, white-collared pastel shirt and throwing on one of Fishburn's bespoke tweed sports coats. It was clear that he was doing so because he didn't have the right clothes for Harvard parties.

Doug had become a preppy, yet remained an outsider—the boy who worked at the country club and watched the pretty members' daughters prance around the pool into which he couldn't dive. At Harvard he was popular, but he wasn't one of them and never would be. Instead, Doug Kenney was a charming chameleon.

In the fall of 1967, Judith Bruce decided to have a romantic relationship with a twenty-six-year-old Frenchman named Maxim and needed to break up with Doug Kenney. Searching the campus for Doug, Bruce located him on Harvard Yard. There, on a gray fall afternoon, Bruce informed Doug that she no longer would be his girlfriend. There was no response. Doug turned away and disappeared into the New England mist.

Soon Doug was dating Bruce's ex-roommate, Alex Garcia-Mata, a striking, dark-haired Radcliffe student who'd graduated from the exclusive Madeira School. Alex was tender, quiet, and not at all flamboyant like Bruce or Doug. The pair quickly settled into a womblike relationship, with Alex filling a maternal role for Doug.

Months later, when Maxim failed to return from a trip to Washington, D.C. (where he was visiting actress Anita Ekberg), Bruce burned one of the Frenchman's expensive shirts every half hour until he arrived. Infuriated, she went to Alex's apartment and found Doug wrapped in a blanket on the couch. Sensing his ex-girlfriend's distress, Doug said, "Oh, sweetie, what's wrong? Did you break up with Maurice?"

* * *

When Amy Carlson went into labor in winter 1968, Doug drove her to the hospital. Though motivated in part by a desire to borrow her car, he was the last person to see Carlson before she entered the delivery room, and he talked his way past security to greet her after she gave birth to a baby boy. Doug brought his friends to celebrate and made the difficult situation a festive one. Having taken on a paternal role as much as anyone, Doug did his best to see that the boy was named Sebastian Dangerfield, after the hedonistic protagonist of J. P. Donleavy's *The Ginger Man*.

* * *

Ever since his 1959 car accident, Doug's brother Dan was living with diseased kidneys. The problem had been fairly manageable until August 1967, when significant problems arose and he was diagnosed with terminal renal disease in Baltimore, where he worked as a hospital administrator and lived with his wife, Sandra.

Dan's heart was enlarged from the trauma of his illness, from his receiving dialysis three times a week, and possibly from spina bifida as well. With surgery not an option, he was put on home dialysis and given a year to live.

Nearly a year to the day afterward, in August 1968, Dan Kenney died. He was twenty-nine.

Shortly after his college graduation, Doug Kenney became his parents' eldest living child.

* * *

Humorists and writers have, in disproportionate numbers, been the younger siblings of beloved older brothers and sisters who died young. The impact on the lives and work of these sensitive souls is indelible.

The ninth of ten children, Scottish author and playwright J. M. Barrie (*Peter Pan*) was seven years old when his brother David died in a skating accident. As David had been his mother's favorite child, Mrs. Barrie sank into a severe depression. Unable to evoke any response from his mother, Barrie dressed in his dead brother's clothing and received attention from his ailing mother for the first time in months. It was, he would recall, the moment when his childhood ended.

New Yorker humorist Robert Benchley was eight years old in 1898 when a newspaper reporter arrived on his family's doorstep to deliver the news that their twenty-two-year-old son Edmund—a beloved West Point graduate—had been killed in the Spanish-American War. In her misery, Mrs. Benchley cried, "Why couldn't it have been Robert?"

Throughout his life, Doug's psyche was continually confronted by the impact of Dan's death. His older brother had been both his beloved hero and a sibling with whom he fought silent internal battles to gain his parents' love—Doug was too polite and lacked the conviction to scream out his enormous needs. The psychological breach was irreconcilable. He adored this individual whose presence on this planet seemingly made it impossible for him to be emotionally whole.

Within this psychic storm, Doug believed that his parents, like Mrs. Benchley and Mrs. Barrie, somehow would have preferred that he—not Dan—had died. In response, he became a Peter Pan of his own making, always attempting, but never deciding, whether or not he wished to grow up. Thus, as he aged and was faced with responsibility, Doug Kenney would maintain control over the adult world and its encroaching need for maturity by creating a safe place in his head and on the page, with a combination of humor and nostalgia for a time when Dan was alive and the world was filled with hope. Yet that place was infused with the bittersweet and never truly safe, as Doug was keenly aware that reality had rendered such a world illusory.

* * *

By 1968, the *Harvard Lampoon* had moved full bore into the parody business, with Chris Cerf's brother Jon as president and the team of Kenney and Beard as its stars. Rob Hoffman was now a business board member and selling ads for a *Life* magazine parody that would cover "the end of the world."

By now Henry and Doug were symbiotic creative forces, bouncing ideas off one another and establishing a rapport that brought out each other's strengths without compromise or confrontation.

"I never, ever saw the slightest hint of disagreement between the two of them," Jim Rivaldo says. "Never even a 'No, it should be this way.' They each had their own self-defined realm and tremendous respect for each other, understanding that the other was totally brilliant and trusting each other's judgment."

Attempting, with arch intent, to demonstrate that humans had been horrifically boring inhabitants of the earth for thousands of years, the pair assembled mundane artifacts (lousy art, workmanlike statues) as evidence of how little humanity had achieved. The issue contained pieces about nuclear war and power, with a dead, overcooked turkey "done nuclear" embellished with upright-standing mushrooms that resembled atomic clouds. A furnishing and design article was shot in the middle of a forest on the grounds of an old New England estate where Doug, the man of the house, smokes a pipe amidst a freestanding fireplace, carpeting, end tables, and lamps—the house destroyed.

*　*　*

In 1968, during the tumult of the Vietnam War, the draft was at the forefront of every college-aged American boy's mind. Henry, who'd been kicked out of ROTC that year, correctly instructed Doug on how to do the same. Henry had decided to fulfill his military duty by joining the National Guard, attending meetings and going on twice-yearly maneuvers. Despite his disdain for the war and the U.S. military, Henry found the experience inspirational, a means by which he could knowledgeably criticize military stupidity. Ground-level access allowed him to mock the slow-moving American institution firsthand. He also developed a fondness for the leisure use of its weaponry.

Returning from maneuvers with stolen explosives and gunpowder, Henry, Rivaldo, and others would go to the Cheever Estate in Wellesley, with brass ashtrays and billiard balls. Creating mortars, the group would blow billiard balls down tubes, ignite the gunpowder, and shoot the balls hundreds of yards. On one occasion, Henry shot his homemade cannon off the Castle dining table, sticking a ball in the rafters that would remain there for years.

Doug, for his part, continually postponed his army physical to the point where it became clear in summer 1969 he had to actually take it. Based on the presumption that doctors couldn't prove that you didn't have epilepsy, Doug feigned a fit prior to the physical and wound up in a Cambridge emergency room where he foamed at the mouth and was given medication for the affliction.

At his physical, the military doctor asked Doug if he was on any medications. "Just these," Doug said, handing him the prescription bottle.

"Do you know what this is for?" the doctor asked.

"No," Doug replied.

"Well, I'd be very interested in this if you weren't already 4F because of your eyesight," the doctor said.

The postponements and the medical ruse had been completely unnecessary. The medication was given to a friend's epileptic dog.

Hoffman joined the Coast Guard Reserves in fall 1968 and set off for a six-month tour at sea. Before he left, however, he, Kenney, Beard, and Rivaldo held informal conversations about a national humor magazine modeled after the *Harvard Lampoon*.

At the time, the *Life* parody was not having the same kind of success as the 1966 *Playboy* issue. Weak ad sales and out-of-control costs were destroying hopes for profitability. Against that backdrop, Hoffman contacted Harold Chamberlain, president of Independent News, America's largest magazine distributor and owner of D.C. Comics. Independent had distributed the *Playboy* parody two years earlier.

Informing Chamberlain of the situation with the *Life* issue, Hoffman was told, "If you need any help on the business end, I know these guys . . . "

3

Here Is New York

“ On any person who so desires such queer prizes, New York will bestow the gift of loneliness and the gift of privacy. It is this largess that accounts for the presence within the city's walls of a considerable section of the population; for the residents of Manhattan are to a large extent strangers who have pulled up stakes somewhere and come to town, seeking sanctuary or fulfillment or some greater or lesser grail. The capacity to make such dubious gifts is a mysterious quality of New York. It can destroy an individual, or it can fulfill him, depending a good deal on luck. No one should come to New York to live unless he is willing to be lucky. ”

—*From E. B. White's* Here Is New York

Matty Simmons was not Ivy League. Not even close. Rather, he seemed the definitive caricature of the cigar-chomping, pinkie ring–wearing, Brooklyn-bred businessman. A little short and a little thick around the middle, Matty didn't buy his clothes at

J. Press. With a broad face and bushy hair swept across his forehead, to the untrained eye he seemed equal parts cartoon *schmata* salesman and *Sweet Smell of Success*. Though both Rob Hoffman and Matty were Jewish, they were different breeds—a well-to-do Texan and a second-generation American *macher* who'd been around the block. Doug and Henry had likely only experienced his type on the streets of lower Manhattan or movie screens.

Matty, however, was more than a stereotype. Bright, shrewd, and self-educated, he'd read the great books on his own, rather than in the dorms on Harvard Yard. One preconception, however, was absolutely true about Matty: he was a gambler by nature.

Born in 1926, Matty was the second son of a poor sign painter and the grandson of Russian immigrants. As a teenager, he had worked to help support his family, and before his eighteenth birthday, he'd talked his way into a job at the *New York World-Telegram*. Serving stateside during World War II, Matty ran USO shows for the troops and got his first major taste of show business. He loved it.

After the war, Matty and his brother Don launched a publicity firm representing Lower East Side Italian restaurants and New York nightclubs—taking free dinners and fifty bucks a week in return for garnering newspaper coverage. Soon their clients included Heineken beer and jazz virtuoso Artie Shaw.

During the 1950s, Matty parlayed his innate smarts and nose for publicity into a position with Diner's Club, as it sought to launch the world's first credit card. Don remained in the business until he died of a cerebral hemorrhage in 1964. The following year, at the unveiling of Don's tombstone, Matty's son Michael saw his father weep in public, something he would not witness again until 1980.

At Diner's Club, Matty met City College grad Len Mogel, with whom he published *Signature*, the company's popular member magazine. As executive vice president, Matty ran editorial and marketing, while Mogel handled the business side—ad sales, purchasing, and production. By the mid-1960s, Matty was chomping at the bit for excitement and new horizons—a gambler seeking action—becoming part owner of the Philadelphia Warriors basketball team and purchasing a string of harness race horses.

In 1967, Matty and Mogel left Diner's Club to found 21st Century Communications, a publishing company they hoped to build into a powerhouse. It was a bold move, as both men abandoned good salaries despite having young children to support and upper-middle-class lifestyles to maintain. Matty had been living his own American dream at Park Avenue and Eighty-third, with a former chorus girl wife named Lee Easton and their three children (Michael, Andrew, and Julie) attending private school. That year, Matty and Mogel drew salaries in the mid-twenty thousands.

21st Century's first effort was a failure. *Cheetah* was an attempt to cash in on the burgeoning youth culture with a slick publication tied to a string of "counterculture" clubs. It lived a short life. At the same time, twenty-one-year-old Berkeley dropout Jann Wenner was trying to finance a music magazine named *Rolling Stone* that would target his own generation. Matty's instinct to go after the youth market was a good one, as no one had yet figured out how to coalesce the exploding demographic of well-educated kids born during the post–World War II euphoria.

The pair's second venture, however, was a success. Trading on their experience with direct-mail campaigns and targeted publications for membership organizations, 21st Century became publisher and half-owner of *Weight Watchers*, whose circulation reached 500,000 by late 1970. Matty and Mogel now had a financial engine to drive the growth of their company.

In early summer 1968, Matty received a call from his friend Harold Chamberlain, who told him that some Harvard kids working on a *Life* parody needed help on the business end. It was the beginning of a partnership that would change the lives of Simmons, Mogel, Beard, Kenney, and Hoffman and alter the course of American humor in ways that no one could anticipate.

* * *

Henry graduated in 1967 and began fulfilling his reserve duty, and Doug got his degree in spring 1968, while Rob Hoffman and Jim Rivaldo both entered their senior year the following fall. All were working on the *Life* parody.

Most other Poonies and Harvard students had made plans for postgraduate life. Treading the path of their predecessors, they were off to law, business, or medical school. Others headed for Wall Street, Madison Avenue, or academia.

Ivers and Mayer stayed in Cambridge, prolonging their college lifestyle, making art, and waiting to be esteemed by the world. Doug and Henry, living on small stipends from the *Harvard Lampoon*, arranged to stick around as well, working on *Life* and *Bored of the Rings*, a parody of J. R. R. Tolkein's *Lord of the Rings* that would sell 750,000 copies. For their work, the pair received a trip to the Virgin Islands and roughly $4,500 a piece in royalties. The success of their book ultimately provided much-needed income to the *Harvard Lampoon*, which was swimming in debt accrued from the *Life* parody.

Life was a financial disaster. Costs were out of control, and printing had been purchased at exorbitant rates, running up a $183,000 tab. Solicitations for ad sales had gotten a late start and the Lampoon was in horrible need of assistance, which came via the principals of 21st Century Communications.

Simmons and Mogel first met with Hoffman, Beard, and Kenney in June 1968 at 21st Century's cramped offices at 1790 Broadway in Midtown. Matty figured that the whole thing was a favor for a friend and a small financial opportunity.

Doug, the hippie, seemed nervous and pleasant. Hoffman was smart and driven, but knew little about publishing. Henry, Matty thought, was reminiscent of George S. Kaufman; quiet, but exuding wisdom and gravitas.

The group agreed that it was late in the game for *Life*, but Matty and Mogel offered to help sell ads for reduced commission and gave last-minute assistance in containing expenses.

Though the meeting was brief and friendly, Rivaldo noticed the seeds of a culture clash. "The *Harvard Lampoon* was a WASPy, preppy institution. Handing over our financial state to these somewhat boorish, somewhat tasteless, New York Jewish types was interesting."

This was certainly not driven by garden-variety anti-Semitism—Hoffman was Jewish, Henry too wise for such things, and Doug loved everyone—but rather from unfamiliarity borne of the insular surroundings of Harvard, Gilmour, Taft, and St. Mark's (Hoffman's Texas prep school), where the children of Moss Hart and Jerome Weidman represented New York Jewdom.

Life sold only half of its 750,000-copy print run, and the *Harvard Lampoon* lost $75,000. Yet amid the ruins, Matty and Mogel couldn't help wondering what might have happened if *Life* had been handled correctly from the start, with experienced hands managing the process and aiming at the right target. Their conclusion: it could have made real money.

Doug and Henry returned to Cambridge, where they worked on *Bored of the Rings* and an upcoming *Time* parody, while Hoffman left for coast guard reserve duty until spring 1969. Living at 118 Kinnaird for the first part of the year, the pair was intent on bailing out the financially strapped *Harvard Lampoon.*

Doug also spent much of the year living on Rivaldo's floor and receiving financial assistance from the Lampoon, as well as Ivers's mother. Here on his floor, Rivaldo thought, was a former Spee president and revered editor of the Lampoon, disheveled and surviving on handouts. Whatever money he received, Doug spent quickly, in keeping with what would be a lifelong indifference to and childlike attitude about finances.

Despite this, Doug told Rivaldo one night, "If I thought or knew that I wouldn't be a millionaire by the time I was thirty, I'd kill myself."

"Somehow, underneath, there was a sense of his being really, really driven," Rivaldo says. "He really had to succeed."

* * *

21st Century got involved much earlier on the *Time* parody and the results were dramatically different. Under the headline "Does Sex Sell Magazines?" the *Time* cover featured a half-naked blond—nether regions obscured by a *Newsweek*-peddler's apron—posed before a newsstand overflowing with well-known publications, all displaying her nubile form. They had learned their lesson from Walker Lewis's *Playboy* venture. Yes, sex did indeed sell magazines, and *Time* earned $250,000 for the *Harvard Lampoon*.

Len Mogel loved numbers. They were his métier. Thus, while early projections started coming in for *Time*, he began messing with figures on a scratchpad, concluding that the parody would quickly sell 90 percent of its print run. At the time only Helen Gurley Brown's *Cosmopolitan* regularly achieved such astronomical results.

Matty and Mogel talked. A national humor magazine, targeting the baby-boom youth culture they had missed with *Cheetah*, seemed like a very good idea.

"They saw possibilities in the Lampoon that we artistes didn't grasp," Rivaldo says.

A meeting with Kenney, Beard, Hoffman, and Rivaldo was called for June 1969 in Manhattan.

***

In previous conversations, Matty had spoken far less than Mogel. Matty handled editorial and publicity while Mogel was the business guy—the primary service they were providing to the *Harvard Lampoon*. Now, however, Matty was ready to become involved. He badly wanted to make a deal with "the boys" (as he called them) to publish *National Lampoon*. Though it was implied that other financing might be available through well-heeled Harvard grads, Kenney, Beard, and Hoffman (Rivaldo dropped out in midsummer) were interested in the same.

Matty's motives were well defined. 21st Century needed a flagship publication to become a meaningful player in the magazine business. They only owned 50 percent of *Weight Watchers*, which was profitable and enjoyed a wide circulation but had a limited reach and appeal. It would never be the cornerstone of an empire.

Matty saw opportunity in two areas: the youth market they'd explored with *Cheetah* and the fact that America was the only major country without a national humor magazine. England had *Punch*.

France had supported *Le Rire* for sixty years. The United States, however, had nothing but a string of failures with such names as *Humbug, Ballyhoo, Judge, Monocle, Grump*, and even *Captain Billy's Whiz Bang*. These magazines were published by everyone from famed writers (H. L. Mencken's *American Mercury*) and successful publishers (Hefner's *Trump*) to gifted cartoonists and rank amateurs. All of them, however, failed.

The two success stories in this area were different as night and day. Founded in the mid-1920s by Harold Ross, *The New Yorker* published humor and cartoons but was really more of a literary magazine aimed at Manhattanites and those who aspired to be from their Omaha and Chicago living rooms. *The New Yorker* was adult in the most sophisticated sense, with journalism and high culture mixed between the work of James Thurber, Robert Benchley, E. B. White, Dorothy Parker, S. J. Perelman, and Alexander Woolcott. It was urban and urbane in the extreme. Mainstream it was not.

Conversely, *MAD* was a smart-ass counterculture comic book-cum-magazine that was the Bible for cool disaffected kids of the 1950s who were confused by the idiot adults running the show. Underground Comix legend Robert Crumb, Monty Python alum Terry Gilliam, Doug Kenney, and innumerable other writers and humorists were greatly influenced by *MAD*—their generation's island of sanity in a seemingly idyllic era that they knew was anything but.

Yet *MAD* was for kids. Smart kids to be sure, but kids nonetheless. It was an "up yours" to the adult world, thumbing its nose at popular culture, government, and grown-ups. By the time readers reached their mid-teens, *MAD* became a thing of the past.

A gigantic void existed between *The New Yorker* and *MAD* that Matty sought to fill by bashing a line drive into the heart of the largest consumer demographic in American history. Simmons and Mogel had the business and promotional smarts, while Doug and Henry possessed the creative talent and instincts that would serve as a pipeline to the baby boom market. The boys could synthesize *MAD*'s attitude with *The New Yorker*'s literate style—all the while aiming the magazine at their peer group. They would term it a "brains and money" deal, with Simmons and Hoffman negotiating on behalf of their respective parties.

Early on, Hoffman set out guidelines pertaining to his alma mater. *National Lampoon* would need to pay a 2 percent royalty to the *Harvard Lampoon* for use of its name, and no single issue could be a direct parody of another magazine, which would conflict with what they were doing in Cambridge.

No problem.

Then they got down to it. With Matty and Mogel putting up $300,000 in startup funds, Hoffman suggested they split stock ownership down the middle, with each party owning 50 percent of the magazine. Matty and Mogel, however, needed to own 80 percent so that they could add *National Lampoon* earnings to their balance sheet and secure public financing in the future. Matty also found the even split hard to stomach, as 21st Century brought legitimate experience to the table, while Kenney, Beard, and Hoffman had only published a few college parodies.

Hoffman stood firm. With personal economic security in their favor, he and Henry knew they wouldn't starve if the deal fell through. Though from less certain circumstances, Doug had full confidence in his own talents and believed Hoffman was doing the right thing.

The group broke for a day to think matters over, with Matty eager to make the deal. As time passed, that eagerness grew, despite his belief that the best deals are those you don't have to make.

Returning to the table, both parties agreed to an eighty-twenty split, with an understanding that Kenney, Beard, and Hoffman's share was actually worth 33 percent of the magazine's value. It broke down like this: one-third for the brains and license, and two-thirds for the publishing expertise and the money.

Matty then proposed a buyout at five years from the date of the magazine's first issue, where 21st Century would purchase the boys' stock at eight times earnings. Hoffman, however, had done thorough research and found that publishing companies were being valued at sixteen times earnings and countered with an offer based on that multiple.

The deal Matty wanted to make was on the table, but the stakes were getting higher—maybe too high—and he worried that *National Lampoon* might be a huge success, yet the buyout would cause him to lose the magazine in five years. The more successful the venture, the higher the payout, the greater the risk.

Matty asked for a clause giving 21st Century the option of paying the editors over a number of years if he had trouble accessing cash. Hoffman said no.

To ease his mind, Matty sought counsel from two business acquaintances—both told him not to worry. One of the men, Manhattan underwriter Graham Loving, guaranteed to secure public financing when the deal came due. The market was good, and if the magazine were a success, Loving said, there was no reason for concern. Investors would be all over it. If it failed? Then Matty's worries didn't matter.

When the parties reconvened, Matty confessed feeling like an idiot for worrying about the magazine being too successful. Doug spoke for the group, assuring Matty that they were partners and that the boys had no intention of damaging them. The deal was struck.

"Rob was the better negotiator than I was," Matty says. "No question."

* * *

Though no one quantified the opportunity that lay before them in precise terms, the zeitgeist gave not-so-subtle hints that the time was right for *National Lampoon*.

On CBS in the late 1960s, the Smothers Brothers made pot references and gently criticized the Vietnam War. For this they were censored. At NBC, two Vegas veterans—the arch, worldly Dan Rowan and befuddled goofball Dick Martin—presided over *Laugh-In*, a chaotic, beflowered '60s-style "happening" that served up laugh lines like "sock it to me" and "you bet your sweet bippy," while the hardly subversive likes of Arte Johnson, Ruth Buzzi, and Joanne Worley chewed the scenery, making the counterculture palatable for the forty-seven-year-old Dayton housewife.

And this is where comedy ran into reality. Bad times make for good humor. In the late 1960s and early '70s, happiness was hardly an apt description for the American mood, where young people were sneering at their parents who thought the world was going to hell in a handbasket.

The cold war and McCarthyism had given way to a youthful vision of the world, ushering in an era of civil rights and a sense of hope and justice. John F. Kennedy spoke to the nation about fairness and doing for your country, helping citizens pass from a culture built around grandfather figures to one of youth, optimism, and vigor.

It was not to be. After Kennedy was shot, Americans transformed from a seemingly united people into a country of well-defined factions—the old guards and the kids. It started peacefully, with hopes for a world free of hate and violence. But "All You Need Is Love" soon gave way to "Burn Baby Burn."

The Summer of Love and Woodstock were anomalies. Instead, there was Altamont, the murders of Bobby Kennedy and Martin Luther King, the Black Panthers screaming louder than the civil rights advocates. There was Kent State, the bloody 1968 Democratic Convention, and the deaths of Jimi Hendrix, Janis Joplin, and Jim Morrison. Dreams of utopia espoused in Berkeley and Madison turned ugly, leaving antiwar singer Country Joe MacDonald to half-joke that the revolution had been a success so long as it was measured by growing one's hair and taking a lot of drugs.

Heading into the 1970s, America was no longer a nation divided. Instead, as the Old South breathed its last furious gasps and women stormed the workforce, the idea of one nation was about to shatter like a mirror thrown to the ground, leaving millions of pissed-off shards, each individual believing the group to which he or she belonged was being screwed. The man who led the charge was Richard Nixon, as demon-filled, angry, and savvy a president as the nation had known.

Nixon's persona was unappealing. He was a dramatic departure from the charismatic likes of FDR, Ike, JFK, and LBJ, each of whom charmed the nation by force of personality as much as political insight and daring. Nixon was different. His appearance and demeanor raised the question "Would you buy a used car from this man?"

Privately, Nixon hated blacks, Jews, hippies, and the blue-blooded Ivy Leaguers who had blackballed him from elite New York law firms, as well as anyone else he deemed a threat. Nixon entered office promising to bring the nation together while enacting policies that pandered to the opposition but cut out their hearts at the same time. Instead of peace and prosperity, he gave us Spiro Agnew, Bebe Rebozo, John Mitchell, Watergate, the Saturday Night Massacre, and G. Gordon Liddy. But before any of that, Nixon understood something that the rest of America (other than George Wallace) didn't seem to get.

Nixon rode into office by harnessing the angry white vote. The forty-seven-year-old Dayton housewife who might think Rowan and Martin were the last word on youth culture had always voted Democratic in deference to her union-member husband. Now, however, she was in play—disillusioned with the liberal party and their fancy educations, as well as the mixing of races in her neighborhood and high taxes. Nixon understood this kind of woman and her family and offered himself as an answer to similar souls across the growing Sun Belt and recuperating South. In 1968, their votes would put this unlikely man in the White House.

Nixon had, at best, an awkward sense of humor (as Hunter Thompson put it, "[I] couldn't imagine him laughing at anything except maybe a paraplegic who wanted to vote Democratic, but couldn't quite reach the lever on the voting machine"), which made him all the more suitable as a subject for comedy. Since the early 1950s humorists had been on to his game. Cartoonist Herblock filled the *Washington Post* with caricatures of Nixon emerging from sewers and burning the Statue of Liberty as if she were a witch. Pranksters arranged much-hyped but poorly attended Nixon rallies on college campuses. Others told Nixon gala bandleaders that the candidate's favorite song was "Mack the Knife." In 1961, *Esquire* introduced its Dubious Achievement awards that to this day feature Nixon, mouth agape, and asking, "Why is this man laughing?" Even Ike mocked him behind his back.

For Nixon it would only get worse, as he was about to provide endless material to a group he disdained: a bunch of overeducated, pot-smoking, Ivy League graduates and their simpatico friends. For Doug Kenney, Henry Beard, and *National Lampoon*, Nixon and his stewardship of a nation in shambles was the gift that just kept on giving.

While the New York publishing world mourned the deaths of estimable, long-running, general-interest magazines such as the *Saturday Evening Post, Colliers, McCall's,* and others, the stars were perfectly aligned for *National Lampoon.*

* * *

In September 1969, Doug and Henry sublet a duplex from a friend's parents on East Eighty-third in Manhattan. Henry occupied an attic/loft upstairs, while Doug and girlfriend Alex Garcia-Mata lived downstairs. Hoffman commuted from Cambridge, where he was finishing school. Both Doug and Henry were confident, a self-assurance born of belief in their own intellects and derived from attending Harvard at a time when it truly meant something to be educated in Cambridge. They were filled with ideas and ready to do something sharper, more outrageous, and less constrained than the *Harvard Lampoon.*

Faced with the task of creating a magazine from whole cloth, they relied on familiar sources, including Harvard friends Chris Cerf and George Trow, with an assist from George Plimpton. Now writing for *The New Yorker*, Trow chose to make his initial *National Lampoon* appearances under the byline Tamara Gould, so as to not alert his employer that he was moonlighting.

Cerf, meanwhile, was working for his father at Random House, where he made the acquaintance of Michael O'Donoghue, a writer who'd make everyone else at *National Lampoon* look mild by comparison.

The pair met in 1968 while Cerf was editing O'Donoghue's book *The Incredible Thrilling Adventures of the Rock*, which was just that: the story of a rock who sat in a forest not doing anything much, essentially just sitting there. Cerf loved him. Tall and physically soft with a prematurely balding pate, O'Donoghue and his sensibilities were, to put it mildly, out of the mainstream. "[Years later] somebody gave him an original painting by John Wayne Gacy," Cerf recalls. "That sort of describes his ethos."

Born in 1940, O'Donoghue was the eldest child of an engineer and his wife who resided in rural Sauquoit, New York. Their home was filled with books, classical music, and Mrs. O'Donoghue's frequently nasty sense of humor, which her only son gladly claimed as his birthright. He was beyond dark or black Irish; he was macabre.

"He aspired to be the anti-Christ," Harold Ramis said of O'Donoghue.

At age six, O'Donoghue came down with rheumatic fever and was confined to his bedroom for an entire year. Living in his imagination during that time, young Michael (known then as Pete) began showing signs that he wasn't like the other boys, perhaps best evidenced by towering rages that could only be controlled when his mother doused him with ice water.

Though he played on the high school baseball team, O'Donoghue—like Doug—was hardly "one of the guys." Rather than fit in and play the gregarious, literate wise guy, O'Donoghue mastered the art of the nasty barb.

"I learned early in the game that some of the kids could beat me up," O'Donoghue said. "But I found that I could make a remark that would keep them crying in their pillows for the next three days."

Tossed out of the University of Rochester for nonattendance and stealing a campus police car, O'Donoghue ran off to San Francisco, where he helped publish an alternative press poetry magazine and took college courses before a brief stint at the San Francisco *Examiner*—where he was fired for brandishing a lead-type bar at a coworker who had crossed him.

Returning to Rochester, O'Donoghue reenrolled and became involved in experimental theater. Briefly indulging in therapy to cool his temper, he soon came to the conclusion that analysis would take the edge off his creativity. Underlying his rage and grandiosity was a profound insecurity regarding women and peers.

On Pearl Harbor Day 1963, O'Donoghue entered a brief marriage to a receptionist named Janice Tripp, who had three children he was ill suited to parent, to say the least. The couple divorced after three months, freeing O'Donoghue to head for Manhattan, where he held day jobs that ranged from store clerk to costume jewelry salesman, all the while submitting work to the *Evergreen Review*, an avant-garde literary magazine. Soon he was collaborating with a mainstream artist named Frank Springer on a bizarre comic serial about a voluptuous, naked, deceased, international superheroine called Phoebe Zeitgeist, which quickly became an underground hit—earning its creator oodles of esteem in Greenwich Village literary circles. Ambitious and protected by an artifice of self-confidence, O'Donoghue had only begun to scratch the surface of his immense talent and the success he envisioned for himself. From the frail, sickly boy with the sharp wit, he was beginning to morph into a character of his own creation—the dark prince of offensive comedy, more interested in provoking reaction than laughter.

"The Adventures of Phoebe Zeitgeist" led to *The Rock*, Random House, and Cerf—a contemporary possessing childlike glee for new things and boundless enthusiasm for talented people. Cerf had been contacted by Abbie Hoffman about publishing a parody sports program for the upcoming trial of the Chicago Seven in Judge Julius Hoffman's courtroom. Trow and O'Donoghue were brought in to collaborate. This, in turn, led O'Donoghue to Doug, Henry, and the early planning of *National Lampoon*.

* * *

Though they had office space at 1790 Broadway, Henry and Doug preferred a casual atmosphere for planning the *National Lampoon*. The first meetings were held at the duplex on East Eighty-third. Cerf, Henry, Doug, Trow, and Harvard friend Michael Frith were all involved. Plimpton helped when he was available.

They discussed what had and hadn't worked at Harvard. A monthly would be a far bigger job than a yearly, straightforward parody of one magazine. Format and content were defined and refined over several months, both at the duplex and at once-a-week dinners at the Blue Ribbon, an old-fashioned German restaurant decorated with pictures of legendary opera stars.

These "playful, mean dinners," as Trow called them, were free-form. Doug worked from a stream of consciousness and off the cuff, tossing out witty ideas and working intuitively; Henry made thoughtful contributions and took detailed notes on an ever-present pad; O'Donoghue, however, was like a quiet predator who'd finally discovered his prey. This was a moment he'd been anticipating for years. Preparation had finally met opportunity—as he'd known it would—and he carefully shared clearly defined ideas that he'd been cataloguing in a metal box in his dingy Soho loft for years.

Though he liked his new colleagues, and appreciated their intelligence and humor, O'Donoghue wasn't intimidated by their fancy background and education or his lack thereof. Instead, he was aggressive and confident—seeing them through his own inimitable lens as "a bunch of Harvard snot faggots who thought it was wrong to shed blood. It was I that taught them the true essence of comedy is a baby seal hunt, that rather than using the épée, try the bludgeon."

Doug immediately took to his new colleague. At the time, O'Donoghue's sartorial style was Lower Manhattan slumming nonchic, all army jackets and crappy ensembles. Trow and Cerf liked him—providing entrée—but Doug saw that he was another teacher who could help him take his writing and sensibilities to places he yearned to go but had not yet found. O'Donoghue was the real thing, embodying the post-beatnik world that Doug could only dream of in Chagrin Falls.

By the end of the year, the opening roster was set: Doug, Henry, O'Donoghue, Frith, Cerf, Trow, and John Weidman were the major contributors, with additional pieces by comedy veterans such as Roger Price of *Mad Libs* fame and Ralph Schoenstein. This, however, left the boys in need of an artistic presence that could provide visual support to their humor.

* * *

The aptly named Cloud Studio could only have existed in Manhattan or San Francisco during the late 1960s. Housed on the second floor of a run-down clothing showroom in Lower Manhattan's East Village, with floor-to-ceiling windows facing the street, Cloud was filled with underground artwork, photo collages, psychedelic posters, and statuary as well as ample amounts of pot smoke—not unlike a set for Peter Sellers's faux psychedelic *I Love You, Alice B. Toklas.*

Cloud was the brainchild of Peter Bramley and Bill Skurski, two talented underground artists who'd met as working-class students at the Massachusetts College of Art. Moving to New York, they went into business with a frizzy-haired photographer named Michael Sullivan, artist's agent Howard Bloom, and a few others, achieving success doing book jackets for *Evergreen Review*, Grove Press, and Avon Books as well as plenty of commercial artwork and some magazine design. In keeping with the spirit of the times, the studio was operated as a collective. Though Bramley and Skurski were partners and owners, the money was shared equally.

Cloud was, as they used to say, "a regular scene." Rock bands and artists of every stripe (Robert Crumb, David Bowie, and Debbie Harry) dropped by while in Manhattan. And at the East Village loft they found a great place to party and hang with like-minded folk. Bramley dressed like a court jester in puffy silk knickers and pirate shirts. With long dirty hair, Skurski resembled a latter-day Rasputin.

Doug was uncommonly attracted to this aesthetic. His vision for the Lampoon was to create something both unlike any other magazine on the market and in keeping with the West Coast's emerging Underground Comix movement. He wanted a completely original look and design, and it was Doug who lobbied hard to hire Skurski and Bramley as the Lampoon's art directors.

Henry was less sold. At meetings in the East Village, he would calmly play with his pipe and give off an air of educated, articulate reserve. Bramley bonded with Henry over a shared affection for Robert Benchley and the denizens of the Algonquin Round Table. Doug wholeheartedly embraced the place. He loved to come down and be among artists and musicians, dropping acid and smoking pot to blow off steam.

With Henry deferring to Doug's instinct, it became clear that the editors didn't share the same creative vision as Matty, who wanted something slick and highly commercial—all the better to sell to advertisers seeking to peddle wares to "the kids." Henry, with his lordly command of English, continually couched any outlandish direction as being "the last thing we want to do . . ." meaning, of course, that it was precisely what he and Doug wanted to do and counter to whatever Matty desired. It was a perfect fit with Cloud, where the whole attitude was that idealistic and unfettered people could create magical things. The Man wasn't going to tell them what to do.

4

You've Got a Weird Mind.

You'll Fit in Well Here.

Sirs:

It says here that you're starting some sort of funny magazine. All I can say is that you people have a lot of nerve. Haven't you looked outside your own selfish egos long enough to see that people are being wronged and oppressed all over the world? Take the fascist military regimes which seem to grow in number every year. In these stricken countries, you can't even look cross-eyed without the secret police writing your name down in little notebooks. It may even be years later that one night you are roused from your sleep by the terrifying sound of rifle butts breaking down your flimsy rattan door. The brutal thug drags you, heedless of your piteous cries, deep, deep into the jungle. Never to return. And you, with your funny magazine.

—*Viola da Gamba, South Orange, New Jersey*
(The first fictitious letter to the editor appearing in
the April 1970 National Lampoon)

The following things happened in 1970: John and Yoko declared it the first year A.P. (After Peace); the Chicago Seven were acquitted; Elvis played Vegas for the first time; a poll found that 61 percent of Americans approved of Nixon's job performance; Diana Ross quit the Supremes; Charles Manson released a folk album; and antiwar protesters began a seventy-five-day fast in Washington, D.C.

* * *

The March 23, 1970, *Newsweek* ran a small item about Kenney, Beard, and Hoffman, describing Lampoon as a brash newcomer that would "cut its teeth on the vaunted sex revolution of the '60s." The editors told *Newsweek* that they were going after a new audience that went beyond bright young college kids, also targeting those who were out of school and the aging college kid in nearly everyone under thirty.

"Putting out a monthly that will entertain the nearly 30s may make these youthful editors old fast," *Newsweek* concluded.

* * *

Before the first issue went to press, there were unresolved details of the deal between 21st Century and the editors of *National Lampoon*. Namely, no contract had been signed.

When the parties met, Hoffman informed Matty that, in the time that had passed since their earlier negotiations, the value of publishing companies had risen to eighteen times earnings and requested that the buyout multiple be bumped up to the twenties. With a strong stock market and expectations that the magazine would perform, at the very least, at a multiple in the high teens, Matty signed the contract in February 1970. The turning point, though, came a year later when Matty and Mogel told the editors that neither could they afford nor did they need to contribute any more than the $169,000 in start-up funds that had already been spent. From Hoffman's point of view, this, by definition, altered the agreement. If the money side was now worth only roughly 56 percent of what they'd originally intended, then the brains side must be worth more than originally thought.

Because 21st Century had $300,000 worth of equity in the magazine, Hoffman agreed to release Matty and Mogel from the remaining obligation of $131,000 if they increased the multiple to between twenty-five and thirty-three times earnings. The buyout figure now stood at roughly thirty times earnings for cash and a multiple of thirty-two for stock. Less than two years from the date of their first meeting at which terms were discussed, a five-year buyout was set at nearly four times Matty's initial proposal of eight times earnings.

* * *

Beard described the first six issues as both "loathsome" and "a nightmare." He also classified *National Lampoon* as "one of the ten worst business ideas of 1969, up there with starting a steel mill or shipping line with American crews," but noted that "we had youth and stupidity going for us."

Working from 21st Century's newly refurbished offices at 635 Madison Avenue, the Lampoon staff consisted of Doug (editor), Henry (executive editor), Hoffman (managing editor), a copyeditor, a subscription manager, an art assistant, and a secretary. These were the full-time employees of *National Lampoon* and just about all that could fit in the fourth floor offices down the hall from *Weight Watchers*.

Michael Frith, Chris Cerf, George Trow, John Weidman, and Michael O'Donoghue were given contributing editor titles but no offices. The idea of no office suited O'Donoghue. Strangely, and much to his credit, Matty adored his bizarre new contributor and badly wanted him to become an official member of the staff. The dark prince, however, driven by something like mild paranoia, or at the very least a profound mistrust of others, preferred to maintain freelance status, affording him control over the rights to and credit for his work.

In the fall 1969 planning sessions, it had been decided that each issue would be loosely based on a theme, with the writers and artists adapting their styles of humor to topics such as: Sex (April), Greed (May), Blight (June), Bad Taste (July), Paranoia (August), and Show Biz (September).

Priced at seventy-five cents, the sex issue covered familiar ground, harkening back to the *Playboy* and *Time* parodies with a barely dressed, tousle-bouffanted enchantress staring at readers from the newsstand. The chosen topic and image of a beautiful woman were pleasing to Matty, who believed, as the Harvard parody had proved, that sex certainly did sell magazines. Yet that was where Matty's admiration for the work of Cloud Studios ended. The raven-haired model was set against a backdrop that drifted between the color of day-old coffee and muddy brick crayon. The result: from more than five feet away, it was hard to distinguish the sultry hottie from the rest of the page. All that stood out was a smiling cartoon duck that Cloud created as a Groucho-esque Lampoon mascot.

This execution displeased Matty immensely, as he knew that the magazine cover needed to pop from the newsstand. It was essential to circulation, advertising, and, ultimately, revenue.

After World War II, the magazine business had entered a losing battle with the consumer world. Television had become the medium of choice for consumers and advertisers, slowly but surely eating away at mass-market, general-interest magazine sales and revenue. The industry responded by specializing and trying to serve niche markets: boat enthusiasts, teenage girls, and the like.

Another factor working against publishers was the death of the newsstand as a source of information and communal gathering place. Along with television, the automobile was the cause of this problem. With cars now being marketed and made affordable to most income levels, commuters had fewer and fewer opportunities to buy and read magazines at railway and subway stations or on the trains that took them to work. Instead, Americans were behind the wheel listening to the radio.

Matty knew better than anyone that they were embarking on a high-stakes gambit. With no direct-mail lists or readership studies available from which to build a subscriber base of cool young people who liked to laugh, *National Lampoon* would have to pull off the toughest trick of all—developing readership through full-price newsstand sales, and then build circulation via content and word of mouth. With a solid circulation they could then attract advertisers and ultimately create a profitable magazine. It wouldn't be easy.

* * *

The April Sex issue sold 225,000 of its 500,000 print run, with many consumers probably thinking they were buying another *Harvard Lampoon* parody. Those who read it found a jumbled mix of humor that had been written to please the sensibilities of the editors, with no regard for target markets, in the hope that readers would laugh as well.

The Sex issue featured, among other things: Weidman's dead-on Dr. Seuss spoof about a masturbating Splurch named Seymour; Aristotle Onassis's lost love letters to Jackie Kennedy—written in preposterously broken English and peppered with odd woo-pitching dominated by an ineffectual metaphorical obsession with goats and mushrooms; a *Playboy* parody featuring a "liberated" centerfold; Trow's, writing as Tamara Gould, silly gossip column, "People Are . . . " ("People are surprised . . . at how quickly the whole Black Power–Civil Rights balloon burst . . . We're not . . . All that talk-talk-talk about 'oppression' . . . So unfun."); and "White House Romance," a comic detailing the sexless marriage of Julie Nixon and David Eisenhower. O'Donoghue's "Mondo Perverto" was a scandal sheet rip-off whose headlines screamed, "The Case for Killing Our Aged" ("'The Eskimos had the right idea—feed them to the dogs,' says geriatric expert Dr. Carl Ahntholz") and "Nympho Wills Heart to Eleanor Roosevelt."

Another O'Donoghue piece, "Pornocopia," parodied pornography in various literary styles, including John Cleland, Jacqueline Susann, the Marquis de Sade, and Anonymous penning a "Fin-de-Siècle British Birching Book," in which Lord Randy Stoker (whose friends include the Sultana of Zosh, Reverend John Thomas, Professor Schadenfreude, and the Duke of Pudenda) greets his new housekeeper, Miss Prissy Trapp, in a manor house adorned with padded walls, barred windows, an immodest fresco, and a bloodstained altar. Before their encounter is over, he unleashes two eunuchs and reveals the workings of "the blind chicken," a sexual device composed of steam-engine pistons, rubber tubing, manacles, a gilded harpsichord, asparagus tips, a whalebone corset, and a vat of scented lard.

O'Donoghue was only scratching the surface of where he would take his humor.

* * *

Henry and Doug introduced the fictitious letters section, the first thing a reader saw after the table of contents. Spiro Agnew wrote in, objecting to references addressing Martha Mitchell as "Binky"; Galsworthy ruminated on that "hot house flower" that is love, only to be refuted in the following letter by the decidedly less scholarly Mayflower Van Lines of Shaker Heights, Ohio; sixteenth-century Dutch painter Hans Holbein asks for a subscription, but only if he can be guaranteed pictures of naked women in each issue; one correspondent recommends an entire issue devoted to the pancreas; and Andrew I sends the following cryptic entreaty from Zanzibar:

> I have done what you asked me with regard to the coconuts and am happy to report that the shipment is safe and once again underway. I was there in person when they were put into the cotton wool and can confirm that every fourth one has been infected, shaved on the tip, etc. . . . etc. . . . as you specified in your letter to Fran.
>
> I wish I could be as encouraging concerning the rest of the matter. If Mueller has not already told you, then I am sure Bankhali will, in his usual detail. All I know is what I saw, or could learn from Geneva.
>
> When Mueller and I had arrived, the huts had already been destroyed and Janson and his little band of toughs had half the tribe in his control. The transmitter tower had been set aflame and two of Grace's cats had diarrhea.
>
> What do you wish me to do with the Anglican minister, who, after all was never directly responsible for what happened at the club, and will, next month have been in the basement a year? And how about Carter? Does he know about Fran, or doesn't he buy those types of magazines? Sometimes he does not appear to be as pure and holy as he would have us all believe. Do you wish me to attend the railway meeting, or should I simply act as if Geneva (and

Fayette, Iowa, for that matter) had never contacted the school? Will this irritate Bankhali all the more, or will it only mean that it will be April 64 all over again.

Write to Frank, if you prefer, as I still have access to the bathhouse and can still always get my hands on her mail. She is still in close touch with Beard and Kenny, but I get the impression that this is only part of being a dentist's wife. Anyway, it is she who has the report, and not Mueller. Thank god for little mercies.

I will be in New York shortly, before Eberts returns from Uruguay, and I will get into 21st publishing myself. I see no reason why we can't sit for a hot-dog, and work out the guilt issue.

Doug also introduced two long-running columns. The first was "Horrorscope," which predicted the future by ever-changing means. He included everything, from palmistry to phrenology, ichthyomancy (analyzing the first fish pulled from a newly thawed stream) to haruspicy (examining the entrails of sacrificial animals), which he employed in the April issue:

"April 30 (stuffing) Reverend Billy Graham performs famous 'walking on waters' finale before 50,000 gaping faithful in Atlantic City, N.J. Later discovered attempting to hide a pair of inflatable pontoons in a suitcase, Graham states, 'the lord works in strange and wondrous ways,' and refuses further comment."

April 1970 was also the first appearance of "Mrs. Agnew's Diary," modeled after "Mrs. Wilson's Diary" in *Private Eye*, where British humorist Jonathan Wells satirized the innermost thoughts of Prime Minister Harold Wilson's wife. Mrs. Agnew showcased Doug's ability to create and inhabit a fantasy world based in the reality of Nixonian politics and an administration that he believed was controlled by the worst of American values. He did this with savagery and wit, but also empathy.

The simple conceit of the diary is that Judy Agnew offers, through innocent and idiotic eyes, a view of the vulgar ghouls running the country. Beyond their politics, Doug sees the Nixons and Agnews and their cronies as people who: devour meatloaf, cottage cheese, and ketchup under the guise of American cuisine; read the worst bestsellers and pass themselves off as curious; and are totally out of touch with everything outside of white middle-class Phoenix and Toledo.

Dear Diary:

Today was so exciting! Pat and Dick called up this morning to invite us to lunch in the upstairs room! Spiggy [the name by which Doug's Judy Agnew refers to her husband] thought Dick had something up his sleeve again because Pat only invites us upstairs when Dick wants to make a big deal impression.

Spiggy emerges as more than a lout. Instead, Doug gives us a man so cynical that perhaps he, and he alone, completely understands what deceitful, conniving assholes Nixon, Mitchell, and Kissinger truly are. Agnew is appalling but also strangely endearing, as he and Judy play Fred (though in truth more like Archie Bunker) and Ethel Mertz to the Nixons' Ricky and Lucy Ricardo, reducing the nation's capital to a ridiculously bland, tasteless suburban neighborhood.

For his part, Agnew hates everyone and trusts no one—most of all Nixon: "Spiggy grumbled all the while about how Dick is such a tight-ass at parties, but I said it was part of Dick's job and he couldn't help it. Spiggy said that he knew how to help it, but I told him to shush."

Judy is the banal town chatterbox who unwittingly writes the truth: "Pat sort of coughed and got up saying that she had to see the maid about the cat, which seems odd now, because I was sure Pat hates cats. Personally, I like cats, but I didn't know Pat and Dick did. I think cats are cute."

Martha Mitchell is the blowsy, mouthy, indiscreet town drunk and political liability: "John says Binky is very opinionated and that's why he loves her. Keeps him on his toes, he says. One thing you can say for John, he's always on his toes."

Kissinger is an obnoxious philanderer, constantly bedding female employees whom he houses in an office he stole from Agnew. He and Spiggy hash out their differences during a rage-filled game of ping-pong in the Agnew family basement rumpus room:

Spiggy blinked and laughed again, but this time, the way he does when he really doesn't think anything is funny. Hey Hank, he said, what exactly were you doing in Germany in 1938? That made Hank a little mad, I think, because he gave the ball a real hard swat and said he didn't understand how somebody could become a household word with a last name like Anagostopoulous. Spiggy sort of winced and asked Hank if he'd ever read the biography of Cardinal Richelieu, because Hank might find it interesting. Hank sort of smirked and said Spiggy would find *Death of a Salesman* just as interesting, that is, if Spiggy could get somebody to read it to him.

All of a sudden I noticed that Spiggy's ears were getting very pink, which around our little roost means he's having trouble keeping his temper.

Pat Nixon comes off as a hypertense freak of a miserable housewife who takes the administration wives on a shopping expedition that consists of a long, unpleasant bus ride to a tacky Korvette's department store in a suburban Maryland mall ("Pat said this place was smart and sensible"), where Binky Mitchell purchases a gold body stocking, two football helmets, and a speargun.

Nixon is strange beyond belief, playing Ouija with Billy Graham (who Doug implies received early training at Ringling Brothers Circus), employing roller-skating waiters for cash-bar White House cocktail parties, and returning tailored suits for fear that he will be charged for working cuff buttons.

The Nixon children are terrified, astoundingly sheltered, pathetic, and just plain weird. At a White House party for the underprivileged (that devolves into Daniel Patrick Moynihan performing a clown act for D.C. derelicts), Tricia weeps uncontrollably over every mishap, including melted ice cream bars, causing Judy to wonder whether Tricia doesn't cry an awful lot for a girl her age.

Three-quarters of the way through the issue, Doug shows his taste for the sacred cows of his parents' generation in a parody ad for the erotic drawings of Norman Rockwell (known as Rockwall in the piece). Modeled after an actual ad for Picasso's erotic works,

Doug takes the master of small-town American nostalgia to places no one could imagine.

In his studio, surrounded by stuffed dogs and apple pies, Rockwall mistakenly takes a drag of paint thinner, thinking that it's his usual tonic of saltines dissolved in warm cream soda. Thus a commemorative product for the Daughters of the American Revolution becomes a group of outlandish porno sketches depicting American archetypes in a variety of perversions. "Voluptuous cheerleaders surrender themselves to lovable and lustful old country doctors, sinewy grandmothers writhe on drugstore counters with pimply soda jerks, and snub-nosed 10-year-old tads are observed behind the corncrib locked in the embrace of love with good old Spot."

Running two pages, it is the work of a young humorist who knows exactly what he is doing and where his ultimate genius lies— in the loving celebration and debunking of the icons and happy memories of times for which the nation was becoming highly nostalgic, a world not so unlike Chagrin Falls.

* * *

Greed and Blight followed the same mold, with the core group taking whacks at a wide cross section of the culture, utilizing their own style with varying levels of success. There were O. Henry parodies; a series of letters between Thoreau and Emerson bandying about various commercial uses for the tract of land at Walden Pond—perhaps a faux woodsy vacation spot or a bottling facility for Emerson's Own Transcendental Vapors; O'Donoghue's mock interview with Howard Hughes, where the reclusive billionaire turns out to be a completely normal and reasonable fellow who confesses to really having enjoyed the Don Knotts cartoon film *The Incredible Mr. Limpet*; an industrial pollutant magazine named *Sludge*; and "Crossing the Rubicam," O'Donoghue's slam on the soon-to-be consumerist lefty youth culture, featuring ads for Che's Pills for Asthma Relief and Up Against the Wall Carpeting.

* * *

On December 31, 1969, Doug asked Alex Garcia-Mata to marry him in the living room of the duplex on East Eighty-third. Surprised, but not displeased, she figured, why not?

Two weeks later the *New York Times* announced the engagement of Douglas C. Kenney and Alexandra Appleton Garcia-Mata, the daughter of Mr. and Mrs. Carlos Garcia-Mata of New Canaan, Connecticut, and Nantucket Island, Massachusetts.

Alex's father was the former commercial attaché at the Argentine embassy in Washington, D.C., and the successful owner of a Manhattan consulting and finance concern. His daughter had debuted at the Darien-New Canaan Cotillion and was educated at the best schools: New Canaan Country School, Virginia's Madeira School, and Radcliffe. The wedding would take place that June at the Garcia-Mata's New Canaan home.

That spring, Doug visited Alex in Washington, D.C., where she lived while teaching at Madeira. Doug attempted to back out of the wedding, but couldn't provide specific reasons. Alex, thinking her fiancé was suffering from cold feet, talked him out of it.

When Doug returned to New York, he was clearly ambivalent about the idea of getting married. Writer Anne Beatts, who soon joined the magazine, met Doug on a visit to the offices at 635 Madison. The first question Doug asked Beatts, after introductions, was whether he should be getting married. With his wedding only a few weeks away, Beatts thought Doug had bigger problems than his impending marriage if he was asking her advice. Nearly everyone at the magazine had heard the same question time and again.

That June, one hundred and fifty guests sat in the garden of the Garcia-Mata's lovely New Canaan home to witness the marriage of a handsome Harvard-educated couple. When Doug's friends showed up, it became clear that this would be no ordinary event. The groom had been out late the night before. Everyone had been smoking pot, and many were dressed in the kind of things one simply didn't wear to a wedding in New Canaan, or for that matter just about anywhere. Outrageous comments were made in voices too loud to be ignored, causing enormous discomfort for the Garcia-Matas, the Kenneys, and their friends.

"I think Doug is having second thoughts," a friend said to Tim Mayer.

"I think Alex is having first thoughts," Mayer replied.

Behind the scenes, nearly everyone close to Doug tried to talk him out of going through with the wedding. Chris Hart, a grooms-man, liked Alex just fine, but he didn't think his friend truly wanted to be married.

Shortly before the wedding, Hoffman and best man Peter Ivers took Doug behind a neighbor's garage, where they shared a joint and tried to talk him out of getting married.

"Why do you want to get married?" Ivers asked.

"No reason," Doug replied.

"No, really?" Ivers said.

Again, "no reason" was the answer.

Ivers offered to get Doug out of the wedding. The best man suggested that he could explain to the bride and everyone's parents that the groom just couldn't do it.

Doug did go through with the wedding. He and Alex tied the knot and returned to the duplex. They weren't alone.

Khosla and a number of Harvard friends joined the newlyweds on their wedding night. In fact, Doug had invited a friend to stay at the apartment—in their bed—leaving the happy couple on the couch. It was a sign of things to come.

After a short honeymoon at the Garcia-Mata's Nantucket home, where Doug worked on the next installment of Mrs. Agnew while Alex laughed, the couple began their life together—with Henry Beard. Though they shared a downstairs bedroom, privacy wasn't in the off-ing. The hermetic Henry, while not intrusive, was omnipresent and lived upstairs. Despite Alex's affection for Henry and overall good cheer, it was clear that the marriage was going to be far from traditional.

Like Amy Carlson before her, Alex acted as den mother to the boys and whatever manner of Harvard classmates, childhood friends, and prospective comedy writers found their way to her Upper East Side doorstep. Alex cooked, cleaned, and made a home for Doug and his coworkers while her husband consumed himself with two tasks: putting out a monthly humor magazine and having fun.

Both Doug and Henry were working immensely long hours, especially Henry. Fourteen- to eighteen-hour days were not uncommon, with long, drunken dinner meetings at restaurants nearly every night. At such meetings, Beatts recalls Doug frequently leaving the table to call his wife, promising that he would be home in an hour, then staying for several more. Beatts thought, "I never want to be on the other end of that phone."

Doug's home and work life had become an extension of his Harvard existence, with a constant stream of visitors generously being offered accommodations by the newly married editor. Doug never asked how long anyone was going to stay and created no boundaries. Some friends arrived and stayed indefinitely, often for months at a time.

While some who came by were also friends of Alex's, many were *Harvard Lampoon* folks or people like Mayer, who thought nothing of nasty barbs directed at the lady of the house, whom Mayer and others perceived as having no sense of humor. She was just another target. Harvard graduate or not, she simply wasn't part of their boys club.

Doug and Alex had much in common. They were attractive, young, well-educated, sweet, and sensitive people. They cared for each other and had settled into the kind of relationship that felt comfortable for Doug. Both were working through difficult relationships with their parents. Doug especially seemed unable to reconcile himself with Harry, both personally and professionally. As he'd chosen to parlay his Ivy League education into something that seemed totally unproductive to a member of the Greatest Generation, there were bound to be tensions. This was compounded by the death of Daniel two years earlier, of whom Doug seldom spoke, and his new role as the great hope for the next generation of the family. Additionally, Doug was troubled by his father's work at Diamond Shamrock, a major polluter and supplier of chemicals to the U.S. military.

The relationship between Stephanie Kenney and her son was considerably warmer, yet Doug often seemed embarrassed by his uneducated, working-class mother who pronounced toothbrush TOOT-brush. During one of the infrequent occasions when Doug opened up to Alex, he told her about Stephanie's violent temper, which had terrified him as a child. His mother was emotional and uninhibited, often throwing frying pans and other kitchen objects at Harry when enraged.

Alex had borne firsthand witness to Doug's evolution at Harvard. From afar he'd been the geek turned preppy. At one moment he could be Gatsby, hair slicked back, wearing a camel hair overcoat, off to a Spee dinner, yet days later transform into the long-haired artiste and bad boy. This flexibility of persona could be dizzying, the shifts sudden and dramatic.

Doug could adapt to meet the needs of those he befriended without openly needing himself; yet he remained the eternal outsider, pressing his nose against the window of those living the American Dream, unable to grasp it. No matter how desperately he wanted to be an insider, he continually distrusted his desire to become just that—in his eyes, he would forever be the boy from Ohio, one generation removed from the servant class. As a writer, this sensibility fueled his unique take on whatever he tackled. Born with profound sensitivity, he was capable of seeing everything through the various angles of a prism—good and bad, happy and sad—all of life's angles as though each coexisted in conversation and on the page without judgment. It was the way he lived and who he was. It was not something that he could turn off. Placed in a marriage, this complicated gift created significant limitations. Alex believed that he was like an onion. Every time you peeled off a layer, you found another—never reaching the core. Never finding the real Doug Kenney.

Years later, Doug would tell friends that his and Alex's union was "a marriage made in Japan."

* * *

The August 1970 theme was Paranoia, with cover art by Gahan Wilson that depicted bulbous, wrinkled, laughing figures (including Hitler in a wedding dress, Jesus Christ, a policeman, and a pet wild boar) tossing a hapless, bug-eyed everyman into a pit of swords. Though circulation had dropped to 175,000 and advertising sales were anemic, several good things seemed to be happening, including the arrival of Wilson and other artists who found a home for their skewed sensibilities at the *National Lampoon.*

A former accountant named Sam Gross sent bizarre, "sick," one-panel comic strips to the magazine, ranging from a board meeting of identical frowning corporate drones seated at a long table with a lone smiling clown at the far end ("And now we will hear the dissenting opinion") to what would become his most famous piece, a legless frog in a rolling box outside a restaurant whose sign reads "Today's Special—Frog Legs." He was a curmudgeonly, chain-smoking man with a prominent vein continually throbbing in the middle of his forehead that some editors believed was the beginning of a horn.

Charles Rodrigues was a devout Catholic who despised humor of a blasphemous or sexual nature yet thought nothing of submitting thick, fuzzy cartoons that made humor out of the handicapped, epileptics, and dwarfs as they tried to use the toilet or perform other everyday activities.

Descended from both William Jennings Bryan and P. T. Barnum, Gahan Wilson had been born dead, knocked out by a "twilight sleep" anesthetic intended for his mother. Blue and not breathing, he was saved by the family doctor—who dipped him back and forth between hot and cold water until he was revived. It was an appropriate beginning for a man who'd make his living with macabre drawings. Contacted by Henry in spring 1970, Wilson, who'd made a name for himself at *Colliers, Look, Playboy,* and *Help!,* became a regular contributor.

* * *

Though Wilson, Rodrigues, and Gross would become well-known contributors, Rick Meyerowitz was as close to a peer and staff artist as Doug and Henry would find. He was one of them.

Raised in the creative ferment of the post-war Bronx, from which Ralph Lauren and Calvin Klein emerged, Meyerowitz was a nice Jewish boy who had decided at age five that he would become an artist, illustrating library books on his father's shirt cardboards—creating scenes that weren't depicted. Discovering *MAD* magazine at age nine, Meyerowitz was blown away, seeing that the world might give him permission to draw the crazy ideas that roamed his mind.

After art school at Boston University, Meyerowitz returned to New York and earned $22 a day as a housepainter before a friend in advertising offered him $200 for a black-and-white cartoon. A professional illustrator was born. By 1970, he was both a hippie and a conventional married man with a young son and a reputation for wild caricature. Meyerowitz's counterculture sensibilities, filled with outsized political and pop cultural imagery, were in tune with the times.

Meyerowitz first learned of Beard and Kenney when he came across a copy of the *Time* parody on the way to an antiwar demonstration in Manhattan's Bryant Park. For the next four hours he sat on a blanket reading the entire issue, laughing uncontrollably as his friends chanted antiwar slogans.

"I had discovered something that touched my soul," Meyerowitz said. "Something that was just like me. A sense of humor that dovetailed with my own and what I was putting into my pictures."

Months later, Peter Bramley contacted Meyerowitz, an acquaintance, to tell him that Cloud had been hired to art direct *National Lampoon*. Shortly thereafter he was in.

* * *

National Lampoon was filled with Harvard friends (Cerf, Frith, Weidman, and Trow), like-minded young men (O'Donoghue), and a wide smattering of those with the requisite talent, reputation, or sensibility, including Wilson, Gross, Rodrigues, and Meyerowitz as well as established cartoonist Arnold Roth and radio legend Jean Shepherd. The result was a dazzling variety of voices and styles that could be sophomoric, overtly literate, bizarre, angry, gentle, pop culture–tinged, elegant, rudimentary, or straightforward parody. There had been no articulated strategy for finding writers and artists. Henry and Doug were simply seeking content that could fill pages and be funny.

Some of the artists came on their own, drawn to the magazine's aesthetic, while others were recommended or contacted by Henry and Doug themselves. None, though, arrived in the manner of Michel Choquette.

In the late 1960s, Choquette and English actor and musician Peter Elbling were partners in a strange act known as the Times Square Two. Under the stage names Mycroft Partner (Elbling) and Andrew I (Choquette)—thus, My Partner and I—attired in Edwardian dress, they performed an old-fashioned routine that was a throwback to the 1920s, with juggling, mind reading, and vaudeville conventions—a spoof of the slickness so pervasive among mainstream comics. After hooking up in 1964, they toured England, were a hit on the college circuit, and opened for Frank Zappa. By 1968, they were doing their act for Johnny Carson, the Smothers Brothers, and Dean Martin's variety show.

In 1969, the act had run its course and the pair went their separate ways. Choquette endeavored to publish an ambitious (and never completed) book of cartoons and artwork by famous people (Fellini, John Lennon, etc.) entitled *The Someday Funnies*, while also attempting to write for *National Lampoon*.

He was eminently qualified on several fronts. The Montreal-born son of a prominent French-Canadian poet, Choquette was well read and filled with mad ideas. Having heard about the *National Lampoon* from a friend, he sat down at McSorley's Ale House in Manhattan and wrote a bizarre letter (on his Times Square Two letterhead) from a kidnapped dentist to the editors that landed on the desk of Henry and Doug, who invited him for lunch.

The pop culture–loving Doug knew of the act and was attracted by Choquette's show biz pedigree. Impressed, Doug wanted Choquette to help bring in comics such as George Carlin and David Steinberg as contributors.

Henry's feeling was the opposite. Patrician and fiercely intellectual, he despised and looked down on popular entertainment. Choquette believed that Henry had either never heard of the Times Square Two or, conversely, if he had seen them, hated the act. Even so, Henry adored the strange letter.

In either case, Choquette was invited to the offices on Madison and became a contributing editor in a matter of days. Attending idea dinners at cheap restaurants up and down Manhattan, he met Trow, Weidman, Meyerowitz, and O'Donoghue.

Like Meyerowitz, he was in heaven. Suddenly, there was a market for the millions of odd thoughts that raced through his head or had been doodled in a spare moment: comics, parodies of maps, dart-boards, and Dickens—it all could work.

"It was wide open," Choquette says. "No matter what your particular humor bent was, Henry and Doug would embrace it. If it didn't get accepted, you just jotted it down and said, 'I just gotta persuade these guys to do an issue on dental hygiene.' If you worked hard enough at it, you'd get your article in *National Lampoon*."

After one early dinner meeting, Choquette found himself on the subway with O'Donoghue. Continuing the conversation they'd begun at the restaurant, the pair discussed collaborating on projects and tossed off article concepts. As Choquette got off the train, O'Donoghue turned to him. "You've got a weird mind," he said. "You'll fit in really well here."

Choquette's first pieces appeared in the August 1970 issue: a "Paranoia Map of the World" and a multiple-choice "Guilt Test." His collaborator was Sean Kelly.

Born on the Feast of St. Mary Magdalene in 1940, Sean Kelly was the son of a quiet man who worked for RCA Victor and mumbled wisecracks under his breath and a Montreal housewife who believed her spiritual home was at *The New Yorker*. The family was Irish Catholic in the tradition of Chicago and Boston Irish Catholics, where the ethnicity and religion were inextricably linked—essentially one word.

When Sean was eleven, Mrs. Kelly decided that her son, who loved James Thurber and S. J. Perelman, was brighter than the average kid and sent him to audition for a Canadian television quiz show called *Small Fries*. Thus, Friday afternoons of his prepubescence were spent wearing a mortarboard and hitting a library bell to indicate that he knew the answer before everybody else.

It wasn't until he was sixteen that it dawned on Kelly that life truly sucked. Educated as a high school boarder by the Jesuits, Kelly caught on quickly to their game, namely, that they encouraged rebellion in order to co-opt the rebel. If you said that the idea of God made you vomit, they would say, "The saints all had the same feeling." The stronger you pushed against them, the more they would welcome it and bring you into the fold. It was the beginning of an intuitive comprehension of all things Catholic.

While attending Loyola College in Montreal, Kelly did voice work for the National Film Board and was a regular on CBC radio's weekly drama. At the school's theater department, he directed his own reworking of *Julius Caesar*, set in Cuba, on the premise that Shakespeare had fucked up the original.

Though it was the early 1960s and the beatnik movement had died out, Kelly tried to live the lifestyle as much as you could in Canada—where things always seemed to him a decade or two behind the United States. He played chess in coffeehouses and dreamed of becoming a poet.

By age twenty-three, Kelly was married with a young child and working as a junior copywriter at McConnell Leafman, the Montreal rival of J. Walter Thompson. Kelly had decided that Thompson wasn't right for him when, during an interview, an adman from the agency had asked him, "Tell me about the man behind the uniform?" Whatever that meant.

"I knew I couldn't work at J. Walter Thompson," Kelly says.

In between writing industrial copy for Caterpillar, Kelly helped create a sixty-second Canadian National Railways ad that featured nothing but plane crashes. The client quickly explained that they were owned by the same company as Air Canada.

When a Loyola professor of Victorian literature had what Kelly calls "a classic English professor nervous breakdown, as professors of Victorian literature will," in the middle of a term, the school asked their recent graduate to take his place. Fleeing the advertising world, he was suddenly teaching Tennyson to juniors and seniors. Above the desk in his office was a framed panel from O'Donoghue's "Phoebe Zeitgeist."

Kelly moved his growing family, which now included three kids, to a flat in the East End of Montreal, where Choquette was living upstairs and working on Pierre Trudeau's campaign. Choquette invited him to help out. Kelly declined. Later, however, when Choquette told him about the American humor magazine he was creating ideas for, Kelly decided it was worth a shot.

The first idea they tried was a piece about the banality of the American space program, including the fact that one astronaut's initial impression of the moon was that it looked like Galveston Bay. "For God's sake," they thought, "they could have sent these guys anywhere and it would look like Galveston Bay to them. Why hadn't the Americans sent someone like Allen Ginsberg?"

Initially, Matty, Henry, and Doug believed Kelly was a fictitious creation of Choquette's, perhaps a device to get paid double for his articles. In fall 1970, however, Choquette produced his partner in the flesh when he and Kelly visited Henry and Doug in Manhattan.

At their Upper East Side duplex, Doug opened by asking Kelly what he got on his SATs. Kelly replied that there were no SATs in Canada. He suspected that Doug, who was lighting one joint off another, was trying to determine whether or not the Canadian professor was smarter than he.

When Kelly discussed the fact that he'd been involved in a faculty strike that culminated in teachers smoking pot in the president's office, Alex asked him how he would be allowed to continue teaching after such behavior. It occurred to Kelly that Doug's wife was pretty straight; not exactly the kind of person he imagined being married to the dope-smoking humorist who was quizzing him.

The following day, Choquette and Kelly visited the offices, where Doug fired up another giant joint and, showing his solidarity with the revolution, the less frequently stoned Kelly indulged as well.

That night he stumbled into his seat on a plane bound for Montreal, still in a haze from his afternoon with Doug. As the plane neared the Adirondacks, the pilot came over the loudspeaker.

"Ladies and gentlemen, I've never seen the Northern Lights as beautiful as they are tonight," and directed the passengers to look out the window. With the sky exploding around him, Kelly had no idea that his life was about to be forever altered.

***

Matty Simmons had pretty much kept out of editorial for the first several issues, letting Henry and Doug run things for better or worse. Still, he was increasingly upset over the work of Cloud Studio. The covers were all over the place, with no visual appeal and little consistency in execution throughout the magazine. No matter the content, nobody would read something that didn't look good, and if nobody read, nobody would advertise.

He'd tried time and again to work with Skurski and Bramley. Matty encouraged them to work at the *National Lampoon* offices rather than their loft in the Village. Defiantly, they refused—Skurski in particular, who claims that Matty tore up and refused to pay invoices from artists the magazine didn't intend to use again.

Doug and Henry had hired them, but it had really been Doug's idea. He continued to meet with Cloud, hang out at the studio, and let creativity run amok. Yet Henry began showing signs of stress, once biting the tip off his pipe during a meeting at the studio. Subtle tensions developed between the editors and artists as well, which may have had more to do with cultural differences. Bramley and Skurski liked Doug and Henry, but they were taken aback when George Trow visited their loft, turned to Henry, and asked if he really liked "slumming it like this."

Whatever the case, in the summer of 1970 Matty had seen enough and fired Cloud. Doug put up an argument, while Henry shrugged. Ultimately, though, both acquiesced, knowing it had been a failure. Doug had even mocked Cloud's disorganized, hazy art direction and behavior in a *National Lampoon* editorial.

Doug was dispatched to the Lower East Side to find Skurski, who'd recently returned from an unsuccessful trip West where he'd intended to persuade Robert Crumb to become a contributor. Doug was unassuming and apologetic. It just hadn't worked and Matty wasn't happy. Though they had never seen it coming, the Cloud guys accepted their fate.

Matty had been right. Cloud was a disaster. In his youthful desire for creative, groundbreaking work, Doug intended to make the *National Lampoon*'s visual execution an East Coast corollary to San Francisco's Underground Comix movement. Instead, he got sloppy cartooning with a chaotic, inconsistent layout that did nothing to enhance the written humor.

With a recently fired design team and fresh out of ideas for the September Show Biz cover, Matty played art director and came up with a picture of Minnie Mouse removing her shirt to reveal tiny breasts covered only by floral pasties.

Colored bright yellow, red, and blue, it is arguable that the Show Biz cover was in any way superior to the Cloud efforts. Certainly, as it trumpeted articles about John and Yoko, Charles Manson, and Raquel Welch, no one could miss it—least of all the attorneys for Walt Disney, who sued *National Lampoon* for $8,000,000 two days after the issue hit the stands. Matty settled with Uncle Walt, agreeing to never again directly parody a Disney character. The publicity, however, was of tremendous value.

* * *

In Show Biz, Henry Beard began to round into form with "Varietsky," a seamless behind-the-iron-curtain parody of the show-business daily trade paper selling for fifty kopeks with headlines blaring "Oh! Kropotkin in Strong Bid for Rubes' Rubles" and "Dir. Yakubovsky Gets Blank Czech"; while body copy proclaimed the awards being showered upon actors for their work in such productions as "The Sound of Threshers" and "Preparing Turnips for Broth Purposes."

It was a perfect demonstration of Henry's gift for taking polar opposites (Communism and Hollywood) and bringing them together inseparably. It was humor where $1 + 1 = 3$. Nobody did that better than Henry.

* * *

While Cloud was licking its wounds and Minnie Mouse revealed her figure, Rob Hoffman was nearing the end of his tether with Matty. Working as a junior executive, Hoffman got on well with Len Mogel. The two became close, with Mogel even trying to set

Hoffman up with his daughter Wendy. Matty believed his managing editor was "smart and tough," potentially even an important future component of 21st Century management, which now owned the nostalgic history magazine *Liberty*. Hoffman, however, did not share the same vision, nor did he care for the way Matty treated him, which was both paternalistic and adversarial. In truth, each man distrusted the other.

Matty viewed Hoffman as the kid who had been obstinate in negotiations, resulting in a deal that he feared would be unfavorable to the economic growth of his organization as well as undermining of his financial control of the magazine. While their interactions were pleasant and professional, there was an underlying resentment that Hoffman couldn't ignore. He would always be perceived as an adversary.

Since the first issue, Hoffman had been trying to come up with business strategies to make the magazine more financially efficient. Most were ignored. During the summer of 1970, he'd discovered that the magazine could save three cents per issue by making a few small changes. Matty took a quick look at his computations and gave Hoffman the equivalent of an avuncular pat on the head. "Oh, thank you, little boy," Hoffman believed was the recurrent message of this and other interactions. Two weeks later, Matty announced that 21st Century had discovered a way to derive the same savings on its own, without reference to Hoffman's original idea.

Not even a year out of college, Hoffman was trying to decide whether to stick with the magazine or attend business school. This encounter tipped the balance, as he believed his relationship with Matty would never afford him respect or the ability to have a healthy adult working relationship with his boss. Hoffman told Matty and Mogel that he was leaving. Ultimately, he joined his father's soft-drink bottling business in Dallas while continuing as a paid consultant to *National Lampoon*.

* * *

Michael Gross learned of the art director opening at *National Lampoon* when his assistant at *Family Health* magazine interviewed for the job and decided that he wasn't interested.

A former student at New York's Pratt Institute, the twenty-six-year-old Gross had seen the *Time* parody and thought it brilliant. Yet when he read the premiere issue, Gross couldn't get through it, mostly because of the layout and art direction.

"I could probably fix that thing," he thought.

Gross was not funny by nature. He had no pretensions to being a humorist. Though young, bearded, and long of hair, he was first and foremost a professional art director and a careerist who had worked at *Cosmopolitan* and its youth-oriented sister publication *Eye* (where Helen Gurley Brown once suggested the headline "Sexy, Nice Girls in Their Summer Underthings"). He'd also helped design artwork for the 1968 Summer Olympics in Mexico City, and art directed such seemingly mundane publications as *Medical Economics* and *Family Health.*

Influenced by *MAD*, George Lois's *Esquire* covers, and his childhood mentor Val Warren (with whom he put out a high school fanzine and made 35mm films), Gross was married at nineteen, and now had two children and a conservative attitude toward life. Though socially liberal, Gross voted for Barry Goldwater in 1964 and was dismayed by the arrogant, impractical attitude so prevalent in the "liberal arts."

Meeting with Matty, it was clear that only one thing was on the publisher's mind: ad sales. Since the first issue, "I'm not gonna put an ad in this fuckin' underground piece of shit" was all *National Lampoon* salesmen ever heard. Gross understood completely.

"[Henry and Doug] had just never done a magazine before," he says. "They didn't even know what an original magazine should look like." Gross did.

Cloud, for all its East Village hippie cred, was not in the magazine design business. Gross saw that they were breaking design rules, which was OK as long as one understood those rules and broke them for a reason, but the folks at Cloud were simply doing whatever they wanted—there were no rules—and the editors were too inexperienced to point them in a different direction.

Matty was sold. Henry was his usual thoughtful, somewhat removed self. Gross walked Henry through the Paranoia issue, stopping at Doug's piece, "America as a Second-Rate Power." The writing and concepts were funny: a Mount Rushmore featuring the visages of presidential brother Milton Eisenhower, failed candidate Wendell Wilkie, and others, and commemorative stamps honoring great American disasters.

Gross focused on the stamps. The concept was hilarious and the presentation was completely straight-faced. But the execution also sought to be "funny" in the *MAD* tradition, with cartoonish depictions of the events.

"You've written the piece straight," Gross told Henry. "But the illustrations don't look anything like real postage stamps. The parody here is the absurdity of the subject these stamps are commemorating, so they must look like real postage stamps. By visually dealing with the subject deadpan, by avoiding a 'nudge-nudge, wink-wink' approach, then the joke is strengthened tenfold."

Henry got it. Doug was a harder sell.

Gross found Doug to be inexplicably strange during their first meeting. Seemingly unfocused, Doug had no idea what questions to ask a prospective art director and was unable to get past the fact that Gross was coming from the decidedly unhip *Family Health*. Neither he nor Henry knew or were able to articulate what they wanted, but Doug (unlike Henry) was stuck in remaining true to the wild spirit of the magazine he'd envisioned. Selling ads for Matty was the furthest thing from his mind. Gross left that day knowing that he'd impressed Henry and Matty. Doug? He had no idea.

Putting up minor resistance, Doug stepped aside and let Matty hire Gross. Within two weeks he was working at *National Lampoon*. What Gross found was a mixture of chaos and freedom. The chaos resulted from the lack of discipline regarding the layout and production process. Lead times were nonexistent, as was often the case with money. Everyone simply struggled to get the magazine out on the fly each month.

Gross, however, was prepared for a chaotic environment. His unconventional early life in Newburgh, New York, was peopled by characters who ranged from his bookmaker uncle (who filed his scratch sheets alphabetically in the pages of Gross's encyclopedia) to the tenants of a rooming house his stepfather owned. There were card games in the kitchen until five A.M. on school nights and Thanksgiving dinners attended by stray residents without families. The result was that Gross became a chameleon—not the same way as Doug, but rather somebody who remained himself yet could deal with all manner of people. His childhood served him well at *National Lampoon*, where he and he alone would make no enemies. They needed him too much.

Undaunted by the crazed, disorganized surroundings, Gross flourished as the Lampoon's art director. It was his magazine, his design, and his baby to put out each month. And it was Gross who would make the parody accurate.

* * *

The November Nostalgia cover was the first of many legendary images that appeared on newsstands during Gross's tenure. Parodying a Norman Rockwell barbershop scene, a balding, jug-eared, small-town barber takes his shears to the head of a freckle-faced hippie boy—peace medallion hanging from his neck. One side of the kid's hair is shaved into a crew cut while the other, uncut, hangs beneath his shoulders. A smiling mustachioed man wearing a vest and smoking a cheroot reads an old *Time* magazine in the background. The picture symbolically captures all that was happening between the Lampoon staff's generation and that of their parents.

Though their introduction had been inauspicious, Kenney and Gross immediately connected over the issue, whose topic was right in Doug's wheelhouse. Having quickly gotten past his misgivings about Gross, Doug saved the new art director's ass by locating the appropriate artist to mimic Rockwell after the first choice had proved that he wasn't up to the task. But their true bonding arose during the creation of a piece about the 1950s for which Gross had seamlessly re-created a high school yearbook named "Cat Calls." Years later, Doug would introduce Gross around Hollywood as the man with whom he'd created nostalgia.

From the small note written beneath a torn corner of the back cover to the cut-off heads in the photo of the Ezra Taft Benson High School Bobcadettes ("who cheered our Bobcats to a respectable 2–6 season, three games of which, while not actual victories were either extremely close or practically ties"), Gross nailed the precise look of what Doug sought to parody. The editor who'd opposed his hiring became his biggest fan.

"I'm sorry. I was wrong," he would tell Gross time and again. "I didn't know you could do this. You're brilliant."

"Cat Calls" was an idea from O'Donoghue's files. But he quickly passed it to Doug, knowing that the 1950s and high school were his specialties. While it is a far cruder editorial product than the *National Lampoon 1964 High School Yearbook Parody* he would later write, "Cat Calls" was the first time that Doug took a direct swing at the happy, sad, nostalgic, and funny "better times" in which he grew up and so thoroughly understood.

The dedication to a deceased teacher is written by a student and innocently touches on Rupert L. Peen's (Doug had a tremendous gift for names) hidden Communist allegiance ("There are few of us who will ever forget your lectures on the little known benefits of the World Socialist League and the slide shows of happy Russian peasants you always brought back from your summer trips abroad"); closeted homosexuality is disguised as love for the Bobcat football team ("We remember how you cheered and cheered at every football game, never forgetting to ask the quarterback for a small memento of victory for your collection . . . a spiked kicking shoe, a damp, mud-caked Bobcat jersey. We remember, too, your warm, wonderful grin and twinkling eyes as you stood watching us in our after game showers"). "Cat Calls" also gets the "stupid and cruel but funny" humor that is the mainstay of the American high school experience, when the writer apologizes for "the unkind jokes we made about your cough and those nicknames like 'Hacker' and 'Old Croupy.' We had no idea at the time you had cancer of the trachea."

An inspirational and instructive letter to the class of '56 from the principal provides frightening insight into the paranoid mainstream mind of a middle manager in charge of educating teenagers and the kind of world he seeks to create.

Dear Seniors,

A famous man once said, "A chain is only as strong as its weakest link." This means that Life, like Football, is based on team effort. Your club, school or country, is a team, and your team can be weakened by even a single, disloyal teammate. As your team goes forth into the promise of the future, be ever vigilant for those "weak links" who spread discontent, habitually "rock the boat" or generally act in a suspicious manner. Keeping your eyes peeled for these individuals is not always easy, but as Thomas Edison said, "Vigilance is 2 per cent inspiration and 98 per cent perspiration." It is sad but true that these individuals may appear anywhere, even in the classroom, and often their subversive ideas are not uncovered until after they have passed from the scene.

On the Team of Life some will be quarterbacks, some will be cheerleaders, and some will only warm the bench; but whatever our position on that greatest of teams, let us all dedicate ourselves to keeping it on the winning side of the scoreboard.

Sincerely Yours,
Ralph C. Krintzler
Principal

* * *

Doug's material and viewpoint in "Cat Calls" illustrate a fundamental difference between him and Henry. Having grown up in a privileged atmosphere, one in which it would be immensely difficult to surpass the financial success of his parents, Henry was constitutionally incapable of relating to a mass audience of Americans with understanding or empathy.

Not that his humor didn't translate; in its own specific realms of parody, literary subjects, and current events, Henry's work was beyond reproach. Yet for the majority pursuing the American Dream, somebody like Henry Beard was an anomaly. His family had achieved that dream long ago and it was unavailable to him. Instead, Henry knew what it was like to always be on the inside. It was his birthright. And though he may have never known the popularity of the high school quarterback, he also never knew what it was like to be ineligible for the club or have Thanksgiving dinner with the cousins from the wrong side of the tracks. He knew one thing for certain: being an elite Manhattanite had its privileges, but it wasn't all it was cracked up to be.

There are many ways to respond to this kind of upbringing. Some are driven to exceed the achievements of their parents. Many fail. Others are crushed by the knowledge that no matter how talented or successful, they will never match the comfort of their upbringing without inherited wealth. It's the same plight that faced the characters in Whit Stillman's film *Metropolitan* years later. They are the Urban Haute Bourgeoisie—well-to-do kids, products of good schools, raised in Manhattan on the debutante circuit, with nowhere to go but down—if not financially, at least in the realm of self-worth.

Henry responded to these circumstances the only way he knew how—by saying fuck it and fuck them. He went to Taft and Harvard, did his thing and held on via brains and cynicism, with an eye to the bigger picture. Yet his upbringing was reflected indelibly in his studied, mannered style of parody. He was the last of a dying breed—the elegant *New Yorker* writers like Benchley, Thurber, and Perelman. Doug, he believed, was the first of something else entirely.

"He was an amazing populist," Gross said of Doug.

Doug was the great hope of his family, which was only beginning to taste the world afforded by a college education and home ownership. In Chagrin Falls, he'd witnessed the all-American life as directed by Frank Capra, starring Jimmy Stewart and Bing Crosby with set design by Norman Rockwell, where every boy cheered on the local team and marched with the Cub Scouts in the Fourth of July parade. This fueled Doug's personality and writing, allowing his work to genuinely connect with his readership. The experience of his parents and grandparents serving families like Henry's was part of his DNA. The world of Middle America, with its promise of a better life and the inevitable disappointment, frantically coexisted in the refracted lens of his mind. One moment he was the greatest humorist who had ever lived, bar none; the next, he wondered if he was even any good. Everything he wrote, Doug thought at some point, might be nothing but a piece of shit. Inside and out, over and over, the debate raged on.

The contrast between the two men was striking. Doug was eternally optimistic but insecure beneath a mellow exterior; believing in the dream, he needed to succeed, no matter his cynicism. He was at once overconfident and riddled with fears of failure. But he was keenly in touch. Henry, though socially awkward and ill at ease, knew exactly who he was and what he thought about everything; being happy or successful didn't seem to drive him. Beneath his sarcasm was clarity and self-assurance.

The impact of this divide was apparent in most of their activities at the magazine. As an editor, Doug led by example. Other writers saw his desire to break boundaries and, inspired by his unfettered creativity, pushed themselves to measure up to him. In practical matters, Doug was enthusiastic but infuriatingly vague. He said, "yes . . . yes . . . yes" to every article, every crazy execution and insane idea. Then he would forget about it, letting Henry deal with whether or not it would go in *National Lampoon*.

Henry Beard didn't just say no; breeding wouldn't allow for it. Rather, hope was mixed with the possibility of rejection. "Tempting," he would say to nearly every idea, which, according to Tony Hendra, who joined the staff full-time in summer 1971, "meant anything from 'that is the most Godawful notion that has been proposed since postwar British socialism,' to 'judging by the lines of this baby, I could be persuaded to have a prolonged intellectual orgasm.'" Then behind closed doors, he and Doug would choose the ideas that truly appealed to them. The only outward indication, perhaps, of Henry's admiration for an idea was a dry comment that something was "funny," which meant that interest was piqued beyond imagination.

All in all, the boys ran a loose ship. Much of the writing that went into the magazine was unedited, appearing as it had been submitted, which offered the contributors an unprecedented opportunity to try new things and flex their muscles. The rough-hewn result was incredibly appealing to the young men who read *National Lampoon*.

Though not a born editor, Henry fashioned himself into a skillful and effective one. He was generous with his time, when he wasn't rushing to avert a deadline disaster. Given his capabilities, Henry faced the task of directing writers on articles that he could have easily rewritten to be ten times funnier and a hundred times smarter. Yet when he did turn his attention to editing, he did so carefully, helping writers with structure and the precision of their parody.

Despite being kind and respectful, Henry's lack of social skills sometimes had awkward consequences. A cartoonist once made an appointment to show him some less-than-stellar artwork. Unimpressed, Henry left the hopeful contributor in the room with a writer and never returned.

Doug, though, was all over the map. He urged people to do their own thing—and have fun doing it—and provided tremendous energy to a creative enterprise. He was an encouraging editor and loved to help others succeed, but was not particularly effective at crafting their writing. When it came to specifics, he was hopelessly vague. On stylistic points, however, he could provide insight into how satire should be approached.

"Doug would sometimes tell writers to 'put in a little schmuck bait,'" O'Donoghue said, "things like a kitten playing with a ball of yarn. People see that and go 'Aww . . . ' It pulls the schmucks in."

Some tuned into his advice easily. One contributor recalls Doug laughing as he read each line of an article, then stopping to say, "It needs work here." Then he would laugh again at the next paragraph. Despite the lack of specificity, he told the same writer that the danger of parody is that writers become enamored of their precision in aping the subject. The real trick, he believed (after parodying a few headlines or paragraphs in the style of a particular author or publication—making the reader think, "I get it"), was to find new and interesting ways to play with the subject and make people laugh. Simply put, there needed to be jokes.

Doug went about this task by outlining his pieces and creating a structure while jotting funny ideas in the margins. While writing the piece he would insert those jokes throughout, then make another pass, inserting more humor wherever he could. Before the final draft, he would again make notes on places where he could insert more and more laughs. His goal was to have at least one funny line, concept, or word in every sentence.

In addition, Doug would always embolden the writer, no matter how badly the piece turned out. Behind his obtuseness was a clear and constant message to respect your work even if, or even because, it was shit. The impact of such encouragement on gifted but unformed writers was incalculable.

Henry's style was diligent and immensely productive. Outside his closed office, Lampoon staffers would hear Henry's typewriter clacking away constantly, as he produced reams and reams of material. Doug needed guilt and pressure to reach a boiling point before he was ready to write. Hence, he maintained the style he'd employed at Harvard, pounding out and editing pieces late at night and on deadline. According to one staffer, he would often disappear for days when article submission time loomed, causing Matty to send out search parties to find his star contributor.

Though both Doug and Henry worked painfully long hours, Doug freed himself to roam and create. He played the role of the brilliant kid, who might disappear but always produced. This left little energy for making the trains run on time—a task he was ill equipped to handle. The magazine was his design, but making sure that it came out each month was Henry's responsibility, one that he took on with industriousness. In keeping with his prodigious capacity to fulfill duties, he said nothing.

Both Doug and Henry were somewhat conflicted over their chosen careers. Henry suffered the notion that he wasn't "doing anything substantial" and perhaps would have been better off as a lawyer, doctor, or investment banker; the kind of careers people like his father and classmates had pursued. Essentially, he wasn't sure that writing humor was a decent way to make a living.

Doug was overcome with the message he'd received from his father and the way it contrasted with his own desires. While he was clearly born to do precisely what he was doing, and was using his uncanny gift for capturing the societal mood of the moment to its maximum, he had the sinking feeling that he was a fraud who would never measure up to Waugh or Graham Greene. Beneath the easygoing exterior was an insatiable need to become a star of the highest magnitude. Behind it all was also a measure of guilt arising from his background and his desire to transcend it. It was a complicated mix of feeling like both the underdog and the insider.

This dynamic within Doug worked out well for *National Lampoon*. He intuitively understood that readers wanted to get to know the guys writing their funny magazine, and he was only too happy to become its public face. While Henry agreed to appear in the odd photo layout, Doug was up for anything, including, years later, providing his naked backside (which held a fake eyeball) for a *National*

Lampoon "surprise poster." The first-year subscription ads showed a picture of an unshaven Doug, holding a tin cup and tattered stuffed pig, crouching in what appears to be a garbage dump above the headline "Little Doug Kenney will go to bed hungry tonight."

> . . . unless you help. Raised in a small village called by the natives "Ohio," Doug has never had the things that your children have had. He was 10 years old before he owned a pair of Florsheim shoes, he was almost 20 before he had his first ride in a Lincoln Continental, and his parents were too poor to send him to a fancy Swiss private school like his playmates. He has never tasted caviar . . .
> . . . If you buy a one-year subscription, little Doug Kenney can have a crust of bread and a cup of milk every day. A two-year subscription will send him to school where he will learn to read, write and play polo. A lifetime subscription will allow him to throw an entire coming-out party for his less fortunate friends, in the south of France. . . .

In keeping with his ability to connect with the public and his lust for social contact, Doug gladly took on the role of showman, promoting the magazine with the media, wherever he went. During one interview, he insisted that a *Soho Weekly* writer refer to him in her article as "the handsomest man in comedy."

Despite the fact that his public role made it seem like most of the credit for *National Lampoon* should go to Doug, Henry didn't seem to mind in the least.

5

What Do Women Eat?

The time has come for us to set straight certain wild-eyed individuals who have publicly accused the *National Lampoon* of harboring chauvinist pigs, sexist dogs, female-exploiting jackals and other unfashionable quadrupeds in its editorial kennels. Nothing could be further from the truth. However, to allay the fears of the 27% of our readership who happen to be female (68% Male, 5% Undecided), we hereby openly admit that certain female staff members of the *National Lampoon* have grown restive of late (under the inflammatory goadings of a certain Managing Editor Mary Marshmallow, no doubt).

The Editors were recently presented with a list of demands by these shrill individuals, which included the following outrageous ultimatums: 1) all female staff members' salaries are to be paid in real money or its equivalent in edible produce, 2) a permanent cessation of corporal punishment for lateness or general editorial pique, and 3) exemption from the *National Lampoon*'s Weekly Purification and Fertility Ritual.

Needless to say, these preposterous prattles of a too-long-pampered platoon of pusillanimous panhandlers were rejected out of hand. Nevertheless, our crack team of negotiators responded immediately with what we, the management, feel was a reasonable, perhaps even over-generous counterproposal that included 1) free dimes for the executive washroom, 2) free track shoes and uniforms for the morning wake-up jog around the Editor's desk, and 3) free medical consultation following any injury resulting from the Weekly Purification and Fertility Ritual.

We are unhappy to report that these magnanimous counter-offers were unceremoniously hooted at by our strikers, not all of whom, we must add, have been a credit to their sex. However, after long sessions with strike representatives and days of haggling, whining and the stamping of stacked heels, an equitable compromise was finally hammered out, and we are pleased, ladies, that we have arrived at a happy solution.

You're fired.

—DCK (i.e., Douglas Clark Kenney), editor's letter
from January 1971 issue of National Lampoon

The following things happened in 1971: several popular, long-running television shows aimed at mainstream family audiences (*Ed Sullivan, Green Acres, The Beverly Hillbillies,* and *The Andy Griffith Show*) were canceled, making room for CBS's *All in the Family,* which forever changed the format and image of the American sitcom by exposing the ignorant curmudgeon inside us all; South Dakota Senator George McGovern announced his candidacy for the Democratic presidential nomination; Idi Amin declared himself president of Uganda; U.S. Army Lieutenant William Calley was found guilty and sentenced to life in prison (later reduced to ten years) for the 1968 slaughter of twenty-two Vietnamese civilians in the My Lai massacre; George C. Scott's tour de force performance in *Patton* won one of seven Academy Awards for the film; the *New York*

Times published the Pentagon Papers, detailing classified documents regarding the Vietnam War that were leaked by government analyst Daniel Ellsberg; Jim Morrison, Duane Allman, and Louis Armstrong all died; Tricia Nixon got married; and a new breed of filmmakers like Peter Bogdonavich (*The Last Picture Show*) and William Friedkin (*The French Connection*) set the stage for the soon-to-emerge careers of a gritty, less idyllic breed of directors such as Francis Ford Coppola and Martin Scorcese.

* * *

By all accounts she was the ultimate hippie chick—warm, gentle, sensual, and maternal, yet keenly aware of the power she held over men. Mary Martello (known in the office as Mary Marshmallow) was curvy, well endowed, and an employee of *National Lampoon*. She was, says Michael Sullivan of Cloud Studio, "a fabulous woman that anybody would love to be close to."

It is unclear how and when she and Doug began their relationship, but at the latest it started shortly after he got married in June 1970. Sexually available, earthy, and kind, she was the perfect woman to play both roles of the Catholic boy's virgin/whore complex.

Late in *National Lampoon*'s first year of publication, Doug recommended (over Michael Gross's objections) the creation of a regular item named "Foto Funnies," a series of one-page, seven-panel, black-and-white photos of the editors that told silly fart, drug, and sex-variety jokes or odd non sequiturs in which they made fun of themselves.

At first, Gross considered them "Polaroids of a bunch of guys bullshittin' around," and thoroughly amateur. As a man who valued professionalism, they seemed undignified and damaging to his pride.

Doug, as Gross would soon understand, thought it was important for readers to believe that they knew the writers—their faces and how they dressed—and had a sense of who they were, thus forging a family-like connection akin to them. These weren't just names on a masthead. They were regular guys with cool jobs who liked to screw around. "Foto Funnies" destroyed the wall between reader and humorist, creating a belief that the magazine and the twenty-two-year-old reader in Omaha were somehow in it together. The instinct was correct and the impact was powerful.

In many of the first "Foto Funnies," the featured players are Doug, the camera-shy Henry, and Mary Martello, whom Doug elevated (without telling anyone) from editorial assistant to managing editor of the magazine (with no change in duties) shortly after Hoffman's departure.

Aside from the fact that he was cheating on his wife, Doug quickly experienced other complications from his relationship with Martello. The main complication was O'Donoghue. Tough and angry on the outside, O'Donoghue had a soft middle when it came to certain subjects—mostly women, with whom he would fall into gushy, sentimental love, sometimes of the unrequited variety. Though no one knows whether or not he and Martello ever actually slept together, or even if O'Donoghue had made his desires clear, the new managing editor was the subject of such a crush. In his mind, Mary Marshmallow belonged to him.

In spring 1971, Doug confided his affair, which had pretty much been a secret, to O'Donoghue. He told the wrong man. O'Donoghue turned his back and froze Doug out with deadly silence.

O'Donoghue disappeared briefly, causing Kelly and Beard to head down to his Spring Street loft where they found the man who could destroy anyone he liked with a put-down, chain-smoking and crying on a daybed under the stairs.

Blindsided by O'Donoghue's reaction, Doug tried to rectify the situation with humor and endless apologies. Nothing worked and O'Donoghue's silent rage cast a pall over the offices.

Later, after much water had passed under the bridge in both of their lives, O'Donoghue forgave Doug and reopened lines of communication. This change of heart was based as much on his respect for Doug's talent as it was on the belief that the chief editor was, along with Henry, his only true peer at the magazine. Others would not be so fortunate.

* * *

The subhead of the January 1971 Women issue was "Would You Want Your Brother to Marry One?" O'Donoghue's "The Censorless Woman by 'F'" parodies the bestselling *The Sensuous Woman* by "J" with chapter titles such as "Don't Wait Until You're Old and Ugly! Live Life Now While You're Young and Ugly," "Put Out the Welcome Mattress," and "The Spanish Fly in the Ointment"—all in the name of cashing in on the women's movement. The Dick and Jane–styled "Mighty Minerva" cartoon takes a young girl through a liberated life where she climbs trees, gets drafted, saves men from fires, fixes engines, sexually dominates (screaming to one hapless conquest, "Can't make it, eh? I might have known! Goodbye!") and becomes president, dropping atom bombs on male-dominated societies during her period.

The headlines of the *Cosmopolitan* parody scream "Do Call Girls Have Orgasms?," "Create a Groovy Orgasm Nook in Your Apartment (On a Budget)," "The Jewish Orgasm," "Small Town Orgasms," "Do Black Men Have Bigger Orgasms?," "Orgasms Burn Calories: How to Fornicate Your Way to a Better Figure (yum!)," and "Orgasms and the Kent State Killings." Under Gross's direction, the cover model and layout were exacting re-creations of the real thing. Among the columns in the body of the parody is a spoof on Helen Gurley Brown's legendary "Step into My Parlor" article entitled "Step into My Bidet," where she trumpets birth control pills but admits that "I myself never had periods, even when I was younger, but, then I think I'm lucky I still feel like a complete woman; I just avoid all that messy blood!!!" Demonstrating that a wealthy, older Manhattanite might not be on the same wavelength as her supposedly liberated, confident young readers, Brown regales them with stories of losing 212 pounds drinking carrot and kohlrabi cocktails (now fortified with prestressed concrete) and the value of hitting on every boss for whom she'd ever worked.

* * *

Before World War II, women such as *The New Yorker*'s Dorothy Parker and screenwriter Anita Loos created a brand of wisecracking,

urbane female humor that would not survive the Truman administration. When soldiers returned home from Europe and the South
Pacific, women's humor and the uniquely female comic voice became
domesticated right along with the wives who were giving birth to
Doug and Henry's generation. Parker and Loos were replaced with
the humor of the suburbs and family life.

Funny women now wrote things like *Please Don't Eat the Dai-
sies* and *Among the Savages*; on screen, Nora Charles, who gave as
good as she got from husband Nick, was replaced by Doris Day as a
female comic heroine, innocently and frustratingly adrift in a man's
world. Comedy was being done to her, not by her.

Television's wittiest woman was Rose Marie on the *Dick Van
Dyke Show*. Her Sally Rogers (a character that Carl Reiner based on
Selma Diamond and Lucille Kallen, who both wrote for *Your Show
of Shows*) was a smart, edgy comedy writer to be sure, but also a
closeted lesbian spinster. The wisecracking, sexy dame was a thing
of the past.

The social reorganization of the 1960s and early '70s, with Betty
Freidan, Gloria Steinem, and others leading the charge, broke ground
for the emergence of a new breed of liberated, funny women like Bette
Midler and Lily Tomlin. Anne Beatts would take up where Parker
and Loos left off and fill that role at *National Lampoon*, despite having arrived as Michel Choquette's girlfriend from Montreal.

"I got into comedy the way Katherine the Great got into politics,"
Beatts liked to joke. "On my back."

Beatts had certain things in common with Doug and Henry. She
was extremely smart and well read, though less intellectually refined
than the Harvard boys. Raised in Somers, New York, her background
was not dissimilar from Doug's. Beatts's family was decidedly working
class and had their share of experience in the service sector. A prodi-
giously bright high school student, she had been a nerd (who graduated
in three years), though a much tougher one than Doug. Like Henry,
she was highly disciplined and possessed an unshakeable belief in the
rightness of whatever she thought. If ever there was a woman ready to
play ball with the boys at *National Lampoon*, it was Beatts.

When her parents divorced, Beatts moved to Montreal with her
mother. She graduated from McGill University and by age twenty-

five had been engaged to the same man twice, though they never married. While working as a copywriter at McConnell Eastman, her colleague Sean Kelly set her up with Michel Choquette. Beatts and Choquette moved in together and began collaborating on articles. In 1970, she traveled with him to New York, meeting Doug and Henry at the office and attending writers' dinners. There was just one problem: nobody wanted her there.

Filled with witty dialogue, intense intellectual competition, verbal fencing, and massive consumption of alcohol, the meals were often held at horrific restaurants like the Steak and Brew, located in the basement of 635 Madison. Other than the stray girlfriend who might be waiting for them to finish, no woman had ever been a participant in the meetings. The whole atmosphere was an extension of the boys' club at the Castle.

Trow and O'Donoghue would trade sharp, nasty banter. Choquette's volcano of ideas sprang forth. Doug cracked everyone up with his riffs on sex, high school life, politics, and whatever was of the moment, while Henry puffed his pipe, took notes, and pitched in his sophisticated parody concepts. Kelly, when he was there, was a master of the format, spouting off so many story ideas and dark Irish jokes that it was hard to keep track of all of the laughter in the midst of the rapid-fire succession of literary references, parody rock lyrics, and disdain for things both great and small.

Arriving early in the game, Choquette had found it easy to gain acceptance. The magazine needed contributors. It had been more work to get Kelly on board. At first, no one could figure him out. Clearly brilliant, Doug and Henry could only classify him as a mad poet. Quickly, however, his Jesuit credentials and wicked, elastic mind (which consumed nearly a book a day) sealed the deal.

Beatts, however, was another matter. She was a woman.

"[The editors] weren't really exposed to women," Beatts recalls. "They thought women were a different species, like horses. It was sort of like 'what do women eat?'"

Doug and Kelly were both married men, but they were hardly experts on the subject of women. Though a cheating husband, Doug truly loved women and they loved him back. Yet his understanding of them at age twenty-five was that of a very smart teenager. Kelly, with a wife and three children back in Montreal, had married young and had a bunch of kids before he knew what hit him. His first marriage would not make it through his tenure at the magazine.

Trow was gay. Doug, Kelly, O'Donoghue, and Henry had been geeks in high school, at an age where brains do not give you access to the pom-pom squad. At Harvard, Doug had figured out how to harness his charm and looks into an attractive package. All four were now at the precipice of realizing that as adults, their collective Achilles heel had become an aphrodisiac. But they were still scared of girls and saw them mainly as potential sex partners and mother figures who held the keys to both unspeakable happiness and searing pain.

"You have to remember," Emily Prager (who later became involved with both Doug and the *National Lampoon*) told one reporter, "emotionally they were about five years old. As soon as it got to boyfriend and girlfriend, it got right back to ninth grade. They were all so bright and directed and just insanely immature. Every one of them must have been just crazy in high school. There was no quarter for anything that happened to you, nothing private. They never viewed each other in terms of their humanity, but they were happiest when they were together. It was like Totie Fields's leg. They were all one-legged people who could make jokes about it."

Henry, still unattached and believed by all to be a virgin, wasn't so sure about Beatts. To Choquette he seemed supremely uptight about having a woman at the table. Somewhere inside themselves, both Henry and Doug believed that women weren't funny in the way that men were.

Beatts was neither a likely sexual partner nor a nurturing maternal presence for the boys. Instead, she was tough and abrasive, and wouldn't take no for an answer. If she was at all intimidated by the intellectual might or verbal jabs of those at the table, Beatts didn't show it. She had a tendency to become undiplomatic and aggressive when she didn't get her way.

"She would propose something and they wouldn't laugh," Choquette remembers. "So she'd say, 'You're crazy! It'll work!'"

While collaborating with Choquette, she demanded not just money but also a byline. Through a combination of raw determination and talent, she wore them down and became a regular contributor.

Beatts would be singular among the women who worked at the Lampoon for not succumbing to Doug's charms. Nearly everyone at the place adored and even worshipped him. Most women were instantly smitten, finding a sensitive man-child who needed a loving mommy-girlfriend. Beatts's reaction was the polar opposite. She tolerated Doug's ambivalence about everything from marriage to editorial matters, but to her it seemed a sign of weakness, as it had when he'd asked O'Donoghue if he "should be for the [Black] Panthers?" It bordered on infuriating for a woman like Beatts, who wasn't about to mother a lost soul like Doug, no matter how charming or talented he was.

In the aloof and decidedly less emotionally available Henry, she found a more kindred spirit and one with whom she could empathize. Henry was clear about what he wanted and had his shit together. He was awkward but also organized and straightforward—at least compared to everyone else at the magazine. Underneath his rumpled exterior, she saw a very lonely young man.

Around the office, Beatts was struck by the subservient role of women, most of whom she recalls as being extremely short—which surely meant something. One was even a dwarf. By the fall of 1971, Beatts was an important comedic voice at the magazine, an essential component of its social-political dynamic and the grande dame of *National Lampoon*. Later, in a tribute to her ability to play the hard-edged Nora Charles to the men in the office, the boys would say, "If you can't stand the Beatts, stay out of the bitchin'."

It was a compliment.

* * *

Henry and Doug would often venture down to Chinatown, where Rick Meyerowitz lived in a loft on East Broadway. The three men would eat inexpensive Chinese dinners, after which Doug more often than not bummed money from his less well-to-do artist friend for taxi rides home.

One of these evenings, Henry and Doug went back to Meyerowitz's place and discussed the cover for their March 1971 Culture issue. Between the covers they intended to run O'Donoghue's "How to Write Good," a paranoiac parody of mail-order writing schools that becomes a fear-mongering attempt to make students submit to the instructor's control, while offering literary devices that involve ending difficult scenes with someone being run over by a truck ("or, if in England, suddenly everyone was run over by a lorry"); Trow's *TV Guide* spoof, "The New York Review of TV," that features shows like *Kaptain Angsteroo*, where kids read *Tale of the Warsaw Ghetto*, and *Tell Me Erik Erikson*; and Doug's "Undiscovered Notebooks of Leonardo Da Vinci," with drawings of early whoopee cushions ("una device joculare! Le Poo-poo Cushine") and vibrators ("una Christamasso presente per Il Papa Innocenti III"). They wanted Meyerowitz to create the cover à la Da Vinci.

Meyerowitz, who feared that his work was becoming too sophomoric, looked at his Harvard-educated buddies and suggested Mona Lisa as a gorilla. Before they could react, he said, "No, no, too sophomoric."

Doug fell off the side of the sofa laughing. Henry's pipe shook from uncharacteristic giggles, spilling ashes all over his jacket. "That's it!" Henry said in his trademark clipped manner, choking back what appeared to be real tears of laughter. Doug was on the floor.

Meyerowitz continued trying to back out, believing the idea was too stupid and that everyone had just been caught up in the moment. Henry and Doug demanded he follow through.

In his studio, Meyerowitz put up a print of the Mona Lisa and began looking through a book of wild animals. Examining the primates, he was struck by the idiotic visage of an orangutan. It was too stupid and funny to pass up. The drawing came with uncharacteristic ease. A few days later, Meyerowitz brought it to the *National Lampoon* offices covered in opaque white paper.

Mike Gross, Doug, Henry, and several others gathered in a conference room, waiting for their March cover to be unveiled. When Meyerowitz lifted the paper, there were screams of joy from the generally cynical and tough-to-impress crew. Big, stupid, and almost obscenely ugly, Mona Gorilla held a banana in her left hand and pursed her orangutan lips in the precise shape of the original's legendary smile.

"It was so gratifying," Meyerowitz says. "It was that moment when you knew you'd hit a grand slam and won the game."

The image was reproduced worldwide in newspapers and magazines as well as on posters and T-shirts; one of the enduring icons of American humor and a growing hallmark for a magazine poised to become the voice of a generation ready to say "fuck it" and laugh.

*　*　*

Although design caught up, covers popped, and editorial gained important new voices, business was still not booming in 1971. With the second issue, circulation had dropped to 120,000. Thereafter, it hovered in the 150,000 to 200,000 range for most of 1970 and 1971. No matter how visually impressive the magazine had become, it was taking time to build word-of-mouth readership and the ad sales that would spring forth.

The March 1971 issue was practically free of paid advertising, save the Psychology Today Book Club, the Freighter Travel Letter, a few odd pieces of stereo equipment, and Benson & Hedges on the back cover. Where were the blue jeans, booze, tobacco, cars, records, and other items that corporate America wanted to ram down the throats of its largest generation?

Gerry Taylor, a successful Chicago publisher's representative, was working with 21st Century on *Weight Watchers* and had been involved with selling the *Life* parody. In tune with the swinging '70s aesthetic, he also understood the youth market, having been the publisher of a college magazine named *Big Ten*. After moving to New York, Taylor was approached by Matty Simmons and Len Mogel about joining *National Lampoon* as ad director when it was only five issues old. To that point, Taylor had been unimpressed by the duck mascot, the weird design, and the quality of the humor. Matty assured him that Cloud had been fired, Gross was on board, and that the boys had just been trotting out old jokes from their Harvard days in the first few issues. Still, Taylor demurred.

By the time Nostalgia hit the stands in November 1970, he was sufficiently impressed. Editorially, he believed the magazine was becoming very exciting and its appearance was cohesive and marketable. Like Gross before him, he looked at *National Lampoon* and thought, "This is something I can really sell."

Taylor began working at *National Lampoon* in spring 1971. One of his first acts was to establish a dress code and image that would translate to advertising and corporate marketing executives. While *Rolling Stone* sent reps to Madison Avenue in jeans and backpacks, Taylor understood that the marketing of *National Lampoon* could not mirror the magazine's content. Instead, it would mirror him.

Wearing three-piece suits and writing notes on conservative letterhead, *National Lampoon* salespeople went out to do business with advertisers, not to make them laugh.

"I wanted our letterhead to look like we were Merrill Lynch," Taylor says. "We aren't about being funny. We are about being marketers. We wanted money from [advertisers] and we had to look legitimate."

Taylor devised a strategy that concentrated on the music business and began by picking what he considered to be the low-hanging fruit. Married to singer Mary Travers of Peter, Paul and Mary, he had contacts and understood the record industry through his work representing *High Fidelity*. The first move was to go after the record business itself. Taylor knew that there was a liberal and bizarre bent to the drug-oriented, irreverent folks who were putting out albums by the likes of Humble Pie.

"I figured, these guys have got to understand the Lampoon," Taylor says.

With a network of contacts and an easy rapport, Taylor knew the labels would listen to his pitch that *National Lampoon* was not just good for selling comedy records but for music as well. "We're entertainment, you're entertainment" was the basic concept. The revenue accrued quickly.

With record producers in the fold, Taylor planned to go after the more conservative makers of stereo hardware, starting with Bernie Mitchell, the innovative president of Pioneer. If he could get Mitchell, other hardware firms would follow—and they did—legitimizing the magazine as a place where mainstream companies could sell their products.

Before he had been there a year, Taylor was making the best of *National Lampoon*'s intensely loyal readership, devising the tagline "There's nothing funny about the way it sells."

* * *

Clad in a robe, with horns spouting from his head, Richard M. Nixon appeared on the cover of the June 1971 Religion for Fun and Prophet issue holding a copy of *Reader's Digest* in place of a Bible.

Kelly's "Utopia Four" comics pit geodesic dome–inventor Buckminster (Super Bucky) Fuller; hot and cold media theorist Marshall (Media Man) McLuhan; bisexual, feminist, social, and literary critic Kate (Karate Kate) Millet; and *The Greening of America* author Charles Reich against a parade of social ills, all of which they were decidedly incapable of dealing with.

"Had any orgasms lately? Raise your consciousness Sister!" Millet screams at a poor black woman with a passel of children, after breaking down her tenement door and thinking to herself, "My God, it's just like D. H. Lawrence around here!"

The woman replies, "Hey, who is yo'? Yo' from de welfare?"

McLuhan screams, "Now that's what I call revolutionary!" as a black youth runs by him with a stolen television. Shortly thereafter, McLuhan is beaten on the head by a riot cop.

The piece had stirred a debate around the offices as to whether it was OK to make fun of Fuller. It was the type of argument that didn't take place anywhere else, the problem being that everyone agreed Fuller was "an asshole" but "he was our kind of asshole." It was a serious discussion about who was worth parodying or mocking. Similar debates would follow, with the inevitable result that everyone was fair game so long as it was funny.

The issue had solid, incisive pieces, including Henry and Trow's "Big Blessings Bulletin," a traditional modern American church newsletter put out by the Reverend Dr. Christ and his Church of the Universal Blessings and Spiritual Well-Being, Inc., announcing that "the meek" sweatshirts are back in stock ("these handsome garments are ideal for work or play"), containing news of the enormously successful Olive Mountain Outing ("a fish fry where the Poor in Spirit learn that they have inherited the much coveted Kingdom of Heaven"), and boasting an "Ask Mary" advice column. The issue, however, is Kelly's, ending with the lyrics to "I Dreamed I Was There in O.D. Heaven," a reverent hymn that mixes old-time religion and rock music in telling how the new Holy Trinity of Brian Jones, Jimi Hendrix, and Janis Joplin made their way to the pearly gates.

> Not one for half measures,
> Janis J. mixed her pleasures,
> Shot up what she couldn't drink down.
> No angels protested
> When the lady requested
> Long Sleeves for her heavenly gown.

* * *

Henry and Doug each had his specialty, a style or brand of comedy in which he was the master of the universe and arbiter of all that was funny. What little organization they could impose upon their staff evolved from this structure.

Henry had predated the *Onion* by some twenty-five years with his mock "News of the Month" and was a master straight-on parodist who loved to deal with intellectually dexterous writers. The fierce minds of Kelly and Beatts gravitated toward his leadership, as did contributor Terry Catchpole, the magazine's one avowed conservative.

A freelance political writer and satirist in Washington, D.C., Catchpole represented the divide in the Republican Party between those who supported the war in Vietnam and those who opposed it on Libertarian grounds. Catchpole, in his mid-twenties, fell into the latter category. After receiving a polite rejection letter from Henry, Catchpole followed up and was soon writing articles like "Gracie Slick's Handbook of Radical Do's and Don'ts" and "But, You Hadn't Heard of Vietnam in 1957," where he makes the case for future military actions in mythical countries.

Doug handled writers with more pop culture–oriented and sexually themed sensibilities. Chief among this group was John Boni, an Italian from South Philly who had once been a Broadway actor and sometime opera singer before turning his attention to comedy writing. Another was Chris Miller.

Miller's first appearance was in the July 1971 Pornography issue, which ran Doug's tour de force classic, "Nancy Reagan's Dating Do's and Don'ts," which begins:

Hi. If you are "twixt twelve and twenty" and a would-be dater, this book is for you. In it, I am going to deal honestly, and sometimes quite frankly, with the joys and pitfalls of teen-age dating in the hope that it may prevent your first corsage from shriveling up into a bouquet of nettles.

A dating manual for this day and age? one of your "sophisticated" chums may scoff. Why all that jazz about moral decency and lofty ideals is a lot of bunk and hooey! Is it? Well, take a good look, fellows and girls, at the dangers that surround you in today's "anything goes" world. Everywhere a teen turns he is assaulted by an avalanche of filth that lurks in many forms—pornographic movies, obscene novels, indecent plays, lurid magazines, prurient snapshots, seductive television commercials, suggestive song lyrics, immodest dances, salacious paintings, lewd advertisements, coarse poems, smutty radio shows, depraved newspapers, indelicate lithographs, perverse sculptures, shady stories, gross cookbooks, tawdry cocktail napkins, ribald postcards, libertine bumper stickers, provocative buttons, meretricious gestures, licentious operas, pandering food labels and shameless zoos.

. . . it is no secret that certain foreign powers would like nothing better than to see our country paralyzed and prostrated by a degenerate Supreme Court that sanctions petting sprees and free love as "freedom of choice" and "harmless kicks." While America rots from within, all the Russkies would have to do is rumble through Washington in tanks with those long nasty things on top and pick up the pieces. Her youth "brainwashed" by so-called "liberated" codes of behavior, a mighty nation would be vanquished, laid low by deep kissing and petting parties.

But, young people all love dates . . .

The guide offers advice like "Dating is like dynamite. Used wisely it can move mountains and change the course of mighty rivers. Used foolishly, it can blow your legs off." Dating, Reagan warns, is like electricity. "Used wisely, it can operate your dad's power tools, fry eggs and run trolley cars. Used foolishly, it can electrocute every member of your family including your goldfish." Masturbation, particularly for girls, can take place even when asleep, when one dreams of degradations involving "beatniks, Negroes or worse." Thus, the future first lady advises children to ask their mothers to keep objects such as pencils, candles, bananas, frankfurters, hairbrushes, and softball bats . . . "on ice."

Ruminating about the anatomy and the wonders of the human body, Nancy confesses that her own cycle is based on the appearance of Haley's comet and suggests that cleanup following a wet dream involves two bath towels, an automobile sponge, a mop, a pail of hospital-strength disinfectant, a five-gallon can of industrial cleanser, a hammer, a chisel, and a two-handed paint scraper. Her description, however, of ovaries as two little "almond-flavored" organs is Doug at his best.

"If most comedy writers wanted to do a joke about this, they would change the shape—in Doug's writing they were almond-flavored organs," recalled David Kaestle, a Pratt friend of Michael Gross's who had joined the art department. "That's ten times as funny as working with their shape. Making a flavor out of it brings in all kinds of lascivious thoughts about a woman's lower anatomy."

"Caked Joy Rag" was Miller's first piece, recounting a frustrating afternoon in the life of a chronic and creative masturbator, the first piece in his *National Lampoon* career as the magazine's ribald master of sexual and fraternity-style humor.

Raised on Long Island and the son of a frustrated jazz musician turned businessman who encouraged his son to forgo the creative life for a solid career, Miller grew up on the radio humor of Jean Shepherd and Stan Freberg as well as the rock 'n' roll Alan Freed played each night. Discovering Bo Diddley, Chuck Berry, and bands like the Midnighters (whose songs were mostly about fucking) helped him ease out of *MAD*, the Marx Brothers, Ernie Kovacs, and Martin and Lewis.

As a business major at Dartmouth, Miller's life changed dramatically sophomore year when he became a member of the Alpha Delta Phi fraternity, where he began to chafe at the idea of being a good little boy at the business school. In his fraternity brothers he found kindred spirits who held booting (voluntary vomiting) and masturbation contests, kept a scientific chart of penis sizes (flaccid and erect), and got roaring drunk while pursuing women and listening to R&B music. Their motto: "Sickness is health, blackness is truth, and drinking is strength."

After military reserve duty, Miller joined Madison Avenue's Dancer, Fitzgerald, and Sample as a copywriter, where he worked on Coco Puffs cereal and Oxydol detergent campaigns. By 1970, he'd grown his hair long, traded beer for pot, and immersed himself in the radical lifestyle that espoused free love and getting high. He began to wonder whether working in advertising made him a traitor to his generation and quit to pursue short-story writing.

He had sent stuff to *National Lampoon*, but hadn't heard back from them until an editor at *Playboy* passed his work to Doug because it didn't fit with Hef's taste. Doug called him in to the office.

"We think you are the find of the year," Doug said, rushing over to Miller when he arrived. Miller became a close friend of Doug's and one of the magazine's most popular contributors. At the offices, he got along with everyone, but avoided the savage wits of O'Donoghue and Kelly—who were often marking territory.

"I was a flower child," he says. "I wanted everybody to love each other with no conflict. That was my thing."

Miller admired Henry, particularly his encyclopedic mind, which any moment could give a detailed twenty-minute explanation of how jet engines worked or hold forth on the lives of monarch butterflies. He likened Henry to the dad of the magazine, while Doug was the mom who kept hitting the cooking sherry. But he bonded with Doug.

"He was like type-O blood," Miller says. "Doug could get along with anyone. This was a very special person with way-more-than-usual amounts of soul, heart, and caring about people. He really listened; he could inhabit the stuff you were saying and you felt you were making a connection."

* * *

"Mom! Dad! I'm home!" Doug Kenney said, arriving on the Los Angeles doorstep of Peter Ivers and Lucy Fisher in summer 1971.

In early July, Doug disappeared. He told no one where he was going or when he was coming back. He only left a note for Henry pinned to the mantel of the duplex fireplace explaining that he was "going to go gonzo" and that "the eye in the sky" would get him if he didn't run away. Some thought it was a suicide note.

For nearly eighteen months, Doug had been *National Lampoon*'s poster boy, chief architect, star writer, and least organized, least responsible, but most productive editor. At the same time, he felt guilty about living in a marriage where he was at a loss as to how to be a meaningful participant. Working long hours suited Doug; he simply didn't know how to be a married man, and really had no idea why he'd gotten married in the first place. Undoubtedly he cared for Alex, but was far from able to commit himself to the marriage. Hence the affair with Martello—which helped him cope by adding a healthy dose of familiar guilt.

"Doug was troubled with guilt about the relationship," Alex said. "If he had a failing it was that he was not great at telling the truth to people."

Alex had prevailed upon Doug to see a psychiatrist, finding one who was favored by celebrities. Doug went only a few times, claiming he didn't want to see a celebrity shrink and that he didn't believe in the commoditization of his inner life.

The affair and Doug's disappearance—which left Alex alone, confused, and penniless—was effectively the end of their yearlong marriage.

There are claims that Doug had shown signs he was about to crack. Some recall that he drank heavily and smoked mass quantities of dope. Other stories had it that he would fail to finish sentences, inexplicably appear to have tears in his eyes, and hated to be alone. Henry had seen the warning signs, but was hopeless to do anything about it. "Slow down," he'd tell Doug. Instead, he only went faster.

More stories emerged, claiming that a jittery Doug often joked around the office that snipers across the street were aiming for him. He would mimic the sound of bullets and fall down, pretending he'd been shot.

Then he was gone. Without a trace. Taking with him a knapsack containing underwear, a few articles of clothing, and a *National Lampoon* American Express card. Not by coincidence, his leaving New York and the magazine came at a time when the *National Lampoon* was on the verge of achieving the kind of success he so desired and that he needed to feel whole.

"He kept running away from things," Chris Hart says. "The magazine. Alex."

Doug's disappearance was fueled by many things, not the least of which was a fear of responsibility and adulthood that was far more complex than what lay on the surface. At twenty-four, he'd perfected the role that everyone wanted him to play. He was the sensitive child with extrasensory perception for what everyone was feeling at all times, always trying to smooth things over with a laugh. At Harvard he'd shed the nerdy kid persona and become a star. And with that came expectations—the expectation that he'd always be perfect. So as his professional life began to soar and his personal life came apart, he fell to pieces, not knowing how to be perfect anymore. The public, socially unacceptable failure of his marriage must have echoed his inability to fit in as a child, his inability to make his parents understand and love him the way he needed. It was perhaps the first public failure of his life, arriving at a time when the magazine was no longer just a lark but a successful ongoing concern where he was depended on to produce time and again.

After a brief stay with Martello (who disappeared with him) in a tent on Martha's Vineyard, Doug set out alone for California. Fisher and Ivers were in Berkeley on the last leg of a cross-country trip that culminated with their move to Los Angeles. With their itinerary in hand, Doug arrived at the Hollywood home of their friends, Howard and Barbara Smith.

"I'm a friend of Peter and Lucy's," Doug said. "Can I stay with you?" In the spirit of the times, the Smiths said, "No problem."

When Fisher and Ivers arrived in Los Angeles, Doug was a basket case, alienated from his life, his marriage, and the pressure of running a national magazine. In addition, Doug seemed hugely conflicted over his success, making money when all of his friends were poor and struggling to get by. He found it immensely confusing, exacerbating an already overtaxed state of mind. Doug was having some kind of breakdown.

For the next several months, Ivers and Fisher treated Doug as if he were their child. They took trips to Yosemite and Disneyland. There were cap-gun fights in the Hollywood Hills. Doug played the funny, lovable little boy to Fisher's understanding mommy who made sure that he was happy and protected.

Fisher knew that Doug needed nothing so much as love and to be treated well. She had seen him attach himself to Ivers's mother and how her maternal warmth soothed him. Fisher would try the same, reading bedtime stories to him each night (*Moby Dick* was a favorite) and literally tucking him under the covers.

"He went from being this responsible person, to 'I can't do any of it,'" Fisher recalls.

After a while, the old Doug started showing his face and having a good time. For nearly a month he had refused to contact Matty, Alex, or Henry. Fisher went to Schwab's Drug Store in Hollywood and bought several postcards, imploring Doug to at least contact them. She even addressed the cards for him. It is unknown if, or what, he might have sent to Henry or Alex, but his card to Matty has become legend. "Next time try a Yalie!" was all he wrote.

* * *

Back at 635 Madison, the reaction to Doug's disappearance included concern, rage, panic, and even some joy. Michael Gross, who admired and respected Doug, was beside himself. "How could anyone be so irresponsible and unprofessional?" he thought. His concern for Doug was not couched in sympathy for a sensitive young man under tremendous pressure who had simply snapped; rather, Gross viewed Doug's disappearance as an act that demonstrated disrespect for his colleagues and, perhaps worse, his own abilities.

"He was a little bit like Marilyn Monroe," Gross said. "[Writing] was so easy, he never saw it as a talent."

Matty, who'd now lost two-thirds of the original Harvard team within the first eighteen months of operation, somehow managed to keep a reasonable lid on whatever he was feeling and turned to Henry.

If Henry had any reaction to Doug's disappearance, it was tough to tell. Since the beginning, his primary response to Doug's irregular work habits and periodic writer's block walkabouts had been to grumble a little under his breath to Cerf or Trow. Having worked with Doug for nearly five years, he'd become used to this kind of thing as an unpleasant but necessary part of Doug's creative process.

What was going on inside Henry was anybody's guess. He essentially behaved as though he didn't care, and, more important, there was a job that needed to get done. Doug's vanishing act, however, had to be devastating, both personally and professionally.

"I think [Doug and Henry] had a love relationship," Beatts says. "Henry had a heterosexual crush on Doug and potentially vice versa."

Henry had been abandoned. Doug left a note that could be interpreted in the extreme as suicide. Not used to dealing with emotions, Henry reacted as the brokenhearted often do—by putting on a brave front and trying to be humorous, while in reality his legs had been knocked out from under him.

"It was mean of Doug to disappear," Beatts says, "no matter how freaked-out or fucked up he was. It was a mean thing to do to Henry."

Beyond that, the idea of leaving the magazine and its staff must have been inconceivable to Henry. Despite having the cynicism of a disappointed idealist and a jaundiced view of human nature, Henry was a man of impeccable manners. He never would have done what Doug had done. It simply wasn't polite.

The not-so-secret fear around the magazine was that things would fall apart. Henry was fine as an editor and de facto manager, but he wasn't Doug. For whatever leadership qualities he demonstrated during the past year and a half, Henry was a less-than-dynamic presence who lacked his partner's energizing spirit and common touch. How the hell was he going to run a magazine?

When it became clear that Doug was not coming back any time soon, Henry called a meeting at the duplex.

Despite their fears and overall affection for Doug, many saw this as an opportunity. Suddenly, within this competitive group there was an opening. The guy who often wrote a third of the magazine was gone, and somebody had to fill the space.

"I was happy that Doug left," Beatts remembers. "It didn't mean anything to me and it made more room for anyone else."

O'Donoghue, Kelly, Beatts, and others would now have a chance to fill the vacuum Doug had left. Henry began pounding out material day and night. O'Donoghue, a star in his own right, seized the opportunity to become the dominant presence at the magazine, even taking an office. And a British comedian named Tony Hendra, who'd been contributing to the magazine for the past year, joined the staff full time.

They would do more than survive. Under Henry's leadership, they would thrive.

* * *

In November 1966, the comedy team of Tony Hendra and Nic Ullett was in the midst of a long run at Manhattan's Plaza 9 cabaret. Just off three guest spots on the *Ed Sullivan Show* and veterans of a short-lived TV show, *The Entertainers*, their act was profiled in *Time*.

Honed to within an inch of everybody's life, [the act] is among other things, a pigeonholer's nightmare, swooping from low burlesque to high camp, from keen wit to Raggedy Ann clowning, from one line gags to intricately orchestrated gags. William Wordsworth's "The Daffodils" is revived, lyrics faithfully intact, as a rock and roll song, with Ullett wreaking vengeance on a mangy guitar and Hendra doing a Cambridge version of Teresa Brewer . . .

Chubby, with one slightly crossed eye and stringy blond hair cut in a modified Beatles mop, Hendra told the reporter that he'd been born in London during a German air raid and that his first toy was a piece of shrapnel that landed in his cradle. After meeting his comedy partner at Cambridge in the formative school days of Monty Python and the aftermath of *Beyond the Fringe* and Spike Milligan's *Goon Show*, the two men created an act that made its 1963 debut at a London nightclub owned by a Lebanese gangster.

Coming to the United States in 1964, Hendra and Ullett were booked in Dallas—not exactly a hotbed for far-reaching, silly humor filled with literary references and liberal sensibilities. They were canceled within a week, causing a tactical retreat to the far more open-minded borscht belt of the Catskills and well-known clubs like Chicago's Mr. Kelly's, which caught fire one night while they were onstage. The band played "Smoke Gets in Your Eyes" while Ullett told patrons, "Don't worry, my partner once quieted down an audience in a fire to avoid panic . . . and they all burned to death."

Hendra was the product of what he calls a "mixed marriage" between a Catholic (with Irish roots) mother and agnostic artist father. Growing up in the British countryside, Hendra's early education took place at schools run by the Dominican Sisters and then some Catholic Brothers who inspired boys under the age of ten to beat the holy hell out of each other when they themselves weren't hitting the boys with belts. Boxing matches in particular were encouraged to settle even the smallest differences.

"You'll settle it with gloves," Hendra wrote in his memoir *Father Joe*, "as Christ intended."

When there was blood or physical damage from the fisticuffs, the Brothers (who employed no nurse) would stitch or bandage up the little boys themselves. Even the Catholic Mrs. Hendra realized this wasn't the place for her son and sent him to a succession of Church of England prep schools.

By age eleven, Hendra was spiritually adrift, without much feeling for any organized religion. At fourteen, however, he began an affair with the wife of a local Catholic man at whose home he did odd jobs. His punishment, or salvation, was to be introduced to a Benedictine monk named Father Joe who resided at Quarr Abbey on the Isle of Wight.

During the next several years, Hendra would wrestle with his faith and go back and forth between a desire to pursue a cloistered life at Quarr or attend Cambridge. Not without soul-searching or internal conflict, he chose the latter.

In 1966, Hendra met Michel Choquette on the comedy-club circuit in Chicago, where their respective acts were performing. Their paths would cross several times until Hendra and Ullett broke up in the late 1960s and Hendra became a writer for television's *Playboy After Dark*. Living in Los Angeles and writing for television wasn't something Hendra particularly enjoyed.

"You're writing for blue-haired septuagenarians and you're constantly trying to second-guess your audience and not offend advertisers," he said. "That's when you stop being funny."

In summer 1971, Hendra was out of a job and the married father of two small children while Henry was in Manhattan desperately trying save the *National Lampoon*. Hendra called Choquette, informing him that *Playboy After Dark* had been canceled and that he was seeking employment at *National Lampoon*, whose counterculture, fuck-the-system-anything-goes style of humor presented such a stark contrast to the world of television.

Choquette told him to come east, where he'd provide formal introductions, inspiring Hendra to pack up his wife and kids in a VW bus and immediately head for Manhattan.

* * *

After Doug disappeared it was decided that a different editor would be assigned to each issue of the magazine. Henry would run things, but somebody else would need to spearhead and deal with the content for each theme, thereby giving everyone a bigger stake in the product, creating greater variety, and lending a unique viewpoint to each issue.

Kelly handled August's Bummer issue, whose cover was another instant classic. Artist Frank Kelly Freas, who'd been the foremost illustrator of *MAD* covers from 1958 to 1962, sublimely morphed the visage of Alfred E. Newman with that of the infamous Lieutenant William Calley (U.S. Army uniform and all) above the headline "What, My Lai?"

Inside the issue were the board game "Welfare Monopoly" by Weidman (with tokens for the Vietnam veteran, the addict, the dropout, the prostitute, and the hardened criminal, and Get Out of Jail Free cards labeled Community Control), where players either hit the numbers and collect $125 or are bitten by a rat and must pay the hospital $50 or die; "As the Monk Burns," Boni's Vietnamese soap opera; Henry and Meyerowitz's collaboration on a computerized "Fight of the Century" between Charles Manson and Calley; and the "Canadian Supplement" by Beatts, Choquette, and Kelly that takes fourteen pages of potshots at The Retarded Giant on Your Doorstep.

The country that would give the world Eugene Levy, John Candy, Rick Moranis, *SCTV*, Jim Carrey, Mike Myers, and the Kids in the Hall was, to Kelly (and all of the other Canadians who brought their brand of humor to *National Lampoon* during the 1970s), a hopelessly bland nation where flour was the favorite spice and secondary status a way of life.

The "Canadian Supplement" is all over the place, with buttons that read "Mounties are strict but fair"; an ode to great Canadian celebrities from Joni Mitchell, Lorne Greene, and boxer George Chuvalo ("who was bested in the ring by no less an opponent than Cassius Clay himself") to the comedy team of Wayne and Shuster ("as Canadian, and inseparable, as ham and maple syrup or porridge and blackstrap molasses"); a Cwick Canada Cwiz that asks readers what happened to the Canadian protest movement (the answer: "he got married and settled down"); and various facts and figures, including the highlights that half of Niagara Falls belongs to Canada, Toronto has only 2.2 rapes every three years, and Montreal, Quebec, is the only French-speaking major metropolis in the North American continent, with the exception of New Orleans.

* * *

While AWOL in Los Angeles, one of Doug Kenney's favorite activities was to wander into bookstores and ask clerks whether they had a book titled *Teenage Commies from Outer Space* in stock and, if they did, how it was selling.

There was no such book. Instead, TACOS (as he liked to call it) was the name of a novel Doug intended to write—the most hilarious, insightful, significant book ever written about being an American teenager. It would be a midwestern public high school version of *The Catcher in the Rye* that measured up to the literary standards of Salinger, Fitzgerald, Faulkner, and especially Waugh.

On these outings, Doug would approach the clerks with a smile and confidence sufficient to convince them the book actually existed. "We don't have it right now," some would say, "but I hear it's great."

* * *

The September issue marked Doug's brief return to Manhattan, where he guest-edited the December issue, moved out of the duplex, formally (but not legally) ended his marriage, and prepared to set off for Martha's Vineyard, where he would write TACOS.

At year's end, circulation had reached 250,000, with revenues of $1.7 million and net income of $197,000. Matty was busy promoting the Lampoon and creating ancillary publications related to his flagship, a book parody entitled *The Job of Sex*, and the first *Best of National Lampoon* collection.

Other things were also improving. Gross's design and execution were now full-fledged policy. Gerry Taylor's advertising strategy was bearing fruit. Pages were filled with work by Beatts, Kelly, Catchpole, Miller, Boni, Hendra, Henry, Weidman, Trow, Meyerowitz, Wilson, Rodrigues, Gross, and Roth. All in all, things were pretty good considering it was a million-dollar enterprise run by people in their twenties who were making it up as they went along.

Doug continued to contribute (he wrote many articles, and "Mrs. Agnew's Diary" never went away), but physically and spiritually he wasn't there. Never again would Doug want, or be asked, to be in charge of *National Lampoon*. That job now belonged to Henry, and O'Donoghue was quickly establishing himself as the preeminent creative and political presence within the walls of 635 Madison.

* * *

Toward the end of December's A Heart-Warming Christmas issue, the editors did a bit of Doug-style self-parody with a piece called "Editorial Fantasies." In a series of cartoons, Henry is depicted inside a television set sitting opposite a shocked William F. Buckley, calmly uttering the words "Yes . . . Your face and my ass"; O'Donoghue is surrounded by buxom women and sophisticated celebrities who hail his brilliance and comment that he's not balding in the least; and a letter-sweatered Doug stands on a podium receiving a sportsmanship award and Kiwanis college scholarship in front of adoring, all-American masses from a place not unlike Chagrin Falls.

"They were," said one female staffer, "the most miserable bunch of guys I've ever known."

6

Hitler Being Difficult

66 Chess is as elaborate a waste of human intelligence as you can find outside an advertising agency. 99

—*Raymond Chandler*

The following things happened in 1972: cigarette advertising was banned from television; Don MacLean's "American Pie" topped the pop charts; *Grease* opened on Broadway; Nixon became the first U.S. official to visit China since 1950 and returned with two panda bears; 69 percent of Americans opposed busing as a means of school integration; "blaxsploitation" films (*Shaft*, *Hammer*, etc.) hit movie theaters; segregationist Alabama Governor George Wallace won the Florida Democratic presidential primary; J. Edgar Hoover and Jackie Robinson died; five burglars were arrested for breaking into Democratic National Committee headquarters at the Watergate Hotel on June 17; and, on November 7, Richard Nixon won over 60 percent of the popular vote and every state besides Massachusetts, defeating McGovern and securing a second term.

* * *

In January 1972, under the editorial guidance of Tony Hendra, *National Lampoon* published the nastiest, funniest issue in its brief history. The theme was Is Nothing Sacred? and the cover was graced by the iconic Che Guevara poster—so favored by well-intentioned baby boomers—being bashed with a cream pie.

Hendra's editorial read:

> To a generation that, when it sees starving babies on the screen, knows it's almost time for dinner, not much is sacred. All around us, the idols, ikons, and cows of six thousand years of Indo-Aryan culture lie shattered and daily another paragon goes down to ignominy (Kissinger, Richard Speck) another cherished tradition is lost (see *Esquire*'s stinging attack on cordovans). And now with Jim Morrison gone, there really isn't anyone left to look up to . . . it is possible that a society to whom nothing is sacred might just be a better one. And that may be the vision, dimly perceived but beautifully expressed, that one of our most famous and enduring leaders had when he sang: don't follow the leaders, watch the parking meters . . .

Not only was nothing sacred, nothing mattered. And nobody took that message more to heart than Michael O'Donoghue, whose "Vietnamese Baby Book" is one of the Lampoon's most savage and socially relevant pieces of humor.

Whether it is funny or not is beside the point. It is more than black humor; rather, it is an evocation of its author's point of view that comedy is indeed a "baby seal hunt." Dark laughter is one reaction. OUCH! is another.

For six pages, O'Donoghue parodies the traditional American baby book, taking the tender original and sending it to the war zone in Southeast Asia. "Time of birth" for baby Ngoc is listed as "morning." Hospital, doctor, and nurse are left blank. The "about the mother" section describes a seventeen-year-old Vietnamese girl who has lost her parents and three siblings to the war ("had friend but he now dead also"). The father's name is unknown, but mom describes him as a tall, blond, all-American soldier with a Purple Heart ("would know more but it hard to see in alley and he knock me cold before I could get good look").

Baby Ngoc, we learn, has experienced many unusual firsts: first whimper at three weeks; first cringe at two and a half months; first nightmares; first unaided limp; all the way to being "able to pimp" and ready to support himself at age five. A weight chart shows that at age one he weighs three pounds less than at birth. Other pages detail "baby's first wound" (with a blank space for sample of first dressing); "first word" ("medic"); and "first funeral." On the last page is a section for snapshots, including one for the baby's grave.

Identical to its subject in form and execution, O'Donoghue's piece is discomfiting and politically incorrect before such a term existed, using the stereotypical language with which xenophobic Americans mocked Asians to both evoke laughs and send a devastating attack on America's involvement in the war.

Laughter, he believed, was the lowest form of comedy.

Equally incisive, though far easier to laugh at, are Henry's intricately rendered "Buckminster Fuller's Repair Manual for the Entire Universe"; cartoonist Stan Mack's drawing of an apron-clad mother entering the kitchen to find her son, pants around his ankles, having sex with a giant apple pie fresh from the oven; Beatts's "The American Indian: Noble Savage or Renaissance Man?" ("the Indians discovered the wheel. But, foreseeing the environmental devastation, mechanistic society, and needless suffering that would arise as an inevitable consequence of this discovery, they admired it exclusively for its aesthetic qualities. They chose to wear it as an ornament"); and "Summer of '44," Hendra and O'Donoghue's fashionista repackaging of the Holocaust's distinctive look and diet secrets.

Choquette and Kelly had long discussed creating a WASP superhero who fights Catholicism. Deciding to do it as a comic, they invented Son O' God as a buff, caped, haloed Jesus (wearing a gold JC belt) whose Clark Kent is a nebbishy Jewish Brooklynite (thirty-year-old Benny David) who still lives with his overbearing parents. Dedicated to the virtues of peace and love, Son O' God sets out to defeat the villain Antichrist and his evil army of religious fanatics. The image they had in mind for Antichrist was the pope himself.

Doug had used Joe Orlando, an artist who drew *Archie*, to illustrate a piece about teen dating. Frank Springer, who had done "Phoebe Zeitgeist," was O'Donoghue's collaborator of choice. Hoping for similar authenticity, Kelly and Choquette sought out Neal Adams, who drew *Batman* for D.C. Comics. No one, they thought, could be a better choice to draw their pope-fighting superhero. Meeting him at the D.C. offices, however, Choquette began to suspect they might not have the right man.

"I get there and see this guy who looks like a big Irish cop," Choquette says, "and I'm going to come in with my anti-pope jokes."

Listening to the concept, Adams didn't smile. Choquette began to sweat. As he and Kelly continued describing the bellicose pope caricature who runs the Boston police and Knights of Columbus while planning a diabolical assault on white Protestant decency, democracy, and fair play, Adams began quietly drawing on a pad. When the pitch was over, Adams turned the paper around to show the writers a precise rendering of the evil Vatican dweller they'd been describing.

"Yeah, I'll do it," Adams deadpanned.

The work Adams, Choquette, and Kelly did on "Son O' God" was painstaking, with intricate and heavily researched renderings of St. Patrick's Cathedral, the White House under construction, the Brooklyn Bridge (complete with city view), Washington Square Park, vaults buried beneath the Vatican, cardboard cutouts of actual former popes, sculptures, religious art treasures, totems, and icons. The entire project took nearly three months. The three lapsed Catholics were serious about their parody.

The comic ends in a cliffhanger, when the devil himself confronts Son O' God on the steps of St. Patrick's (which has a large "Bingo Tonite" banner hanging from its spires) and screams, "Give up you little Kike! You are powerless in the grip of my Jesuit logic!"

Also in the issue are Doug's "Che Guevara's Bolivian Diaries," which parody the writings of the man Jean-Paul Sartre called "the most complete human being of our age." Beginning with his arrival in Bolivia, we find the iconic revolutionary posing, for airport security, as part of a Mexican mariachi band. When one official discovers a Russian mortar in his bass fiddle case, the quick-thinking Communist puts his mouth on the weapon and improvises "Bésame Mucho." When he writes in his diary about the incident during a taxi ride through the jungle, Che suspects that his compatriot Marcos ("a swaggering adventurer who even apes the way I curl my beard") is watching over his shoulder, attempting to steal good items for his own book. Like a girl in chemistry class, Che writes, "you are an idiot Marcos and it is no wonder that your publisher won't give you an advance."

The diary is filled with idiotic military failures, including Che's faith in his German fellow traveler Tanya, who decorates the roof of their hideout with "a gay bulls-eye." Soon misfortune, in the form of precipitation and digestive problems, overtakes the revolutionaries:

Diciembre 15
    Rain.
Diciembre 16
    Rain.
Diciembre 17
    Rain.
Diciembre 18
    Our first loss. Camba, as usual, fell asleep on guard duty with
his mouth open and drowned. . . .
Enero 5
    More rain today. Once again the men are racked with diarrhea
and our patrols are frequently halted, as marching is difficult with
everyone's pants around his ankles. Our situation is desperate. We
have also run out of air freshener.
Enero 6
    The diarrhea grows worse. We have run out of corks as well.

On the road to creating a Communist haven in South America, Che becomes hopelessly addicted to the capitalist vice of drinking Coca-Cola and his efforts move away from politics and toward the takeover of a local bottling plant. All along, he is busy planning the film version of his diaries, wondering if Dalton Trumbo (of *Spartacus* and *Viva Zapata* fame) will write the screenplay and dreaming that John Wayne, Omar Sharif, Steve McQueen, and Candy Bergen might star. He also makes a deal with *Playboy* to sell "Che" tie clips and wallets.

* * *

In early March, the *San Francisco Chronicle* interviewed Doug during a brief trip west. Arriving in his Gilmour letter jacket, he told the reporter that he'd had an unhappy childhood that still provided awful memories, while noting that his given name was Douglas Clark Francis Michael Kenney. This is not Doug's only falsehood; he also recounted how he (calling himself the Duke De Chevrolet) and Dudley Fishburn spent the summer of 1969 conning little old midwestern ladies into paying $200 for lectures by two experts on the medieval homes of England entitled, "Homes in and Around the British Countryside, Plus a Brief Ramble in Marbleton Gardens." In reality, Fishburn and another friend had undertaken such a con and Doug had simply co-opted a great story.

The lecture tour, he claimed, was "an interesting experience in the gullibility of nearly everyone in the world."

The article dwells heavily on Doug's sadness and belief that nostalgia for days past was a generational antidote to the ways in which the world had been fouled up. As for himself, Henry, and the boys at *National Lampoon*, he mused, "Guys who start humor magazines are slightly neurotic and happy-go-lucky and because of that not very well equipped to deal with the world."

* * *

Tony Hendra was in heaven. About to become *National Lampoon*'s managing editor and free from a world of writing corporate-approved jokes that pandered to the little old lady in Omaha, he'd found a band of kindred spirits, most of whom shared his tainted idealism and desire to express whatever the hell he wanted, so long as it was funny.

Hendra possessed many traits common to his new coworkers. He was a lapsed Catholic (like Kelly, Choquette, and Doug), a graduate of an elite university (like Doug, Henry, Cerf, Weidman, and Trow), politically progressive (everyone except for Henry and Catchpole), and by turns charming (Doug) and angry (everyone). He also possessed odd, often nasty sensibilities that were O'Donoghue, Beatts, and Kelly's stock-in-trade. All of this lay behind the veneer of an ambitious, sophisticated Brit who knew the ins and outs of show biz.

The newcomer found the wicked interplay at 635 Madison somewhat intimidating but much to his liking. During one particularly vicious interchange, which he recalled for a *Harper's* article, Hendra suggested a cover image (August 1971) of Nixon with a long Pinocchio-style wooden nose.

"Ouch," O'Donoghue mocked, "so hard hitting!"

"Quiet day at Cliché?" Kelly popped off.

"Satirized for your convenience," another tossed in.

"You know, Hendra," O'Donoghue said, dragging on a Virginia Slim, "I hear the *Village Voice* has really terrific health benefits."

"Wait! Wait!" Beatts chimed in, "Nixon's the emperor, right? And wait-wait-wait, he's got no clothes."

This led into a rapid-fire succession of references to Hans Christian Anderson, Legs Christian Anderson, Hans Jewish Anderson, One-Hand Buddhist Anderson.

"My suggestion," Hendra wrote, "now lay spread-eagled in a puddle of blood."

Of all of the things Hendra loved about *National Lampoon* in the winter of 1971 and spring of 1972, however, none compared to the pleasure of O'Donoghue's company. In O'Donoghue he found a complementary soul, one of the few of his generation who mocked Mick Jagger, Bob Dylan, and Andy Warhol with rage usually reserved for Nixon, Agnew, and Kissinger.

* * *

Beginning in late winter, Doug spent much of 1972 on Martha's Vineyard, where he was determined to finally write *Teenage Commies from Outer Space*.

Before leaving New York, Doug met Gilmour friend Roger Cox at a private men's club in Manhattan's Biltmore Hotel. Lunching in a room that had been imported from an Irish castle, they seemed a million miles from New York City.

The luncheon was a networking event for Gilmour alumni, and Doug showed up in a maroon-colored velvet suit to calmly confront a room where all others were clad in their Brooks Brothers best.

During the meal, Doug chatted up Carlos, the headwaiter, and before dessert arrived was organizing the employees in a revolutionary uprising against the membership—Che-style. What may have seemed an act of snobbery (a Harvard boy lunching in a private club rounding up the Hispanic employees) was transformed into a warm, sympatico routine with Doug at the controls.

"[The employees] felt so included because they were in on and part of the gag," Cox says.

After lunch, Doug and Cox visited the *National Lampoon*, where he stopped an editorial meeting.

"Ladies and gentlemen!" Doug announced theatrically, "let me introduce Mr. Roger Cox."

Days later, Doug was gone.

His first days on the Vineyard were spent in a tent on a wooded West Tisbury lot owned by singer-songwriter James Taylor. When the weather grew cold, he rented a beautiful home in Gay Head on the western tip of the island. Doug was drawn to the Vineyard from visits during his Harvard days and with Martello, who had gone there throughout her life.

Stephanie Phelan, who'd befriended Doug while working at Cloud Studio, had fled New York and was living on the Vineyard at the same time. Returning to her rented cottage one day in the spring, she found Doug in a hammock with Rita, her roommate. In attempting to find Phelan, Doug encountered Rita and they began a brief affair.

Mary Martello was also on the island, but not with Doug. Instead, she was living with a friend and planning a move west, to a California commune established by the fourteen-year-old Perfect Master. Though the relationship had begun as a guilt-ridden and sexually motivated affair, Phelan believed Doug had serious feelings for Martello.

"It's all very complicated," Phelan says. "My feeling at the time was that he was always in love with Mary. I knew him well, but I never knew what was actually going on with him. I know that he really seemed to be in love with her."

Phelan and Doug also had a brief relationship on the Vineyard that evolved into a close friendship. She would come over to the house on Gay Head, with its extraordinary view of the Atlantic Ocean and Nashaquitsa and Menemsha ponds, where they would watch television and eat. Doug taught Phelan to drive a car and the two would often kick around and play with her dog.

One spring weekend, Doug took Phelan to Cambridge and showed her around his alma mater, visiting the Castle and Spee. He took her on a motorcycle tour of Boston, during which they had an accident. Though no one was injured, Phelan felt decidedly unsafe on the back of his bike.

That summer Doug also visited relatives in Newport, getting off the plane in old shorts, ripped high tops, and carrying his belongings in "a bag like you'd get at a shopping center," says Frank Kenney. The first night he took Grandmother Eleanor, Uncle Frank, Aunt Margaretta, and several other Kenneys out for dinner at Christie's, a nice place on the waterfront. They'd barely seen him since he was a teenager.

Frank asked Doug why he hadn't used his Harvard education to do something important. Like cure cancer.

"It's a sad time," Doug said. "I want to make people laugh."

And make them laugh he did, cracking jokes through dinner and reconnecting with his dad's family the only way he knew. After the meal, Doug pulled his grandmother aside and said that he'd like to give her some money, perhaps $1,000. She refused, telling her grandson that she was just fine and that he ought to keep his money. Doug also offered to buy a new roof for a relative's home. Again, he was politely refused.

Back on the Vineyard, Doug had made a few friends and became a minor celebrity—Doug Kenney from *National Lampoon*—at several local haunts. He'd hit the Black Dog Tavern to have a beer and flirt with the waitresses. At a bar on Circuit Avenue in Oak Bluffs, he helped arrange for Phelan to run into a man with whom she was falling in love. To Phelan and the rest of the Vineyard, he was pretty much just a cool, funny, sweet young guy hanging out.

Phelan recalls that Martello's attitude toward Doug had turned disdainful by this point. If he had any intention of getting back together with her, it was quickly dashed.

By day, Doug worked on TACOS. According to Lucy Fisher, the book was a comedy about the ultimate outsiders, "not just teenagers, but Communists and aliens." These "outsiders," O'Donoghue once recalled, spoke a language that, Doug wrote, "sounded like a gun fight in a bell factory."

Having melted down the previous summer, Doug was trying to regain his bearings by legitimizing himself as a novelist. Clinging to the belief that real writers wrote novels, he pounded away at TACOS, intending to create a modern American comic masterpiece by which others would someday be judged. It would be no small task, as he was measuring his performance against that of his idol, Evelyn Waugh.

* * *

With Doug on sabbatical, O'Donoghue became the magazine's enfant terrible, sharpest writer, and most dominating presence. The writing of others fell under O'Donoghue's influence, and he pushed less edgy contributors to new places. In the office he made an equally indelible impression, where he always played the character of Michael O'Donoghue to the hilt.

Stories of O'Donoghue's behavior became legend. With his office door open, O'Donoghue would scream at representatives of the Columbia Record Club, threatening to send them loads of bricks COD and frequently ended such diatribes by slamming his phone against the wall. Emerging from his office and finding a crowd (that he knew was listening) gathered outside, he would smile with sheepish delight as they applauded. When the onlookers dispersed, he would call the phone company and, with no shortage of vitriolic threats, request a repairman for his shattered receiver. "It slipped," he would explain when the repairman arrived.

Nearly anything could send O'Donoghue into a rage, including the art department's failure to follow his precise directions for the layout and appearance of his articles, or the rare correction of his grammar made by one of the female staffers assigned to the task. One recalls that O'Donoghue warmly said he liked her because she was the only one who didn't "fuck up his work."

On one occasion, O'Donoghue was sitting in Matty's office when a call came through from his father. Taking the call at Matty's desk, he was solemnly informed of the terrible news that his diabetic mother had "lost her toe." Without batting an eye, he responded, "Did you look for it behind the refrigerator?"

Perhaps the most famous O'Donoghue story took place in April 1972, when a package bearing his name arrived at the *National Lampoon* offices. Inside were several sticks of dynamite. A letter, which O'Donoghue believed came from a reader in California, stated, "Hi Mike—have some fun with this dynamite."

Such a package would cause most folks to immediately run screaming, or at the very least call the police. O'Donoghue took the dynamite around the office to show to his coworkers and then did something entirely unlikely. He called George Plimpton, a self-described "demolitions expert."

"I told him that you could eat the dynamite and even hit it with a hammer and nothing could happen," Plimpton said, "provided that nitroglycerin had not leaked out and crystallized on the outside . . . which of course it had."

With this, the previously game and amused O'Donoghue turned a ghastly shade of white. The police were called, hundreds of workers were evacuated from several floors of the building, and traffic on Madison was cut off between Fifty-seventh and Sixtieth streets for nearly an hour.

As NYPD demolitions experts examined the dynamite, the color returned to O'Donoghue's face and he began demanding that the package be returned to him. Eventually he was led from the office by a group of people as he screamed about having explosives that were rightfully his taken away without his consent.

Despite his often difficult behavior and disruptive personality, Matty truly liked O'Donoghue and valued his talent, creating a better than normal relationship between editorial and business staff. One Christmas, he and Gross gave Matty a sled, crossing out the Flexible Flyer brand and replacing it with Rosebud.

Matty's teenage son, Michael, worked as O'Donoghue's assistant. He was, more often than not, amused by the explosive antics of his boss and felt that the price of bearing witness was worth the noise. Even more, he found that O'Donoghue could be caring and sweet beneath it all. He was not alone. Kelly, who was experiencing great difficulty in his marriage, always had a home at O'Donoghue's loft.

"I was having a domestic catastrophe in Canada," Kelly says. "He had some kind of weird heart beneath all of that shit."

O'Donoghue's loft on Spring Street was nothing if not befitting of the man who dwelt there. Filled with overweight cats, headless mannequins, a stuffed bear decked out in World War I fighter pilot goggles, odd plastic curios, stuffed owls, a mummified ocelot, and a little girl mannequin wearing a tattered dress staring out the window, it was a kitschy, ironic, slightly terrifying place.

"I was knocked out by the Bohemian-ness of it all," Kelly says. "There were license plates covering holes in the floor, a barrel of white rubber gorillas, and an original unedited copy of *Hollywood Babylon*."

Hendra, who lived several hours' bus ride away from the office at an old stone farmhouse in rural New Jersey, was O'Donoghue's most frequent guest. He spent many a night on the couch at O'Donoghue's, teaching his friend about fine wines, an area in which the Brit was a self-styled expert. O'Donoghue, Hendra found, was immensely interested in learning about all things sophisticated as a means of filling holes in his own persona. That O'Donoghue didn't even care for wine (preferring pot) was beside the point, as his bombast covered what Hendra perceived was "a real social inferiority complex."

Their joy in each other's company was immense—they shared similar worldviews and humorous sensibilities. One evening, the pair tackled the nature of kitsch and camp. They examined every in and out of the subject, including whether "being camp about camp became camp itself," and to what extremes they might take such a concept, including the impact one might have on camp by adding shock value to the package.

"We decided that the most shocking thing you could do was to really, really start liking Montovani," Hendra recalled.

One night, the two decided to drink and listen to an album of schlock classical music covers and found themselves musing, "That's the most beautiful rendering of 'Ave Maria' I've ever heard," almost unable to determine for themselves whether the comments were kitsch or truly heartfelt.

Kelly and Beatts were also drawn to O'Donoghue. Initially a fish out of water, Kelly found Henry, Doug, Cerf, and other Ivy Leaguers to be clannish and WASPy. Trow, he recalled, "seemed like somebody who'd been riding through my ancestors' potato fields for generations." Though he would adjust and come to see that in the game of comedic wit, attitude and bravado were all part of the package, O'Donoghue seemed to Kelly more like a brother who, beneath the madness, was someone to whom he could relate.

"He just seemed like an agreeable guy," Kelly recalls. "He just seemed like somebody who was vulnerable and angry."

As much as two avowed heterosexual males could be, O'Donoghue and Hendra were in love. Not just in love with each other, but in love with being young, funny, smart, and free to do whatever they wanted in the sex-and-drugs counterculture world of 1972 America.

* * *

A friend in Montreal had shown Michel Choquette some photographs of an elderly Swiss ex-acrobat named Billy Frick. Otherwise unexciting, the pictures were notable because Frick bore an uncanny resemblance to Adolf Hitler. His bone structure was almost an exact match for the führer. With a small black mustache, he was a dead ringer and had even done some work as a look-alike in Europe.

"I figured, 'I've gotta find something to do with this guy,'" Choquette thought. The next logical step, of course, was *National Lampoon.*

Choquette approached Doug and Henry with the idea of taking his discovery to a tropical island and shooting him as a fish out of water retiree clad in his military uniform, living out his days in peace.

Doug laughed. Henry immediately jumped on the idea. Matty, however, was reluctant to send Choquette and "Hitler" to Martinique on the magazine's dime, but was persuaded that the project would remain on a $5,000 budget.

Arriving on the Caribbean island, Choquette set about hiring locals to portray island natives. In the photo spread, more than one island taxi driver wore a loincloth. Frick, with his wife in tow, became sick with a painful prostate condition. His frumpy spouse was unsympathetic and rode him mercilessly. Roll after roll of film was burned each day, trying to capture Hitler in paradise. Money became a problem.

A week after they arrived in Martinique, Matty was at the Lampoon offices when a telegram arrived. "Hitler being difficult," it read. "Shoot not completed. Need additional $2,000." Matty wired the money.

Several days later, a second telegram arrived on Matty's desk. "Hitler an impossible human being. Need more time. Need additional $2,000." With art and commerce comically butting heads, Matty replied, "No more money. No more time. No more Hitler. Return at once."

The March 1972 Escape issue features Billy Frick's führer, umbrella drink in hand, tropical shells around his neck and parrot on his shoulder, seated in a wicker chair with palm fronds peeking over his shoulder, and dressed in full Nazi regalia with the iron cross beneath his heart. If Hitler could be funny, Choquette had discovered the joke.

"All of us dream of a return to paradise, an escape from the hustle and bustle of everyday life. But, few of us are fortunate enough to find paradise on earth. Here is one man who has."

Thus reads the introduction to "Stranger in Paradise," a photo spread of Hitler frolicking naked in the surf, tidying up the grounds around his thatch roof hut, peacefully sniffing tropical flowers, standing contemplatively on the beach at dusk, telling stories by the campfire, darning his own uniforms, and leading the natives through morning inspection. Neither his identity nor the name of the Nazi party are ever explicitly mentioned. Rather, the article closes,

> The fervent idealism of youth has mellowed with the passing years. He has stopped trying to save the world, and now he cares only for his own peace of mind. Hidden away in his little Eden, he has his thoughts and his memories to fall back on.
>
> Occasionally he looks up at the migratory birds flying overhead. But he finds himself not longing to leave with them.
>
> It would seem that this stranger in paradise is, by now, very much at home.

* * *

Escape also marked the first appearance of the most skewed and downright odd sense of humor that would ever appear in *National Lampoon*, with a *Papillon* parody by Brian McConnachie, a burned-out adman who'd been sending Henry some of the most poorly drawn cartoons he had ever seen.

The first odd thing about Brian McConnachie was the way he dressed. O'Donoghue wore old army-navy surplus; Henry favored rumpled suits and oatmeal-colored turtlenecks; Doug dressed like a preppy-hippie whose family lost their money and had to enroll him in public school; Gross wore open shirts and chunky fishermen's sweaters. All unique, yet suited to the tenor of the times. Even Henry's disheveled professor look was somehow appropriate.

Well over six feet tall, with neatly parted black hair, McConnachie favored white duck trousers, blazers, and white bucks in the summer, and glen plaid suits when the weather cooled. In his Brooks Brothers staples of shined Oxfords, neatly pressed shirts, and bow ties, McConnachie was the embodiment of the Madison Avenue stereotype. Yet his mode of dress revealed little of the mind lurking within his conventional-looking head. He looked like a skinny, slightly out-of-it Clark Kent.

Raised in Forest Hills, New York, McConnachie was the son of a former newspaperman who ran an independent film company that produced newsreels in the 1940s and "I Like Ike" commercials for Eisenhower's 1952 presidential run. The middle of three children, McConnachie attended Catholic elementary school and an all-boys Catholic military boarding school, while feasting on Thurber and comics that ranged from horror books to *MAD*. As a child he'd even produced his own comic book with a friend. After college at Ireland's University of Dublin and a short newspaper stint, McConnachie was drafted into the Vietnam-era military, where he bathed in the institutional stupidity as Henry once had. While in the service, McConnachie got his hands on a photograph of the post commander, on which he inscribed, "To Brian, Let me know if you ever need anything," and placed it in the locker beside his bunk.

After avoiding a trip to Southeast Asia, McConnachie went into advertising, where he worked for agencies handling the accounts of giant corporations such as General Foods and Procter & Gamble. Thoroughly conventional in manner and dress, he immediately found the work to be completely irrelevant.

At one agency, McConnachie was assigned to synopsize shows appearing on CBS. Forced to read *Mayberry R.F.D.* scripts and determine whether any of the characters made negative hairdo references that could reflect badly on Prell Shampoo, McConnachie was bored trying to convey the intricacies of plots best summed up, "Aunt Bee loses her hat." Then suddenly McConnachie embraced the assignment, giving in to the subject matter; the small-town humor of Barney Fife and Gomer Pyle began to seem sublime. There were no real jokes, he thought, it was all in the attitude. Before long, he was composing intricate analyses of each episode, dutifully sending them to his superiors.

"I went from not caring too much to really scaring them," he says.

Back at the office, McConnachie suspected he would soon be relieved of his position. As a gentlemanly profession favored by men who took the 5:30 train back to Connecticut each night, advertising hadn't yet morphed into the cutthroat, mass-layoff industry of today. Since each executive implicitly understood his fate, the companies preferred not to fire employees, instead banishing them to what McConnachie called "the floor of forgotten men," where you were given a small office and a phone that never rang. Eventually, it was assumed, you would have the good grace to leave.

McConnachie was taken with *National Lampoon*. He knew a writer lurked within himself as he fiddled with a thirty-page short story that he'd written and tucked away in his desk. However, while reading *The New Yorker* one day, he found a cartoon that he believed conveyed more information and meaning in a single panel than he had in thirty pages.

Married and soon to be a father, McConnachie contacted Henry and Doug after sending over some scribbled cartoons that, while artistically inept, indicated the workings of an offbeat mind. Doug was kind and let McConnachie hang out at the offices, where one day Henry asked, "Do you write?" When Doug disappeared, McConnachie joined the staff and moved into Doug's office.

It was much to Henry's credit that he identified McConnachie as a unique talent. At the time, the magazine was becoming well known and humorists were climbing the walls to gain entry. With little to go on beyond the oddly drawn cartoon panels, he followed his instinct and brought McConnachie on board.

McConnachie found a happy home among the misfits. Though the sweet, pixilated Irishman was neither nasty nor cutting, he made his humor part of the mix both in the magazine and at the office. Once, finding out that a *Weight Watchers* subscriber had sent an angry letter of complaint after mistakenly receiving a copy of *National Lampoon*, McConnachie asked a clerk to let him handle the matter, which he did by sending the woman the most offensive issue of the magazine with a note reading, "Sorry for the mistake. B. McConnachie, subscription manager." When another furious letter arrived, he sent the same note and another issue of the wrong magazine. They went back and forth like this for several weeks, ending when McConnachie sent the woman a bill for the issues he'd mailed her.

His story ideas and nonlinear sensibilities were unlike those of anyone else at the magazine. Late one evening, while collaborating on an article, McConnachie called John Weidman at home and asked to meet him at an all-night grocery. Silently walking the aisles, McConnachie pulled a box of laundry detergent from a shelf and excitedly shouted, "See, that's what I've been talking about!"

Wandering into Kelly's office on another late night, McConnachie tried out a cartoon he was writing in which the Pillsbury Dough Boy asks Mr. Peanut, "How's your aunt? The one with the small hands."

"Should it be small feet?" McConnachie asked, leaving the loquacious Kelly temporarily speechless.

"He was a fabulous part of the mix," Kelly says. "He was so off the wall. You could follow Doug; and Henry was firing his dart right down the middle—a perfect imitation of what he was imitating. But Brian, 'small hands or small feet?'"

When he returned to the magazine in the fall, Doug told others that McConnachie wasn't human, but rather a visitor from the planet Mogdar, and was being sent instructions through a vine that grew in his office.

* * *

The April 1972 issue commemorates the magazine's 25th anniversary with articles from the past: 1955's "Commie Plot Comics" by Doug, where dark Marxist forces attempt to turn the Chagrin-like community of Pleasantville into Stalinville by co-opting the unemployed brother of an upstanding suburban citizen; O'Donoghue's 1947 "Frontline Dentists," hailing the heroic achievements of those who fixed the Greatest Generation's teeth while under enemy fire; and the editor's letter by Beatts, parodying James Thurber's *The New Yorker* history entitled "The Years with Henry."

Also appearing in the issue is a catalog for the space-age 1958 Bulgemobiles, with names like Flashbolt and Fireblast and features such as UltraKlimaTron Interior Weather Control, 32 percent more trunk room, and windshields that are 63 percent more transparent. Drawn in a fantastical style recalling the 1950s that never were, their creator was a frustrated adman named Bruce McCall.

* * *

Like many Canadian boys of his generation, Bruce McCall grew up longing to live in the magical country to the south. The third of six children, McCall was raised in a Simcoe, Ontario, farmhouse and a town where everyone knew everyone. The son of a disappointed newspaperman-turned-government-information officer and a mother who always thought she and her husband would wind up in Manhattan, McCall was surrounded by issues of Harold Ross's *New Yorker.*

With an absent father and a disillusioned mother, McCall lived in a room with his brother Hugh, who shared his passion for drawing as a means of self-entertainment. For McCall, however, it was also a way that he could invent his own worlds. From early on, he would seldom be without a pencil in his hand.

When McCall was twelve, his father moved the family to a two-bedroom Toronto apartment. Living in a cramped space with a father who didn't want to be there, it was the beginning of a very unhappy period in which the idyllic farm community of his youth was replaced by a big city where the kids all wanted to beat him up.

Though uncommonly bright, McCall failed ninth grade three times and dropped out of high school. His father told him it was time to get a job and found him work as an apprentice in a Windsor, Ontario, art studio, where Hugh soon joined him.

For the next seven years, the McCall boys toiled in the crappy factory town, illustrating promotional materials for automobile manufacturers. They made little money and worked in a place with, as McCall puts it, "three morons, Hugh, and I." The studio folded in the late 1950s when photography trumped the illustration business on which it depended. McCall bounced from periods of unemployment to short stints at art studios. Then, having long been a car fanatic, he began writing letters to every Canadian car magazine he could think of. A trade magazine, where someone knew his father, offered him a job as a cub reporter. He wouldn't touch a paintbrush for the next ten years.

Suddenly it seemed that there was nothing better than being paid to hang around auto races and write about them. When an attempt to launch his own car magazine flopped after one issue, he joined *Canada Track and Traffic*, where he became editor on his first day.

At a 1962 race, McCall met a worldly adman from Detroit's Campbell-Ewalt who offered him a job working on the Corvette account. In January 1963, twenty-eight-year-old Bruce McCall started his new job in Detroit and doubled his income. He was succeeding beyond his dreams in the Technicolor America he'd imagined was populated by kids on gleaming Schwinn bikes while he was growing up in dowdy, complacent Canada.

Longing for the big time, McCall eventually moved to New York, became an acolyte of advertising legend David Ogilvy, and worked on the Mercedes-Benz account. Living for a time in Frankfurt, Germany, he let his hair and beard grow, smoked pot, and donned the type of clothes worn by Dennis Hopper in *Easy Rider*.

"My God, what an idiot I was not to see how the world was changing," McCall says. "I was a prisoner of the other side."

Returning to Manhattan, McCall was exhausted and disillusioned, having come to realize that clients were like mad emperors with the agency at their eternal whim. Every hero in the industry, he thought, was only in it for the money. Even Ogilvy.

Seeing the Lampoon, McCall realized there was an outlet for the kind of writing and artwork he'd been doing since childhood. In summer 1971, he visited the offices at 635 Madison and met Doug, who was wearing his granny glasses, smoking the ever-present joint, and looking like a bomb had hit him.

Doug was mildly encouraging, but gave McCall the sense that he needed to earn his spurs. A month later, with Doug in Los Angeles, McCall met and hit it off with Henry, whom he recalls as the "smartest man I'd ever met." He showed Beard and Gross the 1958 Bulgemobile catalog and they were astonished. Soon McCall took a leave of absence from the agency, contracted to do twenty-five pages a year for *National Lampoon*, and worked from his studio in the Village, where he avoided the office scene as much as he could.

"I liked everybody, but it was not a pleasant place to be," he says. "It was like my family: a crabby father in a small space. There was never anyplace to sit. I liked to be by myself."

McCall would grow close to McConnachie, Beard, and Kelly. By staying away from 635 Madison, he maintained his own voice and style, rarely feeling the influence of the others.

"I just did what I did and they published it," McCall says.

* * *

Beatts got her chance to edit an issue with May's Men!, which revealed her attitude and style. Less than two years removed from working as a copywriter, she wrote the following editorial:

Did you hear about the Vagino-American movement? No? Well the Vagino-American Movement advocates among other things, that we Vagino-Americans should stop being ashamed of our Vagino-American heritage. We should openly relish ethnic foods like creamed chicken and peas. We should wear proudly the net stockings, garter belts and false eyelashes that are our native dress. We should plump for the establishment of institutes of Vagino-American Studies offering courses in home economics and childcare. We should stop aping the stilted, overly cerebral speech of our oppressors and allow our Vagino-American poets, writers and birthday-cake decorators full freedom of expression in their own words—words that have already enriched the language in phrases as diverse as "My that's terrible," "Honestly now," and "Does ookums wanna cookie."

From Kelly she elicited "Norman the Barbarian," a comic book dedicated to the adventures of Norman Mailer, the last heterosexual who is battling for his very manhood against "no-dork's entrenched army of eunuchs"; Doug's "How to Score with Chicks," a parody of pickup manuals offering insights such as "Women are human beings. Luckily for us they are also stupid beings," and recommending that men wishing to project a romantic, slightly dangerous image should wear a black eyepatch, a jeweled hook, or a stick-on dueling scar "from your undergraduate years at the University of Heidelburg"; and Henry's spectacularly devised Mike Hammer piece, "My Gun Is Cute," in which he creates a hard-boiled female detective ("I looked at the battered Lady Speidel I've been wearing ever since it stopped a slug once when I was scratching somewhere a bullet could do a lot of damage").

Amy Ephron, the sister of writer and film director Nora Ephron, wrote a short piece for the Men! issue entitled "How to Score with Men," as a companion to Doug's article. Somewhat funny, though not notable, the article would be her only actual contribution to *National Lampoon*, yet Amy Ephron soon would forever be etched in the magazine's lore.

* * *

"This is a phenomenon and we're living it," Henry told Gross in 1972, and dryly added, "It won't last."

He was right on the first count. By midyear, all signs were telling Matty that he had a winner. Even with Doug away, the additions of Kelly, Beatts, McConnachie, Boni, Catchpole, Miller, and McCall had editorial clicking along at optimal levels, while Gross had transformed the chaotic underground format into something readers could read and Gerry Taylor could sell. And sell he did. During 1972, ads for record and hi-fi equipment became more prevalent than those for counterculture bumper stickers and condoms, quadrupling ad revenue and nearly doubling the rate per page from $2,000 to $3,600.

During the spring, circulation climbed to 320,000 and reached 530,000 by the year's end. In turn, revenues of $4.1 million represented a 400 percent increase in net income and operating profits—the latter topping $415,000. As a strong indication of its growing appeal and cachet, John and Yoko contributed their own "Foto Funny" to the March Lampoon, which by now had become a staple on college campuses across the eastern seaboard and was rapidly making inroads west.

21st Century owned *National Lampoon*, *Weight Watchers*, and the nostalgia magazine *Liberty*. With business booming at the *National Lampoon* and plans to acquire another youth-oriented title, Matty sold his half-ownership in *Weight Watchers* back to its namesake organization, but continued to manage the publication. An original investment of $50,000 netted him and 21st Century between $1.2 and $2 million.

Having gone public in 1971, Matty now focused his efforts on building the Lampoon brand and on cultivating publications targeted toward the growing baby boom market. Strategically, it was a sound move—Matty intended to make more money from building up what he already had, while expanding in known areas of expertise and competence.

In 1972, special interest magazines were the place to be as the industry was going through a transition in which the last of the true general interest magazines were dying out. That December, having been impaled by television, *Life* would end its thirty-six-year run, while dozens of new specialized publications rushed to fill the void with titles like *Epicure*, *Contemporary Obstetrics and Gynecology*, *Learning* (for elementary school teachers), the diet magazine *Sweet N Low*, *Oui* (*Playboy* for eighteen- to twenty-four-year-old men), and *Doctor's Finances*. The entire industry was learning that boomers and the rest of society had been fractured into thousands of niches for which there seemed to be nearly as many editorial needs and strategies.

In this sense, 21st Century had been a bit lucky with the Lampoon, which was conceived and billed as a general interest magazine but in reality was a special interest publication that focused on the specific (though unquantifiable) amusement of college-aged and twentysomething men. In addition, though selling magazines at full price and making revenue from circulation had seemed an unlikely and difficult strategy in the summer of 1969, it was becoming the path toward profitability by 1972.

"The publishers who will succeed now will be those seeking reader support," former *New York* publisher George Hirsch told the *New York Times* that December. "And reader support means paying real money for the magazine. Let's face it, a guy lays down a dollar on the newsstand, he picks up *Playboy*, he gets no change back—and you don't have to spend too long with documented research to know that the magazine has reader loyalty."

Through letters, newly acquired subscriptions, and growing newsstand sales, Matty knew that reader loyalty was being established with *National Lampoon*. Thus, he thought he might be able to repeat that performance by acquiring *Ingenue* from Dell Publishing. *Ingenue* was a poor woman's version of the popular *Seventeen*, and Matty swung a deal with Dell in which 21st Century would take over the magazine in February and publish its first issue that May.

"We believe in gearing magazines to special audiences," Matty told a reporter around this time. "You can say more and be more informative."

* * *

The expansion of the *National Lampoon* brand had already begun with the "Best of" collections, the posters, and other products during 1971, but the branding was about to move into new areas that would prove profitable, fruitful, and, ultimately, destructive.

Matty, knowing of Hendra's close relationship with O'Donoghue, asked his managing editor to persuade his buddy to join the staff full time. Trying to negotiate, O'Donoghue asked for more than just the traditional raise and perks. Since he was already making good money ($45,000 once he joined the staff, second only to Henry's $50,000—both men earned more than Matty, and made Hendra's $18,000 pale in comparison), O'Donoghue requested that 21st Century invest in a movie magazine where he intended to cross the variety and irreverent worldview of *National Lampoon* with *Rolling Stone*'s emphasis on rock music, producing a product focusing on the world of film. The magazine would have features about penis sizes in Hollywood (contrasting the legendary appendages of Charlie Chaplin and Milton Berle with the assumedly less impressive manhood of Joel Grey);

a parody column with Charles Manson as a film critic who takes action when a movie offends his taste; and odd historical articles, such as one about a film Salvador Dalí directed for Disney.

O'Donoghue also asked to be put in charge of creating a comedy album. Gerry Taylor, married to Mary Travers and working extensively with the music industry, endorsed the idea, knowing he could use it as a marketing tool with clients and help build the *National Lampoon* brand. Ads for comedy records by Cheech and Chong, George Carlin, and others were running in the magazine, and the records themselves were climbing the *Billboard* charts. With the magazine's growing popularity, it seemed a logical move. Taylor also had a childhood friend, Christopher Guest, whom he thought might be a valuable contributor to the project. Matty thought it might make money. Henry was mortified, insisting that they were "literary people" who should get what they were doing right before moving into the hated venue of show business.

Tony Hendra was not afraid of show business, however, and became O'Donoghue's collaborator and coproducer. Hendra was the only creative person at the magazine who knew anything at all about the record business, as he'd produced two albums with Ullett.

Guest was a unique combination of comedic and musical talents, with deadpan delivery and a serious approach to being funny. He could do any number of voices, play several instruments, and brought along Bob Tischler, a sound engineer who could tie it all together.

Taylor made a deal with RCA and the album was cut in their Manhattan recording studios and completed in April 1972.

Radio Dinner is a wide-ranging album, taking swats at everything under the sun. Hendra, with his voice electronically altered by Tischler (who would become the aural equivalent of Mike Gross), plays the irreproachable icon John Lennon in "Magical Misery Tour" as an egomaniac run amok, shrieking about his own brilliance and the idiocy of the rest of the world (the contents of the piece were taken from an interview with the former Beatle); "Concert in Bangladesh" has Hendra and Guest working together as an old-time comedy "tragedy team," their jokes punctuated by triangle rim shots and plucks on a sitar; and O'Donoghue's game show "Catch It and You Keep It," where large prizes are dropped on contestants from one hundred feet above. And of course, there were the usual O'Donoghue touches, such as a series of sketches in which he makes various uses of dead pigeons.

In an October 1972 interview with the *Washington Post*, O'Donoghue discussed the album and its approach, particularly the Lennon piece performed by Hendra. "It's always such a delight when you can hang somebody with his own words," he said, later observing of Joan Baez, "There's one soul everybody wanted to crucify for years."

He was on a roll.

Commercially, the album did relatively well and was nominated for three Grammy awards (winning two). It also convinced Matty that there might be financial gain in similar show business projects. *Radio Dinner* did, however, create some strain in the relationship between its coproducers. Since O'Donoghue had to rely on Hendra's technical expertise, he was often not completely in charge. For a man who took professional pursuits with the greatest seriousness and considered them a reflection of his own personal vision, this was not easy to take. There were frequent flare-ups. Hendra recalls one incident during which O'Donoghue "just went ape shit because I was telling him what to do." Nonetheless, when *Radio Dinner* came out, both men were pleased with their mutual success.

* * *

In the July Surprise! issue, Dean Latimer and P. J. O'Rourke contributed their first piece, "Third World Comics."

While *National Lampoon* had been essentially an outgrowth of college humor magazines, Underground Comix, *The New Yorker*, *MAD*, and the work of Lenny Bruce and Mort Sahl, it also had roots in the underground press movement of the 1960s, which gave the world publications like the *East Village Other*, *Evergreen Review*, and the *Village Voice*. It was from this world that Latimer and O'Rourke emerged.

"Dean was a spectacular human being," Kelly recalls, "but you wouldn't want him around your tea party any more than St. Francis of Assisi."

Latimer was an outlaw—scruffy, sometimes a little smelly, and definitely different. Bohemian to the nth degree, he would have been perceived as such at any place and time in history. Often arriving at meetings in short shorts and no underwear, he tossed off the expression "throw him a turd" to handle any situation.

A brilliant autodidact, Latimer was a productive writer and underground press legend whose work appeared in several New York publications, though he sometimes paid the bills by writing porn novels for mob-linked publishers in rooms filled with men seated eight to a picnic table pounding on their typewriters.

On his second trip to the National Lampoon offices in spring 1972, Latimer brought O'Rourke with him. Often difficult to find (he didn't have a phone), Latimer was the less reliable of the two. By contrast, O'Rourke was eminently reachable and spent many hours hanging around 635 Madison.

A native of Toledo, Ohio, Patrick Jake O'Rourke was the eldest child of a car salesman and his wife. O'Rourke's mother was a Michigan City, Indiana, native whose staunchly Republican, FDR-hating family had lost their money in the Depression, yet never lost the belief that "people are never too poor to pick up their yards."

Born in 1947, P. J. O'Rourke led a a quiet middle-class life until his father died in 1956, after which O'Rourke's mother fell apart and hastily married another car salesman, who brought with him a drinking problem and a bully's demeanor. Beset with financial problems, these were not particularly happy times for O'Rourke.

As a child, O'Rourke loved to read the funny papers and MAD and watch the Warner Brothers cartoons of the 1940s. Even as a young boy, he was struck by Up Front, a collection of Bill Mauldin cartoons from World War II, which showed him that humor could be applied to deadly serious subjects.

After graduating from Miami of Ohio, O'Rourke moved to Baltimore, where he attended a Johns Hopkins graduate writing program. A committed leftist and Maoist, O'Rourke went to work for an underground Baltimore paper named Harry. During his tenure there, a group of local revolutionaries, who called themselves The Baltocong, forcibly took over the *Harry* offices because their editorial content wasn't leftist enough.

Soon thereafter, O'Rourke headed for Manhattan, determined to become a poet, novelist, or—if those failed—a working writer. Contributing to the *East Village Other*, he met Latimer and became smitten with *National Lampoon*.

There was much to like about O'Rourke. He was not only driven and sarcastic but even a little innocent. With long reddish-brown hair, an army surplus jacket, and leftist politics, he was definitely one of them. Additionally, he came with Latimer's blessing and recommendation, which Hendra deemed a "heavy credential." Raw as a writer but filled with bile, O'Rourke was a hard worker who fell under the wing of O'Donoghue and, later, Doug. He became their student and was willing to do whatever was necessary to secure a place at the magazine.

O'Rourke also formed a close relationship with Matty. Though he perceived tension between the editorial/Harvard factions and the former press agent, O'Rourke also believed that those same dynamics were very productive, giving the humorists a lightning rod for venting their displeasure.

"Matty was a really good publisher in this sense that everybody could agree to be mad at Matty. In that way he was a great peacemaker," O'Rourke says.

Within six months, O'Rourke joined the staff full time. At *Weight Watchers* he ghost wrote Jean Nidetch's weight-loss column, despite the fact that he weighed all of 130 pounds. Soon he was an editor on *Ingenue*, contributing to *National Lampoon*, and assisting Matty with various projects.

Before the end of the decade, it would be O'Rourke's job to save *National Lampoon*.

* * *

August, September, and October produced a number of memorable pieces (the Miracle of Democracy with Hendra's Nixon/Pinocchio cover, then Boredom, and Remember Those Fabu-

lous Sixties? respectively). McConnachie's send-up of columnist
Jack Anderson portrays the political writer as a paranoid freak who
can't keep his delusions out of print ("Baldisrohl was originally found
with money confiscated from Jewish refugees prior to our entry into
WWII and has since served as a conduit for PRETEND YOU'RE
JUST READING THIS. DON'T LOOK AROUND"); Doug and
McCall's "The Miracle of Democracy" explains how a bill to kill
the Negroes becomes law; Kelly rips off T. S. Eliot with "The Love
Song of J. Edgar Hoover"; Hendra's "Wide World of Meat" demonstrates his off-kilter fascination with said subject by depicting conti-
nents, beaches, politicians, Mount Rushmore, and the Hindenburg
as roasts, poultry, and burgers; Henry, O'Donoghue, and Trow track
the proud, untold heritage of the white man in America, debunking
its myths and stereotypes, while hailing their achievements ("did you
know that both the Dewey Decimal System and the Cutter Classifi-
cation System were developed by White people?"); and yet another
superhero with Jewish roots is born in Kelly and Hendra's "Ventures
of Zimmerman," which tracks the young life of the great capitalist
Bob Dylan (who comments while watching Little Richard on television, "two chords and a funny haircut, and that shvartzeh must be
worth a fortune").

All seemed well in the world of *National Lampoon*.

* * *

The December 10, 1972, *New York Times* Sunday magazine ran
a feature on *National Lampoon*, written by Mopsy Strange Kennedy.
Clearly prepared for her arrival and the interview, the staff was in
fine fettle.

O'Donoghue held forth on his philosophy of humor. "Within
the medium," he told Kennedy, "a laugh is OK. But, I like rhythms.
I also like Kafka."

Hendra and McConnachie discussed their mutual admiration of
meat as a comedic subject.

"Meat is funny," Hendra said.

"Fish isn't funny," McConnachie added, showing Kennedy a picture in his office of a crown roast made entirely from hot dogs.

When Henry arrived, the crew engaged in some witty banter for their visitor. "I've just been to the zoo," Henry said, feigning a serious tone. "You know that's a jail for animals, don't you?"

"Yes," O'Donoghue chimed in, "they've been found guilty of the law of the jungle."

"Bestiality," Henry shot back. "The court will be composed entirely of kangaroos of course. They should round up all of those dogs that played Lassie on TV, hundreds of collies, and put them all in the zoo for tax evasion."

During his interview, Matty discussed his philosophy of running the magazine. The writers, he said, should pick on everyone. That was part of the formula—nothing is sacred, and the radical leftists were just as repugnant as the John Birch Society. The worst kind of person was the liberal who laughs when they make fun of Nixon, but "draw[s] the line at the Kennedy assassination," saying, "that's not funny."

The overall editorial strategy was best summed up by Hendra, who said, "We write for ourselves and just hope our readers will like it too."

The article did an excellent job of tackling the magazine's intuitive appeal to its readership. Created each month by contributors whose average age was twenty-eight, its voice was not too far removed from that of its readership—young men in their early twenties—yet had a few years of perspective with which to mock that life and place it in context. Henry likened the growing *National Lampoon* phenomenon to the impact of the movie *M*A*S*H*, which fans believed spoke to them in their own language and sensibilities.

"When Bob Hope jokes about hippies, he is talking about something alien to him," Hendra said. "When we write about hippies, it may not be from sympathy, but at least it comes from some experience."

Kennedy's article presciently noted two events that could have an impact on the magazine's lifespan and continuing relevance. First was the fact that two years hence, 21st Century would be contractually obligated to buy out Kenney, Beard, and Hoffman. (With *National Lampoon*'s growth continuing its upward trend, Doug and Henry would become millionaires.) The other, more seriously considered issue, was the potential impact of aging on the editorial staff and how that might affect its connection with its audience. "At the moment the editors of the magazine are writing both to an audience and from an experience that is familiar to them. But the danger of the hardening of the satirical arteries could set in and as they get older they may find themselves hurling their darts from too great a distance."

McConnachie and O'Donoghue both responded.

"Then we'll do older guy stuff," McConnachie said. "We'll buy Toyotas and we won't be afraid to go to the Copa."

O'Donoghue, reigning king of the Lampoon circa 1972, was equally philosophical. "When you smoke four packs a day, luckily you don't have to worry about that."

* * *

During the spring, O'Donoghue fell madly in love with Amy Ephron, who'd contributed to the Men! issue and was working for Chris Cerf on the PBS show *The Electric Company*. In pursuit of a more romantic appearance, O'Donoghue worried about his weight, ceased eating, and replaced sustenance with more cigarettes.

Officemates and friends like Kelly were astounded by the impact the relationship was having on the raving banshee they called "The Presence." In love and suddenly confident of his sex appeal, O'Donoghue dropped the angry persona around Ephron, allowing her to call him by the pet name "Goo."

At one point, O'Donoghue became so filled with self-love and admiration for his new impact on the female of the species that he said to Hendra, "Why don't we start a humor magazine? I'll bring the women!"

The boy who had been ill and sat alone in his room for nearly a year, and then graduated to verbally humiliating the cool guys at high school, was now in command of his love life and was the literary star of an ultrahip magazine. It was an emotional apex he couldn't resist.

The relationship, of course, did not survive. The couple argued frequently. O'Donoghue had an affair with a neighbor. (Hendra, with his friend's blessing, had an affair with the same woman.)

O'Donoghue and Ephron fought and reconciled over and over until The Presence finally declared it over.

"I never want to see that bitch again," he told Hendra. Shortly thereafter, Hendra, O'Donoghue, and Ephron found themselves at the same social gathering. After O'Donoghue left, Ephron invited Hendra to her home. The two smoked a joint and had sex.

The one-night stand was just that. Hendra departed in the morning, probably more concerned about cheating on his wife than any impact the evening might have on his relationship with O'Donoghue. who, in the meantime, had gleaned the details in a phone conversation with Ephron. At the office, Hendra began to see the consequences, which he describes in his book *Going Too Far*:

> [O'Donoghue] came in late in the afternoon, lips the width of piano wire, talking in some odd Englishese: "You owe me an explanation, I feel . . . " "What was the purpose of this, might I ask . . . ?" It was ridiculous. . . . But he was obviously in the eye of some powerful emotional storm, and though it didn't look quite like hurt, I didn't want him to stay that way. If there was any wrong here, I was in it. I told him what had happened and how I thought it had happened, but that to whatever degree he was hurt, I was sorry and regretted it.

This and all future efforts at apology would be insufficient. O'Donoghue had been crossed in a manner that he could not accept. Yes, Doug had slept with Mary Martello, but there were two key differences. First, O'Donoghue's love for Martello was likely a figment of his vivid and insecure imagination. Second and more important in this case, he'd been betrayed by his best friend (one whom he'd let behind the curtain) and, even worse in O'Donoghue's eyes, by a writer of lesser talent, a matter of deadly importance at the time.

Hendra himself was naive, if not reckless and insensitive, in sleeping with a woman who had once owned O'Donoghue's heart. Knowing his friend so intimately and being a man of keen intellectual capacities, he should have foreseen that such a reaction was a distinct possibility. Others saw his motives, unconscious as they may have been, as far more insidious and calculating than he let on.

"Michael may have overreacted in an incredibly melodramatic way, but it was like a power play," says Beatts. "I guess there was something sort of Machiavellian about it. Michael was 'King Baby,' he definitely wanted people to pay attention to him and to get his way. But you knew exactly where he stood. He either loved or hated you—often in the same day. But it wasn't exactly hidden. Tony had more of a hidden agenda."

Beatts claimed that she'd also been the subject of romantic attention from Hendra on one occasion, but rejected him because it was more of a power grab than a reflection of sexual desire.

Hendra and O'Donoghue were done as friends. That much was certain. But O'Donoghue wasn't done with Hendra. The offices became the battle lines for a public war. He insisted that Matty fire Hendra.

Faced with a volatile interoffice squabble, Matty knew O'Donoghue was of far greater value than Hendra, but ultimately concluded that the whole matter was none of his business and moved Hendra's office eight feet farther away from O'Donoghue's.

This didn't settle matters. O'Donoghue continued to tell anyone who would listen that Hendra had to be fired and began dividing the office into factions. There were those who stood with O'Donoghue and those who stood against him, either through support of Hendra or their silence.

Perhaps only Henry remained above the fray, telling Hendra to "keep a low profile," while, thanks to his position and demeanor of quiet reserve, avoiding O'Donoghue's wrath.

McConnachie was astonished by his friend's furious reaction to the realization that Hendra could be a user. Trow simply knew that speaking with Hendra would be the kiss of death to his friendship with O'Donoghue. Kelly, who was close to both men, paid the worst price—forced to choose sides, he begged off a decision on the matter for as long as possible.

The offices had become poisonous.

As war raged at his magazine, Matty took action by giving Hendra an outside project that would take him away from day-to-day operations. With the success of *Radio Dinner* still fresh in his mind, Matty and Taylor decided to do a live album, soon to evolve into the hit stage show *Lemmings*.

O'Donoghue was hardly calmed by this decision, seeing only that they'd punished his enemy by giving him a plum assignment. There was no winning.

7

Show Biz and Dead Dogs

66 We were tight like a family. And I mean that in the worst possible way. 99

—*P. J. O'Rourke*

The following things happened in 1973: the American League instituted the designated-hitter rule; Nixon took the oath of office for the second time; Lyndon Johnson died of a heart attack; Kiss played its first show; the Senate formed the Watergate Committee with Sam Ervin as its chair; Elton John's "Crocodile Rock" topped the pop charts; Picasso died; 63 percent of Americans believed that the Nixon administration had been neither frank nor honest about Watergate; Secretariat won the Triple Crown; Nixon's lawyer John Dean testified about the existence of a White House "enemies list"; and Billie Jean King defeated Bobby Riggs in the "Battle of the Sexes."

* * *

The most famous cover in Lampoon history began as a joke in the nightclub routine of Ed Bluestone, who'd been contributing to the magazine since 1972.

In his early twenties, Bluestone was an angry, abrasive, upper-middle-class Jewish kid from New Jersey who idolized Woody Allen and cut his teeth on early Jerry Lewis. Dropping out of Monmouth College, the former class clown performed in Greenwich Village folk clubs that once hosted Bob Dylan and Joan Baez.

Bluestone's act was entirely verbal—no faces or noises. One of his jokes was about the kind of record club that O'Donoghue berated on his oft-shattered office phone. The bit revolved around a club whose demands for payment got progressively more threatening until they finally sent a picture of their customer's cocker spaniel with a gun to his head.

Henry, on a rare trip out to see live entertainment of a low-brow nature, heard the joke and loved it, and took the concept to Gross. Initially they intended to do a subscription campaign that continually upped the ante. First, a picture of a gun pointed at a kitten's head under the legend, "If you don't buy this magazine, we're gonna kill this kitten." A subsequent ad would show a dead kitten, with the legend, "You didn't buy the magazine. If you don't buy the magazine now, we're gonna kill the dog. We warned ya!" And so on, all the way to children and family members.

Knowing that the January 1973 theme would be Death, Gross persuaded everyone that Bluestone's joke was the perfect cover image. There was agreement all around.

With his keen understanding of visual humor, Gross rejected the idea of using a German shepherd. Rather, if they were going to execute the iconic family dog, they needed an animal beloved by one and all—an adorable mutt.

Gross found a trained, black-and-white mixed breed and went into the studio knowing that the animal could basically sit on command. Yet every time they pointed a revolver at his head, the dog understandably flinched. Finally, after hours of attempts, they learned that the dog couldn't help but freeze when the gun's trigger was pulled. Quickly, they captured a shot with the mutt sitting still, head forward, with his eyes turned skeptically toward the pistol. Gross had the cover.

* * *

The Death issue includes two of Bluestone's best and darkest pieces: "23 Ways to Be Offensive at the Funeral of Someone You Didn't Like" and a series of cartoons entitled "Telling a Kid His Parents Are Dead" (adult: "Here's your Halloween costume. You're gonna be an orphan"). In his funeral list, Bluestone suggests that disgruntled mourners: Walk up to the casket and start comparing the size of the deceased's clothes to your own. Listen to the baseball game on a transistor radio and react loudly to every pitch. Stand around at the cemetery saying, "At least now he'll no longer be tormented over being impotent." Shake the widow's hand with an electric buzzer. With several other articles in the issue, Bluestone was the definitive voice of the Death issue.

"Doug wrote a lot of outrageous pieces," says Louise Gikow, who worked for *National Lampoon* during the early and mid-1970s. "O'Donoghue did a lot of shock pieces, but they were much more political. Brian McConnachie's outrageousness was gentler. But Ed was the most shocking. He was beyond Doug and Michael."

Henry's "Deadman Comics" tells the story of a deceased superhero; Kelly parodies James Joyce with "Finnswake Again"; McConnachie contributed "Children's Suicide Notes to Santa" and "Playdead," which features a series of nude female corpses with heads in the oven, hanging from nooses, and reclining in hospital beds.

Sending up the long-running *Playboy* interview, "Playdead" features a candid conversation with the recently deceased actor Dan Blocker, who had gained fame as "Hoss" Cartwright, the beefy middle brother on *Bonanza.*

Playdead: After fifteen years of high riding, ranch tending, and shout-outs in and around Virginia City, Nevada, you've become an institution and a very wealthy man. How much of the show's success would you say is attributable to your gun vis à vis your brother's and father's guns?

Blocker:

This line of questioning and response continues until the interviewer finally says, "We don't want to put any words in your mouth but . . . "

Seemingly innocuous in the take-no-prisoners world of *National Lampoon*, it caused problems for Gerry Taylor when it turned out that the account executive for Sony's Superscope brand had been a friend of the actor, a fact that he shared with the ad director soon after the issue came out. The Superscope account was lost.

* * *

The release of *Radio Dinner* was, in part, helpful in raising *National Lampoon*'s profile as a legitimate cultural outpost for young people, and ad revenue had grown to $682,000 during 1972. The album was transferred to Blue Thumb Records after RCA attempted to excise from the record a piece about the sex life of Nixon's daughter Julie and son-in-law David Eisenhower. As the corporate giant did significant business with the federal government, they didn't want to be associated with anything that would inspire ill will on the part of the chief executive's family. O'Donoghue freaked out and refused to comply with the request, and Matty agreed, retaining a $25,000 advance from RCA and receiving an additional $25,000 from Blue Thumb. With the production costing only $10,000, this was becoming a pretty nice business deal before *Radio Dinner* even earned a dime from sales.

Blue Thumb now wanted a second album—this time a live, rock 'n' roll–based effort. The project morphed into *Lemmings*, which opened in New York City at the Village Gate theater in January 1973.

In November 1972, Tony Hendra visited Martha's Vineyard to meet with Doug. The intended purpose of the trip was to persuade Doug to adapt "Cat Calls," the Ezra Taft Benson High School Yearbook parody from the Nostalgia issue, into a piece for *Lemmings*.

Hendra had first encountered Doug at the *National Lampoon* offices shortly before his first disappearance. During the brief meeting, Doug told the Englishman that British humor was, by nature, not funny. Within seconds, he was impeccably spouting dialogue à la Thackeray ("and I mean Thackeray," Hendra wrote. "Not Trollope or Mrs. Gaskell or Dickens") before showing Hendra how he could stuff his own hand into his mouth. This meeting, however, was far less antic.

Hendra found Doug, working on TACOS, unhappy and distracted. Living in the house by the water and clearly displeased with his literary efforts, he expressed little interest in adapting the piece, or anything else for that matter, into another medium beyond the magazine or his novel. Unsuccessful, Hendra returned to New York, where he and Kelly were working on *Lemmings*.

With O'Donoghue unavailable for collaboration, Hendra had chosen Kelly, whose facile mind had produced endless musical and poetry parodies. Beyond that, Kelly's literary talents meshed nicely with an astounding knowledge of everything and anything having to do with rock music. He was the natural choice. Woodstock would be their target.

In the few short years that had passed, Kelly and Hendra had gained sufficient perspective on the great countercultural gathering of peace and love, and recognized that it had all been a pile of bullshit, peopled by millionaire performers who reaped financial benefits and hyped their counterculture credibility by participating in the mass event.

Beyond sending up the artists and their motives, the two saw that the festival also belied the inherent hypocrisy of their generation. The counterculture had sold out, trading in ideology and converting it into an ego-driven, self-obsessed fashion and lifestyle statement revolving around sex and drugs rather than peace and love. As only two disillusioned lefties with overactive minds and cynical worldviews could, Hendra and Kelly chose the theme of "self-destruction" for their Woodshuck—A Festival of Peace, Love, and Death.

Death was not an uncommon fascination of both the staff and the culture of the times. Jim Morrison, Duane Allman, Janis Joplin, Jimi Hendrix, and a myriad of others were gone. O'Donoghue played with it endlessly in his work, as, clearly, did Bluestone. In 1972, frequent Lampoon cartoon contributor and Harvard graduate David McLelland hurled himself through the window of a high rise and plummeted to his death. Around 635 Madison they would joke,

"What's the difference between David McLelland and a pizza?" The answer: "A pizza doesn't have shards of glass in it."

One female staffer wondered how they might react when one of their own, somebody from the inner circle, died.

With this backdrop, Hendra and Kelly adapted *National Lampoon* pieces and wrote original material during the fall of 1972, as Hendra started assembling the cast for *Lemmings*, which by now had evolved into a full-out stage show.

Lemmings wasn't the type of show for which Hendra could hold an equity audition. Rather, he'd been assigned to assemble performers who could write, sing, dance, play instruments, improvise (and improve on their improvisations), and create characters from set written pieces. Hendra went about this task in tried-and-true *National Lampoon* fashion—essentially finding people with varied talents, stage presence, and skewed sensibilities that would fit the material. At this he most certainly succeeded.

Christopher Guest, held over from *Radio Dinner*, was on board and brought along his handsome, charismatic friend Cornelius Crane "Chevy" Chase, whom he had met at Bard College.

The son of a well-to-do publishing executive, Chase was, at the time, neither a comedian nor really an actor. A pre-med student, who dated actress Blythe Danner at Bard, he considered himself a writer first and an amateur musician second.

"I was working as a writer for *MAD* and Channel One, an underground television project on East Fourth Street," Chase says. "We did five years of video tapes that were ninety minutes long of television that you couldn't see at home. It was parody and humor much like *Saturday Night Live*, but much, much ruder."

An example of Channel One's approach was a parody of the "Let your fingers do the walking" *Yellow Pages* ads, with Chase's hand moving across a phone book and into the lap of a prostitute, sticking his thumb between his fingers to simulate an erection, and commencing a lurid act as vampy music played in the background. Later he would write political satire for the Smothers Brothers' second network show.

Chase was called into the *National Lampoon* offices early on by Doug and Henry, but he rejected their offer to write for the magazine because the pay at *MAD* was better and he was intimidated by the more literary leanings of the Harvard-educated editors. But Chase was naturally funny and could play the drums, which was essential for a show that intended to tear into the sacred cows and icons of the Woodstock generation.

Guest also brought in twenty-two-year-old musical director Paul Jacobs, whom he'd met at a recording session. Jacobs had learned piano at the age of six, guitar at eight, and performed at Carnegie Hall when he was nine. Having taken courses at Juilliard, he had an intensive classical background from which he'd been liberated by electric guitar–oriented rock music. Growing his hair long and joining the counterculture, he was a versatile studio musician before age twenty.

At his audition, Jacobs wrote an adaptive musical satire of the Crosby, Stills, and Nash classic "Our House" that became the *Lemmings* theme, as well as two other songs that wound up in the show. Jacobs and Kelly created the words and music for much of the show in little more than a weekend.

"Sean would just come up with fifty variations of everything in a minute," Jacobs says.

Soon, Hendra traveled to Chicago to meet a young Second City performer named John Belushi, whom Peter Elbling, Choquette's former partner, had recommended. Desperately craving a trip to New York and the big time, Belushi was ready for his arrival.

At Second City's space on Chicago's North Wells Street, Hendra was treated to a wild performance. Belushi not only chewed the scenery, he broke every rule of performance in the cloistered world of improv (where one is never allowed to say "no" on stage). That night, fellow performers be damned, Belushi was "the show" at Second City, performing for one poker-faced member of the audience.

"John thought Tony hated him," Belushi's widow, Judy Belushi Pisano, recalls.

Knowing that Hendra wanted actors who could play music, Belushi had asked the brother of Second City performer Joe Flaherty to teach him the guitar. By the time Hendra arrived, he'd mastered only "Louie, Louie" and played it for Hendra twice to demonstrate his musical chops.

Charmed, overwhelmed by the actor's performance, and in need of talent, Hendra hired Belushi, who soon moved to New York with Judy.

Next came Alice Playten, who had first appeared on Broadway at age nine as Baby Louise in *Gypsy*. Before long she was an old pro, landing parts in *Oliver!* and *Hello Dolly!* with Carol Channing. Petite and with a little girl voice, she played adolescents until she was nearly twenty. Despite her impressive resume, Playten's best-known role was on a frequently aired Alka Seltzer commercial of the early 1970s, where she portrayed a young newlywed whose husband had overeaten her first home-cooked meal. In need of women who could perform onstage, Hendra called her in for an audition. Guest was there and did his extraordinary Bob Dylan.

"I don't do imitations," Playten told Hendra and Guest. "I can only do Brenda Lee and Mick Jagger."

The men stopped dead in their tracks. "You can do Mick?!"

Having once mimicked Jagger while *Sticky Fingers* played on a friend's turntable, she went into a dance that aped the British rocker's use of the microphone and tendency to look away between musical phrases.

Moving on to the hard-edged, highly political, death-oriented world of *Lemmings* was a terrific opportunity for Playten to squash what she called her "apply-dapply image." Based on the Jagger number and her acting credentials, Hendra hired her.

With Playten cast, actress Mary Jennifer Mitchell, who had been romantically involved with numerous Lampoon employees, filled the other female role. The final male cast member was Gary Goodrow from *The Committee* in San Francisco.

The second act of *Lemmings* was fairly well set to revolve around the Woodshuck Festival, with Belushi as a wild, bearded master of ceremonies. The first act, however, was ever evolving, which did not sit well with Playten, who was used to intricately staged, highly professional Broadway musicals and was shocked by her new work environment.

"There was no script and everybody was rude at first," she recalls. "I just kept waiting for a script."

Much of the act would have to be developed through improvisation, something with which Belushi and Goodrow were more than familiar. Guest, who could improvise in any language and was very structured in his approach, could do it, and the inexperienced but energetic Chase was up for anything.

For Playten, it was a substantial adjustment. The environment was intensely male and competitive. Everyone else, it seemed, was hooked into the fascination with drugs, death, destruction, and danger, "which was not exactly the place I was coming from," Playten says.

Then one day, while improvising a scene, Playten found herself portraying a music exec to Belushi's wannabe, desperate-for-fame rock star.

"If you could just cut your record and then die," she said, "I know I could sell it." She'd clicked in and was now an official member of the team. She got it, but would still ask for a script nearly every day.

For as much as he wanted to be in New York, Belushi was not happy. Living on a friend's sofa, he and Judy missed their comfortable life back in Chicago, where the cast of John's shows hung out at one another's apartments, called each other every night while watching old B-movies on television, and met each morning at the same restaurant for breakfast and to go over the newspaper for material. It was the same routine with the same people, always leading up to that night's show. The show and the cast were your life and family at Second City.

"You lived for the show and everything was about the show," Judy Belushi says.

New York, however, was much edgier and competitive. They didn't know many people and those they were meeting had chips on their shoulders and fought for stage time wherever they could. Everyone was always "on." Scene partners left you hanging. To make matters worse, Judy didn't have a job.

Belushi told Matty he was heading back to Chicago because Judy was miserable and they needed money. "What does she do?" Matty asked. "She's an artist," Belushi replied. Within minutes, Judy was hired as an assistant in the art department.

Though Doug was absent when she was hired, he and Judy became good friends almost immediately upon his return.

Judy had only seen pictures of the AWOL editor and founder, but after returning from lunch one day, she suddenly saw Doug, with long straggly hair and a pronounced slouch, standing by a copyeditor's cubicle. Upon introduction, however, Doug stood up straight, shook her hand, and said, "How nice to meet you."

"This is Doug Kenney?" she thought.

"He was the first person in that group that we met who was so warm right away," she remembers. "Partly because he was from the Midwest. But mostly he was just being Doug."

* * *

Lemmings was scheduled to open on January 25, 1973, for a two-week run at the Village Gate, a jazz club that had been booking theatrical and avant-garde acts for several years. It seemed the perfect venue for the upstart musical. Shortly before opening, however, Dale Anglund—one of two theater professionals helping to manage the show—called Matty from a phone booth before rehearsal.

The club's owner, Art D'Lugoff, had failed to pay some of the tax on the cash he took in each night, and a government collector had padlocked the door, refusing to let anyone in. With the cast going insane on the street, Anglund told the man he needed to make a phone call.

After explaining the situation to Matty, he put the collector on the phone, and Matty agreed to immediately cut a check for $18,000 if the padlock was removed. The doors opened and D'Lugoff paid Matty back several weeks later.

After the first show, Matty, the cast, and numerous *National Lampoon* employees gathered at Manhattan's Minetta Tavern to toast the performers and await the reviews.

The *New York Times* ran a special feature that evening, demeaning portions of the first act's improv-based script as "brainless" and "a supposedly comic assault on sex and politics [that] suffers from a serious case of the puerilities." Particularly savaged was an operating room piece about surgeons on acid who kill a patient, laying blame on the hands of fate: "You can't fight Karma and you can't fight Ghia." The opening act's most positively received number was Guest's stand-up Jackie Christ bit, in which he played the Son of God as a tummeling, old-fashioned Catskills comic:

> Thank you. Hey, it's been tough being the Son of God. You know. Take the inn for instance. It wasn't that there was no room at the inn. The inn was restricted. But mom was very cool. She pretended to be Catholic. Then the desk clerk caught her reading from right to left. Thank you very much. You've been a beautiful multitude.

The second act got raves. Guest did dead-on send-ups of Bob Dylan and James Taylor (performing a song that made repeated reference to the latter singer's intravenous drug dependency and during which Belushi feigned sleep onstage). The Dylan number billed the folky rebel icon and generational voice as sellout Jesus Zimmerman singing his classic "Positively Wall Street." Crosby, Stills, Nash, and Young were sent up as Marx, Engels, and Jung. Playten's Jagger was "devastating," while Mary Jennifer Mitchell played Joan Baez, baby on her shoulder, droning on about her imprisoned husband, and singing a protest song with the lyrics, "pull the trigger niggers/we're with you all the way . . . so many grievous wrongs/for me to right with tedious songs."

As master of ceremonies, Belushi introduced the All-Star Dead Band, with Janis Joplin and Jim Morrison on vocals. Brian Jones on rhythm guitar. Jimi Hendrix on lead guitar. Duane Allman on slide. Ginger Baker at the drums. Paul "Is Dead" McCartney manning the bass. And on the keyboards . . . Harry Truman. After announcing the band, Belushi would count "one . . . two . . . three . . . four," and would be met only with silence.

Belushi got the best notes of all, with *New York Times* critic Mel Gussow writing, "The discovery of *Lemmings* is John Belushi—a bushy bearded clown with a deceptively offhanded manner."

"I can remember coming out of my apartment on Thirteenth Street and Third Avenue just after it opened, buying the papers, and sitting down in a greasy spoon," Belushi told *Newsweek*. "I opened the *New York Times* and there was something like 'new discovery John Belushi.' I felt like I was three feet off the ground."

Reading the reviews at the afterparty, Matty was overcome with pride. The evening, however, was not without its unpleasant moments. Somewhere O'Donoghue was seething over Hendra's success. Kelly, who still lived in Montreal at the time, found that the program noted his contributions in small print, dwarfed by the name of director Tony Hendra (which Hendra explained away as "a mistake" in the printing). In addition, the show biz–averse Henry had mouthed "I hate it" to Matty at intermission.

Lemmings became a smash and the hottest ticket in town for 385 shows at the Gate. It attracted celebrities like Barbra Streisand, as well as those parodied in the show, such as Dylan, John Denver, and James Taylor, who sat mortified at his table while wife Carly Simon held him and laughed.

In May 1973, Eric Lax would write a follow-up piece entitled, "Why Do Young People Love *Lemmings*?" for the *New York Times*. Deconstructing its appeal, he noted,

> For the first few weeks after *Lemmings* opened, the first act, at its best, wasn't even sophomoric, perhaps freshmanic would apply. But Hendra and the cast have re-worked much of the material, dropped other parts and now most of it is quite funny. A recently added lecture on the art of comedy that ends the act is a clinical deadpan, wonderfully timed and executed.

* * *

In late winter 1973, Doug left the Vineyard and came back to the offices at 635 Madison with a manuscript for his novel, which he asked Henry and O'Donoghue to read.

Sitting silently across from Henry, Doug said, "It sucks, doesn't it?" Henry nodded. Doug tossed a year's worth of work in the garbage, and it was never discussed again.

Though no copy of the manuscript survived that day, O'Donoghue and others felt that Doug had frozen while trying to write his novel.

Measuring himself against the work of Waugh and Salinger, he was overwhelmed by pressure to be great in a new medium. For the first time in his life, he'd found something meaningful that he couldn't do perfectly on the first try, even with hard work and dedication. The impact of such failure was devastating. To many, Doug seemed broken. During a nearly yearlong sabbatical, when he'd hoped to finally shed the burden of outside expectations and cast off the shroud of his beloved older brother, Doug had come to the realization that he wasn't ready for life after *National Lampoon*, nor was he the writer that he hoped he could be.

For all of his flakiness and disappearing acts, Doug took his writing and his relationship to the written word very seriously. He'd been born with a gift but seemed to take his talent for granted. Yet all outward appearances to the contrary, he defined himself through his ability to write.

"He never just tossed something off," O'Rourke says. "He took it very seriously, always pushing the form. Doug was an artist. He could do regular sorts of magazine humor very easily, but he was always looking for something more difficult to do."

Doug and Alex met to discuss the dissolution of their marriage. The interaction was pleasant and Doug even made a halfhearted attempt to win her back. Sensing his ambivalence and knowing the marriage was irretrievably broken, she refused. The divorce became final.

Doug moved his belongings into a brownstone at 28 Bank Street in Greenwich Village. The place wouldn't be much of a home for him. Doug barely unpacked, pulling his clothes each day from a suitcase and furnishing the place with secondhand sofas and orange crates. When Chris Miller tried to eat some food from the refrigerator, Doug called to him, "You might want to carbon-date that."

Around that time, Rick Meyerowitz visited Doug's apartment, still completely in disarray. On the living room floor was an illustration of the Nixon family that Meyerowitz had drawn as a wedding present for Doug and Alex. The frame was broken and the glass was cracked.

"Take this back," Doug said. "I don't deserve it."

Meyerowitz refused.

"I can't take care of it; you have to take it back," Doug implored. Meyerowitz reluctantly agreed.

Throughout their friendship, Meyerowitz found Doug to be immensely interested in his life, frequently asking about the artist's wife and children. How were they doing in school? How did Meyerowitz manage to work so hard and still have a loving family life? "He would say that I was lucky," Meyerowitz says. "There was a wistfulness there—as if he was incapable of getting there. He asked me about my marriage. I said, 'It depends on what you want.' And he wanted to ask me what he wanted."

It was hard to know what to do with Doug now that he was back at the magazine. So much had happened in his absence— albums, a stage show, and sharp increases in both circulation and advertising revenue. Within him lurked the talent that could take things even further and the willingness to continue to be a significant part of the magazine, but something indefinable was now gone, forever.

Henry knew it. Though it was never discussed, he could no longer rely on Doug. Doug could still be part of the magazine and hailed as a genius. But never again would he be in charge.

Doug knew it too.

Freed of responsibility, Doug would stay on at *National Lampoon* as the magazine's star writer, éminence not so grise, and creative soul—handling special projects, writing spectacular pieces, and roaming as he pleased without being tied to any singular role.

Len Mogel taught a magazine publishing class at NYU and asked Doug to give a lecture about his work at the magazine. Entering the packed classroom, Doug immediately walked into a closet, closed the door, and began to lecture from inside. When he emerged, he jumped on Mogel's desk and declared, "Actually I want to be a rock and roll singer." With that he began singing. The students went wild, getting exactly what they anticipated.

When things calmed down, Doug sat cross-legged on a desk and the students brought out their pens and paper to record his publishing wisdom. Doug told them that an issue generally ran one hundred and fifty pages. The masthead was one page, thus only one hundred and forty-nine pages needed to be filled. Fifty pages of ads brought it down to ninety-nine. Doug confessed to writing thirty pages per issue. As for the other sixty-nine?

"We just fill up the rest," he explained, going on to say that he and Henry would beg, "Come on Sean, twenty pages please?"

The NYU episode, no matter how bizarre, got Matty's publicity juices flowing. Regardless of Doug's behavior, the students adored meeting him and seeing the improvised floor show. Doug himself had enjoyed being the center of attention and went on to give occasional lectures based on the theme of his failed novel. Launching into free-form rants, he'd begin with "Teenage," discussing life in Chagrin Falls, his brother Dan's high school, and Gilmour. Then he'd riff on "Commies" and "Outer Space" for a while, tying it all together by recollecting how he found meaning in the TACOS sign above an L.A. restaurant. Soon, Miller and Kelly were being sent out on campus lecture tours all over the country. The schools would pay a few thousand dollars for the guest speaker, while the writers received plane tickets, a decent fee, and a weekend of adulation.

The most memorable of these appearances was one of Miller's final engagements at Southwest Missouri State, in a region where the adults didn't exactly embrace blasphemous, sexually explicit, and icon-shredding humor.

Speaking from a small riser in the lunchroom, Miller soon realized that the hundreds of students listening to his talk (which often featured slides of some of the magazine's more outrageous spreads) were enthralled, while the administration seemed less than thrilled. Barely into the lecture, he saw a woman exit the room in a huff and knew that a shit storm was brewing.

Within minutes, she returned with a large, ominous man whose job was to end Miller's appearance. Abruptly turning off the microphone, he shot an unpleasant look at Miller, announcing, "This is over!"

Undeterred, Miller gathered his notes, screamed "Follow me!" and led hundreds of students from the cafeteria across campus, stopping on the quad. During the march, the procession picked up more and more students, who now numbered into the thousands. Camera crews from television stations had been alerted and were now on the scene to cover the event.

Miller stopped at a large tree and the crowd settled.

"Now," he said, calmly gathering his notes and finding his place. "Where was I?"

With the speaking tours garnering further publicity and solidifying the magazine's impact on college students (again, giving the magazine a public face—à la "Foto Funnies"), the question remained: what to do with Doug?

* * *

To assuage O'Donoghue's furor over Hendra's stewardship of *Lemmings*, Matty gave him permission to work on a long-discussed pet project, *The National Lampoon Encyclopedia of Humor*. In addition to total creative control, he asked for billing on the front cover, with "Edited by Michael O'Donoghue" played under the title. Though the magazine's efforts had always been credited in a fairly nonhierarchical, collective manner, Matty acquiesced.

O'Donoghue began the project shortly after the November 1972 issue had been finalized and tore into it with his usual intensity. Around the same time, he was also entering a creative and romantic partnership with Anne Beatts.

Upon first meeting him, Beatts had concluded that O'Donoghue was cruel and more than a bit creepy. Yet by late 1972, as her relationship with Choquette faded and she became friendly with O'Donoghue, Beatts began to see that his exterior protected a far warmer, sweeter man who'd been so kind to Kelly in his time of need and had fallen so deeply in love with Amy Ephron.

For two years, Beatts had been a woman among men, fighting to prove that she was just as good at writing humor as any guy. Unafraid to ruffle feathers, she was determined to assert her equality while not losing her femininity. Though many women worked in subservient roles at *National Lampoon*, Beatts was never one of them. Full of raw talent, she did everything possible to refine her work and transcend the pervading attitude about female humorists.

Thus intertwined, Beatts set out to give O'Donoghue style. Though he saw himself as a sophisticate in the manner of George Sanders, he dressed in army surplus. Beatts changed all this.

"I got him out of those Hush Puppies and torn shirts," Beatts told *Mr. Mike* author Dennis Perrin.

Soon O'Donoghue the trashcan beatnik became Michael O'Donoghue the writer, dressed in ironic deco couture discovered in the second-hand shops of Manhattan. Gone were the army jackets and slouchy shirts, replaced by elegant white suits, vintage Hawaiian shirts, and carved walking sticks. He was shod in old-fashioned wing-tips and spectator shoes.

"It was a form of serious camp," Perrin writes. "A foppish exterior that augmented the dark thoughts within."

Beatts also transformed her own style to complement her angry Eliza Doolittle. Attired in wide-brimmed hats and backless dresses that brought to mind the 1930s and '40s, Beatts became a contemporary Zelda to O'Donoghue's burgeoning F. Scott.

The relationship was symbiotic, though not infrequently explosive, with the two becoming a creative team. Beatts sharpened her comedic sword under O'Donoghue's tutelage, while she gave him a completely fitting persona that complemented his talent and demeanor. They were a force to be reckoned with, and O'Donoghue's fragile self-confidence soared.

While McCall, Kenney, Gross, and many others would make significant contributions to the Encyclopedia, it was O'Rourke who made the project happen.

With O'Donoghue consumed by the project's design (to which he was well suited), he left most of the tactical groundwork (for which he was not so well suited) to O'Rourke, with whom he had a good relationship and who was more than willing to get the job done.

The process of putting the Encyclopedia together was painfully slow, and several deadlines were missed before O'Rourke came on board. Relentlessly hounding contributors for pieces and writing material to fill alphabetical holes (it was organized as a comprehensive, A to Z guide), O'Rourke was invaluable.

"There was no way Michael would have gotten that encyclopedia done without P.J.," Kelly says. "[Working on a foldout map] we sat at P.J.'s apartment naming every place in the world something funny. It wasn't inspiration, it was perspiration. But he just kept to it. 'Now we've got to do Africa.'"

Doug's most important contribution to the Encyclopedia was "First Blowjob." Written in *Saturday Evening Post* style, the story appears under the subhead "A Young Girl's Senior Prom Can Mean Many Things: A Bouquet of Memories . . . Or a Pillow Full of Tears . . . "

The story begins with a 1950s mom calling upstairs to her daughter on prom night, "Connie! Connie Phillips! You better hurry, Jeff will be here any minute."

Still fretting over her nails, makeup, and dress, Connie is a cute, young, middle-American teen prepping for the most exciting night of her young life—a date to the Senior Bounce with Jeff Madison, football captain, student senate chairman, and coordinator of Hi-Tri-Y activities who is going to State in the fall.

Finding Jeff jovially chatting with her pipe-smoking, cardigan-wearing dad on the couch, Connie descends the stairs to a cry of "Ho-ly Bananas! I didn't know I had a date with a movie star!"

Mr. Phillips tells his daughter what a lovely young woman she's become, while Connie assures him that she'll always be his "little girl." Then, just as she is about to leave, Connie's dad pulls her aside for one last father-daughter moment.

> "Just promise me," said Mr. Phillips, fumbling for his pipe clean-ers, "that no matter how wonderful the dance may be tonight and no matter what Jeff and you may be feeling . . . promise me that you won't give him a blowjob."
>
> "A w-what?" stammered Connie, backing away slightly.
>
> "A blowjob," Mr. Phillips repeated. "You know when a fellow forces his dork down your throat and makes you suck on it until he eventually shoots his pecker-snot all over your tonsils."

When Connie comments, "Th-that's . . . horrible . . . sickening . . . " Mr. Phillips replies, "You bet it is. Just ask your mother."

Connie regroups and sets off on an evening that begins with a romantic trip down Lakeshore Drive, followed by frequent flattery from her date, and her admonition that Jeff "better've eaten [his] Cheerios because I'm not going to sit out a single dance."

Before the evening is over, Connie is dosed with Dramamine, proposed to, discovers that Jeff is headed to the State Mental Hospital in the fall (rather than old State College), forced to perform the dreaded act her father described ("Connie saw Jeff's tan, athletic penis straining toward her"), chained to her date's steering wheel (while he changes into a Nazi uniform), and lashed with a car aerial.

"Gee," exclaims Jeff, "I've been wanting to try this ever since I first heard Negro music."

Returning home, covered with welts, Connie is greeted by her father, who calmly says, "Well, it certainly looks like you've had your fun. Do you have any idea what time it is young lady?"

Noting that he can sympathize with today's young people, Mr. Phillips says, "I'm even 'hep' to a lot of your kookie teen lingo," and sends Connie flying through the door and onto the lawn with a punch in the eye. "'Padiddle for example,' chuckled Mr. Phillips."

The broken, fragile, unreliable, disappointed failed novelist and dethroned founder of *National Lampoon* had regained the voice he'd never truly lost. Instead, with precision, he'd found a new way to take Eisenhower, the family dog, Jim Anderson, Ward Cleaver, Ozzie Nelson, Chagrin Falls, and all of the asshole jocks who went on to sell life insurance in Cleveland and toss them amiably on their asses with the evocation of what every way too smart, unable to be cool high school boy in America had envisioned happening to the prom queen when she meets with that psycho quarterback who we all know is lurking in each of our high schools.

Finally released in September, the Encyclopedia sold 315,000 copies by the end of 1973. Painstakingly assembled, it included McConnachie's "Swamp Sluts"; a lesbian, sado-masochist comic called "Cowgirls at War"; a goofy O'Rourke–O'Donoghue collaboration named "The Battling Buses of World War II" (loosely parodying patriotic consumer ads during World War II); and O'Donoghue's "The Churchill Wit," an assemblage of vulgar witticisms allegedly uttered by the British prime minister.

Churchill was known to drain a glass or two and, after one particularly convivial evening, he chanced to encounter Miss Bessie Braddock, a Socialist member of the House of Commons, who, upon seeing his condition, said, "Winston, you're drunk." Mustering all his dignity, Churchill drew himself to his full height, cocked an eyebrow and rejoined, "Shove it up your ass, you ugly cunt."

Beatts's numerous contributions included a two-page ad spread that depicted a returning soldier holding his daughter aloft as his beautiful young wife smiles with glee.

"He's Home. With maturity, ambition, skills, and a hundred-dollar-a-day habit." Beneath it read: "Hire the veteran. He needs the money."

This piece and others resulted in numerous hate and protest letters arriving on O'Donoghue's desk. Yet none provoked as great a response as Beatts's phony Volkswagen ad, depicting the legendary Bug floating in water (one of the auto manufacturer's marketing claims) with the headline, "If Ted Kennedy drove a Volkswagen, he'd be President today."

Almost immediately, Volkswagen began receiving angry letters from consumers who, despite the fact that the parody ran in a something other than a periodical, believed it was the work of the automaker.

"I'll be damned if I buy another Volkswagen after seeing an ad like the one attached," read one.

Kennedy's press secretary Richard Drayne commented, "We found the ad very offensive. Certainly Senator Kennedy and his political fortunes are subjects for the Lampoon's scrutiny, but not the death of a young woman."

Volkswagen responded with a $30 million lawsuit for violation of copyright and trademark laws as well as defamation. Matty settled out of court, agreeing to withdraw the remaining copies of the Encyclopedia from the newsstand, destroy the plates for the ad, and allow VW to run a statement in the January 1974 issue of the Lampoon.

"Of course it'll be sold out by then probably," Matty told the press, "so I wouldn't describe the situation as arduous for us. Besides, the ad wasn't untrue. If the car had floated, he might be president."

* * *

On April 1, 1973, Manhattan's New School for Social Research welcomed a panel of experts to discuss "the primal laugh and the cosmic giggle" in honor of April Fools' Day. On the dais with O'Donoghue and McConnachie were writers Cleveland Amory and Calvin Trillin, along with psychotherapist Ilana Rosenfeld.

According to the *New York Times*, O'Donoghue looked like "James Joyce on a prosperous day—light beige suit, green cap, and a fancy walking stick." That day he would sum up his comedic philosophy by telling the audience, "It's very easy to laugh at myself. The important thing is to laugh at others." He went on to explain that satire is the least effective manner of changing the world. "The real sin," he said, "isn't sodomy or adultery. It's non-returnable bottles."

Asked if they took anything seriously, O'Donoghue, with McConnachie's tacit assent, said "no" to the audience of two hundred.

"I believe them," Trillin commented.

* * *

In February, Matty Simmons had told the *New York Times* business section that 21st Century, on the strength of *National Lampoon*'s performance, was growing too fast for him to make any forecasts for investors, who were suddenly seeing an oddly sound financial opportunity with the magazine created by Henry and Doug.

"We're growing too quickly and contemplating too many new publications to make predictions," Matty said. "However, I can comment on Wall Street estimates when I know that the estimate is reasonable based on the information available to them."

One of those new publications was *Ingenue*. To get the project off the ground, Matty assigned O'Rourke to the new magazine and assembled a management team that included Joanna Brown and Elliot Marion from *Glamour* to serve as editor and publisher, respectively.

With a paid circulation of 750,000, *Ingenue* was losing money, but Simmons, Mogel, and all others involved had high hopes that they could put it back in the black by the close of business in 1973. It was not to be.

For the final issue (April 1973) published by Dell, the soon-to-be deposed editors of *Ingenue* had dumped many spiked articles from the past into the magazine. This was bad enough, but one of the prominent features was by a renowned adolescent psychologist who advised teenage girls to shed their inhibitions regarding heavy petting and premarital sex.

"The reaction was akin to the dropping of a large bomb," Matty recalls.

The magazine, which O'Rourke characterized as something "a maiden aunt buys for her favorite niece," immediately lost thousands of subscriptions and advertisers. After recovering $500,000 from Dell in an out-of-court settlement, Matty folded *Ingenue* in 1974.

Well before that settlement, the *Ingenue* debacle forced O'Rourke to pursue projects more befitting his skills.

* * *

The April 1973 Prejudice cover features two rough-looking black men sitting on a tenement building's front stairway among empty beer cans and garbage. In front of the steps is a white lawn jockey wearing a gray business suit, shined black shoes, and a conservative striped tie.

John Boni and Rick Meyerowitz contributed an illustrated spread of "Inverted Stereotypes" that includes: Those Shiftless Germans, Those Meticulous Arabs, Those Menacing Jews, and Those Greasy Swedes ("the passionate but sloppy Swedes spend their days drinking wine, growing fat and shaving their mustaches. . . . When not singing, having fun or wringing the oil from their hair, Swedes indulge in their national sport of suicide").

Henry collaborated with Chris Cerf on a piece called "Americans United to Beat the Dutch." Modeled on racist hate literature, the newsletter-style article graphically depicts a traditionally dressed Dutchman (wooden shoes and all) next to the typed warning KNOW THE ENEMY and enumerates his recognizable characteristics: weak chin, florid face, shifty eyes, beer and/or cheese breath, and chocolate under fingernails. They also give a paranoid breakdown of the word *Dutch*:

Dike-building schemes
Unrest everywhere
Tulip Scourge
Cheese-mongering
Hex signs

And that was just the cover. Inside, a picture of the Dutch royal couple is tagged "The Bandit Prince and his evil Queen, the Grand Dike Juliana, enlist more willing dupes into their vicious drainage schemes."

Given the tenor of the piece (broad, to put it mildly) and the issue—along with the fact that the Dutch had neither invaded nor menaced anyone in hundreds of years—no one expected Henry and Cerf's newsletter to create much rancor. Indeed, the cover alone was far more objectionable. Yet Heineken, whom Matty had represented in his press agent days, was not amused. "You called my queen a dyke," one marketing exec told Gerry Taylor. Despite the fact that Matty had become personal friends with importer Leo Van Munching, the company pulled its advertising.

* * *

Another adman, Gerald Sussman, contributed both "The Joys etc., of Yiddish" and "Profiles in Chopped Liver: Our Greatest Jewish Presidents" to the Prejudice issue. By far the funnier of the two articles, "Profiles in Chopped Liver" runs next to Gross's drawing of a Mount Rushmore where scaffolding holds up the prodigious noses of Washington, Jefferson, Teddy Roosevelt, and Abe Lincoln.

In Sussman's piece, Washington is the son of show biz parents (who perform as The Virginia Hams) named Jacob and Rebecca Washington. Despite his legendary military career, the first president is a showman at heart who longs for a career on stage and tosses off Yiddish with frequency and aplomb ("maybe I'm meshuga," he writes in one diary entry, "but how the hell are we going to beat the most powerful country in the world?" and later refers to Patrick Henry as a "goyisheh kop"—which translates to "Gentile head"). After the long winter at Valley Forge, Washington is never the same, always worrying about having enough food on hand at the White House and driving Martha crazy by purchasing too much smoked sturgeon.

Jefferson (a doctor and a lawyer), Lincoln ("as a boy he walked miles to the tiny one-room Yeshiva and studied the Talmud by candlelight"), Teddy Roosevelt (a transsexual), Franklin Roosevelt (whose Borscht Belt Trust included comedian Jackie Joey, dancer Monte Mark, Negro Cantor Jesse Wayne, and ex-boxer Tony Rocky), Ike (in Yiddish, Sussman claims, the name Eisenhower means "happy baking pan"), JFK, and LBJ ("even for a Jew, Johnson was bigger than life") all get the same treatment.

Unlike his presidential subjects, Sussman was indeed Jewish. And, unlike Bluestone, Weidman, and Meyerowitz, it was an essential part of his humor and personality. His life experience was far more akin to Matty's than it was to the editors'. At the magazine, he would become to Judaism what Kelly, Hendra, and Doug were to Catholicism.

Born in 1933, Sussman grew up a stickball playing, sex-obsessed kid in the Bedford-Stuyvesant section of Brooklyn. He read voluminously and adored the Marx Brothers. The son of a waiter, Sussman attended Brooklyn College, dropping out to help support the family when his father died.

Through a cousin, Sussman entered the advertising world where, as a successful copywriter, he thrived on talent, street smarts, and self-knowledge. When advised to attend a focus group for a product aimed at teenage boys, Sussman said, "I don't need a focus group to tell me what fourteen-year-olds are thinking."

Wanting more from his life, his writing, and his checkbook, Sussman began freelancing for *Playboy* and wrote the book *Sussman's Sex Manual*, a successful parody of the popular sexual self-help genre of the late 1960s and early '70s. One chapter was notably titled "Jellies, Jams, and Marmalades." He was born to write for *National Lampoon* and soon discovered by Henry Beard.

Sussman was older than the other contributors, married, and more socially mature. Staying out of office politics, he befriended nearly everyone, preferring to drink espresso and write instead of matching wits with O'Donoghue. Still, before long he would become part of the magazine's social framework, growing close to Kelly, Weidman, and others.

"He was funny even when he wasn't being funny," Kelly says. "He just thought funny."

In keeping with his adult lifestyle, Sussman had far greater financial obligations than Doug, Henry, and O'Donoghue. He was always in need of money to pay the bills, resulting in an arrangement with Matty by which Sussman was on a draw that provided him payment for articles and ideas before they were actually delivered. At the end of each quarter, however, Sussman often found that he owed his soul to the company store as he regularly took more money than he had produced in actual writing, which is not to say that his production wasn't enormous. Writing day and night, he was capable of pounding out voluminous amounts of humorous material. And, as he was paid by the word, Sussman made it a habit to deliver work that was nearly twice as long as it needed to be.

Within a few years of joining the magazine, Sussman divorced his wife to marry *New York Times* writer Elaine Louie. Soon after, the couple moved into an expensive loft downtown on Horatio Street ("we found an apartment and turned it into a loft," he'd say), making his financial life even more complex. This necessitated more and more writing.

One of the articles he banged out was "Bernie X," a running column written in the voice of an angry, offensive cab driver who embodied the New York City everyman. By the second half of the 1970s, Sussman would be working full time at *National Lampoon*.

* * *

As *Lemmings* raged through the spring of 1973, the first act began to take shape over the course of the brewing Watergate scandal that had Nixon, the magazine's beloved sacrificial lamb, continually in the news, thereby providing daily fodder for the show.

The mushrooming scandal became the focus of the first act, giving rise to pieces like "Mission Impeachable," which Henry had developed to brilliant effect in his "News on the March" section by turning Peter Graves's television character into Watergate coconspirator E. Howard Hunt: "Your mission, E., should you choose to accept it, is to stop these men once and for all, by ensuring that the weakest of them, Senator George McGovern, wins the nomination— and then by sabotaging his campaign with any possible means." The speech closed with "this administration will self-destruct in sixteen months." Less sophisticated, but equally hilarious and apropos, was Goodrow's trou-dropping Nixon impersonation.

"I got to do something that I'd never get a chance to do again," Goodrow says. "I got to play the president of the U.S. with my asshole."

Before Watergate carried the show, however, Hendra contributed a piece called "Humor Lecture," the excellence of which was noted in Eric Lax's laudatory article about *Lemmings*. Used to close the first act, the piece was an instant hit with audiences, cast members, and critics. Essentially a slapstick number in which a comedy expert and three assistants deliver an academic lecture on the history of humor, Hendra describes it thus in *Going Too Far*: "From the earliest japes (getting hit in the head with planks) to the complex ones of the Industrial Revolution, [it is] a long series of every conceivable combination of pies in the face."

Years before, Hendra and Ullett had occasionally performed the piece, though preferred not to—as it required significant postshow cleanup. The two had used the lecture, Hendra contends, with the permission of its creators, Terry Jones and Michael Palin of Monty Python, who, as students, had originated it for a show at Oxford.

One day in spring 1973, Hendra arrived at rehearsal having typed the script from memory. Introducing it as a potential closing number for the long-suffering first act, Hendra's piece was the first thing that everyone in the show loved immediately. No explanation had been given as to its origins. For all they knew, Hendra had written it himself.

"It was the only thing [in the first act] that was fully conceived," Playten remembers. "It happened overnight."

The lecture was inserted right away and played brilliantly, with Goodrow, Guest, Belushi, and Chase ripping through it each night for about a week, during which Kelly received a call from a friend in Canada who'd seen *Lemmings* and informed him that Monty Python was ripping off their first-act closing number on a tour running in their homeland. Almost simultaneously, Matty opened a registered letter from Monty Python informing him that 21st Century's hit show was using part of their act without permission. Matty quickly wrote back, apologizing and making it clear that *National Lampoon* had no knowledge of how the piece originated. It was immediately removed from the show.

Hendra believed that Jones was no longer using the piece, and that because he and Ullett had previously performed it, on television no less, they had tacit approval for future usage. Moreover, Hendra said, he figured Jones would be happy to get some royalties and he intended to try it out on stage before bothering the Pythons with a request. Caught up in the day-to-day operations of the show and the excitement of how well the piece was doing, he never got around to making the call.

"It was unprofessional certainly," Hendra wrote of the incident, "a bad judgment, even a stupid gamble. What it wasn't was grand larceny, which is how the word ran around the editorial offices."

In Hendra's recollection, Henry had almost no reaction until months later when, while renting a summer house on Hendra's property in New Jersey, the usually reserved editor turned and said, "How could you do it? How could you do it?"

Matty recalled Henry's response differently, with Beard rushing to his office and insisting that Hendra be fired. Subsequently, Hendra explained to Matty that he'd made a bad assumption about using the piece again, after having performed it with Ullett. Matty wrote of the encounter, "I remember shaking my head in disbelief, thinking to myself, 'Does he believe this shit, or does he think I'm stupid enough to believe it?'"

Whatever the case, Matty didn't fire Hendra. But stories, rumors, and acerbic commentary about Hendra spread around the office. O'Donoghue was happy as a clam.

***

Whenever she'd see her therapist during the run of *Lemmings*, Playten would talk about how unsafe the backstage and onstage atmosphere made her feel. Though she liked everybody, there seemed to be a pervading aura of danger around the show that was more than a little threatening to a young woman who stood roughly five feet tall.

Belushi loved to work and was very dedicated to the show. He, Chase, and Guest began to see *Lemmings* as more than a successful piece of entertainment—it was something approaching their own personal band. They had a chance to act out the rock star dreams common to nearly everyone of their generation.

With this conceit came prodigious use of drugs. Chase was dating a cocaine dealer at the time, while Belushi had grown enamored of Quaaludes. Playten was assigned to watch the drugs each night, because she alone could be trusted not to run off with them. This led to some uncomfortable moments.

One night, Belushi, who was generally sweet, told her he'd taken fifteen Quaaludes and was incapable of performing without cocaine. She reluctantly gave in. Later, Belushi would tell Playten that he had dreamed about a giant 'Lude the size of a pillow that he was desperate to consume—yet, still asleep, he kept reminding himself that Playten would kill him if he did. When he awoke, Belushi found himself holding tight to his pillow.

"It was 1960s drug use, so that meant it was a way of life," *Lemmings* stage manager Dale Anglund remembers.

Another evening, the Quaaludes were giving Belushi no little trouble standing up, forcing the entire cast to pool their cocaine to revivify him for the show. Though Belushi was able to perform, Anglund was infuriated, asked Judy Belushi where her husband kept his stash (in the pocket of his jeans backstage), and took it.

Later, Belushi stormed into the box office and raged at Anglund, who threw the drugs in his face and told the actor that he was going to be brought up on charges with Actors' Equity.

"We've got to control you some way!" he shouted.

Properly chastened, Belushi, with Judy's encouragement, flushed the remaining pills down the toilet and promised to be a good boy.

With pot smoking and alcohol use rampant in *National Lampoon* offices—and pretty much everywhere else among hip young people who had lived through the Summer of Love—the *Lemmings* folks were simply an extension of the magazine's prevailing aesthetic. Doug, most of all, enjoyed running away from the office whenever he could to attend rehearsals, hang with the performers, and smoke some dope.

Though they were friendly, Belushi and Chase were extremely competitive with each other. Chase had learned how to do the show by sitting at the feet of his friend Chris Guest, who mentored him through the rehearsals and performances. Guest was a consummate gentleman who worked hard, didn't overindulge in drugs, and was serious about his craft. Yet Guest often seemed personally unhappy and possessed a nasty sense of humor. Neither warm nor cuddly (qualities Belushi demonstrated in spades), he generally stayed out of the way and did his work in extraordinary fashion.

Chase was far wilder than his friend, achieving both notoriety and accolades for his energetic stage work. Compensating for his dearth of experience with intensity and a total lack of regard for his own safety (and that of others) while on stage, one night Chase smashed Playten's nose during her Jagger routine.

The aura of violence was not unintentional. It was a key component of the act, as in a bit in which Chase and Belushi slammed their heads together endlessly, searching for a buzz. In another piece, Chase did an unruly Hell's Angels impersonation, indiscriminately spilling beer on audience members in the front row.

One evening, as Matty's son Michael was working the door at the Gate, five genuine Hell's Angels showed up in full colors and requested seating for the sold-out show.

"That's OK," Michael said, escorting them to a table in the front row where Chase routinely doused the customers.

He turned white as a sheet when he saw them. Chase uncharacteristically underplayed the scene. Not a drop was spilled.

"There was tremendous excitement in being dangerous," Playten says.

The evening after her first day of work at *National Lampoon*, Janis Hirsch went to see the show. Stricken with polio as a child, she needed crutches to walk.

"Don't let Chevy see your crutches," she was warned.

Within moments of her arrival at the theater, Chase seized Hirsch's crutches and was walking around the Gate using them as stilts. Blessed with a thick hide and well-developed sense of humor, Hirsch couldn't help but laugh.

"They all played so well together," she says. "They had so much fun."

At rehearsal and backstage, Belushi and Chase would torture each other unmercifully. They were the stars of the show, but for different reasons: Belushi for his craft and natural but well-honed stage presence, Chase for his pure charm and unrefined talent. Both were jealous of what the other had. Belushi wished that somehow he were movie-star handsome, and Chase hoped to act and improvise as well as his counterpart.

In true *National Lampoon* fashion, this took the form of needling each other where it hurt most. Upon arrival at rehearsal, it was not uncommon for Chase to ask the extremely hairy Belushi whether or not he had shaved his back that morning. The son of Albanian immigrants, this cut him to the quick and demanded response, which came quickly and referenced any number of Chevy's weaknesses to devastating effect.

Guest was not immune to such behavior himself. Jacobs recalls that they would walk down the street and encounter homeless men, whom Guest would loudly identify as his attorney, or scream, "Ladies and gentlemen—Lou Gehrig!"

By the time *Lemmings* was ending its run at the Village Gate, Matty wanted to put together a road troupe and take it around the country. With a talented former Miss Arkansas named Rhonda Coullet and the singer Meat Loaf added to the mix, *Lemmings* went on tour. Playten declined to participate, fearing for her health and well-being.

One night her therapist came to see the show. Playten, who won an Obie for her role, had long begged the psychologist to let her quit *Lemmings*. The therapist had encouraged her to remain, arguing that she was simply running away from success and trying to avoid the kind of discomfort that is natural in a new or different work atmosphere.

After the show, the therapist came to see Playten. "Now I understand," she said.

The initial run of *Lemmings* not only extended the Lampoon brand and generated even greater publicity for the magazine, it also made a profit of $180,000. Hendra assumed that this money would go into whatever entertainment project he would next helm. Instead, it went to the man who hated him more than anyone in the world.

* * *

On July 16, *Newsweek* again took notice of the Lampoon phenomenon:

> Some may call it tasteless, sophomoric or plain outrageous, but the Audit Bureau of Circulation calls *National Lampoon* "the fastest growing magazine in America." In just three years, circulation of the monthly humor mag has vaulted from 165,000 to 685,000 while its annual pretax profits have passed $1,000,000. Lampoonmania is fast becoming a mini-industry. When not snatching up *National Lampoon* paperbacks, posters and t-shirts, its youthful disciples are making instant hits out of such Lampoon-produced spin-offs as the record album "Radio Dinner" a zany collection of pop-culture parodies and the off-Broadway musical review *Lemmings* . . .
>
> Today the Lampoon's most fervent loyalists are the collegians and post-grads who can no longer identify with the teenage hysteria of *Mad*.
>
> "The *National Lampoon* is getting to be a myth among the people I know," says one 25-year old fan, "It's a common point of reference because it mocks both generations. It finds the worst in every camp."

"It was like being able to purchase Lenny Bruce's act at your local bookstore in Omaha," says *Spy* magazine cofounder Kurt Andersen.

* * *

"It got dumped on me and Doug," P. J. O'Rourke says. "It was Matty and O'Donoghue's idea. They had done the 1958 yearbook ["Cat Calls"] and Matty wanted to do it as a whole yearbook. A special publication. [Doug and I] said, 'The joke's too thin. We can't pad this up to the size of a whole yearbook.'"

From this seemingly inauspicious beginning, Kenney and O'Rourke would spend much of the next year creating a classic of American humor and the most precise, meaningful, and hilarious parody in Lampoon history—the *National Lampoon 1964 High School Yearbook Parody*.

Doug was in the doghouse, due to his disappearance and nearly yearlong leave. With no clearly defined role, he was a man in need of a project and had little political capital to spend on rejecting one.

O'Rourke was the magazine's most junior contributor, and was making a name for himself through sheer tenacity and a willingness to shepherd projects that ranged from the extraordinary (the Encyclopedia) to the ridiculous (*Ingenue*).

Everybody said that they'd help. Almost no one did.

Doug and O'Rourke prepared for the project by sitting around the Bank Street apartment, smoking dope and talking about high school. Doug discussed his brother's life at a traditional American public school and his own interest in the middle America of the 1950s. Before long it dawned on them that there were only a certain number of personalities or archetypes that were universally common and applied to nearly every high school this side of Andover. Together they drew up a list of thirty-five personality types that they could parody and make easily recognizable to readers.

"By the end of the evening we realized—Oh, fuck! You really could do this," O'Rourke says. "Once you had the characters and personalities—you had a Trollopian or O'Haraian universe in which things could happen."

Gathering yearbooks from staff, friends, and family, they saw that their perceptions were on the money, with social meanings from which they could derive humor.

"It was chilling to see how much they were all the same," Doug told one reporter about looking at the yearbooks' stereotypes. "Bully, clown, intelligent introvert, politician, protohomosexual. It was Nazi social engineering. By weight of social pressure these people became these things."

Realizing that the project was not only possible, but likely something that could be truly funny, Doug and O'Rourke began scouting around New York for schools that might provide students and an appropriate backdrop. No administrator would have them.

Matty approached the headmaster of Manhattan's Columbia Prep, where one of his sons was enrolled. After initially balking, the headmaster gave in to Matty's argument that it would be a great experience for the students. When the project was brought up at an all-school assembly, the student body exploded. After school each day, they'd be transformed from well-to-do New York teens into students of the Dacron, Ohio, C. Estes Kefauver High School circa 1964.

David Kaestle, Gross's closest friend from Pratt, was a big, mustachioed man who joined the art department in October 1971. As Gross's chief lieutenant, he was completely in tune with the art director's approach to visual humor. Precision and accuracy were the order of the day. He had art directed O'Donoghue and O'Rourke's Encyclopedia project and was assigned to handle the Yearbook as well.

Doug, Kaestle, and O'Rourke took over Columbia Prep for nine weeks, working from 3 to 6 P.M. every school day. Assigned to make the trains run on time, O'Rourke carried a clipboard enumerating everything that had to be done. Kaestle arrived early and tried to keep everything ahead of schedule by prelighting rooms while making sure that kids were dressed in period clothes with appropriate hairstyles, and coordinating who needed to be in each shot. The undertaking was a logistical nightmare.

Doug's role was to be a genius. It was a job that he took on with great energy and to astounding effect. Kaestle recalls prelighting the language lab, in anticipation of Doug's arrival. With nine kids seated in their stalls, Doug arrived and told them a funny French phrase that would make their mouths contort identically to convey that they were stumbling through a foreign language. Then he turned to their headsets. Doug approached each kid and, keeping their yearbook personae in mind, arranged the headsets in a humorous manner consistent with the character they were playing. The entire process took less than a few minutes. Kaestle was astounded.

"He just materialized and did it," Kaestle said. "He had the spastic kid. The wiseass kid. And there are three to four absolutely funny jokes built into how they wear headphones. There aren't people that can do that. And he was doing that constantly on that project. He would take a situation that wasn't inherently funny, think about it for fifteen seconds, and make it funny."

Though he had always respected Doug's talent, Kaestle came to see the depth of his gift. Not only could Doug write enormously entertaining humor that worked on several levels, but he could also visualize how that humor should play out in photographs and layouts. In this area he surpassed every other editor, including O'Donoghue, who was legendary for specificity regarding the visual elements of each piece he wrote.

O'Rourke was the perfect balance to Doug's free-form approach. Thinking everything out in advance, he was anything but seat-of-the-pants. Arriving each day with a firm plan, O'Rourke created enough order that Doug's direction could be built into the process without becoming disruptive.

"If I had done the whole thing it would have been too mechanical," O'Rourke says. "If Doug had done it, things would have been too messy. We came together fortuitously."

The working relationship was remarkably effective, and O'Rourke drove the train with tremendous efficiency and understanding of his collaborator. His drive to succeed and dedication to both Doug and the magazine took him to great lengths. One Sunday afternoon, when Len Mogel was riding his bicycle through the Village, he found O'Rourke desperately wandering the streets in search of Doug, who was supposed to be working.

* * *

With the profit from *Lemmings*, Matty planned to fund another project near and dear to O'Donoghue's heart—the *National Lampoon Radio Hour*. A studio was built on the eleventh floor of 635 Madison and designed according to O'Donoghue's specifications.

"The Radio Ranch" featured cactus-shaped furniture, desert murals, and a hallway filled with blown-up pictures of contributors dressed as old-time radio personalities, all in tribute to O'Donoghue's great affection for the medium's golden age in the 1930s and '40s. Due to budget constraints, it would never be completed as O'Donoghue envisioned.

Like the Encyclopedia, O'Donoghue took to the project with grand plans and a desire for exacting detail. Attempting to create structure at a place where structure was at best only an illusion, he devised a schedule and sent out the following memo: "All material (save music) must be in at least one month before a theme's air date. This is an absolute deadline and . . . cannot be changed."

O'Donoghue, though, had no idea just what an undertaking the show would be. With Tischler, with whom he had worked on *Radio Dinner*, as his chief engineer, the creation of the radio show would take up all of O'Donoghue's time. The studio became not just his workplace, but on many nights his bedroom, as the two men stayed until the wee hours trying to master precise sounds— like a screen door in the American South circa 1930 and similar aural images.

What no one had taken into account was that O'Donoghue really only had one coproduced album under his belt and a perfectionist's temperament. The combination would play havoc with his new obsession.

Only Tischler truly knew what he was doing and served as the one person who understood how to translate O'Donoghue's vision into a weekly hourlong show.

Janis Hirsch and Judy Belushi were assigned to help get things in order. Neither had radio experience.

"We were making it up as we went along," Hirsch recalls. "Bob Michaelson [who syndicated the show] asked if we wanted to syndicate. He literally showed me a book that explained how it worked and we called stations and said, 'Do you want the show?' It was that haphazard."

O'Donoghue dubbed Hirsch "Wobbles the Duck" because of her crutches. As with Chase's jibes, she didn't mind.

O'Donoghue's management style provided creative energy that could be transferred into the show, but also grated on many nerves.

Polly Bier, who later married Bruce McCall, was brought in to run the *Radio Hour* offices. She enjoyed O'Donoghue, but understood the parameters of working for The Presence.

"Michael was the giant genius behind the show. He was this wonderful, crazy, very intense, very compulsive guy," Bier says. "He was very clear about what was funny and what wasn't funny. He thought he was the arbiter of funny. You couldn't argue with him about what was funny. 'Why would I care what you think?' [was his attitude]."

Yet O'Donoghue could be warm and was entertaining to work with, even when enraged.

One evening, Trow and O'Donoghue began to have an argument about the show (the subject of which no one can recall) and they started hurling everything that wasn't nailed down at each other.

"Judy [Belushi] and I were in the office together and they were throwing furniture," Hirsch recalls, "[and] these two effete, scholarly men with great vocabularies were throwing chairs and filing cabinets. I never knew what all of the feuds were about—I'd just come in one day and pictures [of *National Lampoon* contributors] would be ripped in half."

It was not a place for the weak of heart, as Bier learned one day when O'Donoghue commented that she looked "like Gloria Steinem—if she ate a lot of cheesecake." Such was the price of his company.

O'Donoghue had a gurulike quality that convinced everyone that he was brilliant and that it might rub off on them if they stuck around and did what he said. Moreover, he was often uncharacteristically kind to Bier and others. The combination was enough to engender a great deal of loyalty.

Before long, the *Radio Hour* offices became a place for Doug, McConnachie, and other Lampoon writers who weren't on the Hendra team (or whatever was left of it) to congregate and contribute. Amazingly, they perceived the place to be far less contentious than the editorial offices downstairs.

* * *

While working with O'Rourke on the Yearbook, Doug met Emily Prager, the daughter of a well-known Manhattan academic and author. They quickly became a couple.

A few years younger than Doug, Prager was an attractive brunette who was working as a soap-opera actress when she came upon a copy of *National Lampoon* while sitting in the makeup chair.

"I want to know these people," she thought. "I want to work there."

Her boyfriend knew Anil Khosla, which led Prager to call Doug, who invited her out to dinner as an audition for the *National Lampoon Radio Hour*.

"We went to dinner," Prager laughs. "That was the audition!"

Prager found Doug extremely handsome and very, very nervous, completely uncomfortable in his own body. This sense continued throughout their relationship. Doug seemed incredibly driven to succeed but unable to take in that success, or much of anything else.

"Once in a million years he was comfortable," she says. "It was always like 'Are we having fun yet?'"

During the next two years the pair would spend their time "making jokes, having sex, and having a good time." Doug loved to dress up and go dancing, or hear Bobby Short play piano. "He was entranced by the high life," Prager recalls. While visiting the apartment of Chris Hart's mother, Kitty Carlisle (Moss Hart's widow by that time), Doug's face seemed to say, "This is it!"

Prager became a part of his work life, having dinner with Meyerowitz to discuss a piece on dinosaurs that hadn't survived (The Dodosaurs) or hanging out with O'Rourke to come up with jokes for the Yearbook. Other times, Doug would look up the names and addresses of New York–based artists and writers he admired, seeking out their company and insight. One night the two attended a dinner for Monty Python, an opportunity for Doug to meet the humorists he so admired.

Doug Kenney, Prager found, was a man who was deeply respectful of talent and was generous both financially and with his ability to create opportunities for those he believed in. And though disorganized and irresponsible, he became totally focused when he worked.

Doug was keenly aware of writing for mass appeal while maintaining high standards.

"I'll never forget one time with Doug. I made a joke and he said, 'Jesus, that's terrible,'" Prager told a reporter. "And I said, 'I didn't realize this was a business.' I just make jokes for the fun of it. I forgot it is a business."

Yet when Doug Kenney wasn't writing, dancing, meeting talented people, or having sex, he seemed to be a man who couldn't maintain control over his internal state. Doug, she found, was complex, often dropping into deep depressions, from which he would emerge with great energy.

During the relationship, Doug expressed profound regret over the failure of his marriage. He hadn't liked being married, he told Prager, but had behaved badly and was guilty about what he'd done to Alex.

"He felt responsible for the failure of the marriage," Prager says. "He called himself a dumb blond."

Moreover, Doug constantly examined the ins and outs of everything happening around and within him, never quite sure of how he felt or should feel. Everything was questioned. It wasn't ambivalence, Prager believes, it was an inability to hold his moods steady in any consistent manner.

"He was born with a big brain and sensitivity to everything," Prager says. "But he was unable to keep it steady. He could be thrown off. But the things he really cared about, you couldn't throw him off."

* * *

The *National Lampoon Radio Hour* debuted on a few hundred stations on November 17, 1973, with the national 7-Up Bottlers as sponsor. Billed as a combination of skits, blackouts, and other routines that would call to mind old-time radio comedy, the opening announcer told listeners they were in store for "sixty minutes chockfull of mirth, merriment, and racial slurs," adding, "it will be more fun than feeding Julie Eisenhower a puppy biscuit."

"Basically," Tischler says, "our assignment was to do whatever the hell we wanted to do. [We] promised Matty they'd be good."

The initial shows were astounding. O'Donoghue did a piece in which he promised an Ed Sullivan impersonation. The hitch was that he would be doing Sullivan with nine-inch needles being driven into his eyes, followed by a series of hideous screams that went on and on. McConnachie, Trow, Beatts, and O'Donoghue conceived a piece about a nonexistent gilded age in Manhattan, when people played polo on Clydesdales through the Palm Court and out the south entrance of Central Park, while every taxi was inexplicably equipped with butter.

"Butter in taxicabs, oh, yes, an odd touch but nice to know it was there."

One early show headed into a commercial break with Doug announcing, "The National Lampoon Radio Hour will be back with a word from insincere Nazis who are just after your parents' money."

Soon the show would be heard on six hundred stations.

In December, O'Donoghue and the show outdid themselves with a "Special Impeachment Day Spectacular." Utilizing several veteran radio actors (courtesy of Tischler), old records, tapes, and various National Lampoon talents, the show included a Pat Nixon–led tour of the White House where she points out the hidden microphones; commentary from a Barbara Walters sound-alike; a special edition of Sesame Street in which the math lesson explains the subtraction principles at work when eliminating two secret tapes from nine; a cast of 500 "loyal but clumsy Cubans"; Henry's "Mission Impeachable"; a soap opera based on "Mrs. Agnew's Diary"; and a swearing-out ceremony led by a wrathful Reverend Billy Graham—all looking back sorrowfully at how Nixon's impending demise could "mean an end to vicious and accurate satire as we have come to know it."

It was brilliant radio humor of the first order, whose creator would implode after only thirteen shows.

* * *

By the close of business in 1973, *National Lampoon* had an average circulation of nearly 800,000 and pretax profits approaching $2 million, while the *Radio Hour*, *Lemmings*, and the Encyclopedia were taking 21st Century to places never believed possible. Matty had a burgeoning Motown of comedy on his hands and a humor empire within his grasp.

Late in the year he visited Graham Loving, who had taken him public a few years earlier and promised financial support at the buyout date. If 1974 looked anything like 1973, Matty would be on the hook for roughly $5 million when the deal came due. The company's cash assets were in the neighborhood of $2,500,000, leaving him 50 percent short of what would be owed.

Given the company's financial state and the current national buzz surrounding its flagship magazine, Loving assured Matty that financing was "a lock."

Matty was somewhat reassured. He had a growing, phenomenally successful enterprise on his hands that was hitting line-drive home runs nearly every time it came to bat. What could go wrong?

Starting with the office, he might have been able to intuit that there were problems. Matty had mostly kept his hands out of editorial. He supported Doug, Henry, and the staff in their legal battles and didn't freak out when Heineken and Superscope bailed. Matty let the boys do what they wanted with minimal interference.

As a manager, however, Matty was not particularly attuned to the impact of his chosen role upon his unique group of employees. He truly viewed the writers as his "boys." With Doug, he had forged a close, paternal relationship. Doug was happy to glom on to anyone offering a congenial and warm child–parent relationship and had great affection for Matty and his family, often coming over for what Michael Simmons recalls as "Doug Nights," which consisted of hanging out, eating dinner, watching movies, and listening to records in the kids' rooms.

Matty had also developed a close friendship with O'Donoghue. The two men respected each other, and Matty put up with a great deal from his explosive contributor—probably much more than most publishers this side of Jann Wenner and Hunter Thompson.

Matty's goodwill relationships with Doug and O'Donoghue thus created the blueprint for how he dealt with others. He admired Henry's work ethic and high standards, but they weren't close. No matter, Matty imagined, it's just not Henry's style. He was wrong about this, as somewhere beneath his polite, hard-working exterior, Henry was burning up. He just hadn't told anybody, perhaps least of all himself.

Matty was also wrong about applying this unique publisher–contributor relationship to people such as Hendra, McConnachie, Kelly, and Beatts. The cynicism that made them humorists was also completely resistant to warm relationships with authority figures, particularly with those who were so dissimilar from them. Matty, Beatts thought, seemed like he was a thousand years old. Being considered their boss's children did not sit well, nor did Matty's growing self-image as a media mogul and his style of handling financial arrangements.

"I've never seen this kind of father–son, love–hate relationship in publishing. Matty was a father figure," Gross said. "He thought of them as his sons. He was a nurturing guy. O'Donoghue would beg for salary. [Matty] held it over our heads like a father. He doled it out. If people got in trouble he gave personal loans. If you were cynical, you'd call it Machiavellian—but I don't think it was. He could never understand why they were pissed at him. 'I'd do anything for these kids.'"

By the end of 1973, Matty was having fun; with the magazine expanding into show business, he was getting respect around Manhattan and was recognized around town as the publisher of *National Lampoon*. He believed that some credit was also due to him inside the walls of 635 Madison, which caused problems.

"Matty somehow managed to make it seem as though he thought this all up," Cerf says. "That's probably OK, but not with this crowd."

Yet as the boss, he would tell one reporter, "The only semblance of order comes in [my office]." No matter how devoutly he wished for this to be the case, it was not so. *National Lampoon* was a madhouse, and he was the lightning rod for much anger from the staff.

He was playing the role of a lifetime and living a dream. A man who thrived on chaos, he was able to maintain a sense of authority amid the insanity. Yet he was doing it with a staff ill suited to give him even an ounce of respect.

In editorial matters, Matty was continually trying to save money—less expensive paper, two-color spreads instead of four, cheaper rates on everything he could negotiate. Cutting costs was a skill at which he excelled. He also could explain very quickly why you were overpaid. Frugality was part of his nature, an inherent part of his experience as a driven businessman who had clawed his way up from poverty to owning a basketball team. Cutting corners was not uncommon in the world of magazine publishing, where profit margins could never approximate those accrued in television or film.

Doug, Henry, and Gross worked around this. They had the authority and self-possession to do so, putting out the magazine that they wanted while fighting for the rights and fair pay of their contributors. When speaking with writers, Doug would often dismiss Matty's suggestions about editorial, particularly those aimed at not offending advertisers, and simply say, "Bullshit, bullshit. This is our magazine." Henry stood in between and negotiated. O'Donoghue had enormous gravitas, courtesy of his talent, tantrums, and special relationship with Matty. Sussman played by the rules because he was older and needed the money. Others, though, didn't follow suit, particularly when it came to their financial well-being.

"I remember [Matty] saying to me, 'How come you need money, I just gave your boyfriend $1,000?'" Beatts says. "'Yeah' [she responded], 'he promised to take me out to dinner and buy me roses. But who's gonna pay the rent?'"

The process of getting paid by 21st Century was laborious. Needing each check to be countersigned by Henry or Doug as well as by Matty, Beatts would leave notes for Henry, begging him to expedite the process. After it was signed by editorial, she would march the check to Matty and then on to the accounting office—where the bookkeeper always seemed to be in the hospital with a broken arm or wrist.

"I think there was a low-level rumble at all times," Chris Miller says.

* * *

Whatever his faults, Matty served as a convenient scapegoat for an editorial staff that was beginning to experience serious problems of its own.

The atmosphere at 635 Madison was becoming a bastion of what O'Rourke calls "heterosexual bitchiness." With so many sharp, angry young men working under pressure and in competition with one another, the cracks were beginning to show.

"You can't have a bunch of people with that sensibility in one place at one time," O'Rourke says.

There can only be one clown in each classroom. Assembled at *National Lampoon* were the best class clowns that both America and Canada had to offer. After three years of creative bliss, they were beginning to behave like a sack of cats.

After O'Donoghue and Hendra's various travails, the staff had become factionalized. And now, like their own generation, they were moving even farther apart, taking sides on everything, tearing into colleagues in public and behind one another's backs.

"People would be mad at you if you talked to others," Cerf remembers. "It was impossible to stay out of the feuds."

O'Donoghue's diva act was beginning to wear thin. Deep down he may have respected his colleagues, but even close friends were beginning to feel the sting in a new way. Chris Cerf, who was working on *Sesame Street*, was often the subject of snide commentary in which O'Donoghue insinuated that he'd sold out. Years later, when working at *Saturday Night Live*, O'Donoghue refused to write sketches for the Muppets. "I don't write for felt," he would say.

Others simply found him to be kind of a jerk. Miller avoided O'Donoghue at all costs.

"Guys like O'Donoghue were savagely marking their territory. He was this perennially angry guy," Miller says. "I couldn't have been more different from Michael. To be angry in public was a total breech of decorum for me. Michael lived for that."

Further complicating matters was O'Donoghue's relationship with Beatts, who had become the magazine's self-appointed grande dame and wasn't afraid to wield the power that accrued to her.

"She was very harsh about other people," Bruce McCall says. "[She was] a very tough cookie, [with] not all that much love for the rest of the world. But capable of being very funny."

Though not always around, Trow was capable of ruffling feathers on his visits to the office in the name of both humor and spite, once commenting on the wide 1970s necktie of an ad salesman, "Some say it's a necktie, while others think it's a board game."

"I was always afraid of [Trow]," McCall says. "[He was] the worst kind of Harvard snob asshole. He thought I was some kind of bug."

Kelly, now an integral part of the *National Lampoon* fabric, was either genetically or temperamentally compelled to take others apart for sport.

"He was dangerous. I absolutely adored him," Louise Gikow says. "But you didn't want to leave the room because you knew he'd be talking about you. He's so smart that he could completely rip people apart and was likely to do that at some point." With Kelly, that was a fact of life. Everyone knew how he was and his comments were out in the open, even if they were said behind your back. Hendra was another matter.

"You knew where you stood with Sean," Gikow says. "With Tony it was more shock and surprise. If Tony was going to get you, it was more stealth."

Hendra had major credibility problems. Though more mature than the rest and a polite, charming companion, he was now viewed warily by the others, who feared they might become his next victim.

Henry stayed above the fray. McConnachie was simply too obtuse to get involved in a destructive manner. Doug joined in, but mostly for sport.

The interoffice dynamic was underscored by the background they all shared as humorists, with each contributor bringing his own sadness and complicated life to the party.

Kelly and Hendra were forever tangling with their Catholicism, difficult marriages, and children. O'Donoghue and Beatts were frequently angry and bitter about something. Doug had the divorce, Henry his untapped rage, and what might have been happening inside McConnachie was anybody's guess.

"I think a lot of these guys were the smartest guys in their class and weren't the most popular. Now they were doing this extraordinary thing," Gikow says. "But it never makes up for the reason you were doing it. You never got paid back."

It was a divisive brew.

* * *

During 1973, Matty was approached by building management about renaming 635 Madison "The *National Lampoon* Building." Fearing an endless string of pranksters at their doorstep, he opted for calling it the "21st Century Communications Building."

Playing on this theme, the December 1973 Self-Indulgence issue included artist Alan Rose's depiction of the *National Lampoon* Building, which would tower over the Manhattan skyline (taller than the Eiffel Tower, Empire State Building, and Great Pyramid of Cheops), complete with blimp docks, botanical gardens, airport, national forest, and the Kenney Towers—a federally subsidized high-income housing project.

That month, McConnachie debuted "Tell Debby," an advice column containing letters from "a worried father" or "upset mother" telling of various domestic tragedies that received responses ranging from "oh, how awful" to "that's quite tragic," only veering from this formula to chide one writer who uses "crap" in her letter: "Don't you ever use that ugly word when you 'Tell Debby' something! Debby does not like vulgar expressions. None the less, I do sympathize with your unpleasant situation, but it never has been, nor will it ever be, an excuse for using coarse language."

The height of Self-Indulgence was "humor's official teen fan mag" called "PoonBeat," whose headlines roar, "The Night Michael O'Donoghue Broke My Heart, My Cloisonne Vase, Somebody's Pelvis and Both My Legs"; "You Can Have Sean Kelly's Next Baby"; "Dougie and PJ Fun Fux"; and "Where to Kiss Chris Miller."

Inside, readers can "find out who isn't talking to me this week" by Hendra; discover "which editor's girlfriend pisses me off the most," by Kelly; view a seductive, autographed photo layout of O'Donoghue, Henry, Doug, and Gross; and read a piece in which female staffers answer the question, "If I could fuck any editor in the world it would be . . . "

The editors further parody themselves in "Our Sunday Comics" where Henry becomes "Hank Beard" à la Dick Tracy; McConnachie is sent up as a modern-day Dagwood Bumstead; O'Rourke is the hero of "PJ and the Pirates"; and Beatts is "Little Beattsy" who continually tries to break into the *National Lampoon* boys clubhouse, where childhood versions of the editors toss around ideas like "naked women served up like food," and "deadly dump trucks of World War II."

Doug's contribution is a Ripley's-style series of panels that depict the sign welcoming people to beautiful Chagrin Falls, tell the potentially true 1953 story of "The Frog That Wouldn't Die" (tied to a bike and dragged two miles to Tony's house), and credit the founding editor with the World's Speed Record for writing this parody piece in four minutes and forty seconds.

Under a cartoon of Doug at the typewriter it reads, "Douglas C. Kenney (1946–197?).

8

Guns and Sandwiches

66 It is you who remains 'President of the Class of '64' in our hearts. You who might as well have said, 'Ich bein ine Kefauver Senior.' 99

—From the dedication to John F. Kennedy in the
National Lampoon 1964 High School Yearbook *parody*

The following things happened in 1974: newspaper heiress Patricia Hearst was kidnapped by the Symbionese Liberation Army; Barbra Streisand's "The Way We Were" was the top pop single; gasoline shortages crippled the nation; Watergate Judge John Sirica's grand jury handed down indictments against a number of Nixon aides; a streaker ran through the Hawaiian legislature; *The Sting* won best picture at the Academy Awards; Hank Aaron surpassed Babe Ruth as baseball's all-time home-run king; the House Judiciary Committee passed three articles of impeachment pertaining to

Nixon, causing the president to resign; the Ramones debuted at New York's CBGB, launching the punk rock movement; and Gerald Ford became the 38th president of the United States.

* * *

A new Henry Beard was beginning to emerge. Though his mother still dropped off his laundry at the office in a big purple Bergdorf Goodman bag, Henry was a man in his late twenties who suddenly seemed interested in life outside the magazine, in things like clothing, women, and socializing.

A few years earlier, Henry had visited Sean Kelly at a rural Quebec vacation home. There, Kelly's wife saw Henry walking around, dressed down only a tad from his usual turtleneck uniform, and commented, "It's Holden Caulfield."

That day, Henry lay in the grass, drunk, staring at the overhead power lines. Silent for a while, he told Kelly that a properly placed charge could black out the whole East Coast. It was just how he thought.

"Henry's politics were always nonexistent," Kelly says. "He always liked to think of how you could do the most damage to whatever it was."

Henry was a man trapped within the constraints of his upbringing. Generally quiet and reserved, he became verbally, but never physically, pugilistic when he drank. *National Lampoon* photographer Pedar Ness remembers a soused Henry sitting alone at the kitchen table of P. J. O'Rourke's Greenwich Village apartment, repeating over and over to himself, "I showed them. I showed them." When asked what he was talking about, Henry said that his entire family had attended Yale, while he threw caution to the wind by enrolling at Harvard. As rebellions go, Ness thought, this was a fairly small one.

Though raised in New York, Henry had hardly experienced the Bohemian nightlife of Greenwich Village until Kelly took him to see Kris Kristofferson at the Bitter End. For all of his education and sophistication, he lacked a worldliness possessed by his comrades.

Then, in late 1973, Henry grew his hair beyond the close-cropped, prep-school cut he had long favored. Suddenly it dangled dangerously over his ears and near the neckline. Henry's taste in booze now tilted toward high-end whiskey, replacing the endless stream of cheap beer, the empties of which filled his bathtub. The Beard lexicon also grew saltier. Words like *fuck* and *shit* regularly emerged from behind the pipe. The oatmeal-colored turtlenecks remained a staple, but there seemed to be a move toward less somber dress—perhaps even colors. Moreover, he found a girl.

In 1974, Henry Beard met Gwyneth Cravens, an editor at *Harper's*, at a gathering for young New Yorkers in the publishing business. Cravens and Beard realized that they'd both recently read John McPhee's *The Curve of Binding Energy* and engaged in a lengthy conversation about the construction of atom bombs.

Up until this point, one could say that Henry's greatest love affairs had been with the written word and *National Lampoon*. Despite having had an artist girlfriend for a time, the magazine, Doug, Matty, and the staff served as his demanding spouse—to whom he dedicated more than ninety hours a week. This was about to change. He would continue to put in the hours, but his heart lay elsewhere.

One friend recalls that in spring 1974, "He came and confessed to me with this loopy grin on his face: 'I'm in love.'"

The divorced Cravens had a young daughter whom Henry adored. She and Gwyneth provided him with instant normality and a real life.

Hendra calls it "The Greening of Beard": the emergence of a real human from the reclusive humor machine that spent endless days and nights pounding out parody on a typewriter with no "E" key.

Free from what ailed at least part of him, Henry became a different man. Visiting Hendra's rural New Jersey home in summer 1974, he swam naked and indulged his continuing love for destruction and explosions that harkened back to the pool ball stuck in the Castle's rafters. Henry typically would show up at the home he rented on Hendra's property with two bottles of Mount Gay Rum, then borrow Hendra's shotgun, which he often discharged into the trees covering the peaceful countryside.

In 1974, Henry was intent on catching trout from a stream that ran through Hendra's land. Having little success, he hooked two copper tubes to an outlet and placed them roughly ten feet apart in the stream to create a force field that would kill the fish. When that didn't work, he placed the tubes closer together, again unable to impact the trout population in the slightest. Puzzled, he connected the tubes to Hendra's fuse box, hoping to pump one hundred amps into the stream.

"What about the people downstream?" Hendra asked.

"All Republicans," Henry replied.

Upstream, Henry said, were mostly small animals that would be unaffected as the current wouldn't flow in that direction.

With that, Hendra pulled the switch on the fuse box. No dead fish came to the surface.

"I'm going to put my foot in," Henry said. "See if I feel anything."

Rightfully fearing that his friend would get fried, Hendra shouted, "Are you insane? Think of the magazine."

"Fuck the magazine," Henry responded, putting his foot in the water and realizing that his force field was completely nonexistent.

Puzzled, Henry asked Hendra if he had any dynamite. Hendra provided a shotgun, which Henry stuck in the water and discharged several times. Dead and unconscious trout exploded to the surface. Flush with success, Henry could rest easily and return to his bottle.

In years past, *National Lampoon* editors would think, "Christmas is coming. Somebody should invite Henry." Now, explosives aside, the tightly wound Henry was coming out of himself and had a place to go during the holidays.

Exhausted from negotiating with Matty over budgets and salaries, while playing older brother to a bunch of bratty wiseacres, his priorities were beginning to shift. The inward transformation was subtle, but the *National Lampoon* would no longer be his consuming passion.

* * *

Doug had far less reason to be exhausted. But, though exhilarated by working on the Yearbook, he was also showing signs of wear. Possibly speaking for much of the staff, he told a reporter, "The first year was fun. Twelve issues, great. The second year, twelve more issues, that's OK. But then the third year, guess what? Twelve more issues. Four specials, paperbacks and college tours. Unmentionable places, unspeakable hosts. I'm old. I thought I could make it three years the first time out. I made it two and a half."

Against this backdrop, O'Donoghue was about to make his spectacular exit. As was Michael Gross.

* * *

Among his many contributions to the *National Lampoon*, Gross had created the "Funny Pages," a section in the back of the magazine that featured the "Nuts" by Gahan Wilson, which took on the scary world of childhood with morose glee; the soon-to-be-deceased (asphyxiated in an act of autoeroticism) Vaughn Bodé's "Cheech Wizard"; Rodrigues's Siamese twin Aesop Brothers; the work of Shary Flenniken, Bobby London, M. K. Brown; and the highly unlikely stick-figure drawings of Ed Subitzky.

The daughter of an admiral, Shary Flenniken grew up in Seattle. After taking commercial art classes at a school where the best graduates designed *Yellow Pages* ads, Flenniken set off to join the counterculture and helped put out a daily publication (living for eleven days, without bathing, in a geodesic dome) at Oregon's Sky River Rock Festival, where she met Dan O'Neill, the Svengali-like L. Ron Hubbard of the San Francisco–based Underground Comix group The Air Pirates. Moving to the Bay Area, Flenniken shacked up in the old building that housed O'Neill's group and tried to make a name for herself as the lone female in an intensely macho environment where art was created day and night, then criticized intensely by one and all.

One fellow Air Pirate was Bobby London, a Jewish kid from suburban Queens who taught himself to illustrate and studied the work of Laurel and Hardy, Buster Keaton, and the Marx Brothers, frame by frame.

After dropping out of college, London made his way to San Francisco, where he joined the Air Pirates and created Dirty Duck, a cigar-smoking, sexually active, Donald Duck look-alike that became a raging success. It also earned him a multimillion-dollar lawsuit from Disney.

Inside the Air Pirate studio, London was berated for having sold out. The self-published cartoonists, led by O'Neill, gave him endless grief.

"I was typed as being an impressionist," London says. "Not like Monet, but like Frank Gorshin."

Flenniken and London became an item and soon entered into a tumultuous marriage. In 1972, Michel Choquette showed up on their doorstep soliciting work for *The Someday Funnies*, his never-completed book of cartoons and artwork by famous people. As a teenager, London had seen the Times Square Two open for Jefferson Airplane at the Café Au Go Go and so agreed to do the book. Choquette told the couple that if they were ever in New York, he would introduce them to Doug and Henry.

As the door closed, London and Flenniken began planning a trip east. Shortly thereafter, Dirty Duck and Flenniken's "Trots and Bonnie" became regulars in the "Funny Pages."

"Trots and Bonnie" follows a young, innocent, somewhat pre-pubescent girl (based on Flenniken) through the trials and tribulations of childhood, emerging sexuality (including masturbation and an odd lesbian encounter with a gym teacher), and just about everything else, all in the company of her loyal dog Trots, who offers sardonic, knowing commentary. It became a "Funny Pages" staple for many years, and even provided masturbation material for some teen readers.

Artist B. Kliban and his then-wife Mary K. (M. K.) Brown—who had grown up in Darien, Connecticut, hoping to marry Ernie Kovacs—were both living in the North Beach section of San Francisco during this time. Spending summers at her family's farm in Canada, Brown developed a love of horses and other animals that would become an important theme in her work, particularly with regard to a western hero named Beans Morocco.

In 1971, after doing some work for Paul Krassner's *Realist* and having a few batches of cartoons published by *Playboy*, Brown discovered the *National Lampoon* and sent her strips to New York. Gross bought them all, including a long-running cartoon entitled "Earl Porker Social Worker." After that, she became a regular. The freedom of working with Gross was tremendous.

One day, Gross called Brown and asked for a five-page color strip. Looking above her desk, she saw a title she'd written: "Snakes in the Bathroom." She repeated the completely unformed idea to the art director, who immediately accepted.

"I don't think they ever edited anything that I did," she says.

Then there was Ed Subitzky, a shy, college math major who lived with his parents until age twenty-seven and looked every bit the part. Inside his nerdy head, however, was the brain of a mad Bohemian. Like his colleagues, Subitzky had subsisted through childhood on *MAD*, racing to the newsstand when each issue came out and imploring the vendor to open the box immediately.

"*MAD* was sanity to me back in the 1950s," he says. "I don't know what would have happened to me if it weren't for *MAD*."

The son of a glazier, Subitzky was both a geek and class clown in his hometown of Mount Vernon, New York. Immediately after graduating from college, he accepted a job writing junk mail and later moved on to the Wonderman Agency, specializing in the decidedly unglamorous world of direct marketing. (Not suited to the life of a starving artist, he would hold onto the job throughout his tenure at *National Lampoon*.)

Wonderman was located two blocks from 635 Madison, and Subitzky frequented a newsstand between the two buildings. One day, he saw several Lampoon editors asking the vendor how the magazine was doing. Too shy to introduce himself, Subitzky walked away sad and jealous, knowing they were making a living at something he longed to do.

Having drawn his whole life, Subitzky took a Manhattan-based workshop in comic art (taught by *National Lampoon* contributor R. O. Blechman) for twelve semesters. One evening, Choquette came in to the class to discuss his book. Assigned to do a piece for the book the previous week, each student handed their cartooning in to Choquette, who liked two of the submissions. One was Subitzky's. After an introduction, he overcame his anxieties and began hanging around at 635 Madison.

The first of his pieces the magazine accepted was April 1972's "Anti-Comics," a crudely drawn strip that showed characters talking to the balloons that usually contained words. Soon the Lampoon was taking nearly everything he submitted, and Subitzky wrote "Don't Reveal the Trick Beginning," a backward piece of detective fiction (with all the sentences in reverse order) for the May 1973 Fraud issue.

Subitzky's closest contacts were Gross and Beard, the latter of whom connected to the socially awkward adman. Everyone around the office seemed nice, though most seemed to suffer from the occupational hazard of being in humor. They never stopped telling jokes.

"Any line you gave them turned into a punch line," Subitzky says. "It was impossible to have a serious conversation."

Subitzky also began doing some of the campus lectures. As his work was considerably stranger than most of the stuff running in an already strange publication, the students were shocked to find that their speaker looked like a mild-mannered actuary, instead of a drug-addled lunatic.

"When people meet me they expect the biggest freak on the face of the earth," he says. "But most think I'm an accountant. They were always disappointed that I didn't live up to the experience of reading my strips."

Like Flenniken, Brown, London, and countless others, he'd found a place for his ideas, a place where they were never edited and always embraced. On one occasion, Subitzky submitted a piece to McConnachie with several lines and weird images crossed out. McConnachie put them back in.

With the "Funny Pages" in place, the magazine was solid from front to back.

* * *

During his tenure, Gross and *National Lampoon* won countless design awards, including the 1974 Columbia School of Journalism Magazine Award.

Gross and Kaestle had been together at the magazine for two and a half years and nearly forty issues, as well as innumerable special publications and projects. But no matter how exciting the atmosphere and their coworkers had been, routine had set in. Neither perceived himself to be a humorist. Rather, they were artists and designers who now had an amazing portfolio built upon one of the most innovatively designed and visually interesting magazines in the country.

At the end of 1974, they left *National Lampoon* to set up their own design firm with another partner, continuing to do special projects for the magazine and hoping to capitalize on the phenomenon they had brought to life. One of Gross's last duties was to hire Peter Kleinman, a twenty-two-year-old *Esquire* staffer, as his replacement.

Receiving word from Gross and Doug that he'd been hired at $20,000, Kleinman gave his two weeks' notice and met with Matty to iron out final details. In this meeting, Kleinman says, Matty informed him that he'd be taken on at a salary of $16,000, which was $2,000 less than he was earning at his previous job. When he told Matty about the salary promises from Gross and Doug, Matty said that the pair weren't "in charge of the budget" and that he'd receive raises commensurate with his performance. Kleinman brought the matter to Doug, who kidded, "We love to get 'em when they're young, before they know about money."

Unable to go back to his old position and intrigued by working at *National Lampoon*, Kleinman took the job at $16,000.

Doug immediately took to Kleinman, while the other editors reserved their judgment, wondering how a twenty-two-year-old would replace the man who'd delivered the magazine from its initial hideous design.

As the magazine was growing at breakneck speed, it seemed a loss that Matty, Henry, and Doug could handle.

***

The loss of Michael O'Donoghue was far more explosive.

The *Radio Show* now included pieces like Trow's Winchellesque "Mr. Chatterbox," McConnachie's bizarre "Public Disservice Messages," Chris Guest's idiotic space hero Flash Bazbo (written by Doug), and various memorable pieces performed by Belushi, including a teenage perfect master named Craig Baker who got in touch with his own personal god by drinking beer with his high school buddies. One *Waiting for Godot* parody has the elusive titular character stuck in traffic and greeted like an old friend when he does actually arrive. McCall frequently contributed "The Camera Club of the Air," which had callers describing their photographs to a panel of experts on the radio.

Once, after midnight and at a loss for material, O'Donoghue called Chevy Chase and asked him to come into the studio, explaining that he was five minutes short of material for an upcoming episode.

"I came in and improvised," Chase says. "'We get a lot of letters at the *Radio Hour* and they're not always nice and some of them say we're not a tight show, we're not a show that's put together tightly—and that sometimes let's say we wing it—this hurt my feelings, Chris Guest's feelings, and Michael's and John's,' and then I'd take a little pause."

This went on for the prescribed five minutes. The show was complete.

But after producing thirteen episodes of the *Radio Hour*, with long nights turning into early mornings, many screaming matches, and the never-ending cold war with Hendra, O'Donoghue was emotionally piqued and beside himself with exhaustion.

The "Impeachment Day Special," combined with Doug's "insincere Nazis who are just after your parents' money" commercial lead-in, had destroyed the relationship with 7-Up, who ended their association with *National Lampoon*. Kelly dubbed them "the Unsponsor." The show was cut to thirty minutes, but O'Donoghue elected not to tell the audience. It just went to commercial and never came back. The second week without a sponsor, O'Donoghue ended the show by addressing complaints that flowed into the office during the interim, informing listeners that the second half hour wasn't being played on certain stations, one of which was claiming that the show had actually switched to a half-hour format.

"Now, I don't know who they think they're kidding—the show is called the *National Lampoon Radio* Hour."

Sadly, he reported, most of the good stuff came in the second half of the show, particularly the really adult humor. This was followed by an admonishment that listeners not let themselves be pushed around by their local station.

The next week Doug followed suit, chiding the "fascist pig station managers," and calling claims that the show only ran for thirty minutes an "outright lie." Enjoying every minute, O'Donoghue and Henry announced that, out of the kindness of *National Lampoon*'s heart, they were donating the second half of the show to the United Council of Churches.

In spring 1974, O'Donoghue was negotiating with Matty for a new contract that would offer significant financial rewards. One night, the two had a friendly dinner and walked for hours discussing O'Donoghue's future. Matty wanted him back at the magazine and suggested bringing in others to assist him on the radio show, over which he would maintain creative control.

On Easter Sunday, Beatts and O'Donoghue visited the *Radio Hour* offices before meeting friends for brunch at the Stanhope Hotel. Beatts found someone else's belongings in her desk, went ballistic, and implored O'Donoghue to call Matty and demand an explanation.

Home watching a ball game on television, Matty was not particularly pleased to receive an irate call from O'Donoghue, who was screaming about some injustice involving an inanimate object that had been done to his girlfriend. Matty suggested they discuss things that week at the office. O'Donoghue refused, insisting they discuss it immediately or he would quit. Matty took him up on his offer. It was Michael O'Donoghue's last day in the employ of *National Lampoon*.

In subsequent weeks, O'Donoghue laid in state at a stylish new apartment he and Beatts had dubbed "The Winter Garden." Lounging in his bed, smoking dope and watching television, he was crushed.

* * *

O'Donoghue's departure was dramatic and ugly. People whispered in the halls, taking sides and wondering about their jobs. No matter what a pain-in-the-ass O'Donoghue could be, he was a friend and, in his own way, something of a leader. Janis Hirsch cut the tension by borrowing a roller-skating chimp named Zippy from a friend.

At 635 Madison, Simmons, Mogel, and several others were having an uncharacteristically somber meeting. Hirsch knocked on the door. Simmons and Mogel turned, looking at Hirsch as if she were insane to interrupt their proceedings.

"Michael's replacement is here," she said, letting Zippy in, where he skated around the office to torrents of laughter.

* * *

The cover of the *National Lampoon 1964 High School Yearbook Parody* shows three teenage cheerleaders, with big Ks (for Kefauver) on their bright white turtleneck sweaters, twirling before a crowd with their golden skirts floating around their waists. The two dark-haired girls in the background are wearing large, red panties. The pig-tailed blond in front is bare-assed. The whole crowd stares in awe. The image had come to Matty Simmons at three A.M.

The rest of the Yearbook was all Doug and O'Rourke.

Ostensibly belonging to Larry Kroger (Kefauver class of 1964), a middle-of-the-road senior too bland to even be classified as a geek or nerd, the Yearbook is more than funny—it is a revealing piece of cultural history.

In his opening letter, Principal Dr. Humphrey C. Cornholt (portrayed by Mogel) implores graduates to become like the "silent doer who makes the cent" and to "bear down hard" upon every task and when asked to pay the price "no matter what the outcome," to "pay it proudly." His handwritten inscription to Kroger reads: "Dear Mr. Kroger, The only true human waste is a waste of time." Cornholt's words are a clue that he, and not a Kefauver student, is "The Mad Crapper," a humorous fecal artist whose work runs throughout the parody.

Nobody needed to tell Doug or O'Rourke how to think and write like a typical high school student. As extraordinary as previous parodies were at re-creating the precise look, feel, and tone of its subject, the Yearbook would stand alone, capturing the crudeness, innocence, shallow thoughts, and inherent conflicts of being a teenager in the American education system. Doug had become so deeply involved in the project that Weidman claims, "He would have used Clearasil if he could."

In a brief message, Assistant Superintendent Durward Chromel tells the Kefauver '64s that they are leaving high school, but entering "Life School," complete with "superiors and supervisors" who will be grading them. "So be glad that you've passed in high school but remember not to flunk your future."

The sheer mediocrity and white middle-class nature of Kefauver runs throughout. The sports teams are horrific. The football team scores only eight points all season, winning one game on a bizarre play where the opposing defender slips on a drinking cup. In the team photo, the school's lone black student, Madison "Zippy" Jones (a newcomer from Nashville Lincoln Roosevelt, who not surprisingly plays every varsity sport and is voted best dancer in the senior class), is shown lining up in a football stance five feet away from the rest of the closely huddled crew. Zippy thanks Kroger for hiding him from classmate Purdy Lee "Psycho" Spackle, a new student from Juvenile Work Farm High. "You are my friend," Zippy writes to Kroger.

Team quarterback Bob "Flinch" Baxter, the school's all-American boy and projected future astronaut, signs Kroger's yearbook: "Glad to see you came out for football again this year. You really gave it a good try. Hey, you know we were laughing with you, not at you. —Bax."

One of Doug's many gifts was that he never forgot a great name. He also had a tremendous ability to create monikers that were completely telling of the person to whom they were assigned. Thus, the Dacron superintendent of schools is Philo M. Doggerty, the sexy Dolores Panatella teaches Romance languages, stern Mara Schweinfleisch handles art, and Edith Girkins, a blowsy divorcée, is the sex ed instructor. The faculty also includes the chain-smoking school nurse Mrs. Edna Krupp and career counselor Hubbard Lunger, while the

Doug in the Gilmour
yearbook circa 1964.
Photo courtesy of Greg Nash

Doug's
inscription to
classmate Greg
Nash. This
worldview would
remain a running
theme for the
rest of Doug's
life. *Photo courtesy
of Greg Nash*

Doug Kenney's Gilmour
Mentor, Brother Ivo Regan.
Photo courtesy of Greg Nash

The Kenney brothers, Dan and Doug, in the 1960s.
Photo courtesy of Sandra Kenney

Doug and girlfriend
Judith Bruce at Harvard.
Photo courtesy of Judith Bruce

The ever-evolving Doug Kenney
at Harvard circa 1964–68.
Photo courtesy of Judith Bruce

Henry Beard hard at work in his office at *National Lampoon* in the early 1970s. *Photo courtesy of Michael Sullivan*

Doug Kenney
hard at work in
the mid-1970s.
*Photo courtesy
of Pedar Ness*

The many moods of a comic
genius circa 1971. *Photos courtesy
of Michael Sullivan*

The wedding of Doug Kenney and Alex Garcia-Mata, summer
1970. (Stephanie Kenney is at far right, and Harvard friend Anil
Khosla is in background wearing a blue blazer.) *Photo courtesy of
Alex Garcia-Mata*

Mary Martello with Cloud Studio's Peter Bramley (center), early 1970s.
Photo courtesy of Michael Sullivan

From left, the legendary Michael O'Donoghue, Michael Sullivan of Cloud Studio, and Emily Prager, mid-1970s.
Photo courtesy of Michael Sullivan

Art Director Michael Gross at the National Lampoon office in early to mid-1970s. *Photo courtesy of Mike Gross*

Henry before the greening
of Beard, early 1970s, in the
National Lampoon offices.
*Photo courtesy of
Michael Sullivan*

. . . and after, in
the mid-1970s.
*Photo courtesy of
Pedar Ness*

Brian McConnachie in his traditional work dress in the *National Lampoon* offices, early 1970s.
Photo courtesy of Brian McConnachie

A woman among men, Anne Beatts, on Martinique during the infamous Hitler shoot in 1972.
Photo courtesy of Michel Choquette

Rob Hoffman and Doug Kenney on vacation in Mexico, mid-1970s. *Photo courtesy of Rob Hoffman*

(From Left): National Lampoon Editors from the mid- to late 1970s: art director Peter Kleinman, Tony Hendra, Peter Kaminsky, Danny Abelson, Sean Kelly, Gerry Sussman, and Ellis Weiner. From a faux–Richard Avedon photo shoot. *Photo courtesy of Chris Callis*

Matty Simmons and P. J. O'Rourke at the *Animal House* premiere, 1978. *Photo courtesy of Pedar Ness*

P. J. O'Rourke on break from a mid-1970s photo shoot. *Photo courtesy of Pedar Ness*

Ellis Weiner (seated) and Matty (far right) hanging at the *National Lampoon* office late on a Friday afternoon, late 1970s. *Photo courtesy of Pedar Ness*

The craziest of them all: Ted Mann on the day he brought a tank of nitrous oxide to an editorial meeting in the late 1970s. *Photo courtesy of Pedar Ness*

Doug "Stork" Kenney, John "Bluto" Belushi, and Chris "Hardbar" Miller on the Eugene, Oregon set of *Animal House*, summer 1977. *Photo courtesy of Chris Miller*

Stork, Bluto, and Hardbar kidding around with Stephen "Flounder" Furst. *Photo courtesy of Chris Miller*

Doug Kenney
at the *Animal
House* premiere
in 1978.
*Photo courtesy
of Pedar Ness*

Tony Hendra (left) and Rick Meyerowitz (right) at the
Animal House premiere. *Photo courtesy of Pedar Ness*

Doug Kenney and Kathryn Walker, late 1970s. *Courtesy of Kathryn Walker*

Hanapepe Lookout, Kauai, Hawaii, the site of Doug Kenney's death.
Photo courtesy of Brian Fujiuchi

intimidating Vernon Wormer runs the athletic department. Wormer (who reappears in *Animal House*, as does Kroger) was a derivation of Vernon Weber, the athletic director at Gilmour with whom Doug was close. At long last, the sanitation crew ("Custodial Engineers") is manned by three bumbling fools in odd hats named Stanislau Dupa, Norton Weevil, and Humboldt C. Cornfrey (portrayed by Mogel, who holds three rolls of toilet paper and sports a fake moustache in the photograph, with the caption reading, Temporary Lavatory Maintenance).

Larry Kroger is a pale, mildly greasy-haired, high school every-man who pines after Tammy Ann "Twinky" Croup, Kefauver's peppiest senior. A smiling blond with a cute bob, she lists her pet peeve as "pesky little brother" and longs for cool guy Bob Baxter. After finally getting up the nerve to ask her to the prom, Kroger is rejected ("to a really swell guy," she writes in Kroger's yearbook. "Sorry about the prom, I really did think I had to wash my hair!"), and instead goes with the chubby Naomi "Eggy" Eggenschwiler, whose accomplishments include Oven Club and participation in the Ohio State Crisco Fry-Off.

The senior class is made up of every conceivable archetype: the rich kid (Woolworth Van Husen III), the crippled girl (Hirsch as Ursula Jean "Wobbles" Wattersky, who is noted as a "big help at rummage sales"), the artistic closeted homosexual (Forrest "Swish" Swisher), the beatnik chick (Faun "Weirdo" Rosenberg, who appears as Faun Leibowitz in *Animal House*), and class ice princess (Amana "Fridge" Peppridge, also recurring in the film as Mandy Peppridge), the spaz (Rufus Leaking), the brawny frowning lesbian (Francine "Half-Track" Paluka, a dominant Purdue-bound athlete and big Paul Hornung fan), and the idiot jock (Bruno "Lurch" Grozniac, who loves to give Indian burns). There's even future success Charles "Chuck" U. Farley and class slut Maria Teresa "Quickie" Spermatozoa, who is listed as Jayvee Tongue-Wrestling Champ!

Included at the back of the Yearbook are Kroger's D+ effort on an English final and his permanent record.

When asked to write an essay agreeing or disagreeing with whether or not *Macbeth* is "not so much the tale of a thane's ambition as it is a lesson in politics," Kroger responds:

That the great William Shakespear's famous play Macbeth (which I may add is one of my personal favorites) is "not so much a tale of a thane's ambition as it is a lesson in politics" is a statement that may be easily agreed or disagreed with. Remarkably enough, the real answer to this question has a great deal to do with how the playwrite might have felt about "ambition" and "politics" himself!

Certainly, as the world's most famous writer, Shakespeare himself must have had some "ambition," but is it the same "ambition" felt by the thane mentioned above? I think not. . . .

While in other fine plays by Shakespeare his view of "politics" is often hard to put your finger on, in Macbeth which I enjoyed reading and rereading it is not.

To prove this, one must support one's findings by citing the specific scenes and quotations the main character in "Macbeth" makes in regard to his own feelings about "ambition" not to mention "politics" . . . scenes and quotations often too numerous to mention in an essay of this type but which will be listed below, time permitting.

The essay rambles on, pointing out that there is little reason to believe Shakespeare was ever involved in politics or ran for office besides Bard of Avon, and includes a paragraph that characterizes Scotland in Macbeth's time as a place known for its "excellent plaid kilts" and "penny pinching misers," who must have been ambitious to accrue so much money.

Though it is straight parody, the Yearbook demonstrates Doug's innate talent for transcending simple one-for-one comedy and re-creating a world filled with people we recognize. Kroger's essay is more than funny; it allows the reader to empathize with its writer because we've all been in his shoes. We all wrote, imagined we wrote, or knew someone who wrote some variation of this rambling, bullshit-filled response to a question about a book we never read, padding it with irrelevant and inconsequential bits of information and restating the teacher's original question over and over in hopes of filling the page and somehow passing.

Kroger's permanent record captures the era with frightening verisimilitude. After learning Kroger's height, weight, birth date, and racial status (with a box for Negro, Mulatto, or Colored, and Acknowledged, yes or no), we find that his last name was changed from Kroggerski and his mother's "real age" is forty-one (under Role Model Deportment, the box next to Cigarettes is checked, but empty are the boxes next to Working Mother, Previous Marriages, Excessive Dress or Makeup, Female Trouble, Miscarriages, Etiquette Difficulties, and other random indicators of good parenting). The value of the Kroger home and various debts, wages, and other private financial data are revealed, along with the fact that Kroger's dad failed to volunteer for combat.

The medical report logs Kroger's vaccinations, while noting that he's seen a doctor for persistent rectal itch, suffers from dandruff, non–socially debilitating acne, and athlete's foot. On the bright side, he's not a mouth breather, bed wetter, poorly coordinated, or guilty of bad posture. Personal Hygiene includes grades for perspiration (excellent), toilet habits, underwear, notebooks, locker (poor), private parts, spittle, and friends. Under Pride in Personal Appearance, we find that Kroger occasionally wears blue denim pants, no socks, odd expressions, tight pants, and that his sideburns have exceeded a half-inch. Though a milquetoast, he's being watched.

It's all there, including analyses from every teacher he's ever had, all noting that he frequently fidgets or talks out of turn, picks at himself, suffers from spontaneous penile arousal, keeps an untidy desk (which causes his fifth-grade teacher to suspect that he "may not be college material"), and has looked at other boys while dressing.

One running theme throughout the Yearbook are the wiseass inscriptions of class clown "Wing-Ding" Weisenheimer, who circles the number on page sixty-nine and makes every juvenile joke imaginable. And of course there is the mysterious identity of the devious campus vandal "The Mad Crapper," likely none other than Dr. Cornholt, demonstrating that even the administrators feel beaten down and restricted by the world of Dacron. It is the seventeen-year-old boy that resides within every adult—as Doug suspected or hoped.

The *National Lampoon 1964 High School Yearbook Parody* sold over one million copies (the single bestselling special issue of any magazine) and was hailed as "the finest example of group writing since the King James Bible" by *Harper's*. Doug and O'Rourke had taken nostalgia to another level, making the American high school experience universal, relevant, and hilarious. In creating the parody, the pair seized on the tremendous force of Doug's coiled tensions.

O'Donoghue's stuff was dark but definitive—whatever he was shredding got it with a razor-sharp knife. The eminently studious Henry mastered direct parody. But Doug was more circumspect. His writing was tight but came at subjects from several angles. Kefauver is a horrific, socially engineered nightmare, where people are typed for life before they've turned twenty. The hopelessly inept administration underscores this mission by encouraging mediocrity and filling a drone's role within American society. The cruelty of teenage America is flushed out into the open and lampooned unmercifully. Yet the man who flitted between thinking he was Waugh and thinking he was a miserable failure—often in the same moment—was able to create fond nostalgia from the very same material, tying together the rituals of high school in an easily relatable package that was both sympathetic and hysterical while it indicted the high school experience and its context. It is the circumspect nature of his writing that give his humor depth and significance in a way that no one else at *National Lampoon* was capable of.

* * *

The Yearbook's "In Memorium" section is dedicated to Howard Lewis Havermeyer, a recently deceased student whom almost no one knew ("just because we did not know him, however, does not mean that he was not a real nice guy"). He often missed school and is best remembered for his frequent coughing.

"He used to smile at people when he wasn't coughing, and he was supposed to be really good at baseball when he wasn't coughing. . . . They say he was even supposed to have been good at touch football, although he was supposed to stay away from dust, and a lot of the girls thought he looked like a Master of Ceremonies."

The picture of Howard Lewis Havermeyer that appears above the memorial is a crew-cutted, handsome, tuxedoed Doug Kenney at Gilmour Academy. Next to the picture, Wing-Ding has written, "What a dipshit!"

* * *

The Yearbook, with its use of nostalgia and the content of its humor, offers insight into Doug's fragile psyche, perhaps more than anything else he ever wrote. The fact that the deaths of John F. Kennedy and the fictional Havermeyer, the horrors of the preceding three years, and the hopelesslessness on the horizon are all fixed here in the same time frame as Doug's own youth feels particularly poignant.

On the surface, the Yearbook seems to echo the *National Lampoon*'s fascination with death, and its ability to make humor out of tragedy and the banality of how people respond to it.

The Class of 1964 History section reads, "Junior year ended on a sad note as popular and handicapped Howie Havermeyer went into the hospital and Senior year started on a sad note as he died. And so did President Kennedy." Three of the historical events of their Kefauver experience pictured in this section are: the 1961 murder of the Freedom Riders in Alabama, the Buddhist monk who burned himself to death in 1962, and Lyndon Johnson's swearing in aboard Air Force One in 1963, as Jackie Kennedy—her husband's blood on her dress—looks on. This was the era of hope witnessing the beginning of a tumultuous and destructive time.

Nineteen sixty-four is recalled as "the best Senior Year for the best Senior Class ever at C. Estes Kefauver Memorial High except for the tragic deaths of Howard Havermeyer and President Kennedy and the car accident after prom."

Nearly every poem in the Leaf and Squib section, written by Sean Kelly, relates to death. The last words of the entire Yearbook are "to die," the concluding words of a poem written by Larry Kroger.

A close read of the Yearbook reveals that the world expects great things from Howard Havermeyer—not unlike Doug's brother Dan. Both are physically handicapped and unable to do things they were "supposed to be really good at."

"[W]ho knows to what dizzy heights he might have risen on the playing field or in the classroom, if Death had not hip-checked him into the boards just as he appeared ready to break alone into the goal?" reads a note about Havermeyer in the "Prism" section of the Yearbook.

That 1964 was also the year of Doug's Gilmour graduation and the year he gave his speech to the student body is no accident. That his nostalgia resides in this era in a country caught between Kennedy's murder and the destruction of an idealized, hopeful world is hardly coincidence either. It was a representation of his polarized inner life.

Beyond the obvious context and comedic value of Doug's nostalgia, it metaphorically expresses a longing for a shared sense of home, commonality, and belonging. By creating nostalgia, he was grappling with everything that had eaten at him since birth. Too smart not to know its meaning but simultaneously unconscious of his intentions, Doug used his humor to conduct an in-depth exploration of the idealized world that he had dreamed of, a world that never truly existed anywhere except in his mind. That is how he made sense of his life. Although the themes of death, destruction, and hope lost are only one layer of the Yearbook, it's really no wonder that Doug and O'Rourke found their work to be just as sad as it was funny.

* * *

The June and July *National Lampoon* issues dealt with Food and Dessert. In one article, Beard, Hendra, and Sussman created a parody of people who subsist entirely on goats and their by-products: goat kraut, goatsup, goat bock beer, and goatmeal cookies, with articles about "the new goat substitutes—sham or shammy?" Sussman also contributed "The Cooking of Provincial New Jersey" which discriminates between Bergen County, where "you will be enjoying a cuisine heavily influenced by powdered foods and mixes, with frozen foods, food helpers and canned foods equally as popular," and Essex County, which "seems to like frozen foods although it boasts a strong following for powdered mixes, food helpers and canned foods"; Meyerowitz drew a *Last Supper* where Christ is left with the check; and Doug's educational comic "The Story of George Washington Carver" tells the politically incorrect tale of how a brilliant man born into slavery discovered the many uses of the peanut.

The piece opens with a newborn Carver in the cradle, spouting scientific terms for peanut ("Leguminosae! Arachis Hypogaea!"), while his mother and an Aunt Jemima–like mammy holding a crucifix cry, "dat chile mus' come from de debbil! H-his th-thumbs . . . d-dey's all green!"

Sold into slavery, Carver eventually joins a traveling carnival where he sells peanuts, feeds the elephants, and runs a shell game. As a traveling salesman, he peddles legumes as a cure-all for emphysema, dysentery, and colds. His fascination with peanuts ultimately frees Carver from the grasp of some Klansmen ("don't throw me into dat peanut patch yonder!") and earns him a professorship.

Then, in his laboratory, Carver runs an experiment that jolts a bushel of peanuts with an electrical current, hoping to provide a more efficient brand of electricity ("ten times as good as dese ole lightbulb! . . . Den comes the hi fi phonopeanut, an' after dat de long-distance, direct-dialin' telepeanut"). Aided by a boy named Goober, Carver watches the peanuts turn black and explode, filling the lab with the "brown gold" of peanut butter, which they try in a sandwich with sauerkraut. Finally Goober asks what the scientist will call his creation. "Why George Washington Carver's EEEEElectrical Peanut Oleo, O'Course!!"

By parodying the type of historical comics used to teach children, Doug's broad, *Amos 'n' Andy*–style humor doesn't come off as racist. Rather, it is funny because it takes on and broadens the attitudes of the genre's creators, imagining, as does the reader, that behind closed doors the white, middle-of-the-road educators would have a hard time envisioning the great black inventor as anything but Stepin Fetchit or Uncle Remus.

The most stunningly original piece in these two issues was the magazine parody called "Guns and Sandwiches," which could have only been created by McConnachie.

McConnachie conceived the piece as the merger of two failing magazines, a gun owner's publication named *Guns and Butter* and another dedicated solely to sandwiches. Both magazines were poorly run, receiving mild letters of complaint from readers about their content. Sitting in his office, McConnachie cracked himself up by holding editorial meetings for each magazine in his mind and imagining how they would meld both titles into one publication.

Kelly, for one, was mystified by the concept, but knew it would work, just as he did later, when McConnachie proposed another magazine parody entitled "Negligent Mother," whose cover shows two moms talking over a fence while a small child lays facedown in a kiddie pool.

Billed as "The Finest in Its Field," the cover of "Guns and Sandwiches" has a woman on the phone by her baby's cradle. Next to her is a checkerboard cloth–covered table on which rest a pistol, some bullets, and a partially eaten BLT.

The letters to the editor section alone is worth the price of admission, with Martin Miller of Duluth, Minnesota, writing, "In your May issue you ran a story on the sandwiches that Charles Whitman brought with him to the University of Texas tower in Houston [from which he famously shot several innocent people with a rifle], but the picture that accompanied the story was not of Charles Whitman, it was of James Whitmore, the television actor. What has he got to do with it?"

The main feature takes the pulse of the St. Louis Police Department and their sandwich preferences. One paragraph reads, "Just as St. Louis has played an important part in the history of this country, sandwiches have played an important part in the lives of St. Louis' citizens. There isn't a person from eight to eighty who is unfamiliar with this famous mealtime treat."

From his office window, McConnachie could see a large financial institution across the street. Frequently, he would examine the beleaguered gray-suited men who emerged and thank the people back on his home planet Mogdar for saving him.

By 1974, however, he began wondering "How long can this last?"

* * *

With O'Donoghue gone, McConnachie and Kelly took over the radio show together for the summer of 1974. When O'Donoghue had been too exhausted to produce one episode during his tenure, Kelly took the laid-back approach, recycling old material, playing cuts from Spike Jones records, and having his small children come to the studio where they complained on air about how much they wanted to go to bed.

After *Lemmings* closed, Matty decided it was time to put up another stage show, this one named *The National Lampoon Show*, with Kelly slated to direct. The cast included Belushi and Guest as well as four new Second City–trained actors: Gilda Radner from Toronto, and Chicago's Brian Doyle-Murray, Harold Ramis, and Joe Flaherty, who'd been brought in by Belushi.

During rehearsals, Doyle-Murray fell in love with Radner, who was by all accounts charming and delightful and evoked this response from numerous male coworkers. Radner, no matter how much she liked Doyle-Murray, did not reciprocate. Heartsick and spending all of his time in the presence of a woman for whom his love went unrequited, Doyle-Murray told Kelly that he couldn't go on and suggested that they bring in his kid brother Bill from Chicago's Second City to replace him.

A few days later, Kelly came into the radio show offices one morning to find what he thought was a homeless man (whom he described as "the most unkempt, fucked-up looking human I'd ever seen") snoring away on the sofa. Hours later he would be introduced to that man as Brian Doyle-Murray's little brother Bill Murray, who had taken an overnight bus from Chicago.

Murray spent much of his first day in New York with Laila Nabulsi, who'd been dating Chris Guest. Together they ran around Manhattan, with Murray manically performing the entire time, directing traffic, collaring strangers, and doing an old routine of his known as "the Honker." Nabulsi barely had time to breathe between laughs.

Born into a large Irish Catholic family in the northern suburbs of Chicago, the Murrays became *National Lampoon* staples, willing to do anything for a buck. Doyle-Murray was a quiet, gifted writer who did terrific voices and characters. Both men worked for the radio show, Murray joined *The National Lampoon Show*, and they were frequently called in for outrageous photo layouts. If you needed them to make out with each other, one staffer recalls, the Murrays would do it so long as they got paid.

Regardless of his older brother's talents, Bill Murray immediately established himself as a force around *National Lampoon*—in both his abilities and his behavior. One time he ran into Matty's office loudly demanding to know why a nominal sum (under $2) had been removed from his paycheck. He was also known for doing "the Honker" all day long in the hallways on Madison. Uncommonly charming when he chose to be, Murray made friends with Kenney, Beard, and much of the staff.

Chevy Chase also became friends with Doug and others at the magazine, but he had bruised many feelings during *Lemmings* with his scathing humor and ability to instantly size up the weak spots of others while satisfying his congenital need to poke at them. Underneath it all, Chase wanted to be liked. He simply went about it in a curious way.

Murray, though, didn't care if you liked him or not.

"He's an incredibly gifted and funny guy, but Bill doesn't want your love," Kelly says. "He just wants to scream, 'THERE'S A LOBSTER.'"

His talent for comedic improvisation was undeniable.

While working on another Lampoon album (Matty had signed a long-term deal with CBS Records) named *Goodbye Pop*, Kelly decided to wing it, and called Murray and Guest into the studio. Running tape, he let the two improvise, which turned into brilliantly funny dialogue between a seedy agent and a goofy FM-radio DJ, which he simply edited down to size for the album. It was hardly the O'Donoghue way.

McConnachie's approach was more ambitious, and in the second show under his direction, Belushi, Doug, Emily Prager, Brian Doyle-Murray, and Harold Ramis performed a musical send-up of *Moby-Dick* entitled *Moby!* Written by McConnachie and Louise Gikow, *Moby!* parodied nearly every style of Broadway musical number, from Sondheim to Gilbert and Sullivan.

The show was created over the course of a week at the radio show studios, where Tischler had placed a long board that served as the ship's deck. Belushi portrayed a depressed Ahab with Doyle-Murray as his archetypal first mate Starbuck, who calls out such nautical nonsense as "I'll have you pin swiggled" and "Do you know what nub spurlies are?" to a young boy named Frankie (played by Prager), whom he is continually attempting to bugger.

With O'Donoghue's departure, a heaviness lifted from the studio. Rules about who could and could not work on the show were gone. The result was more fun than McConnachie had experienced in his working life, and he became enraptured with the process of putting *Moby!* together.

"The more we did it, we fell in love with the process," McConnachie says. "We actually became those people we were mocking."

During the recording of *Moby!*, McConnachie would run to the hallway and fall to the ground laughing uncontrollably at what they were creating in the studio, the high point of which was Belushi's Ahab, mournfully singing a *Porgy and Bess*–style number to himself on deck, believing that the crew has forgotten his birthday.

> I keep us afloat, I keep us on cue.
> I care for the boat, I care for the crew.
> Nobody cares about me, I'm the unhappiest man at sea.
> Today is my birthday, I've turned sixty-three.
> When they're in their berths, they don't dream about me.
> "Ahab?" they'll ask you, "Who's he?"
> I'm the unhappiest man at sea.
> When he bit my leg off, I'm certain Moby knew,
> That in my pants I kept my money.
> Now the mortgage payment on my ship is due.
> When I lose my "ves-sile" to bankers in town,
> I'll sink and I guess I'll most probably drown.
> And then I'll certainly be
> The unhappiest man at sea.

By the end of the summer, Belushi took over the radio show, and McConnachie returned to the magazine.

* * *

On November 11, 1973, the stock market began to slide. Within a year, bad news from Vietnam, the Watergate scandal, and the Arab oil embargo would cause the Dow Jones Industrial Average to dip 45.1 percent, the seventh worst crash in market history. Graham Loving, who'd assured Matty that funding was "a lock," shut down his firm and left Manhattan. Other underwriters were far from eager to provide Matty, or anyone else, with cash to fund their business deals.

In summer 1974, Matty sat down with Beard, Kenney, and Hoffman (who came up from Dallas, where he worked for his father's bottling business) to negotiate the final buyout, scheduled to take place the following spring. Simmons, Mogel, and 21st Century had absolutely no leverage. The deal was on paper, they didn't have the cash, and there wasn't enough stock authorized to use in the payoff. Meanwhile, *National Lampoon* stock was selling at a multiple of roughly two-and-a-half-times earnings and they were on the hook for a buyout at almost ten times that figure.

Matty met with his attorneys. They discussed the possibility of arguing that Kenney and Hoffman had breached the deal by not fulfilling their obligations. After all, Hoffman was gone after less than a year and Doug disappeared once without notice, subsequently taking a yearlong leave. Matty wisely decided against this option, feeling that the financial, personal, and morale-lowering costs of a lawsuit would be too large.

When the five men sat down and Matty described his predicament. Hoffman said, "Sorry. What do you suggest?"

Matty told them 21st Century would hold up its end of the bargain, but wanted to wait until the market recovered and they could secure financing. When Hoffman rejected the proposal, Matty offered a combination of stock, long-term notes, and cash. Again Hoffman said no. Countering with $1 million in earnest money to be paid on the due date and ten years' worth of payments covering the remainder, he was rebuffed even after suggesting a slight increase in the numbers. Tension filled the room.

Hoffman made two suggestions. First, he brought up the idea that the five men could take the company private. In the alternative, he, Henry, and Doug would be glad to take the entire payment in common stock, effectively giving them control of the company. These ideas did not ease the atmosphere.

Matty was aghast at the hardball he believed Hoffman was playing. Henry and Doug hadn't spoken at all. Hoffman most likely knew that Matty would never go in on a deal where he would effectively cede control to the boys, nor did Matty intend to work for them. Angered as he was, however, Matty was over a barrel due to the magazine's success, bad luck with the financial markets, and Hoffman's astute understanding of the deal. Matty offered nonvoting stock. No one was biting.

From Hoffman's perspective, he was doing all that he could to accommodate Matty, but was not going to act against his, Doug's, and Henry's own interests.

"It had become our problem because they couldn't pay us off," Hoffman says.

After hours of offers and rejections, things came to a head. Hoffman, according to Matty, pointed out that if 21st Century was unable to make their scheduled payments in accordance with the contract, default or a bankruptcy would result in the boys taking over *National Lampoon* anyway.

"What happened to 'We'll never hurt you'?" Matty said to Doug.

Quiet throughout the proceedings, Doug stood up and began screaming, "I want my money! I want my money!"

Mogel, a profoundly good-natured man, rose to meet him, barking, "I'm gonna punch you right in the mouth!"

Suddenly, the five men were standing around the table, holding back their friends and trying to prevent violent confrontation. Then, struck by the incongruity of two gentle, sweet-tempered men preparing to square off, they began laughing. Only in the halls of 635 Madison could threats of violence ease the tension.

A deal was hammered out by which 21st Century would pay out $100,000 in 1974, then $3 million in cash the following March 18. Notes totaling roughly $3 million would be paid out over a period of several years.

After a brief recess, Doug apologized to Mogel and Simmons. Hoffman assented to the deal with two provisos. First, the $3 million in debt to be paid out after 1975 should bear interest of 8 percent. Matty agreed. Second, Hoffman wanted an additional $1.5 million added to the buyout price and paid on the March 1975 due date. The total value of the buyout was now $7.5 million.

The meeting adjourned, with Matty flummoxed. He'd agreed to the deal that day with only $1.5 million in cash, leaving him to face the task of finding an additional $3 million in less than one year.

Matty called Warner Communications boss Steve Ross, an old friend with whom he'd done business at Diner's Club and whose company distributed *National Lampoon*. Ross invited Matty to his office and agreed to have Warner lend the $3 million at prime interest rate with the ability to repay the money during a realistic time frame that wouldn't bankrupt 21st Century. The deal could close.

It was a tremendous haul for three college kids who'd entered the business less than five years earlier, all taking the same chance as Matty did, recognizing the possibility that it could fail. Nobody had any idea of how much money they would make. Beard, Kenney, and Hoffman had been betting on a multiple of earnings that didn't exist. But between 1969 and 1974, the same combination of factors that screwed Matty had fallen in their favor. The cultural shifts, the influx of talent, the changes in the publishing industry, and the sudden precipitous decline in the stock market had all worked out perfectly for them.

"We didn't make any mistakes. That was due to luck. The way the market worked out gave us a lot of leverage," Hoffman says. "It could have worked out the opposite way. Nobody had any control over that."

In March 1975, Doug Kenney and Henry Beard became millionaires, with their ultimate payout at roughly $2.8 million apiece. Hoffman walked away with $1.9 million.

Later, Henry told a reporter that he'd forgotten all about the contract, concentrating on the task at hand, knowing that if he succeeded, "some result, not entirely unpleasant, would occur."

Doug put it thus: "Hardly anyone reads contracts. I certainly don't. We lucked into something that I don't even totally understand."

The financial implications of the final agreement were only the start of the fallout from the deal the group had struck five years earlier.

* * *

In August 1974, Doug introduced a new column named "Baba Rum Raisin" in the Isolationism and Tooth Care issue. Poking fun at his generation's search for self-actualization (including Mary Martello, who was off in California with the fourteen-year-old perfect master), he created a Maharishi-like leader, as cynically obsessed with his own gain as he is in pursuing oneness with God.

My Beloved Ones,

Greetings from New York City, my devoted sheep. And I know that I may call you "my sheep" because who else would follow an old wrinkled goat scrotum such as my humble Self and bleat so piteously when they are reminded of their back Baba Rum Raisin Membership Dues! Baaaaah Baba Rum Raisin, they bleat, we have no pennies in our knapsacks. We have no nickels in our overalls. We are but doomed ninnies addicted to costly marijuana jags and Snickers Bars. We deserve to be reincarnated as Henry Kissinger's hemorrhoids. Baaah. . . .

My stopover here until I am beheld in Long Island with Commander Cody and his Lost Planet Airmen (a very popular swing orchestra with you young people, yes?) has been marred by recent events. Once again, through an easily explainable misunderstanding, much bad karma has arisen between your beloved 173-year-old perfect master and the Credit Manager of the Plaza Hotel. A small thing, really, concerning certain signatures on certain Travelers' Checks that miraculously teleported into my possession, but this tiny thorn has plunged Baba Rum Raisin, his guileless Raisinettes, and his Very Talented Road Manager Miss Jill St. John into this yet tinier Sixth Avenue phone booth.

The Baba tells his flock about opening for the Bee Gees at Carnegie Hall, meeting Jill St. John in the dressing room of The Dick Cavett Show (where he encounters Senator Sam Ervin, Jane Fonda, and a fifteen-year-old perfect masturbator who begins to speak, only to find his mouth filled with Baba's "humble sandal which was in need of a lodging place"), and plying her with wine at the Oyster Bar.

Talk turns to the need for money from the Baba's followers, due to uncollected receipts from the Baba Rum Raisin's Death Valley Kohoutek Festival, and threatens them with his brother-in-law's Kohoutek's Kurse of 10,000 Pustules in a clip-out payment form, which he contends is a tantric exercise.

The letter closes with Baba Rum Raisin trying to simultaneously avoid a summons from "the impish minions of the fine Immigration Department and the respected Better Business Bureau" and a crowbar–wielding hotel manager.

* * *

On August 8, 1974, Nixon resigned in a televised address. The following day, he stepped on a helicopter and headed home to California, leaving Gerald Ford as the thirty-eighth president of the United States of America.

It would be hard to find anyone at *National Lampoon* who hadn't voted for George McGovern. But in the back of their minds, Doug, Henry, and the rest knew that Nixon's departure would leave an enormous void. He'd been a treasure, bringing with him a group of would-be civil servants and hangers-on who were unparalleled in their capacity to be parodied. And now they were gone.

* * *

"He was our Huckleberry Finn," Sean Kelly says, regarding the initial attitude toward P. J. O'Rourke at *National Lampoon*. "He was a deeply committed Marxist-Leninist up from Ohio."

The previous year, O'Rourke ascended from hanger-on and occasional contributor to executive editor, due in no small part to his eagerness for handling any job, no matter how grinding or small. Nearly everyone on staff was ambitious, but it was hidden behind their various personalities and cynical attitudes. A cynic of sorts himself, O'Rourke's ambition and the very eagerness that were essential to putting out the Encyclopedia and the Yearbook were not well received by his comrades. No longer was he the little boy from Ohio, nipping at the heels of Kelly, Hendra, and Beard. He'd worked and cajoled his way onto the staff and, rightly or not, some of the editors were suspicious.

Previously, they'd kept O'Rourke in a box. He was green but willing to learn and do shit work. Matty encouraged the staff to find a permanent position for the hard-working kid he so liked. Those like Kelly couldn't imagine what capacity that would be.

O'Rourke had grown personally close to both Doug and O'Donoghue during their work together. Despite viewing him as a junior varsity talent, O'Donoghue appreciated O'Rourke's work on the Encyclopedia and valued what he brought to the magazine.

Being friendly with Matty, however, caused much suspicion among Hendra, Kelly, McConnachie, and others. It was OK for stars like Kenney and O'Donoghue to have good relationships with the publisher, but for anyone without their gravitas, it was a problem.

With the authority of a title, O'Rourke began hounding Kelly, Hendra, and others for articles, and they bristled as their former lackey carried around a clipboard and, according to some, tossed around the term "man management."

Even McConnachie began to feel that O'Rourke was becoming like the outwardly sweet but divisively ambitious title character of the Bette Davis film *All About Eve*. When the crew adjourned for drinks each night, they would often tell O'Rourke that they were going home and then meet at a new place that he didn't know of.

The old Harvard ethos of effortlessness had taken hold. After going out each night after work, the editors would write into the wee hours, or at home in the mornings, trying to give the impression that they pounded out humor without sweating. Hendra believed the office was where he "came not to work." But whatever O'Rourke's faults, they didn't include lack of caring about the magazine or his work. This flew directly in the face of the entire editorial staff and conflicted with their projected attitudes about producing humor. Within the walls of *National Lampoon* such naked demonstration of desire and ambition was an unforgivable sin. Understandably, O'Rourke wanted to be respected and welcomed as one of the team. But he had aligned himself with Matty, who represented the business side, where commercial concerns came before art and humor. And for this O'Rourke was punished with indifference and nonacceptance. It began quietly, but it was clear that he was not one of them and never would be, no matter how much he tried.

* * *

In October 1974, O'Rourke edited his first issue. The theme was Pubescence. Its cover image was a fetching young girl clad in a knit halter top and very short hot pants. Sitting at a soda fountain, she holds a hot fudge sundae in one hand and a cherry in the other.

The issue's most significant piece is by Chris Miller, who pulled an old fraternity short story from his drawer while dealing with writer's block on deadline. It was called "The Night of the Seven Fires."

The Adelphian Lodge of Miller's story ("which was to Dartmouth social life what the Yankees had been to the American League pennant for the last fifteen years") is peopled with characters like Stu the Jew, Pinto (a stand-in for Miller himself), Mumbles, Bag, Mouse, Otter, and Charlie Boing Boing. They travel through a raucous evening of initiation rituals that involve immense liquor consumption and frequent booting, which Miller defines as "recreational vomiting" (not a product of illness, but rather a choice to regurgitate with élan and style). On a frigid evening, the story recounts, the Adelphian pledges trot through the New Hampshire mountains, stopping at campfires where they participate in a veritable booting Olympics.

"[Pinto] remembered power boots and dribble boots; spray boots and gusher boots; beer boots, wine boots, and even a warm-salt-water-with-cigarette-butts boot. He felt that no other pledge could possibly be putting on half the show he was."

The evening ends with Pinto being asked to warm a frozen hot dog in Stu the Jew's ass, after which Stu becomes a legend by booting out a campfire. Hearing of his pledge brother's exploits, a hungover Pinto is crestfallen that his efforts have been trumped.

"I got drenched," remembered [Adelphian Lodge brother] Scotty dreamily. "It knocked three of us down, like one of those water cannons they use in East Germany. It must have gone fifty or sixty feet!"

Much of the issue is driven by sexual material. Subitzky did a "Foto Funnies"–style layout of nude women entitled "Three Pretty Girls Doing Just What You Want So You Can Masturbate." Another photo shows a naked female's backside with a pest strip dangling from the front. A special "Pubescence Section" has comic strips of uniformed schoolgirls stripping in front of the class.

Pubescence sold over a million copies, making it the most successful issue in the magazine's history and further endearing O'Rourke to Matty. The November Civics issue, whose cover showed Gerald Ford clumsily sticking an ice-cream cone on his bald head, sold under 800,000.

Though the magazine had long featured material of a sexual nature and run countless images of nude women, many of the editors felt their work was not demeaning to the fairer sex. True, they didn't understand women very well. Yes, they often viewed them as sex objects, both inside and outside of the office. But they were socially and politically liberal men who understood what they were doing. Somehow they had (or believed they had) managed to be winking with their female counterparts: parodying an obsession with sex while at the same time indulging it. And for the most part, they'd pulled it off.

Long before the Minnie Mouse cover, Matty had believed that sex sold magazines. There is no question that pretty, sometimes naked, girls produce results on the newsstand, especially when they are on the cover. And hadn't Doug and Henry done the same with their *Time* parody? It was not a theory to which Kelly and Hendra subscribed, despite the fact that neither had the slightest aversion to taking his clothes off and joining naked women in a photo spread.

On more than one occasion, Kelly and Matty had the following discussion:

Matty: "You know what sells? Sex!"

Kelly: "Heroin sells too. But we're not in that business either. Anyway, what exactly do you mean by sex?"

Matty: "You know what I mean. Tits!"

Kelly: "If sex is tits, how did you have children?"

It was endless. But the contrast between the sales of Pubescence and Civics was proof enough for Matty that sex/tits did indeed sell magazines and that all of his instincts about P. J. O'Rourke had been right.

Much of the staff believed that Matty was totally disconnected from the magazine's purpose and had no bearing on its success. Matty was "living in a fool's purgatory," someone once said, and many believed it was apropos. Here was a guy they considered a lucky promoter who paid them a marginally decent wage, overworked them terribly, and believed that the success of the magazine was due to his genius, rather than the talents of those who actually did the work.

To complicate matters, Henry and Matty had spoken of huge financial opportunities that would accrue to various editors in the future due to the ongoing success of the magazine. From Henry, there were veiled promises (often made while drunk) of everyone making out when the deal came due. Everyone would get rich, they believed. Matty, for his part, spoke of a royalty pool that would eventually compensate them for their hard work and the phenomenal income the magazine had provided to 21st Century.

That, and a growing mistrust of O'Rourke, hung over the magazine as 1974 came to a close.

* * *

From the day he arrived in New York, John Belushi was a force to be reckoned with at *National Lampoon*. His personality and ability to charm were the stuff of legend. People loved Belushi and he was a natural leader who had easily adopted the *National Lampoon* mind-set.

"Thank God he wasn't religious," McConnachie wrote. "He could have done some real damage."

By turns sweet ("He'd be late if a kitten fell asleep on him," Janis Hirsch said) and powerful, he was a natural choice to assume responsibility for the radio show after O'Donoghue departed and Kelly and McConnachie were needed back at the magazine.

Belushi used several magazine writers to help with material, but most of the work he produced on the radio show was created by the extraordinary stable of performers he'd assembled for *The National Lampoon Show* and holdovers from *Lemmings*. Harold Ramis, Brian Doyle-Murray, Bill Murray, Chevy Chase, Gilda Radner, and Chris Guest were all active participants, with Tischler, joint in mouth, holding things together on the technical end.

Murray and Guest made magic from nothing. Within weeks of his arrival, Murray was creating indelible characters. He developed a healthy competition with Guest, whose ability to improvise was legendary. Murray went to great pains in developing characters and lived to embody them. He would often play straight, but with a unique brand of recklessness. Guest was more casual, going with the flow and channeling the moment flawlessly, creating outlandish characters who became believable within the purview of his talents.

"Watching the two of them do improv was a real treat," McConnachie says. "It had a wonderful, flip reversal, the ambience of, say, the Beastie Boys play John Philip Sousa."

Belushi's contributors came up with funnier material than the stuff that Kenney, Beard, and McConnachie could write for radio, and did so with lightning quickness, taking ideas right into the studio, where they were taped and edited in a matter of hours.

Doyle-Murray became Dr. Howard "Bear" Barnes, a child-abusing coach; in a mock interview with the Hollywood Gay Alliance, Chase was a flamboyant Charles Bronson to a lisping Lee Marvin and effeminate Clint Eastwood; Belushi did his Marlon Brando anywhere and everywhere, from a baby Brando rehashing his famous taxicab scene with Rod Steiger in *On the Waterfront* as if they were small children to a Maurice Chevalier Brando singing "Gigi"; Guest created over-the-top talent agent Ron Fields, who prattles on about his newest discovery—a group of seafaring European crooners for whom he shamelessly flogs "The Sperm Whale Song."

The end came in late 1974 when Belushi and Doyle-Murray wrote an entire episode dedicated to the Death Penalty, viciously lampooning the practice and outraging station managers and advertisers alike. Nearly 400 stations dropped the *National Lampoon Radio Hour.*

When Matty complained about the fallout, Belushi smiled broadly. "You know 400 stations, that's the record."

Believing that the show should remain on air as an outlet for the unbelievable collection of talent Belushi had assembled, as well as realizing its importance in keeping the *National Lampoon* name alive in another medium, McConnachie begged Matty to reconsider. This resulted in lunch at the Manhattan Friars Club, where Matty explained that he understood show business and knew when it was time to cut bait.

McConnachie pleaded over and over that even though the show wasn't making money, it wasn't losing it either. Moreover, it was a free weekly advertisement for the magazine that ran on hundreds of stations and underscored the message that *National Lampoon* was the beginning and end of hip counterculture humor in the United States. Matty continually assured him he knew what he was doing. Simmons and Mogel had decided that, with the loss of so many stations, the show was dead.

"There was no commercial aspect to it that we could figure out," Mogel says.

For a time, Matty replaced O'Donoghue's creation with *The Mary Travers Show*, featuring Gerry Taylor's then-wife. The high point of its eight-episode run was the moment when, in the eleventh-floor studio, Bill Murray insisted that he was a lobster and Travers the human equivalent of melted butter. Pulling a turtleneck over his head, Murray repeatedly rubbed against a mystified and annoyed Travers. With low ratings and a difficult star in Travers, Matty bailed on radio for good.

* * *

To coincide with the celebration of the birth of Jesus Christ, the editors chose the Judeo-Christian Tradition as the December 1974 theme. Beginning with the cover image of Mary's father tossing the mother of god and her infant son from his ancient suburban home, they intended to take apart religion piece by piece, leaving bloodshed in their wake.

Kelly brought back "Son O' God" for a "special origin issue"; Sussman refined his cab driver, Bernie X, in "The Goyspiel According to Bernie"; the "Protestant Section" includes "CosmoProtestant," with headlines such as "Potato Chips You Can Eat with a Knife and Fork;" a cartoon of the pope being lynched; and "On Trays of Gorham Silver," a prayer that ends "you are the perfect guest, because of all mankind you still love me the very best. And if you love me from now till then, I know you'll stop by soon again, for we must do this more often."

The sacraments are savaged in a pamphlet that depicts gay priests checking out sailors, a baby drowning in holy water, and a vampire cleric about to chomp into a corpse; Hendra's "Catholic Sex Index" defines the "crass motivation" for contrition as "being sorry for your sins, purely out of fear of the loss of heaven and the pains of hell"; while O'Rourke's two-page cartoon spread of "Denominational Hells" depicts Catholics (for masturbation), Methodists (allowing crabgrass to seed), Baptists (using the flag as bunting), and Episcopalians (eating oysters with a dinner fork) all damned for eternity.

And then, says Gerry Taylor, "The roof caved in on us."

As viciously funny as the issue was to readers, a one-year-old Catholic lay society known as the Catholic League for Religious and Civil Rights, headed by a renowned law professor, was not amused. The issue had taken care of pretty much every religion—but, as Kelly, Hendra, Kenney, and McConnachie were all Catholic, the faith of their childhoods got it the worst.

In the course of a few years, Taylor (now assisted by Bill Lippe) had dramatically increased advertising revenue. With the record and hi-fi businesses in place, he had begun to get results with the keepers of the big advertising dollars—the liquor, automotive, and cigarette companies.

Taking the same approach they had with the music industry, Taylor and Lippe sold the magazine as a vehicle to access the huge market of young males. In the men's field, only *Playboy* and *Penthouse* sold better than *National Lampoon*. The numbers were undeniable. At first, the advertisers were not interested.

"They didn't read it. They hated it," Lippe says of approaching new, larger advertisers. "They thought it was an anti-establishment cult magazine that made fun of everything that was sacred to them and it insulted them."

Initially, it was difficult to even get appointments with larger clients. "Why would I want to see anybody from the Lampoon?" they would ask.

"We'd go in and they'd literally start to throw up on their desks," Lippe says, "and we'd say, OK. That's cool. That's fine. It's not for you. If you liked it we'd be in trouble, but what's important is that we're not here to sell you a subscription. This is a vehicle for selling your product to a very viable market."

Once in the door, Lippe and Taylor laid out research that put *National Lampoon*'s numbers into the same language as other magazines'. They provided syndicated studies defining their readers' behavior. Hearing their own language, executives on the other side of the desk began to listen, particularly those in the liquor and spirits industry who were suddenly being educated on the size, value, and attitudes of the college market.

Budweiser's marketing people imagined that their primary customer was a working-class guy who tucked into a six-pack each night after work. That was where they'd been spending ad dollars. Taylor and Lippe showed them data demonstrating that the age eighteen-to-twenty-four market consumed at least as much if not more beer than all of the auto workers, laborers, and union members they'd been targeting.

With Bud persuaded, Lippe flew to Louisville, where he'd been invited to an exclusive two-day dog and pony show held by Jack Daniels. Arriving in a blizzard, Lippe realized he'd left his creative presentation back in Chicago. Nonetheless, Lippe's time came, and he again explained the age eighteen-to-twenty-four market for hard liquor, which producers had long assumed was based on brand loyalty handed down from parent to child—kids drank whatever mom and dad did.

Lippe told them that college boys and recent grads preferred premium brands like Chivas Regal and Johnny Walker, demonstrating an understanding of the difference between quality and something poured from the well. After detailing their consumption patterns, Lippe produced data indicating that Wild Turkey had made significant inroads into the young adult market, leaving Jack Daniels behind.

When it was over, the president of Jack Daniels stood up and told him that it was the best presentation they'd seen during the entire session. Three weeks later, they got a contract for nine pages from the distiller.

"We had good, sound information about what our market was doing and how they were different and hard to reach," Lippe says. "Moreover, we had a special rapport with this market and we were the best vehicle for getting to it."

The message was simple. Like it or not, *National Lampoon* got to the market better than anybody else. The strategy had achieved at least 25 percent growth in ad revenue during each year of the magazine's existence.

Now, however, the Catholic League for Religious and Civil Rights intended to put a stop to that hard-fought success. The league ran an ad in *Our Sunday Reader*, the major Catholic weekly newspaper, detailing *National Lampoon*'s crimes and asking readers to boycott. Additionally, they sent letters to nearly every advertiser with an ad in the magazine, telling them they'd be listed in the newspaper if they didn't pull out of the Lampoon.

Taylor called the League's director, telling him that his actions went against everything he stood for as a professor and author of legal texts. It didn't work. He followed up by offering the League as many pages as they wanted in the magazine to respond. It had worked with Disney, so why not the Catholics? Again, he was rebuffed.

After getting nowhere, Taylor spoke to Bernie Mitchell, the president of Pioneer, the hi-fi equipment maker who had helped build their ad base.

"No fucking way [I'll go along with the boycott]," Mitchell replied. "This is a free speech thing. The Catholic Church ought to know better. No wonder they're losing people."

Others weren't so easy. Taylor wrote letters to each advertiser and flew around the country, hat in hand, making a businesslike appeal to every client. For the liquor companies, he proposed a sensible drinking program called "good sense, good times," positioning them as responsible corporate citizens. This had some effect, but wouldn't be enough to stanch the bleeding. The Lampoon lost $500,000 in advertising that would take six months to get back on the books. After a while, though, nearly every advertiser returned.

But the boycott was not a good sign. Beyond the short-term losses and costly efforts to lure advertisers back to the magazine, the tide was beginning to turn, in both American culture and the corporate world.

With the nation's identity in tatters, inflation, a depressed stock market, and no clear leadership coming from the clumsy new president, Americans were seeking solace in all kinds of earlier fringe movements, many of them religious. Hence the growth of the Moral Majority and the numerous evangelical, devoutly religious organizations that cropped up during the 1970s, headed by the likes of Jimmy Swaggart and Jerry Falwell. This was where many of Nixon's Dayton housewives and their spouses had taken their problems. By the end of the decade, they would coalesce into an even greater political force under the leadership of a bad movie actor-turned-presidential candidate. The culture was turning on its head and that didn't bode well for the relationship between corporate America and the nation's funniest magazine.

A harbinger of this shift was the magazine's relationship with the Ford Motor Company, whom Taylor and Lippe had long sought as an advertiser. After getting Ford's agency to recommend an ad in *National Lampoon*, Lippe heard nothing for several weeks.

Finally getting his agency contact on the phone, Lippe learned that the magazine had been shot down.

"Come on!" he responded.

The adman then told Lippe that Ford's director of marketing had come into a meeting to deliver the news personally, bringing a handwritten note from Henry Ford II that read, *"National Lampoon?* Do we really need this?"

9

The Pirates

66 To me the *National Lampoon* was an end. To Doug it was a means. The magazine almost inevitably became the larval stage of a butterfly. Doug was really a genius, he saw so far beyond what we were doing—he always saw the butterfly, I never did. Everybody except me thought the idea of doing television and movies was fabulous. Doug was the only guy who understood whatever was going on all the time. 99

—Henry Beard

The following things happened in 1975: John Mitchell, H. R. Haldeman, and John Ehrlichman were sentenced to prison for their Watergate involvement; Cher divorced Sonny Bono and married Gregg Allman four days later; America began its twenty-two-month bicentennial celebration; Gerald Ford announced the end of U.S. involvement in Vietnam; Ron Wood joined the Rolling Stones;

New York City teetered near bankruptcy; *Sanford and Son*, *All in the Family*, and *Chico and the Man* were among the most popular shows on television; moviegoers lined up to see Steven Spielberg's *Jaws*; Jimmy Hoffa disappeared; Glenn Campbell's "Rhinestone Cowboy" topped the pop charts; and, in October, George Carlin hosted the first episode of *Saturday Night Live*.

* * *

In 1975, one of the odder fixtures on late-night television was Tom Snyder, host of NBC's *The Tomorrow Show*. A chain-smoking, arrogant but ill-at-ease graying bachelor, Snyder had come from the world of radio with a deep announcer's voice and wide variety of nervous tics that would make him fodder for Dan Aykroyd on *Saturday Night Live*, whose impeccable Snyder impersonation responded to nearly everything with "Fair enough, I'll buy that."

Running after Johnny Carson and into the wee hours, Snyder's format was intimate—just a few chairs in an empty studio where the host interviewed everyone from Charles Manson to the Sex Pistols' Johnny Rotten, often achieving tremendously uncomfortable results, including one occasion where he seemingly challenged the mass murderer to a fistfight.

Doug and Chris Miller were scheduled to appear on the January 15, 1975, episode of *The Tomorrow Show* to discuss the themes of "religion and morality." To prepare for his first network television appearance, Doug smoked an enormous quantity of hash.

A few questions into the show, it became apparent to Doug that Snyder knew almost nothing about *National Lampoon*. Addled by the hash and riled by the host's ignorance, Doug decided to have some fun.

"What do you think of yourself as?" Snyder asked. "A satirist? A writer? A comedian?"

"Actually none of those things, Tom," Doug replied. "I think of myself as a cheap hustler. Just like you."

Snyder snapped back in his chair, speechless for perhaps the first time in his career. Uncomfortable silence followed.

"[Doug] was nervous and weird," Chris Hart recalls of the appearance. "He had no respect for Snyder, so that was that."

As the show came to a close, Snyder signed off by saying, "You've just heard from Doug Kenney and Chris Miller of *National Lampoon*. That's a humor magazine. Doing very well." Then he paused. "Maybe we can do something about that."

* * *

In January, the Lampoon's theme was No Issue, with a scythe-wielding Father Time in a 1974 sash on the cover, holding a droopy, filled condom in his left hand to represent the New Year.

O'Rourke wrote the editor's letter, lampooning his Ivy League colleagues and the political left within the magazine's editorial ranks. It was a harbinger of things to come.

I didn't attend a certain fancy pants educational institution whose name you'd know in a minute. And believe me I harbor no grudge against my fellow editors who did have the opportunity to spend four years in that prestigious ivied manse of erudition, clasping their books to their chests with both hands, drinking Pink Ladies, and learning to ride sidesaddle. So what if they emerged from sixteen years of expensive private education with a set of pansy mannerisms that, had I displayed them back in Ohio, would have bought me a skull full of 30/06 soft points and a verdict of justifiable homicide for my dad?

[W]hat they don't know (and aren't likely to find out since you bet they'll be in tears before they get this far down the page) is that some friends of mine and I have been secretly diverting millions of dollars of *National Lampoon* profits into a Swiss bank account for the Earth People's Park! Can you dig it?! Just like Che said, we're "inside the belly of the pig" turning their own weapons of mass destruction against them for the good of the oppressed masses! Soon we will have enough money to unleash the forces of revolution in a relentless war on imperialist neo-colonialism and buy some land near Taos for building geodesic domes out of smashed car bodies where we can smoke all the dope we want.

Beginning his move to the political right, O'Rourke had co-opted the *National Lampoon* ethos and used it in the same manner as O'Donoghue and others had throughout the previous four-plus years. He'd learned the game and was embodying the aesthetic set down before he ever set foot in 635 Madison. Yet in his hands, encompassing his shifting perspective, it had to sting—at least for some.

Doug contributed "First High Comics," which takes a nerdy college student at "State" on a wild evening trip through a paranoid drug netherworld (a guitar-playing hippie pulls his stash from behind phony copies of *Howl*, *Catch-22*, *The Hobbit*, and other dangerous counterculture classics); Bluestone's bizarre "Touching Demise Comics" have parents taking their dying child to the "Iceless Capades," where they watch skating bears suffer horrific injuries while attempting to perform on a melted rink; "Negligent Mother," McConnachie's bookend to "Guns and Sandwiches," promises stories about "Getting Your Kid into TV Commercials—In Saudi Arabia" and "Whooping Cranes Are Not Endangered—Just Delicious" and an ad for Mutual of Toyland baby insurance that begins, "Sometimes we don't always remember to cover electric sockets or lock up the power tools or put away the ammonia, and then when we least expect it, tragedy will strike"; and O'Rourke's "*National Lampoon* 1974 New Year's Resolutions," made up of articles the magazine didn't publish. Having learned from Doug, and adding his own acerbic touches, it's a written-word "Foto Funnies" that lets readers see a parody of the magazine's inner workings.

O'Rourke also took on the staff's editorial predilections: McConnachie's "Songs That Can Only Be Played on the White Keys"; Kelly's "Dylan Thomas Under Watermelon"; Henry and Weidman's "The Law of Thermodynamics," explained as "like 'The Law of the Jungle,' but more thorough, man gets hauled into physics court after it's discovered that his system of constant mass has lost more kinetic energy than it passed to its environment"; a musical called *Nam!* with the song "I'm Gonna Wash What's Left of the Man Right Outta My Hair"; and Hendra's "Jokies" ("addicted to humor, just can't stop"), which promises "a barrel of monkeys on their backs," "mock-ings" in Central Park, and other concepts related to the affliction of always making jokes.

Throughout are fictitious handwritten notes from various editors, including one from Doug about the Hendra piece, where O'Rourke sends up his mentor:

"Peej—Whew, man, let's do this for the self-indulgence ish! Cause you know, it really tells some important inner truths about ourselves and ever since I got back from Martha's Vineyard, I think inner truths are what's really important—that's where the magazine should really be, cause laughing at people is, you know, like a defensive trip and we should be more open! Did ya score the coke?—Doug"

* * *

Kelly was initially assigned to direct *The National Lampoon Show*. Quickly, however, he learned that there wasn't much direct-ing to be done with a cast that included Belushi, Murray, Radner, Joe Flaherty, and, eventually, Harold Ramis.

Early on, Kelly tried a sketch about how classic humor is timeless, which of course it rarely is. The premise was that the actors would say, "We'd like to do for your enjoyment a scene from *A Country Wife*," and begin spouting incomprehensible period dialogue: "Oh, lord, I see your snuffbox is open." With no response from the audi-ence, the performers would become desperate and devolve into old Three Stooges routines.

Flaherty liked the piece and worked on it with Kelly, endlessly trying to get it right. The rest of the crew was less interested, prefer-ring to improvise and recycle concepts they'd performed at Second City. Eventually, Kelly stepped aside and it became Belushi's show.

After debuting on Long Island, *The National Lampoon Show* went on a tour booked by the William Morris Agency. Operating on a miniscule budget and pulling props from a steamer trunk, the cast opened in Philadelphia and made their way to Toronto. Though the show was funny, it had been created in a half-assed manner, rely-ing almost completely on the talents of the performers rather than combining them with the cultural acuity of the magazine's writers, as they'd done so successfully at the Village Gate. It would not be another *Lemmings*.

Matty sent his nineteen-year-old son, Michael, on the road as company manager. Despite the occasional bitching about his father, Michael's mellow personality and ability to bond with Belushi won over the cast and relieved him of the "boss's son" burden.

When Michael turned eighteen the previous year, Belushi invited him to his place where he laid out two large rails of cocaine. Smiling like a proud papa, Belushi said, "Today, you are a man."

On tour, it was Michael's job to handle the financial end of the show and whatever operational problems arose, no matter how odd. One of his chief tasks was to figure out how to get Gilda Radner from one place to another. Deathly afraid of flying, she refused to travel by plane from Philly to Toronto. Michael attempted to get her on a train, but for some reason it didn't work out. Ramis offered to step in. Giving her Valium, pot, booze, and cocaine, he kept Radner up all night at their hotel.

As the cast checked out the following morning, the lobby elevator opened to reveal Ramis emerging with Radner, eyes as big as golf balls, in tow. Wasted beyond recognition, she wore a sign around her neck reading, "Hi. My name is Gilda and I'm not afraid to fly."

In less-intoxicated but equally desperate moments, it was Radner who kept the cast together and served as its infectious cheerleader. In London, Ontario, the show was booked at a club that didn't turn the tables between shows. Scheduled to perform two sets each evening, this meant that the cast would have to do the same show twice for the same audience.

Michael told the club's owner that they only had one show, and thus couldn't just perform it again. His explanation fell on deaf ears and the cast improvised an entire second set, which was often hit or miss.

One evening, as the second act bombed before a stone-faced audience, there was a lone voice in the back of the theater laughing hysterically at everything the cast did. Slowly at first, the audience began laughing as well. Before long, the laugher in the back of the club had transformed the entire audience into an appreciative crowd that was convulsed in hysterics.

Walking from backstage into the audience, Michael found Radner, seated by herself, tears rolling down her cheeks and doubling over in her chair.

At Toronto's El Mocambo Club, an awkward, big-toothed young man approached Michael.

"Are you Michael Simmons?" he asked.

Michael nodded.

"Hi, I'm Ivan Reitman."

Reitman, the son of Czech immigrants, had been making B-grade horror and biker flicks in Canada, many of which had been financed by friends of his parents. At the time he met Michael, Reitman was producing Doug Henning's *The Magic Show*, which was enjoying a successful run in Canada.

Enjoying a less successful run was *The National Lampoon Show*. Bookings weren't coming easily and by the time the cast got to Toronto, a discouraged Matty was preparing to shut it down. The performers were panic-stricken.

Ambitious and astute, Reitman saw potential in *The National Lampoon Show*. Michael put Reitman in touch with Matty and the pair struck a deal to open it in New York as an "Ivan Reitman Production." With Reitman taking on much of the financial risk, Matty happily agreed to give him billing and the show.

The agreement with Reitman eased the anxiety of most cast members, with the notable exceptions of Belushi and Flaherty. Reitman, hot off his success with Henning, had definite ideas about injecting more "theater" into the show. Flaherty wasn't interested and left.

Not wanting to give up creative control, Belushi was less than thrilled by Reitman's presence, made worse when the producer brought in theatrical director Martin Charnin, who subsequently directed *Annie*, to run the show. Aside from his creative efforts, Charnin had had an affair with Mary Travers, which ended her marriage with Gerry Taylor.

"The Lampoon craziness had risen to the Jewish ranks of the office," says Dale Anglund.

The collective attitude toward Reitman was exemplified by the first day of rehearsal. Arriving at the theater on a winter day, he was bundled up to fight the cold. As he took off his warm clothing,

Reitman said hi to each member of the cast, but on completion was greeted by Murray, who redressed the producer piece by piece, first the coat, then the hat, and finally the scarf—escorted him to the door, slid him out, and closed it behind him. Reitman didn't return for two days.

Opening in March 1975 at Manhattan's Palladium Club, in the basement of Rockefeller Center, the show did well, but didn't approach the critical or financial success of *Lemmings*.

During the run, various celebrities and artists came to see the production, including Martin Mull, who was performing his odd satirical show *Martin Mull and His Fabulous Furniture* in Manhattan. A friend of O'Donoghue's who possessed an outrageous sense of humor, Mull arrived drunk and heckled the performers throughout the show, so incensing Bill Murray that he leaped from the stage almost directly into Mull's lap with the intent to kill or maim. Only Belushi's quick physical intervention saved Mull from a murderous attack.

As *The National Lampoon Show* ended its run, it became clear that Reitman intended to use his involvement with the project as a springboard into mainstream American filmmaking. Through his connection with *National Lampoon* he hoped to find a platform and the talent to make a comedy. Behind the scenes, he and Ramis began making plans for such a film.

When the show closed, with no theatrical prospects in the offing and the radio show canceled, Matty and Reitman let the entire cast go. Kelly, Anglund, McConnachie, and others pleaded with Matty to keep them on a small retainer, believing there was a real need to keep such talent affiliated with *National Lampoon*.

Instead, Matty let them go, allegedly saying, "Guys like Belushi are a dime a dozen."*

* * *

_____

*Simmons denies that he ever made such a comment and, if he did, that it was in jest.

On March 18, 1975, 21st Century cut checks totaling $4.5 million to Rob Hoffman, Henry Beard, and Doug Kenney. The remaining $3 million would be paid out over an eight-year period.

Wanting to congratulate their friend and anticipating their long-deserved financial reward, Kelly and Hendra waited in Henry's office while he collected the check from Matty. They couldn't wait to find out what lay in store for all of them.

When Henry entered the room, he seemed anything but happy. Rather, he began opening and closing drawers loudly, pulling out papers, and stuffing them in his briefcase. He sat down only briefly, appearing tense and uncomfortable. What came from his mouth stunned the men with whom he'd spent nearly every waking hour for the past several years.

Barely looking at his colleagues, Henry launched into a monologue about money and *National Lampoon*, speaking in what Hendra characterized as the "careful, confident manner [of] a mill owner explaining to the mill workers that they can't possibly understand the larger financial implications of their petty grievances." There would be no money, he was saying, with the additional veiled assertion that they'd made his life miserable.

Finally, Henry stood, looked around the room and said, "I haven't felt this happy since the day I got out of the army." And with that he was gone, never again to set foot in the offices at 635 Madison.

"We ate together, we went everywhere together, we finished each other's sentences," Kelly says. "And all of a sudden Henry wasn't there."

Attempting to divine the inner workings of Henry's psyche had become something of a parlor game at *National Lampoon*. He was admired by all; they'd come to think of Henry as both a friend and an automatic humor machine who would always be there to hold things together. Though Doug had been *National Lampoon*'s soul, Henry provided the brains and willpower. Henry, and Henry alone, was the one who made sure the magazine hit the newsstand each month. What they hadn't considered was the toll it had taken on him. Though they cared for Henry and invited him for Christmas dinner, it hadn't occurred to anyone that he was a human being.

There are several reasons why Henry Beard disappeared from the lives of nearly everyone he had come to know at *National Lampoon*. He was hurt, exhausted, guilty, and finally free, sick of dealing with Matty Simmons and a bunch of demanding, brilliant wise guys. And perhaps most importantly, he was a nearly thirty-year-old man who'd never really lived.

Many wish growing up with money were their biggest problem. From the other side of the fence, it always appears as if generational wealth and the security of knowing that you won't ever starve (or even need to stop shopping at Brooks Brothers) is the kind of issue that could only cause angst in someone who has never known misfortune. The truth is often quite a different story.

Henry, like many before him, bore the need to prove himself and break free of his family's wealth as a means of financial and psychological support. Rather than go through life crippled by the burden of his father's success, he, like Doug, really needed to succeed. The money he got from Matty on March 18, 1975, was his—not his parents'. Nor did it belong to anyone else. And for the first time, Henry was truly on his own and able to start his life. Coming from middle-class families, where immense wealth always seemed a faraway and devoutly conferred dream, the other editors could hardly have anticipated the self-imposed pressure that Henry was under and from which he was now, at long last, relieved.

With the money most likely came some guilt. Coming from wealth, Henry always had access to nice homes, meals, and clothes (of which he did not avail himself). That in itself causes guilt when your comrades are relying on their paychecks for the rent. But when he was paid off by Matty and realized that Kelly, Hendra, and others were expecting a payout, Henry likely also felt guilt at not wanting to reward them. Whether the promises of profit sharing from his windfall were illusory, imagined, or real, this money was his. He had earned it. Yet they had helped get him there. Socially awkward and loathing confrontation, Henry took the path of least resistance. He did nothing. He just left, not wishing to explain or debate why he wasn't sharing his money, nor whether any debt was owed. He knew that everyone would be jealous and angry. It was something he felt he'd earned the right not to deal with.

Hastening Henry's departure was the fact that he hadn't taken a vacation from the unrelenting pressure of running the magazine since its inception. He'd weathered Doug's disappearances; the overwhelming force of O'Donoghue's tantrums; haggling with Matty over budgets, pay for contributors, and the magazine's content; sex scandals; and the innumerable other personal and professional storms that churned around the offices. He'd had it with all of them. For years, nobody wondered how he might be feeling about things or holding up under the pressure. He'd been doubted and rose to the occasion. Silently, his resentment of Matty and everyone else had been building up inside him like steam in a teakettle. Somewhere within his adept brain, he was hurt. So he cut them to the quick with his closing line and was done with the lot of them. He was ready for a real life.

"He realized that he didn't have to define himself that way anymore," Louise Gikow says. "He could open the door and actually leave for the first time."

When Henry left his office that day in March 1975, he headed back to his apartment on Central Park West, finally ready to figure out who he was. It was a luxury Doug would never afford himself.

For the next five years, the name Henry Beard would hardly be spoken within the walls of 635 Madison, except in anger. Nearly everyone on the editorial staff was furious, believing they'd been betrayed. Everyone, that is, but Doug.

* * *

Doug didn't leave the *National Lampoon*, nor did he keep all of his money. Instead, he told Matty he'd like to stay around, and bought his parents a house in Connecticut, a condo in Florida, and two cars. Later, when Harry complained about mowing the huge lawn, Doug bought him several goats to maintain the grounds. Doug also gave $30,000 to O'Donoghue (he wrote "for school supplies" in the memo line) and several thousand to Trow. He lent a thousand to the Belushis. When they repaid him, Doug said, "You're the first ones who paid me back." Doug also began leaving huge tips that would grow and grow as the 1970s wore on. Always generous and viewing money with a mix of desire, dismay, and nonchalance, this was his way of assuaging whatever guilt he most certainly felt about being a millionaire.

After the buyout, Doug visited a midtown Manhattan Porsche dealership. Wandering in, clad in his uniform of Gilmour jacket, torn jeans, and high tops, Doug inquired about a Red 911 Targa.

"I think I want that car," he told a salesman, who responded with a dismissive look.

"No, I'll take it and I'll pay cash," Doug said.

By the beginning of 1976, he had broken up with Prager, softening the blow by saying that he had a fast car and would die young. As a breakup gift, he gave her a trip to Greece. He also gave money to Alex, who needed it to repair her car.

Kelly asked Doug what he intended to do with his newfound riches. Doug said he'd probably put it in the bank and visit Disneyland. Kelly was flabbergasted. "How about going to Tibet?" he thought.

But for all of his intelligence and keen instincts about American culture, Doug was not terribly sophisticated. Well read and educated, he was still a middle-class kid, not far removed from the seeming comforts afforded by Chagrin Falls and Harvard Square. America was what he understood. The wider world made him uncomfortable.

Doug did find his way to London, where he visited Dudley Fishburn, stayed at the Savoy, and went out each night. Keenly aware of the country's establishment, he mockingly doffed his cap at everyone he met. Purchasing a bespoke suit, he returned home.

Arriving at 635 Madison in his Saville Row suit and Italian leather driving gloves, he asked Lippe to go for a drive. Veering around Manhattan, barely able to shift his expensive sports car, the pair laughed and laughed at Doug's ineptitude and good fortune.

Within days of arriving home he was back at the office, wearing his Gilmour jacket and borrowing lunch money from administrative vice president George Agoglia. Still living in the barely furnished apartment on Bank Street, he realized that *National Lampoon* was his home, at least for the time being. And after all that had passed, it was Doug who loved *National Lampoon*. That Ash Wednesday, as he had most years before, Doug walked around the offices, dip-ping his fingers in a dirty ashtray, consecrating both Catholics and non-Catholics alike.

* * *

Kelly believes that, metaphorically, Henry was indeed Holden Caulfield, with Doug playing the role of his older brother D.B., an accomplished writer who moves to California and works in television—creating profound disillusionment in the young protagonist of Salinger's novel. "[Doug] wrote the perfect short story and then went to Hollywood and became a prostitute and Henry stayed in New York City to find the sword he'd lost with the fencing team," Kelly says.

* * *

Doug always loved to pose for pictures. He had readily agreed to portray a priest, a proctology patient with an eyeball in his anus, a Spanish soap opera star, a man receiving oral sex in a heart-shaped Poconos bathtub from a snorkel-clad model, and just about anything else.

Thus, with some of the money from the buyout, he asked Peter Kleinman if he knew anyone who would paint his portrait. The art director recommended his friend and infrequent *National Lampoon* contributor Matt Goldman.

Every third or fourth day for much of 1975, Doug visited Goldman and posed for portraits. Some sittings lasted five minutes, others half an hour. Each was an emotional impression of Doug, depending on the mood of both parties and whatever substances they'd ingested that day. The paintings were done in nearly every conceivable style—expressionist, realist, impressionist, Picasso, Kandinsky, and Cézanne. For Doug, it was both a means of supporting an artist and mock entertainment for himself in the style of the well-to-do. Later that year, he paid out of his own pocket for a group of underground artists known as the Ant Farm to create a photographic re-creation of the Kennedy assassination that ran in the magazine.

Kleinman, ever the street-smart New Yorker, was always looking out for Doug, and suggested that his friend buy some midtown parking lots. With the city in financial crisis, he figured they'd come cheap and would eventually be worth untold millions. When he suggested the idea, Doug just laughed. "I'm a comic genius. What am I going to do with a parking lot?"

* * *

For some time, Kelly had been receiving bizarre letters and postcards from a funny, clearly insane kid from Vancouver named Ted Mann. Kelly wrote back telling him to drop by if he was ever in New York. In late 1974, Mann did so and became the first among a new breed of writers who joined *National Lampoon* after Beard and O'Donoghue departed. He would also become one of its most colorful and amusingly disruptive figures.

Mann brought a unique version of O'Donoghue's energy to the mix. With lanky blondish hair and standing somewhere around six-foot-four, he was dark and physically menacing. Where O'Donoghue specialized in verbal jibes that cut where it hurt most, Mann brought an intensity and physical presence that indicated that he was not a man to be fucked with. Quieter than O'Donoghue but equally cutting, there was always the sinking sense that if you pissed him off, Mann might disassemble you. Unlike O'Rourke, Mann didn't seem to be ambitious or have a desire to belong. Rather, the *National Lampoon* ethos seemed part of Mann's DNA. He didn't give a damn about much of anything and seemed dangerously uncontrollable, a cause for great admiration from the other editors. He fit in perfectly, and added a new flavor to the environment. Mann respected and disrespected everyone equally in accordance with the situation and his whims. It was a powerful combination in the factionalized, post-Henry environment.

The son of a lawyer, Mann grew up in an idyllic but bland section of West Vancouver, where implicit cultural understandings disciplined and repressed its institutions. Though intelligent, Mann avoided those institutions by never graduating from any school beyond eighth grade. During brief stints at several high schools, he was disgusted with the entire scene, preferring drugs, alcohol, reading (Nabokov, Wodehouse, and Irish humorist Flann O'Brien), and mischief to parties, sports, and classes. Mann wrote a sex-filled novel when he was twelve and sold comics to underground newspapers.

Wanting to be a writer, Mann longed to live in New York, where there were impolite folks, busy streets, and vibrant artist communities. The opportunity to get there presented itself when Vancouver's Pulp Press had trouble soliciting payment for ten thousand copies of their *Mini-Manual of the Urban Guerilla*. The nonpaying customer was Harlem's Liberation Bookstore, run by the Black Panthers. They were two hundred days overdue. Being Canadian, the publisher assumed it was a misunderstanding and dispatched Mann to collect.

Arriving in Harlem with a bag of Maoist literature on his hip, Mann was mildly surprised to find that he was the only white person as far as the eye could see. Yet his surprise could hardly match that of the Panthers' when Mann walked into the bookstore requesting payment. Astounded, they gave him $13.

While visiting the *National Lampoon* offices, he sold a cartoon to McConnachie, and Henry bought another. But it was Doug with whom he bonded.

Residing at the Times Square Motor Hotel, Mann's lone male guest was Doug, with whom he cooked scallops on the grill of the room's radiator. Mann was mostly making ends meet by writing for *Screw*, *High Times*, and the occasional pulp sex publication, so Doug arranged for him to receive a $750 monthly draw from *National Lampoon*. Doug also helped him get an apartment on Hudson Street and referred him to a doctor friend from Harvard who ran a medical magazine. As the doctor was looking for some humor to spice up his publication, Doug immediately thought it could be an opportunity for Mann to make a few bucks. Mann, however, wrote an outrageously filthy and scatological piece.

"I did something so horrible that they were insane with rage," he says.

Doug couldn't stop laughing as the doctor/editor ranted about Mann's offensive submission. Years later, Doug helped Mann land a job at *Saturday Night Live* that would last only one night.

"Doug was like an older brother to me," Mann says.

Mann became a powerful force around the office, as no one had any idea what his agenda was and knew, deep down, that there probably was none at all.

* * *

One person who didn't take the buyout well at all was Matty Simmons. Feeling that he'd been betrayed and now suffering from Henry's sudden departure, he was in a jam and deeply hurt. Worse yet, he was on the hook for a gigantic loan, and out of cash to fund the growth of his enterprise.

In the space of eighteen months, Matty had lost two of the three members of his A-team in Beard and O'Donoghue. Doug, for whom he had endless affection, was around but certainly wasn't going to take charge. All that remained, therefore, were Kelly, Hendra, and McConnachie, the only full-time editors capable of running the magazine. While Hendra had ambition, Kelly was intellectually brilliant, and McConnachie possessed a unique sensibility, none was particularly suited to being anybody's boss or running things in as organized and professional a manner as Henry had.

That left the young and inexperienced O'Rourke, who, in the interim, had cut his hair short and assumed the duties of executive editor. Whatever Matty knew, it is clear that in 1975, putting O'Rourke in charge would alienate the remaining talent simply by virtue of O'Rourke's youth and lesser status. Thus, for the bulk of the year, Kelly and Hendra—neither of whom cared for Matty— became de facto editors in chief.

The financial implications of the buyout put an enormous strain on the magazine. Matty had taken a big chance in starting *National Lampoon* with unproven writers. On most days before 1975, he'd kept his hands off editorial. Matty would get upset and kvetch when advertisers dropped from the magazine or an inordinately offensive piece drew notice, but in his promoter's heart, Matty knew that it was all good publicity and trusted the boys to do their thing—which they would have done anyway, evidenced by Doug's attitude when Matty complained about a piece to Chris Miller. When told of Matty's apprehension, Doug simply responded, "Bullshit! Bullshit! Bullshit! It's our magazine!"

Likely knowing that they were disregarding him, Matty let them go about their business. It was part of the creative tension that fueled the magazine. They needed to disobey Matty. But still, he trusted Doug's explicit promise that the boys were partners who'd never hurt him, which meant there was always the potential for pain and disillusionment. Both were triggered by the buyout.

Surely Matty, the avid negotiator and shrewd businessman, was not happy that Hoffman had out-negotiated him and had a superior understanding of the deal's inner workings. Under pressure from the markets and trying to keep a hold on the future of the business, Matty had been anxious about what would happen when they sat down to finalize the deal. In fact, he'd been anxious since the day they first outlined the buyout in 1969. Thus, when Hoffman took a hard line and refused to budge—making the implications even more onerous by insisting on the higher payout—Matty's worst dreams came true. The institution he had funded and gotten off the ground was about to be taken away unless he ponied up money he didn't have. Worse yet, this was all happening at the hands of a green kid, not some savvy business veteran.

To Matty, the situation was as much about aggressive, ungrateful kids, whom he loved and thought of as sons, as it was about a bad business deal. They had screwed him. Rob Hoffman made out like a bandit for doing little or nothing, Henry left without so much as a word, and Doug had thrown a fit at the meeting. What kind of gratitude was this?

"Like everyone in those days we exploited the talent as much as we could, because it was a business," says Gerry Taylor. "Yet in a sense Matty felt that he had their love. But he didn't. They were loyal to themselves."

Though he and Doug remained close, Matty would forever perceive the boys as having betrayed him. After March 18, 1975, he would refer to them as "the pirates" and often deny requests for money, pay raises, and other financial output because "the pirates" had looted all of the swag.

And, though they were immensely pissed off at Henry, the editors viewed his behavior as a confirmation of their belief that Matty was a cheap hustler, someone who only wanted to save a buck. They rightfully desired equal credit for helping turn the magazine into a multimillion-dollar enterprise.

Now, suffering financially and lacking a true editor, Matty was facing a world in which he needed to keep putting out the magazine with a group of lesser (though significant) talents. Moreover, he needed to make a ton of money to pay off the debt and get the business back to its former strength.

* * *

The June issue included "Boy O Boy" Comics, Bruce McCall's parody of innocent 1930s cartoons for young boys. Drawn in McCall's inimitable style that reflected an elegant brand of hypernostalgia for times that perhaps never were, it included "Ten Commandments for the Normal Boy," straight from Cap'n Jasper's (a pipe-smoking old sea salt) Crow's Nest:

1—The Normal Boy will never stay more than five minutes in the bathroom alone.
2—The Normal Boy will never smell his or anyone else's bodily functions.
3—The Normal Boy will never look in a toilet or other sanitary receptacle.
4—The Normal Boy will never kiss a man or other boy.
5—The Normal Boy will never use rouge or lipstick, or dress up in ladies clothing or foundation garments, even for "fun."
6—The Normal Boy will never allow his fingers to enter his own or others' bodily openings.
7—The Normal Boy will never touch sheep, cows or other farm animals, except on the head.
8—The Normal Boy will never bring unguents, jellies, salves, drawings, postcards, pictures, magazines, fresh meats, mirrors, lingerie, or toilet tissue into his bed.

9—The Normal Boy will never examine his underwear.
10—The Normal Boy will never drink an unpasteurized
beverage.

Over the years, McCall had been one of the magazine's most
consistent contributors, delivering smart, devastatingly accurate text
and artwork for several issues each year. His "RMS Tyrannic," a
parody of gigantic luxury cruise ships, and other pieces had garnered
a large following and made him an important flavor in the thrown-
together but complicated editorial mix.

During those years he'd been protected from the magazine's inner
workings and politics. He simply did his work from a garret in the
Village and brought it in on time. Now, however, Henry was gone—
as was Mike Gross—which removed the layers that stood between
editorial and Matty.

The "Boy O Boy" piece was produced as a three-quarter-size
insert. When it came time to settle up his year's billings in late 1975,
McCall found that Matty was intent on paying him only three-fourths
of his usual rate. The normally quiet Canadian became incensed,
demanding his full-page rate and explaining to Matty that he'd done
the same amount of work as he ordinarily would, it was only the size
of paper that was different.

Matty suggested that McCall surely didn't want to be paid for
work he hadn't done. The stalemate ended with McCall receiving his
usual rate, but not without tremendous strain and tension. It would
effectively end his affiliation with *National Lampoon*.

* * *

In 1975, the business of humor was slightly off, primarily the
result of an overall downward trend in the magazine industry. In a
Wall Street Journal interview, Matty assured a reporter that *National
Lampoon* was suffering far less than the average publication.

First-half earnings were $453,095, which was $25,000 ahead of
what it had been for the same period in 1974. Ad revenue for the year
was projected at $2.6 million, up from $2 million the prior year.

"We believe we're back," Matty said, "particularly with the July
issue."

* * *

The July issue promised "X-Rated, 3-D Entertainment" and showed a picture of Stevie Wonder, in bicolored 3-D glasses on the cover. Peter Kaminsky, a Princeton graduate who'd been campus chairman of Students for a Democratic Society and entered *National Lampoon* through its advertising department, had suggested the cover image.

The son of a Jackie Gleason writer, Kaminsky moved to New York after college, where he drove a cab and enrolled at NYU to pursue a master's in anthropology. Then, through Guest, the twenty-six-year-old received an introduction to *National Lampoon*.

"Chris told people I was OK," he says, "and you very much needed that. It was pretty hard to crack that group."

After a stint writing sample advertising copy, Kaminsky became friends with Kelly and Hendra, who took him under their wings. He was intelligent and openly shared their politics—he was bound to fit in. Kaminsky, like Mann, was another in the new group of writers who emerged during the next few years. Yet unlike Mann and his predecessors, there was something different about Kaminsky. Shockingly, he appeared to be a rather happy and well-adjusted young man.

"Peter was quite a bit sunnier and much, much less angry than most of the people at the Lampoon," Mann says.

Kaminsky, however, was about to enter a work environment that didn't reward those who viewed the world in a positive light. Since Henry's departure, the tension had grown exponentially. Kelly and Hendra were devastated by Henry's exit. Already cynical and angry, the pair upped the level of divisiveness. Most in editorial held a jaded view of Matty, who was upset in his own right and under colossal financial pressure. Meanwhile, few trusted O'Rourke, especially with his growing authority. The vicious interplay expanded by the day. If you arrived at the office unprepared for battle, you would leave in tatters.

"It's like when you see the movie depiction of English prep schools," Kaminsky says. "It was fun, but you had to be on your game. If you weren't, you were meat."

* * *

Perhaps the funniest piece in the July 1975 issue is Sussman's "Mel Brooks Is God," illustrated with a chopped-liver sculpture of the man who created *Blazing Saddles* and *The Producers*.

Sussman, who grew up in the very same Brooklyn as the comedy auteur, shreds Brooks, envisioning him as an egomaniacal lunatic with such exalted status that he is worshipped in temples bearing his name and operates adjunct businesses that sell Mel-emblazoned T-shirts, candy bars, sneakers, and the Spaldeen rubber balls that he whacked in stickball games as a boy.

The religious leader of each "House of Brooks" is called "The Bernie," who directs Mel's minions through a service consisting of "Horseplay" (where congregants shoot paper clips at one another and create slapstick havoc), a blessing entitled "Blessed Art Thou, O Brooks Our God, Creator of the Comic Universe and the Nectarine," followed by a call-and-response prayer where the Bernie shouts such Brooksisms as "I love your face!" to which the masses reply, "You're so pretty!"

This only serves as an introduction to the interview, where Brooks (after a breakfast of a kosher salami omelet served pancake style and a dish of stewed prunes with heavy sweet cream) greets Sussman clad in a fuzzy bathrobe and cozy slippers.

In a devastating parody of the maniacal Brooks's public persona, Sussman shows him digressing continually, suddenly trying to hump the reporter because, from the back, he looks like Sheila Fliegelstein, whom he once dated in Brooklyn. Soon Brooks recounts how his album *The 2,000 Year Old Man* was so funny that people (including an entire family in Iowa) literally died laughing and their survivors brought lawsuits.

"They threw it out of court," Brooks tells Sussman. "Couldn't get a judge or jury to stop laughing once they heard the evidence."

A few years later, Sussman and Rick Meyerowitz were walking through Manhattan when they saw a large limousine from which Brooks emerged. Meyerowitz turned and shouted, "My God! It's Mel Brooks!"

"It is!" Sussman responded, then screamed, "HEY MEL! FUCK YOU!"

* * *

In the mid-1970s, Herb Schlosser, a former Wall Street attorney, became president of NBC. One of his early tasks was to help the network gain a foothold against CBS, which, through its deep penetration into rural areas and mainstream programming, had long been the leading network.

Perhaps the only significant area of strength for NBC was its late-night programming, with Johnny Carson representing the zenith of middle-American cool and easygoing humor. But Johnny only appeared on weeknights and wanted to pull the plug on NBC's habit of rerunning his shows on the weekend. If they could find a program to fill Carson's space on Saturdays, they would be able to make their network into an almost weeklong habit.

Dick Ebersol, a young ABC sports executive and Yale dropout, was hired to lead NBC into a new world of late night. To solve the Saturday night problem, he believed they needed to attract the youth audience, which was not as enamored of Carson as their parents. He considered Richard Pryor, Lily Tomlin, and George Carlin. One agent suggested teaming a then-unknown Steve Martin and Linda Ronstadt as cohosts. Then Ebersol met Canadian comedy writer and *Laugh-In* veteran Lorne Michaels, who pitched the idea of a Second City/Kentucky Fried Theater–style comedy show.

Before long, O'Donoghue was hired as head writer and Beatts was added to the staff. Chase, Belushi, and Radner all signed on, while Dan Aykroyd, Garrett Morris, Jane Curtin, and Laraine Newman rounded out the cast. Debuting on October 11, with George Carlin as guest host, *Saturday Night Live* quickly became a long-running phenomenon.

Earlier in 1975, before Ebersol hired Michaels, Matty was approached by an NBC executive who inquired about taking a ninety-minute, *Lemmings*/Lampoon–style show to late night. Suffering from the loss of Beard and O'Donoghue, and with a staff that was overwhelmed by the needs of the radio show, Matty declined. Instead, he negotiated with comedian Alan King, who was producing an hour-long show hosted by Howard Cosell. The magazine would only be responsible for producing a far less burdensome two sketches each week. The deal broke down, however, when it became clear that King would hold firm creative control over whatever the Lampoon wrote.

* * *

There were numerous consequences to Matty's decision to forgo television, the most obvious being that *Saturday Night Live*, trading on the brand of humor created by *National Lampoon*, was being written and performed each week by talent that had once been under the magazine's banner. The phenomenal success of the program was a crucial lost opportunity for revenue, exposure, and the ability to brand all-American youth humor under the *National Lampoon* name. Less apparent, however, was the creative impact the show would have on the market for young, talented humor writers and the existing *National Lampoon* staff.

"When *Saturday Night Live* started," McCall says, "you could feel the energy go right out of the Lampoon."

There was major fallout. The staff was immensely jealous of the people at *Saturday Night Live*. To be seen or heard liking the show was sacrilege. That a seeming half-talent like Lorne Michaels (he had worked on *Laugh-In*, after all) was wrestling with them to be the humorous voice of American youth—and doing so with their formats, talent, and attitude in a forum whose audience was ten times that of the magazine—was beyond infuriating. And to see O'Donoghue rise from the ashes (he'd been reduced to writing restaurant reviews for the *Village Voice*) was a lot to take. Underneath it all was a real but unspoken sense that they were being trumped and that the logical medium for expansion had slipped from their grasp.

"We were a group of young guys who were part of something that was important to the culture. We had so much energy that exploded outwards," Meyerowitz says, "but they couldn't sustain that kind of creative output in the presence of others and in competition with others. It was the crest of a wave. An incredible moment in time. And it passed in five years."

They had created the beast and now had to save themselves from a monster of their own invention.

* * *

The August 1975 issue included one of Doug's last pieces for the magazine. "Trespassers Will Be Violated" is a Jack Londonish, *Boys' Life*-style story of a father-son hunting trip in the Wisconsin woods. Dark and beautifully written, it is perhaps the only thing Doug wrote that wasn't funny.

Tod Turner, sick with a cold and fearing a school report on weeds that's due the following Monday, is finally old enough to accompany his father and their retriever Dave on an overnight duck shoot. During the course of a rain-soaked weekend, Mr. Turner drinks bottle after bottle of Jack Daniels and rapes Tod each night as he sleeps—using Sterno as lubricant.

Sneaking into a bird sanctuary and hunting with a gun specially reconfigured to fire thirteen rounds, Mr. Turner decimates the ducks in a blood-soaked flurry that also wounds his retriever, who he executes moments later with several blasts from the same rifle.

"I drink, son," Mr. Turner explains to Tod, "t'forget the pain of being a man."

Each day of the trip includes long fatherly lectures on the virtues of hunting and slams against the Jews who allow "Negroes to reproduce unchecked" and the Liberals in Madison who don't "even know they're alive."

As the trip nears its conclusion, Mr. Turner apologizes to Tod for what's happened between them, puts a gun in his mouth, and kills himself.

* * *

"Most magazine publishers are wearing dour expressions these days, reflecting a drop in advertising revenue of 3% for the first nine months of the year, coupled with a 9% drop in ad pages. But Matty Simmons is grinning," read the lead for a November 1975 *Business Week* article.

Despite all that had befallen Matty and the magazine, *National Lampoon* was running 30 to 35 percent ahead of 1974 and was positioned to hit $3 million in advertising revenue during 1975. Pages were selling at 400 percent of 1971 rates. Advertising studies showed that the magazine outranked *Playboy, Penthouse, Newsweek, Time*, and five other publications in CPM (cost per thousand readers) for college graduates with incomes over $15,000 who regularly purchased records, stereos, and other youth-market staples. Circulation was hovering around the million mark established by the Pubescence issue, and an astonishing 85 percent of its copies were selling off the newsstand at full price. To make the financial outlook even brighter, revenue for the Yearbook parody was in the neighborhood of $2 million.

As Matty was putting the editors to work on numerous new products, *Business Week* concluded that he was "building himself a miniature empire based entirely on laughter."

These ventures were targeted to help 21st Century net $1 million after taxes on revenues of $10 million in fiscal 1975. They included: a book of art-poster parodies, a bicentennial calendar that listed tragic events in American history, several musical shows and albums, and a series of paperbacks that parodied anthologies, novels, and other publications.

With the nostalgic history magazine *Liberty* folded, and only a small managerial interest in *Weight Watchers*, *National Lampoon* now accounted for 97 percent of 21st Century's revenue.

"We've thought about changing the company name from 21st Century to something like NL Enterprises," Matty said, "but not until Len Mogel computes what it will cost to paint the new name on the front of our building."

To pull the company out of a financial bind, Matty needed more and more product. The Lampoon name was enormously marketable, and whatever they pounded out sold—and sold well.

The human and strategic cost would be large. The talent-drained staff needed to put in greater efforts to churn out all of the projects. Despite their belief that, one day, they would bathe in the royalty pool, they also remained cynical and angry. The overwork only magnified their growing resentment of management.

Worse yet, in the pursuit of profit—and lack of a firm editorial hand—*National Lampoon* was imperceptibly beginning to trade quality for quantity and engage in a fight against not only Lorne Michaels's television show, but also against its own products each month on the newsstand.

Closing out a year of emotional, financial, managerial, and competitive turmoil, *National Lampoon* would head into 1976 with high hopes for continued success—yet the short-term aftermath of the buyout would be chaos.

10

The Cultural Revolution

66 Hey Guys: Look fun's fun and everything and I can take a good ribbing as well as the next guy, sure. But, come on there are some things that just aren't funny. I mean, I do not eat other fellows' shit off of plates with a fork. I don't ever do that. **99**

—*Fictitious letter to the editor from Chevy Chase in the April 1976 issue of* National Lampoon

The following things happened in 1976: a New Jersey family sought to have their comatose daughter, Karen Anne Quinlan, legally removed from life support; *Frampton Comes Alive* topped the pop charts; Patty Hearst went on trial for bank robbery; Georgia governor Jimmy Carter swept to victory in the Iowa caucuses, becoming the Democratic presidential front runner; Steve Jobs and Steve Wozniak founded Apple, Inc., in a Silicon Valley garage; Howard Hughes died; North and South Vietnam reunified as the Socialist

Republic of Vietnam; America celebrated its 200th birthday; Texas congresswoman Barbara Jordan was the first black person and the first woman to deliver the keynote address at an American political convention; Frank Robinson was named manager of the Cleveland Indians, becoming Major League Baseball's first black manager; Jimmy Carter became the nation's thirty-ninth president; and a band named Starz released "Pull the Plug," a song whose lyrics evoked a startlingly similar situation to that facing the family of Karen Anne Quinlan.

* * *

In early 1976, Susan Devins, who'd just completed her master's degree in library sciences, was hired as an assistant copyeditor at *National Lampoon*. Early on her first day she received a phone call.

"Cheeseface is dead," the caller said. "Cheeseface the dog is dead."

Someone had tracked down the black-and-white mutt from the January 1973 cover at the farm where he lived and shot him. After initially thinking the call was a joke, Devins realized the bizarre event had actually taken place and that indeed Cheeseface had been assassinated. She burst into tears, thinking, "Oh my God, what have I gotten myself into."

Before the week was out, Matty's daughter Julie came by Devins's desk and offered a single piece of advice: "Don't trust the editors."

Among Devins's duties was to fact-check things in the magazine like whether *motherfucker* should be hyphenated. Copy came in all forms; there was no format, no margins, and all manner of spacing. Articles were covered with stains, eraser marks, and typos.

"It wasn't the *New York Times*," she says.

Barely removed from grad school, she found herself calling the typesetter in Kansas, asking to move words like *cunt* from one paragraph to the next. Each month, she was amazed that the magazine actually went to press.

"It was like we put it in this spin cycle and it came out hilarious," Devins says.

* * *

In early January 1976, Tim Mayer invited Doug to a thirtieth birthday party for actress Kathryn Walker at her Upper West Side apartment.

Walker met Mayer in the late 1960s, when she was a Harvard graduate student appearing in his shows at the Aggasiz Theater. She combined a husky voice, physical elegance, and a deep intellectualism with a persona that seemed powerful and mature beyond her years.

The late 1960s were a rich time for the Cambridge theater community, and Mayer served as dark, charismatic genius and leader to the talented group of performers who'd congregated there. During that time he'd directed shows such as Brecht's *What a Lovely War* and he cast Walker as his existential heroine, with Stockard Channing as her voluptuous counterpart and John Lithgow and Tommy Lee Jones filling the male roles. With Mayer as their champion, they believed they were breaking barriers, creating new forms, and changing the world of theater.

The group became a tight-knit artistic tribe around Cambridge, providing the kind of satisfaction that can only be achieved with kindred spirits in one's early twenties. It was the kind of love and fulfillment Doug had found with Henry and the *Harvard Lampoon* around the same time. Though both Walker and Doug were friends with Mayer and their days in Cambridge had coincided, they hadn't ever met each other.

Walker had other things in common with Doug. Raised in Philadelphia, she was one of two daughters in what she characterizes as a dysfunctional family. Her father was a political professional who served in the Pennsylvania governor's cabinet and later commuted to Washington where, under Eisenhower, he designed the Department of Housing and Urban Development. Her mother, who hated politics, kept Kathryn and her sister in Philadelphia, away from the father Walker perceived as her only ally in the family.

Walker felt ambivalent about wanting to be an actress. After attending Wells College, she considered moving on to Yale Drama School, but instead chose Celtic Studies at Harvard because there were few scholars in that area and she received a large endowment.

While studying Beckett, Walker's department chair noticed her theater background and encouraged her to meet Mayer. Within weeks, she became part of his group. When she left Cambridge, Walker headed to England on a Fulbright to study at the London Academy of Music and Art, after which she did a season at Princeton's McCarter Theater under the direction of Lithgow's father. Eventually moving to New York, she performed at the Public Theater and by the mid-1970s won an Emmy for her portrayal of Abigail Adams in PBS's *The Adams Chronicles.*

Like Doug, Walker was fiercely intelligent, curious, attractive, damaged by her family, and by turns both ambitious and ambivalent. They were, in many ways, a matched set.

At his apartment on Bank Street, Doug frequently whiled away his afternoons watching her PBS series in reruns, unaware that the woman playing Abigail would eventually become his girlfriend.

Doug's invitation to Walker's party was not completely innocent. In fact, Mayer had arranged for Doug to attend so that he could "give" his friend to Walker as a birthday present. The gift was a success.

"I remember opening the door when [Doug and Mayer] arrived at the party," Walker says. "I recall Doug was standing there and I felt this great sense of relief."

Equally taken, Doug attempted to impress Walker that evening by munching on a crystal wine glass, as if it were the most normal thing in the world.

"He was a once-in-a-lifetime experience," Walker says.

In Doug, Walker found someone who was capable of providing others a great deal of inner calm while they were under his protection. His impact on her was often Zenlike, re-creating the relief she had felt upon first greeting him at the door.

Outwardly mature and serious, Walker found Doug to be a light-hearted and romantic presence that helped her access the lightness within herself. On an early date, Doug took her to a toy store and sang along with Jiminy Cricket's "When You Wish Upon a Star" on a toy record player.

Doug's humor came from everywhere and nowhere—it was constant, but unlabored. Entering a Bavarian restaurant, he dubbed it the "Enchanted Ski Lodge," perfectly capturing its ambience. When Walker complained about the pressures of theater and film, he would say, "You have to learn to roll with the bullets." Any occasion that confirmed diminished expectations received a somber, Hollywood Indian–style, "Once many buffalo." Attending a film-industry event where Motion Picture Academy of Arts and Sciences president Jack Valenti was speaking, Walker asked, "Who is Jack Valenti?" Doug whispered back, "He's the guy who killed Jimmy Hoffa."

Having worked with so many actors and artists, she found his lack of narcissism and pretension refreshing. Seeming at ease with his feminine side, he put on no airs of ultra-manliness. Though his personality had always been fluid, he was at home with her—never playing a role, exercising his charisma for sport, or being "Doug Kenney, Editor of *National Lampoon*." Physically, he was slender, delicate, beautiful, and comfortable with himself, even if he was still "the male Hayley Mills."

"He was always the most beautiful woman in the room," Walker recalls.

With a strong, sophisticated personality and success in her field, Walker provided the kind of partner Doug needed—someone who was intellectually challenging and going through many of the same struggles.

"He needed to move on," Emily Prager says of their breakup. "Kathryn was very successful. I looked up to Doug. He looked up to Kathryn."

Thus, they embarked on a sometimes stormy, but symbiotic relationship.

* * *

The first two *National Lampoon* issues of 1976 featured nudity on the cover. The January Secret issue exposed a woman's breast (with an eye peering from the nipple) from behind a trench coat, while February's Artists and Models showed a painter standing before an easel and a room full of naked models.

In the early 1970s, O'Donoghue had discovered a woman named Danielle on a sex-trade flyer in Manhattan. With gargantuan breasts that hung to her waist from their colossal weight, she became a regular in the "Foto Funnies" section. Though she was always naked and occasionally in bed with an editor, the panels gave off a whiff of self-parody and mocking obsession with sex.

Now, however, each issue seemed to have more and more nude girls of every stripe within the photo layouts, and the material had taken on an overtly sexual nature. Distinguishing between funny sexual material and exploitative sexual material is a tricky business, and Kelly believed they were crossing the line. This only led to frustrating conversations with Matty, office bitching, and a creeping belief that the magazine was turning away from its original intent. It was one thing when high school boys wrote in to say that they beat off to Trots and Bonnie; to sell sex in and of itself was another.

This new development had many causes, not the least of which was the absence of Beard, Kenney, and O'Donoghue's strong editorial guidance, which would have cast this material within a satiric context. It also lacked effective art direction to translate that intent into the visual execution. Peter Kleinman was gifted, but young. Mike Gross was sorely missed.

Later that year, when Gerry Taylor left to take a job at *Harper's Bazaar*, a disillusioned Kelly would tell the ad director, "You're like a ship leaving a sinking rat."

* * *

Matty's solution to Henry's departure was to have a group of senior editors run the magazine. Sussman, Kelly, Mann, Hendra, O'Rourke, McConnachie, and Kenney would form a committee that rotated with a different editor in charge of each issue. It was an absolutely horrific idea.

"It was insane," Ted Mann recalls. "It was like the Cultural Revolution."

Often, individuals from different perspectives can buttress each other's weaknesses, shore up their strengths, and help colleagues grow by example. This was not the case at *National Lampoon*.

Though talented, McConnachie was far too obtuse to lead or give effective direction. Sussman just wanted to be funny and pay the rent. Doug, in O'Rourke's words, was "around, but not around," completely lacking the will to manage anyone and too tired to be more than an emeritus presence. Mann was young, too subversive, and prone to unpredictable behavior—definitely not management material. This left the battling parties of O'Rourke, Hendra, and Kelly.

The divide between the three editors was as much political as anything else. O'Rourke had cut his hair short, started wearing a tie and sports coat to the office, and was no longer the eager Marxist-Leninist who had been taken hostage by the Baltocong. Though he hadn't fully turned Republican ("It wasn't like I was defending Nixon," he says), he was an equal who now felt comfortable to let his leftist buddies know that he thought they were full of shit.

"I just perceived that [their agenda] was an easy, collegiate point of view on things," O'Rourke says.

Having been nominally in charge for several months, Hendra and Kelly believed they'd marginalized O'Rourke, figuring he'd continue to do the grunt work, carry a clipboard, and bitch to writers about deadlines while they ran the show. Instead, the vacuum created by Henry's absence, when combined with O'Rourke's growing ability to write humor and his successful collaborations with more senior writers, emboldened the junior editor. This led to tremendous ideological conflict and power struggles with Hendra and, by extension, Kelly.

"I didn't get along with Hendra," O'Rourke says, "and Kelly sided with him."

The atmosphere of tension became unbearable, with endless sniping and wisecracking at the expense of others combined with occasional trips to bars where reconciliation was attempted but never completely attained. There were frequent screaming matches and nearly every kind of conflict short of physical.

"It was like one of those families where everybody was always mad at each other," O'Rourke says. "It was no way to run a magazine."

✳ ✳ ✳

Ellis Weiner and Danny Abelson met while working at Manhattan's Strand Bookstore, where every employee believed they were headed to life as a rock star, artist, or poet. Rocker Patti Smith worked at the Strand, which was frequented by Saul Bellow, Phillip Roth, and photographer Richard Avedon. It was the place to work when you were young, smart, artistic, and devoid of direction.

Weiner was a Jewish kid from Baltimore who'd attended a nearly all-Jewish public high school and moved on to the University of Pennsylvania, where a stunning percentage of the student body were Jews as well. Graduating in 1972, he joined a rock band, then moved on to the Strand, figuring that's what aspiring writers did.

Also Jewish, Abelson spent the same four years "smoking pot" at U. Penn, but didn't know Weiner. Raised in South Africa and Australia, Abelson grew up on Peter Sellers, *Beyond the Fringe*, and *MAD*. Living under the repressive South African government, attending stifling boarding schools, and serving in the army, Abelson viewed humor as a weapon to help him survive an idiotic life. Cultivated, but a born wiseass, he listened to Lenny Bruce and tried to keep his own perspective in a world where the government frequently listened in on your phone calls.

Once he arrived in America, he was enchanted by a country where students were taking over the dean's office. In his innocence, he believed this was the true nature of being American.

"I thought that youth ruled and it was an anarchist's picnic," Abelson says. "Norman Mailer and Allen Ginsberg seemed as important as the president to me. I wasn't even aware that the counterculture was a subculture. I thought the world was run by the cool people and we were really taking over."

At the Strand, the pair learned that they shared a common worldview and similar interests, particularly art. Together they wrote a humor piece about Marshall McLuhan and a parody of *ArtNews* magazine, which struck both men as funny and worth parodying. Doug called them in.

"He liked esoteric humor," Abelson recalls. "He was perverse in that way."

Doug told them that he was leaving the magazine fairly soon and that *National Lampoon* needed new editors. Weiner had been to the offices earlier, after writing a Richard Brautigan parody in 1974. Having read that submissions must be sent to the submissions editor, he visited 635 Madison, where he met the receptionist, who was also "submissions editor." Later, he was turned over to McConnachie.

"I'd phone Brian and ask, 'What are you working on?' and he'd tell me—or he'd think he'd tell me," Weiner says. "As an editor he was kind of hard to understand. Then the issue would come out and I'd say, 'Oh, that's what he meant.'"

Contributing their *ArtNews* parody and several other pieces to the Artists and Models issue, they were given an office and made members of the staff, becoming protégés of Kelly's, who appreciated their eclectic interests.

"He liked the idea of publishing something because it was funny, smart, and interesting," Abelson says, "and because it would drive Matty crazy."

Abelson and Weiner were suddenly being paid to act like teenagers and write stories that poked fun at authority. They were avoiding the regular adult life, working with overeducated smart-asses like themselves, and essentially leading a highly indulgent existence. And they knew it.

"We were getting away with something and it was thrilling," Abelson says.

The atmosphere was staggering at first. Weiner was amazed to find that many of the editors were angry ex-Catholics, a group with whom he'd had little experience. When the Israelis successfully raided Entebbe, Hendra made a point of congratulating the Jewish duo.

More astonishing was Weiner's realization that most of the editors were smarter than he was—another novel experience. Making them laugh brought about a tremendous feeling of accomplishment— particularly if the amused party were Hendra or Kelly. Weiner even began to enjoy rubbing Matty the wrong way. During an editorial meeting, he told Matty that one of his suggestions was "completely wrong." Later hearing secondhand that the publisher said he was "pigheaded," Weiner recalls being "flattered that anyone had such a strong opinion of me."

The creative freedom at *National Lampoon* remained a huge perk. All ideas, if potentially funny or interesting, were accepted. When Weiner suggested a Heidegger parody that included compulsory sex scenes, it was immediately scheduled to run, as was the comic

"Sgt. Nick Penis and the Brass Balls Battalion." Having spouted the idea without even wanting to write it, Weiner was told, "OK, that'll be six pages."

Among their new coworkers, Weiner and Abelson were especially impressed with Mann, who wasn't a nice liberal like them, but rather a nihilist who did whatever he pleased.

"He just didn't care," Weiner says. "Grudgingly I liked and approved of the fact that he didn't care. His stuff just wasn't nice in a way that I admired and could never do myself."

What separated Mann from the pack was that there was no sense of his actually being a romantic at heart. Whereas Hendra was a former monk-in-training and Kelly a would-be poet, there appeared to be no source for Mann's disillusionment. Weiner was fueled by a desire to parody bad writing that was successful. Such things infuriated him, and it was romantic to think good literature should be rewarded and bad writing dismissed, if not punished.

"A cynic is a disillusioned romantic. The middle ground is where everybody else is," Weiner says. "To feel betrayed or angry at injustice is to start out with some kind of romantic sensibility. I don't think Ted was that way. I think Sean was. Tony was . . . he started out to be a monk. You're going to be an angry Catholic if you started out to be a monk and wound up someplace else."

* * *

In 1976, anger became *National Lampoon*'s prevailing sentiment. The emotion that had always driven much of the content now took center stage, with rage flowing in all directions, having moved beyond Nixon, Vietnam, and the Catholic Church.

The April "Letters" column got personal, taking shots at O'Donoghue, Beatts, Chevy Chase, and others. An editor pretending to be Anne Beatts, who had just edited the women's humor collection *Titters*, wrote in to ask if her new book about Negro humor should be entitled "Sniggers," adding in a P.S., "Please don't tell Mr. Michael O'Beatts I wrote this, he'd cry and cry. . . . "

In June, they took a poke at O'Donoghue by writing a letter in which their former colleague parodies Barry Manilow's "I Write the

Songs," claiming he invented humor as they know it—"I am humor and I write the jokes."

The May issue was a perfect example of where the magazine was willing to go. Now managing editor, O'Rourke wrote "Foreigners Around the World," which summarizes various foreign cultures thusly: "Africans: Probably not people at all. . . . They eat each other and worship bundles of sticks and mud. You can never remember the names of their countries, which have a new main nigger every half hour and too many snakes and bugs anyway. . . . They put bones in their noses and wear plants for clothes." Under "good points," it is noted, "Africans: don't feel pain the way we do" and proper forms of address include "soot-back and fishmouth."

Everyone gets hammered. Australians, English, French, Germans, Indians, and Arabs, who "burp and fart during meals and wash themselves in sand." Their "good points" include the fact that if "they had any country clubs they wouldn't let Jews in." They are to be properly addressed as "desert Irish."

Canadians are "hard to tell . . . from an extremely boring white person unless he's dressed to go outdoors." Chinese are characterized as "hordes of incomprehensible rat eaters. . . . No one can possibly know what dark and grotesque thoughts pass through the minds of this hydra-headed racial anomaly."

The entire July issue lashed out at the American South, with Mann's "Christian Crusader International Newspaper of God," where one columnist interprets the biblical passage about all men being brothers as a call to anticommunism and hatred of minorities. "Does it mean that all men are comrades? Or that black is whitemen? No, not when you get down to chapter and verse. For comrades is a Communist word derived from Communism, viz, commo-rads, being a shortened term for radicals. Jesus was a strong anti-communist."

An ad for the Reactionary Book Club sells "How to Survive Your Liberal School," where most teachers are "radicals or ink worshippers." The book argues that "we should bounce anti-Commo slogans and Budweiser cans off freshmen who feel sorry for Negroes who can't go to college" and boasts that it "doesn't shrink from thorny issues like 'Education to do with matters involving the reproductive process in higher mammals . . . [and] God isn't dead: no thanks to Jews.'"

The targets were all similar to those of the early years, as was much of the language and style, but there was a shift—as with their treatment of sexuality—from commenting on hatred, atrocity, and stupidity to making fun of its victims as well. It may have been splitting hairs, but there was a new sense of rage within the pages that lacked the righteous indignation, sophistication, and wit that marked the first five years.

To hear Hendra, Kelly, or any of the other more liberal editors tell it, this move was all due to the presence of O'Rourke, leaving one to wonder about his motivations. *National Lampoon* had been O'Rourke's grad school. Understanding that he lacked the natural gifts of Kenney or O'Donoghue, he learned from them. He never considered himself on their level, and he understood that he lacked their complexity. But he did have something that the current staff did not—intuition about where the country was going. He was reacting to the shifting culture, the perceived emptiness he'd found in the platitudes he'd embodied, and the liberals within the *National Lampoon* offices.

Just as Hendra had considered becoming a monk, O'Rourke had his flirtation with the left. The Marxism of his youth, however, had likely been a rebellion against his upbringing and Roosevelt-hating forebears. And therein lies much of the explanation for his shift to the right. He was disillusioned with the ethos of the editorial staff that disliked him. At heart, P. J. O'Rourke was a reactionary.

And what better way to evoke a reaction from Kelly and Hendra than to do something really politically incorrect. O'Rourke aimed to try and prove that liberals weren't funny—not from an insider's perspective that mocked Woodstock-style hypocrisy and silliness, but by going after their core beliefs through pieces that really made fun of minorities in a way that made everyone uncomfortable, yet resonated with the racist that resides somewhere in every American.

O'Rourke was trying to shock, in the long-held *National Lampoon* tradition, Kelly, Hendra, and probably himself. In doing so, however, he'd tapped into what was coming down the road. While his work seemed to echo H. L. Mencken, it also foretold a world in which Sam Kinison would become a successful comedian and Chris Rock would talk about "niggers" the same way a Klansmen might and get away with it because he was black and hilarious. To label him a racist was far too easy. In an environment where Hendra's occasional anti-Semitic comment was explained away through his bad experiences working for cheap Jewish nightclub owners and where even Henry Beard's distaste for Matty could be similarly excused, O'Rourke had tapped into the essential ugliness beneath the well-educated, white male, "too smart for racism" superiority.

Ugly as it seemed, O'Rourke hit on perhaps the single unexplored taboo. His predecessors had worked death and destruction over until there was nothing left. Nixon had been shredded beyond recognition; middle-class white people had been mocked as Kate Smith–loving fools that were crazy for Chicken á la King; and the horrors of Vietnam and the Holocaust had been reduced to comedic fodder. This was shock comedy's final frontier.

* * *

There was much to be angry about. Nixon was gone, replaced by Ford, and soon the equally unfunny Jimmy Carter. The editors were working like dogs. O'Donoghue and Chase were becoming famous, and Beatts had a book. Though circulation hovered near a million, revenues were down substantially because *National Lampoon* hadn't produced anything like *Lemmings*, the Yearbook, or the Encyclopedia in over a year—and then there was always Matty.

As editorial power became less centralized, Matty began involving himself in the process to a greater extent, with many editors resenting the intrusion, thinking that Matty believed he was as funny as they were. And with money getting tighter, there was less to go around and no one had the authority to argue effectively about salaries and budgets. Beard and Gross's departures had badly thrown off the balance of power in the publisher-editorial relationship, where it is standard practice for the writers and artists to want more money (for both salary and budgets) and for the publisher to hold tightly to the reins. This tension is simply part of the game, but without Beard or Gross, the editors were at a loss to handle matters on their own.

McConnachie had never been close to Matty, but was fairly non-confrontational. Over the years, Matty frequently gave him fatherly lectures intended to increase his productivity by suggesting McConnachie not try to hit so many home runs with his writing, but instead satisfy himself with a larger number of singles, doubles, and triples. The result, of course, was that the Irishman swung for the fences every time he came to bat.

"You said it, Buster," McConnachie thought. "That effectively ends my career as a singles hitter."

While taking a leave of absence for part of 1976 to write a Lampoon parody of Hollywood tell-alls called "The Naked and the Nude," McConnachie received pressure-filled phone calls from Matty, who wanted the book finished. Finally, one conversation ended with threats of legal action if he didn't deliver the manuscript. That was the end of McConnachie, who soon joined O'Donoghue, Beatts, and McCall (during a brief stint), at *Saturday Night Live*.

The resentment of Matty came to a head at the office Christmas party. Receiving a miniscule bonus and finding a spread of cheap booze, crackers, and lousy cheese, Hendra was pushed to the brink. Raising a glass to Matty, he rambled off into a long, invective-filled, profanity-laced tirade (which, despite its blue nature, some thought sounded like Shakespeare coming from the erudite Brit's mouth— "the Taming of the Fuck," one editor called it) that ended with something like:

"So I raise this glass to you, Matty—you cheap fuck!"

* * *

Spending minimal time at the office, Doug sought new outlets for his creativity and ambition. With time on his hands, he auditioned for the lead role in *Between the Lines*, Joan Micklin Silver's film about the staff of an underground newspaper loosely based on the *Boston Phoenix*.

Neither Silver nor casting director Juliet Taylor can recall how Doug became involved, but they ultimately cast John Heard in the lead, with Jeff Goldblum, Bruno Kirby, and several other soon-to-be-successful actors taking parts.

Doug was given a small part at the end of the film, as a fan of the newspaper who encounters Goldblum in a bar. With his hair hanging around his shoulders, he utters only a few lines, and flashes a smile that Louise Gikow recalls as being "a zillion watts."

According to one woman who dated Doug on and off, he always had feelers out in the world of entertainment. Now free to pursue whatever he liked, he decided to give acting a try—and the role of a counterculture editor was a natural fit. Let down by not landing the lead, Doug had likely been a bit too nervous to dazzle Silver and Taylor the way he had nearly everyone else.

The idea of getting into movies as a performer was indicative of Doug's long-standing but rather unassuming desire to be the center of attention and the focus of every camera lens. It was the same instinct that drove him to pose for so many promos and spreads and to perform on the radio show whenever he could. He was fearless and more than a little possessed by the idea of being onstage in any way possible. He had an almost compulsive need for exposure. He couldn't resist trying to become an actor the same way he had tried to become a novelist. This pursuit, though, was far more half-assed than his work on TACOS. He likely figured that he would do it and be brilliant right away, while simultaneously preparing for the fact that he might suck.

Yet this desire to be seen and to achieve some substantial measure of fame sharply contrasted with an equally significant wish for privacy and creative autonomy. He still needed success as he had seven years earlier on Jim Rivaldo's floor. He wanted to be cherished by the world and was willing to perform in any way necessary to attain it on a grand scale. His life was often a performance based on the half-truths that he chose to put out in his public life. Yet there was always his deep desire to be the kind of person who didn't need fame at all. Somewhere inside, he wanted to be normal.

* * *

Doug and Walker spent a great deal of 1976 socializing with O'Donoghue, Beatts, Laila Nabulsi, and the *Saturday Night Live* cast. During the next four years they would see Henry Beard no more than twice. Occasionally the pair played poker with O'Rourke.

At an SNL cast party one evening, Lorne Michaels, now the toast of New York, engaged Doug in conversation. There was a stark contrast between the young millionaire who didn't know quite where to go and the man who'd seemingly taken his place as counterculture comedy's boy wonder. During the discussion, Michaels archly offered Doug a job, saying, "Let me help you pick up the pieces of a shattered career."

Doug, who generally had no discernible temper, fumed.

Shortly thereafter, Doug told Matty he was planning to leave the magazine. His work had run its course and he was ready to move on with something else—the nature of which was unclear.

Wanting to keep his surrogate son and star writer with the magazine, Matty told Doug he was planning a *National Lampoon* movie with Ramis and Reitman. If Matty knew anything about Doug, it was that he loved show business and would jump at the opportunity. Matty sold Doug on the idea of writing a film with Ramis, to be loosely based on the Yearbook parody.

Meanwhile, Reitman and Ramis had been working on a script entitled "Freshman Year," based on the latter's fraternity experiences at Washington University. Unsatisfied with the results, Matty paired Ramis and Doug, who'd become friendly. Matty and Reitman simultaneously came to an agreement where the *National Lampoon* would get 75 percent of the producer's money, and 25 percent would go to Reitman.

After messing around on a drug- and sex-filled script called "Laser Orgy Girls" (set in high school, it boasted both a Charles Manson–like figure *and* space aliens), Doug suggested they bring Chris Miller onto the project and use his fraternity-based stories like "Night of the Seven Fires" and "Pinto's First Lay."

The collaboration between Miller, Ramis, and Doug began at a Greenwich Village brunch, where the three writers related their favorite college stories while Ramis furiously jotted notes on a legal pad. All agreed on one idea of central importance: "At the heart of any great fraternity, there is a great animal."

"The moment after we said that, we did that thing where we all looked at each other and said, 'Belushi,'" Miller says.

With Ramis's notes, they set out to write a treatment. None of the three had ever attempted to write a feature-length screenplay. Knowing nothing about Hollywood norms, they produced a 114-page treatment, exceeding the industry standard by roughly ninety pages.

With a finished—albeit gigantic—treatment in hand, Matty approached several studios about making *Animal House*. He failed everywhere. The Warner Brothers production chief, who'd received a hand-delivered copy, at the behest of Steve Ross, pronounced, "It'll never make a movie." Then the treatment fell into the hands of Thom Mount and his assistant, Sean Daniel, at Universal.

* * *

In mid-1976, twenty-three-year-old Thom Mount reported for his first day as assistant to Universal's famously explosive production chief, Ned Tanen. An undiagnosed manic-depressive, Tanen had founded the studio's much-lauded young directors program, but frequently flew into unexplained rages, once publicly dressing down George Lucas after the successful first screening of *American Graffiti*. At Universal, it wasn't uncommon for employees to leave his office ashen-faced, fearing for their jobs and physical safety.

Mount's first assignment was to find an executive named Jerry Miller and fire him, before assessing the various projects Miller had been working on. Mount did as he was told, with a rageful Miller telling him that he wouldn't last six months working for Tanen. Refusing to be fired, Miller quit and stormed out of the office, leaving Mount to sift through a pile of scripts and treatments. Among them was the 114-page monstrosity written by Doug, Ramis, and Miller.

"It was all over the map," says Mount. "It was essentially about frat parties, initiations, and throwing up a lot."

Though it lacked a clear story line, Mount found certain basic elements in place. There was a renegade fraternity bent on fun and destruction in equal parts, an overbearing Nixonian administration, and an unchecked desire on the part of the characters to create chaos. He believed the project had huge potential.

"It was inspiring, though decidedly nonlinear," Mount says.

Mount and Daniel convinced Tanen (who alternately loved and hated the treatment) that *Animal House* was a worthwhile project. Acquiescing, Tanen told Mount to get the script moving and locate a director.

At the same time, Mount was paying attention to the phenomenal success of *Saturday Night Live*. Prior to SNL's 1975 debut, only two shows had successfully captured the "youth culture": *American Bandstand* and *The Monkees*. Mount was also aware of the *National Lampoon* and the humorously aggressive and raw ethos of the times. If *Animal House* could capture that spirit, he believed it would be an enormous success. He was not alone.

Doug went into the project completely confident that he, Miller, and Ramis would write the ultimate youth comedy—subversive, funny, smart, and sophomoric—and create a hit.

The writers devised a work arrangement by which each would compose ten pages (Miller the first ten, Doug the next ten, and Ramis ten more) that would be exchanged, discussed, and edited by each collaborator, after which they would exchange pages again, lending each writer's voice and viewpoint to every page. The entire project was collaborative and noncompetitive.

"It worked because we all had a lot of subversive sensibilities in common," Miller says. "We didn't like authority and thought it was more important to have fun than worry about your permanent record."

When Ramis read Doug's pages, he laughed out loud. The standard of his humor and the polish he put on the text was setting an enormously high bar for his partners. Doug, he found, was writing the movie as if it were a counterculture adult Disney film with sex, drugs, booze, and all manner of antiestablishment mischief throughout.

"[Doug] could get laughs even in his scene descriptions," Ramis said.

They set the film in the innocent world just prior to the Kennedy assassination and meaningful U.S. military involvement in Southeast Asia (again, drawing on Doug's sense of nostalgia for that era), while melding elements of Miller's stories, their own political sensibilities, and the Yearbook. That way they could simultaneously capture both the hope and repression of the country right before the whole place went boom. Their desire was to tear down institutions they despised while celebrating the anarchic, sex-obsessed, beer-swilling teenager that they believed was within every decent red-blooded American male.

Kelly got a look at the original script, which he says was like "a Céline novel," hilarious, dark, weird, and incredibly outrageous, filled with booting contests and culminating with an ROTC siege of the Delta House in which Neidermayer (the evil ROTC commander) moves on the house while driving a papier-mâché float replicating John F. Kennedy's head. Standing atop the roof, Belushi's Bluto defends his fraternity by hurling a keg at the float, which enters Kennedy's head at the exact entry point of his fatal wounds.

"It was unspeakably outrageous," Kelly says.

* * *

When it came to locating a director, Tanen recommended Mike Nichols, John Schlesinger, and Jim Frawley (who had directed *The Monkees* for television). Mount was directed to immediately drop a script at Frawley's house. He did so reluctantly, leaving the script in Frawley's mailbox with a business card.

A few days later, Frawley called.

"This is garbage," he said. "I hate it."

Relieved, Mount began following up on Tanen's other recommendations, none of which seemed remotely viable or appropriate and all of whom he found terrifying.

Daniel's girlfriend, Katherine Wooten, was working as the script girl on the independent film *Kentucky Fried Movie* (shot in twenty days), which was essentially a series of blackout sketches organized together into a feature-length film—a hilarious group of skits spoofing television shows, commercials, and movies—including a legendary kung fu scene. The movie was being directed by a twenty-seven-year-old high school dropout and longtime film junkie named John Landis.

Wooten's stories intrigued Daniel, while at the same time Mount's ex-girlfriend, who'd also dated Landis, encouraged him to go look at the *Kentucky Fried Movie* dailies. After just a few minutes of the screening, Daniel, Mount, and Matty knew that they'd found a director with Lampoon sensibilities. When Mount told Tanen about Landis, however, the studio chief's response was, "Get out of here! Fuck this guy!"

Mount and Daniel eventually convinced Tanen to meet Landis and watch portions of *Kentucky Fried Movie*, after which Tanen gave in, but only if they could deliver the movie for $2.5 million.

"It was some number Ned pulled out of the air," Mount says, "which was status quo at the time."

Later, Matty negotiated a contract that gave *National Lampoon* 5 percent of the gross revenue up to break even, 10 percent up to $15 million, 15 percent until it reached $20 million, and 17.5 percent after that. Clearly, Tanen never imagined the film would be any kind of significant revenue generator for Universal or *National Lampoon*.

* * *

Over the years, Doug maintained close but strained relations with his parents. After buying them the house, cars, and condos, he also put his sister through private boarding school and college. His parents were frequent guests on vacations to the Hamptons and the Vineyard. There were moments of singing and laughter that harkened back to his childhood, but always a profound sense of remove.

When he turned thirty on December 10, 1976, a female friend arranged a small dinner party in Doug's honor to which she invited the Kenneys. Attempting to make the evening a happy event and provide some of the warmth he so desired, the woman toasted Doug and asked Harry if he was proud of his son who had achieved so much success before the age of thirty.

"Actually it would have been the same if he'd never been born," Harry responded with bitter sarcasm.

11

Fuck the Proposal

66 It was the stuff that people in mental institutions talk about, but we were getting paid. 99

—National Lampoon *contributor Chris Cluess*
describing a 1977 editorial meeting

The following things happened in 1977: Jimmy Carter was inau-
gurated with Gregg Allman, Cher, Aretha Franklin, and Linda
Ronstadt in attendance; the following day, Carter pardoned most
Vietnam War draft dodgers; *Chico and the Man* star Freddie Prinze
committed suicide; *Hustler* publisher Larry Flynt was found guilty of
obscenity; the Sex Pistols and the Clash both released their first U.S.
albums; Sylvester Stallone's *Rocky* won the Oscar for best picture;
Studio 54 opened in New York; *Beatlemania* opened on Broadway;
Son of Sam was arrested; Groucho Marx, Bing Crosby, and Elvis
Presley died; advertisers boycotted the ABC sitcom *Soap* due to Billy

Crystal's portrayal of an openly gay character; and *Star Wars* became the top-grossing film of all time.

* * *

A distinguished, graying John F. Kennedy appeared on the cover of the February 1977 *National Lampoon*, which celebrated (as if he had never been shot) the beginning of his fifth term as president of the United States. The issue is a smart blend of nostalgia, cultural commentary, acute political insight, and effective parody.

With the visual imagery and editorial feel of the now-departed American staple *Look*, the issue, named, simply, Kennedy, peeks inside a political dynasty where Camelot has reshaped the United States in its own peculiar fashion. The tragic November 22, 1963, death of Jacqueline Bouvier Kennedy in a Dallas motorcade is depicted in frozen images from the Zapruder film. As Jackie climbs over the trunk to avoid an assassin's bullets, we see JFK kicking her from behind, causing the first lady to be crushed by a press bus being driven by Martin Luther King Jr.'s assassin James Earl Ray. In her memory, Idlewild airport becomes JBK and Bloomingdale's runs an eternal display of the first lady in her famous pink outfit and pillbox hat in their store windows, because, as the widower president says, "She would have wanted it that way."

John-John Kennedy is photographed as a zitty teenager, still in his jammies playing under dad's Oval Office desk, while a voluptuous, topless Caroline is shown giving daddy a kiss good-night.

The issue envisions a world where Kennedy is not just president for life, but also a randy bachelor—whose sexual prowess is a matter of national pride. Forming the "War Corps" after his success in Vietnam (Woodstock is recast as a celebration of Kennedy himself), Kennedy turns his attentions to halting the atrocities in Northern Ireland.

A *Jet* magazine parody, inserted inside the Kennedy issue, is named "Tar," with Martin Luther King Jr. reinvented as self-help guru "Reverend M."

* * *

Though the Kennedy issue is well written and hilariously conceived, it stands in stark contrast to the problems facing *National Lampoon* in 1977. Though it was still not crystal clear that the magazine was entering decline, several factors did not bode well for its future.

For Abelson, Weiner, Kaminsky, Mann, and other new contributors (including future ABC and CNN political commentator Jeff Greenfield), it was a dream come true. They were being paid to smart off. All talented in their own right, they had come of age as writers in a world that had *National Lampoon*. That world, however, begat new outlets for equally bright and more visionary writers to ply their trade—exhibit A being *Saturday Night Live*.

From 1970 to 1975, there had been no place else for people like McConnachie or Miller to take their work. The Lampoon created the market. It also created the career path for counterculture humor writing in all forms, encompassing the work of such people as McCall, Sussman, Bluestone, and Kelly (the last of whom would probably still have been teaching literature had he not found the magazine). *National Lampoon* was the gathering point for all that talent, in the same way Thurber, Benchley, and Parker had been attracted to *The New Yorker* or Mel Brooks, Neil Simon, and Woody Allen were drawn to Sid Caesar's *Your Show of Shows*. Young, angry, funny, overeducated guys who rejected the conventional culture had no place else to go.

But the magazine grew into *Lemmings* and the radio show, which grew into *Saturday Night Live* and provided glamorous, lucrative careers for undermatured geniuses. Instead of attracting new McCalls, McConnachies, and Kenneys, the magazine was gathering talent with a less distinctive voice.

Once *National Lampoon* had boasted a roster of giants: Kenney, Beard, O'Donoghue, McCall, McConnachie, and others. Now it had a bunch of intelligent wiseasses who were gifted, but hardly the A-level talent that passed through 635 Madison during the first half of the 1970s.

Another self-created problem was that the brand of humor to which the magazine gave birth was now five years old and available in mainstream radio and television. America was becoming unshockable. Where they had once asked "is nothing sacred?" the culture now responded with a resounding "no." The younger contributors couldn't possibly have seen that their employer was heading into decline. They were just happy to be getting paid for what they did. But as Carter would soon declare that the nation was having a "crisis of confidence," those who'd been at *National Lampoon* during its recently departed glory days sensed a similar problem within its own pages.

The three individuals in editorial who best understood this problem were Hendra, Kelly, and O'Rourke. Kelly and O'Rourke both had visions for where *National Lampoon* ought to be going. Caring little for business, Kelly believed himself to be fighting the good fight—aiming to maintain editorial quality, not pander, and focus on literate, well-conceived humor aimed at deserving targets. Hendra sided with Kelly out of both a shared worldview and friendship, yet Hendra's level of respect at the magazine was greatly diminished by past behavior and a growing drinking problem.

O'Rourke, on the other hand, saw matters in practical terms. He wanted more than anything to preserve *National Lampoon* as an institution by whatever means available.

The allegiances within the office tilted toward Kelly and Hendra. O'Rourke, though friendly with Mann and Sussman, did not socialize with the rest of the group. Kelly and Hendra, by contrast, were perceived to be mentors and the strongest editorial link to the era of Kenney, Beard, and O'Donoghue.

Though philosophically they appeared to be leaders of opposing camps, there was a sense that O'Rourke respected Kelly's intelligence and desired his acceptance—which would never be forthcoming. Thus Hendra, thanks to his alliance with Kelly, his distinctive persona, and his reputation as being a problem, would become O'Rourke's main combatant.

The situation had to come to a head.

* * *

Tanen's objections aside, Landis was the perfect man to direct *Animal House*. As brilliantly conceived as the script was, Landis, like

Michael Gross, gave it life, translating the *National Lampoon* style of humor to a new medium.

Landis came on board and immediately suggested changes to the script. Though he loved the anarchy and wit of the original draft, he found it too angry, hateful, and downright harsh. The conservative, well-connected, high-achieving Omegas were assholes. That was good. But the Deltas were disgusting beyond belief and despicable in their own way. It was the kind of thing that worked in the magazine, but not on screen, where viewers need someone to root for. Landis therefore insisted on a simple "us against them" conflict. The Deltas needed to become more of a "good guy" fraternity.

The young director also eliminated all scenes of projectile vomiting, to the delight of Matty and the dismay of the writers. Unaccustomed to being second-guessed and unfamiliar with the workings of Hollywood (where directors refer to projects as "my film"), a certain amount of tension developed, particularly between Landis and Ramis, who wanted a lead role in the film. Yet despite these initial setbacks, Landis's take-charge attitude and kinetic energy proved to be a blessing.

A few years earlier, studio executive Barry Diller called Landis to potentially direct a comedy called *The Big Bus*. With only the low-budget *Schlock* under his belt, Landis was presented with an *Airplane!* before its time, a disaster-film spoof with a terrific script. Diller asked Landis how he might cast the project.

"As the bus driver, I saw Rock Hudson, and for the female lead I wanted Elizabeth Taylor," Landis says.

Mystified, Diller wanted to know why you would cast straight dramatic actors in a comedy. It didn't make sense. Landis told Diller that serious actors would make the audience believe the characters, thus making the parody accurate and eminently more funny. Ultimately, Landis didn't get the job, which, in a strange twist of fate, went to Jim Frawley, who cast comic actor Joe Bologna in the lead. *The Big Bus* was a critical failure and tanked at the box office.

Landis refused to give up on his idea of straight actors in comedy, and *Kentucky Fried Movie* had succeeded, in part, on getting straight actors to do outlandish things. He intended to apply the same principle to *Animal House*. Tanen had other ideas. He, like

Diller, wanted comedy stars and comedians. Landis stood his ground and held out for character actors and unknowns.

"They wanted Dom DeLuise to play the [mafia-connected] mayor," says Landis. "I love Dom DeLuise. I just didn't want him for the part."

Rather than DeLuise, Landis hired character actor Cesare Denova, who had been in *Cleopatra* and *Mean Streets*, where he convincingly played a mafia don.

As the evil Dean Wormer, Landis wanted Jack Webb, the dead-pan, crime-fighting *Dragnet* star. Over a booze-soaked lunch, however, Webb couldn't understand why anyone would want him in a comedy and turned down the role, after which Landis turned his sights to veteran character actor and film heavy John Vernon, whom he'd seen in Clint Eastwood's *The Outlaw Josey Wales*. At one point in the film, Vernon, with a blue-eyed squint, delivers the unforgettable line, "Don't piss down my leg and tell me it's raining." Landis thought, "Dean Wormer!"

For the dean's bored, drunken wife, Landis suggested lavender-clad former leading lady Kim Novak. Tanen and other Universal execs began to suspect their director was insane. Instead he cast Verna Bloom, a gifted stage actress who made her film debut in Haskell Wexler's independent film classic *Medium Cool*.

As casting continued, Universal executives began to fear that the film lacked star power. Belushi at the time was considered only a supporting ensemble actor, and the prevailing opinion was that he couldn't carry a film at the box office. Tanen and Reitman desperately wanted Landis to cast Chase (the first true "star" at SNL) as Otter, the charming Delta lady-killer, which had been written with him in mind. Landis hated the idea.

"The role [of Otter] was so close to Chevy," Landis says, "it would have thrown off the balance of the film."

The decision, however, was made for Landis when Chase chose to star opposite Goldie Hawn in *Foul Play* rather than appear in *Animal House*. With Chase out of the picture, the role went to Tim Matheson, a handsome former child actor whose most recent role was on *The Quest*, a short-lived TV series costarring Kurt Russell.

To appease Universal's growing fears, Landis and Mount called on Donald Sutherland. Landis had worked with Sutherland on *Kentucky Fried Movie* and Mount knew the actor from his days as Jane Fonda's script reader. Sutherland agreed to appear as a favor to the pair, taking the role of Jennings, the English professor who turns Katy, Boon, and Pinto onto pot.

Sutherland spent two days on the film's Eugene, Oregon, set, commuting from San Francisco, where he was shooting *The Invasion of the Body Snatchers*. He turned down an offer of profit participation and opted for a fee of $50,000, ultimately costing himself somewhere around $15 million.

Sutherland's decision to commit was crucial. Universal was no longer concerned about the star quotient. Landis says, "It was Donald Sutherland who essentially got the movie made."

The rest of the leads went to several unknowns and stage actors, just as Landis had hoped. Karen Allen was cast as Katy; Peter Riegert landed the role of Otter's sidekick, Boon (which Ramis had envisioned for himself); stage actor Tom Hulce became Pinto; Kevin Bacon got his first film part as smarmy Omega pledge Chip Diller; and, in one of those "it could only happen in Hollywood" stories, Stephen Furst won the role of Flounder when he delivered a pizza to Matty Simmons. He always taped a headshot to the inside of the box and, upon opening it, Matty saw Flounder staring him in the face.

* * *

Less successful was the stage show *That's Not Funny, That's Sick!*, which seemed to have been thrown together for one purpose—to make money. This was the kiss of death at *National Lampoon*, where unfettered, mildly directed creativity and anarchy were the unlikely predecessors to success. This show, however, was perceived as simply another cash cow to generate much needed revenue for an enterprise buckling under the weight of the buyout and amortization on the loan Matty had secured.

That's Not Funny, That's Sick! was little more than a theatrical "best of" album or year-end compilation of articles. This had become a tried-and-true recipe for revenue, as it simply involved repackaging old material without any new writers fees. In the world of theater, it achieved less than stellar results.

Made up of recycled gags from previous shows, the show starred several gifted but not transcendent performers. There was no Belushi, Guest, Murray, Radner, or even a Joe Flaherty.

"We were keenly aware of this pantheon of guys who came before us," says actress Sarah Durkee, "but we were what Joe Piscopo was to John Belushi's *Saturday Night Live* cast."

A cute "Lily Tomlin wannabe," Durkee joined a cast that included a rubber-faced Arkansan named Rodger Bumpass, Yiddish theater performer Eleanor Reissa, actress Wendy Goldman, and Andy Moses, a Jersey-born Jewish kid who'd been appearing in theaters all over the East Coast. *Curb Your Enthusiasm* and *Seinfeld* creator Larry David auditioned, but didn't make the cut.

Performing reheated pieces from *Lemmings*, the *Radio Hour*, *The National Lampoon Show*, and the odd article, the show toured with middling success. Bookings were scattershot; sometimes the venues were terrific, though not infrequently they performed at places such as one Baptist church in the Northwest where Moses did Guest's "Jackie Christ" routine before a stunned audience. In Columbus, Ohio, they were scheduled to perform at a 2,500-seat coliseum, rather than the Ohio State campus; fourteen people showed. An unruly crowd of angry bikers showed up at Tampa's Papa Joe's. "They didn't want to hear comedy," Moses says, "they wanted girls shooting ping-pong balls." The tattooed audience yelled at the cast the entire evening, drowning out the show. In Rochester, New York, they performed on a stage "the size of a bathtub" and a drunken Moses had to be supported by actors on either side of him lest he fall into the audience.

During a successful run at the Roxy in Los Angeles, stars like Jack Nicholson turned out and laughed, while *Laverne and Shirley* star Cindy Williams upbraided the cast for "Jackie Christ" and another piece in which the cast gave the crowd the finger.

"That was the least funny thing I've ever seen in my life!" she shrieked.

"You clearly don't watch your own program," Moses shot back.

* * *

Chris Cluess and Stu Kreisman began their entertainment careers as CBS pages. Cluess, tall and Italian, had just gotten out of the navy. Kreisman was short, Jewish, and a recent NYU graduate. A self-described "Larry Kroger type," Kreisman was a quiet wallflower who sat in his high school hallway making fun of everyone after they passed by. He knew little about what he wanted to do, just that he wanted to avoid working at his father's wallpaper store.

The pair made a name for themselves at CBS cracking jokes for broadcasting giants Walter Cronkite and Douglas Edwards. This reputation was further solidified the day Ed Sullivan died, when they wrote a memo from the network president, on CBS letterhead, asking employees to leave work and go directly to their houses of worship to pray for Sullivan's eternal soul. When someone mimeographed the memo and posted it all over CBS, many employees departed the office and headed for temples and churches across the tri-state area.

Somehow, the pair was kicked upstairs into sales, where they listened to Bob and Ray on New York's WOR radio and tried to crack each other up. Then, one Monday morning in October 1975, Cluess asked Kreisman if he'd watched the *Saturday Night Live* premiere that weekend. He had. That evening, they wrote endless pages of sketch material that they took up to the SNL offices the following day at lunch.

Arriving at 30 Rockefeller Center, the pair found Lorne Michaels's secretary and introduced themselves as funny guys who wanted writing jobs—immediately. "Do you have an agent?" she asked. When they responded in the negative, the secretary said she'd be throwing their sketches in the garbage, after which the despondent pair headed to the nearest bar and got drunk. Believing he'd lost his one opportunity, Kreisman told Cluess that he was doomed to remain in television sales, have 2.3 kids, and die of a heart attack before he was sixty.

Too drunk to go back to work, they decided to drive home to Queens. With Kreisman behind the wheel, they saw Belushi, Aykroyd, and Garrett Morris getting into a cab at Fifty-seventh and Seventh. Kreisman gave chase and followed them back to NBC. As the actors paid for their ride, Kreisman turned to Cluess. "If you're ever going to make an impression on anybody, do it now!"

A hammered Cluess rushed across the street, looking straight at Belushi, Morris, and Aykroyd and yelling, "Stop! I'm not going to hurt you!"—not exactly a reassuring comment in 1975 Manhattan. Belushi threw himself against the cab, Morris ran away, and Aykroyd took a boxer's crouch, prepared to deck the tall inebriate. Sensing that his approach wasn't working, Cluess begged Aykroyd to listen and recounted the interaction with Michaels' secretary.

Aykroyd rescued their portfolio from the trash can. Calling Cluess that evening, he said that much of their work was crap, but that some of it was funny and invited them to visit the show, where they were soon hanging out whenever possible. During one of these visits, Aykroyd called Kelly and set up a meeting at which the pair was asked to write letters to the editor for a few months. They soon joined the *National Lampoon* staff.

Working primarily for Kelly, both men became friends with Abelson and Weiner. Before long, they joined an editorial meeting to plan the October 1977 issue dedicated to the Beatles, with a cover parodying the *Abbey Road* album. Kreisman and Cluess were soon witness to a heated debate as to whether the barefoot McCartney should be stepping in shit as he crossed the street. Despite the crudeness of the topic, the discussion was held, as Cluess recalls, at an extraordinarily high level, with a head-spinning, rapid-fire exchange of historical and popular culture allusions all aimed at discerning whether the British rocker should be stepping in feces.

"It got down to what should be in the shit? Should there be corn in there? If not, what?" Cluess says. "I thought, 'This is where I was born to be.'"

Cluess and Kreisman were assigned to work on a Beatles catalog that marketed the band's ridiculous inventions and other crap they wanted to sell. Capturing the voices of each musician, they parodied how base and commercial the iconic band had become, writing descriptions to hawk the "I Am the Eggman Egg Cup" and a "Nowhere Man Notepad" that sold for $69, as well as "Paul's Fixing a Hole Handyman Kit" and a perfume called "#9" whose copy reads, "It's perfume. It's perfume."

The pair immediately aligned themselves with Kelly and eventually warmed to the now cranky and intimidating Hendra, whose office was always freezing cold, with wet jockstraps and athletic gear littered about on the chairs. ("He'd go play whatever English guys go play in the middle of the afternoon," Cluess says.) O'Rourke, they thought, was removed and Teutonic. Most editors and writers, it seemed, were bonded in their opposition to Matty, who was now involved with Hollywood and fending off attacks from the burgeoning religious right.

* * *

In 1975, *National Lampoon*'s *199th Birthday Book* celebrated the bicentennial a year early, with a forgettable piece by Hendra that referred to Mormons as "Morons." The result was the loss of nearly 2,000 drug and convenience store outlets in the West. Since that time, the magazine had teetered around a million copies a month, but circulation was beginning to trend downward. With fewer seasoned writers capable of knocking out parody books and special publications, the company showed its first year of negative revenue in 1977—a loss of $25,227.

For his part, Matty was spending more and more time in California working on *Animal House* and establishing himself in the entertainment community. The chaos back at the office, however, was apparent in daily phone calls.

On a trip back to New York, Hendra and Kelly took Matty to lunch at a nearby Japanese restaurant they called "The Robota" that served as a hangout for the staff. The pair told Matty that they were getting burned out and felt that there was a need for newer, younger blood to lead editorial. That year, Mogel had discovered a French fantasy magazine named *Metal Hurlant* on a trip to Europe and, with Matty's approval, decided to publish it in America as *Heavy Metal*. Kelly was acting as de facto editor while attending to his other duties at *National Lampoon* as well as various entertainment, publishing, and music projects.

Clearly chagrined by his work environment, Hendra had been mortified to see teenagers sniggering on the subway as they read *National Lampoon*. He was now at least twenty years older than a readership that seemed to get younger by the day. Dismayed by his perception that the magazine was now trading on sex and angrier, more offensive humor aimed not at the establishment but at the disenfranchised minorities of the world, Hendra was in no mood to pander to a new audience.

Matty sat silently as the pair laid out a plan by which they would become editors emeritus, putting Abelson and Weiner in charge of the day-to-day operations. Hendra and Kelly would handle general oversight of the pair, while Kelly worked on *Heavy Metal*, and both turned their attention to future projects that might expand the Lampoon name into television, recording, radio, movies, and other venues.

The meeting ended with little resolution and nearly no commentary from Matty.

* * *

A diehard baseball fan, Kelly formed a *National Lampoon* softball team that competed in the Central Park Broadway Show and Publishing Industry leagues.

On a cool spring afternoon, while playing against *Penthouse*, John Weidman and Cluess looked up into the stands to see Matty's wife, Lee, with a deep, dark tan that belied her Manhattan residence. Cluess turned to Weidman, "My God, look how tan that woman is," to which Weidman responded matter of factly, "Matty had her bronzed."

One evening, as he and Cluess were tossing a ball in anticipation of that night's game, Kreisman saw O'Rourke working in his office, wearing a suit and tie. Feeling bad about how he'd been ostracized by the staff, Kreisman entered and asked O'Rourke if he wanted to join the team. Looking up, he politely declined and went back to work.

O'Rourke now realized that he was not going to be part of the gang, nor did he want to be anymore. Rather, he'd thrown himself even deeper into his role as managing editor, telling one colleague that he was going to beat Hendra and Kelly by outworking them. Though he had a girlfriend and an active life away from the magazine, O'Rourke knew that Hendra and Kelly had homes, children, and family commitments. Moreover, though both were productive, neither was known as a particularly hard worker, preferring to hang around and shoot the shit with other writers rather than actually produce on a daily basis. He would outwork them—to death.

* * *

Mount, Landis, and Reitman sent the *Animal House* script to university presidents and college administrators across the United States, meeting with rejection everywhere but the University of Oregon, whose dean of students, while working at another university, had refused to let Mike Nichols shoot *The Graduate* on the campus because he didn't like the script. Realizing that his strength was in academia and not film criticism, he let Landis have the campus for thirty-two days in summer 1977.

Landis brought the Deltas—Matheson, Riegert, Hulce, Furst, Bruce "D-Day" McGill (in a role written for Aykroyd), and Jamie "Hoover" Widdoes—up to Eugene, Oregon, a week and a half early to rehearse the script and bond like real fraternity brothers.

One evening shortly after their arrival, Matheson, McGill, Widdoes, Riegert, and Karen Allen found their way to a real-life Omega-style party, where the brothers of an uptight young Republican fraternity did not welcome them. Trying to get out before anything started, Widdoes accidentally dumped a beer on one of the brothers and a melee erupted, with McGill, Matheson, and the others receiving bruises, black eyes, and chipped teeth in a brawl on the lawn.

Mercifully, Universal had provided Cliff Coleman as Landis's first assistant director. A crusty, cowboy boot–wearing SOB and veteran of several Sam Peckinpah films, Coleman was accustomed to this type of situation. Acting as the grizzled old sergeant to Landis's buck private, Coleman found medical care for the actors and made sure that nobody told the director that a fight had even taken place. For a young director, having somebody like Coleman around to shield him from terrifying and chaotic situations was essential.

When actors Jim Daughton (the smooth, arousal-challenged Omega president Greg Marmalard), Mark Metcalf (the paranoid Omega "Sergeant at Arms" and ROTC instructor, Neidermeyer), and Kevin Bacon (Omega pledge Chip Diller) arrived in Eugene, they were greeted by an openly hostile group of Deltas—their fellow performers throwing food at them in the cafeteria and calling them dickheads at every turn.

Housed at a motel near campus, McGill wheeled the lobby piano into his room, where he, Doug (who took on the role of Delta's possibly retarded, nerdy oddball "Stork"), Miller (in the role of chronic masturbator "Hardbar"), and the other Deltas smoked dope, drank, and played loud music well into the night. Metcalf, living a floor above and deprived of sleep, got into character by angrily shining his military boots for hours on end.

The thirty-two-day shoot was decidedly low budget. Landis had no trailer or office on the set and was unable to see dailies for three weeks. His wife (costume designer Debra Nadoolman) purchased the circa 1961 costumes at local thrift stores and sewed togas with Judy Belushi. The film was such a low priority that Universal refused to give Landis a crane for more than two days, lest they take it away from *The Incredible Hulk* television show.

Landis, however, had worked since high school in nearly every aspect of film production. He knew how to shoot, edit, and work every piece of equipment necessary to make a film. Though not expert, he'd done almost every job that there was to do on a movie set. He knew what could and could not be done. No crew member could bullshit him about the boundaries of their capability.

Nowhere did Landis's understanding of the process become more evident than in the shooting of the famous courtroom scene where Hoover pathetically defends the Deltas, while his brothers cough "blow job" in the background. Reitman, an experienced low-budget filmmaker himself, bet Landis that there was no way to shoot the overwhelmingly long scene in a single day. The director responded by keeping the camera in one place and moving the actors around for reaction shots, cutting time wherever he could and winning the bet.

Landis also showed extraordinary skill at handling his actors—particularly Belushi. In order to pull off his larger-than-life, cartoonish Bluto character, Landis boiled down the role to a cross between Harpo Marx and the Cookie Monster. The key element, he believed, was appetite. Both Harpo and the Cookie Monster were characters of voracious appetites (for sex and cookies, respectively) who somehow came off as lovable. On the page, Bluto was a disgusting pig, yet the audience needed to love him. There needed to be an essential sweetness to the character for the film to succeed. Without that component, the audience would see a vulgar, primitive animal with no redeeming qualities.

Belushi, whose copious gifts included the uncanny ability to convey warmth while doing unspeakable things, intuitively understood the concept and delivered a performance that cemented his stardom. Landis cut the part down to its bare essentials, using Belushi as punctuation, doing nothing but making entrances and exits, like "a meteor flashing across the sky," Landis says.

The young director also made room for a great deal of improvisation. Though only playing a bit part (for which he cut his hair in proto-dork style), Doug joined in and even wrote Sutherland's classroom speech about the need to read Milton (no matter how boring) on the set as the actors waited to do the scene.

Doug's gift for this type of quick, brilliant, improvisational humor had been apparent in both his professional and personal life from the start. He had done off-the-cuff Thackeray for Hendra and, upon first meeting Harold Ramis (who took a vacation to Greece rather than taking a smaller role in *Animal House*), took a book off the shelf in the actor's apartment, read a page, and then improvised dialogue that maintained the tone, voice, language, and plot of the text, challenging Ramis to determine where the author left off and the performance began. When Ramis expressed amazement, Doug shrugged and said, "I can do that with any book on the shelf."

Landis himself improvised during the scene where the Deltas go to the grocery store and Matheson's Otter tosses food items over his shoulder to a bedeviled Stephen "Flounder" Furst. Not knowing exactly what was about to happen, the chubby, sweating Furst followed Matheson, as Landis, off camera, threw more and more food into his arms. Refusing to cut, Landis kept it up while Furst, in real desperation, tried to catch each and every item without dropping anything. It would become one of the film's classic scenes.

Perhaps no one enjoyed the *Animal House* shoot more than Doug, who'd driven across the country to Eugene and was reliving his college days at the motel with the cast and crew, even smoking pot and watching boxing matches on television in the unlikely company of John Vernon, who played Dean Wormer to perfection.

Despite initial misgivings about Landis's attitude that it was "his film," Doug made himself completely available to the director. A frustrated actor and exhibitionist, he threw himself into the character of Stork, a choice that paralleled the use of his picture in the Yearbook parody and its "What a dip-shit!" caption. Miller thought that Doug consciously, or subconsciously, chose the role because, deep down, he feared that he truly was Stork.

Though he'd only appeared briefly in *Between the Lines*, Doug created an indelible character in Stork. Whether it was his "What are we supposed to do, ya moron?" line during Bluto's ranting speech about their impending expulsion or leading the homecoming marching band down an alley, the tiny role is remembered by everyone who has seen the film.

During the toga party scene, as rain poured in through a leaky floor and everyone sweated profusely, Doug looked at Belushi, screamed, "Hey John, we ought to do the gator," fell to the floor, and appeared to have an epileptic seizure. Landis had no idea what was going on and asked Doug about it, who explained that it was, in fact, a real dance. Confirmed by Belushi and Miller, the moment stayed in the film.

At the end of a rain-soaked shoot, Landis was suffering from walking pneumonia and went to Mexico, where he literally dried out. Getting in his car to leave Eugene, Landis said good-bye to Doug, who told him, "John, my heart is breaking." He had found a new muse and medium. Doug Kenney was going to Hollywood. And so was Matty Simmons.

* * *

At Universal, Tanen and his executives generally ignored *Animal House* and hoped it would stay on budget. Returning from his vacation, however, Landis sent Tanen into convulsions by hiring Elmer Bernstein (who created the scores for *The Ten Commandments* and *The Great Escape*) to create a straight-faced film score. Using the same principle that guided his casting choices, he wanted a professional and serious score to make the satire more effective.

As Bernstein worked on the score, Landis showed the rough cut to Tanen, Mount, and Daniel. Tanen loved parts, but absolutely despised others, particularly the scene in which Otter is viciously beaten by the Omegas. Standing up, Tanen demanded that the film be stopped and the screening room lights turned up. Staring at the now silent Landis, Mount, and Daniel, he said, "That's not funny."

"It's not supposed to be funny," replied Landis, dumbfounded.

"We're making comedies that aren't supposed to be funny?! Is that it?!" Tanen screamed and stormed from the room, leaving Landis, Mount, and Daniel in stunned silence.

During another screening, Tanen insisted that Landis remove the scene where Boon, Pinto, Otter, and Flounder visit the all-black Dexter Lake Club where Otis Day and the Knights are playing. Believing it would be offensive to African Americans, Tanen claimed that it would start race riots in theaters showing the film. Promising Tanen they'd try to remove the scene, Mount and Daniel spent several weeks wondering whether it might be objectionable to black audiences. Mount then called in Richard Pryor, with whom he'd worked on *Car Wash*.

Pryor and Mount watched the film alone in a screening room on the Universal lot. As the lights came up, Mount asked Pryor whether he considered the scene offensive.

"No, man," Pryor chuckled. "It's just fucking funny. And you know what else is funny?"

"No," Mount replied.

"White people," Pryor said. "White people are funny."

The scene stayed.

* * *

By early 1978, *National Lampoon* circulation dropped below 700,000. As 1977 came to a close and he spent more and more time in California, Matty realized he needed to do something about the rotating editor system that was essentially being run by Kelly and Hendra, both of whom hated him.

The staff was a wild, flaky group that could be counted on to (a) be funny and (b) fuck with Matty as much as they could. Kleinman, though talented, was not Gross or Kaestle; where the two men commanded considerable gravitas and respect for their stewardship over the design, Kleinman was younger and more erratic. He didn't have the same ability or authority. No one seemed to be in control. Moreover, while the new staff was gifted and funny, they didn't live and breathe funny as Kenney and O'Donoghue had. The energy was waning. Matty needed someone to take over the ship immediately.

By his own admission, O'Rourke had been angling for the job. He was sick of missed deadlines and the incoherence of the magazine's content and design. No two issues seemed to be alike. Unimpressed by Kelly and Hendra's pitch, Matty asked O'Rourke to write a proposal detailing his plans for running the magazine and recapturing its former glory.

About to leave for a vacation in Key West, O'Rourke decided to spend the entire week in Florida writing a twenty-page proposal. He envisioned a *National Lampoon* that could grow older with its audience, perhaps something like a slicker version of Britain's *Private Eye*. Most of all, however, he wanted to make it funnier and less self-indulgent—framing the insanity within a grown-up magazine.

Upon returning to New York, O'Rourke received an early morning call from Matty, informing him that he was the new editor in chief. "I haven't shown you the proposal," O'Rourke said. "Fuck the proposal!" Matty responded.

Before they knew what hit them, Kelly and Hendra had been marginalized just as they had marginalized O'Rourke a short time earlier. O'Rourke, much to their dismay, brought in a secretary. Only Matty had ever had one. In suit and tie, with his feet up on the desk, he would call from his office for Betsy Aaron to take a memo. Kelly thought O'Rourke was aping the mannerisms of Superman's big city editor, Perry White.

Though they disliked each other, Kelly found something oddly touching about O'Rourke being in charge and taking on a managerial role. O'Rourke looked like a kid in his uncle's suit, acting the way he thought an adult male was supposed to behave in the real world.

"He had no dad," Kelly says. "He'd seen some movies, but he had no model for what a guy in a suit did."

At the first editorial meeting under his guidance, O'Rourke sat at the head of a table in *National Lampoon*'s tiny boardroom. Rather than bouncing ideas around with the staff, he issued edicts. In Kelly's recollection, there was a constant stream of "I want! I want! I want!" No discussion of whether it was the right thing to do or what anyone else might think. If O'Rourke wanted it, it would come to pass. Kelly decided that he would not work under these circumstances. He took over *Heavy Metal* and collaborated with Hendra on entertainment projects. *National Lampoon* was now P. J. O'Rourke's magazine.

12

Round Up the Usual Jews

❝ Tip the world over on its side and everything loose will land in Los Angeles. **❞**

—Frank Lloyd Wright

The following things happened in 1978: *Saturday Night Fever* topped the pop charts, cementing the emergence of disco; a gunman shot and paralyzed *Hustler* publisher Larry Flynt; Woody Allen's *Annie Hall* won the Academy Award for Best Picture; *Dallas* premiered on CBS; Sid Vicious covered Sinatra's "My Way," murdered his girlfriend, and committed suicide a year later; thousands of gay and lesbian marchers celebrated Pride Week in New York and San Francisco; popes Paul VI and John Paul I died within the space of two months; *Science* magazine published a study in which monkeys eschewed food for cocaine; jogging became a national obsession; Anwar Sadat and Menachem Begin signed the Camp David accords;

San Francisco mayor George Moscone and gay city supervisor Harvey Milk were gunned down by an assassin; the Supreme Court upheld FCC sanctions against a New York radio station that had played George Carlin's "Seven Dirty Words" routine; 900 members of Jim Jones's People's Temple of the Disciples of Christ died after intentionally drinking poisoned Kool-Aid; and Studio 54 co-owner Ian Schrager was arrested for possession of cocaine with intent to distribute.

* * *

A 1978 *New Times* article detailed the fallout at *National Lampoon*, focusing on the precipitous drop in circulation (1 million in 1975 to 659,000 in August 1978) and the human carnage among the editors.

Since the buyout, the following people were no longer on speaking terms: O'Donoghue and Beard; Trow and Beard; Hendra and Beard; O'Donoghue and O'Rourke; O'Donoghue and Kelly; and O'Donoghue and Hendra. Not noted was the strain between Hendra and Kelly, the latter still openly complaining about his tertiary billing on *Lemmings*.

Though *Heavy Metal*'s circulation had risen from 90,000 to 240,000 since its acquisition and was making a contribution to the company, it wasn't nearly capable of offsetting difficulties at *National Lampoon*, which was now forced to derive more and more income from advertising without Taylor to offset the mounting pressure from religious groups and growing right-wing sentiment that would peak with Ronald Reagan's 1980 election.

O'Donoghue mocked the magazine, claiming that the editorial department was too well aligned with the business side and had "bent down for the soap for too many Japanese stereo producers."

O'Rourke's secretary, Betsy Aaron, also saw the slippage. Though the average reader was still twenty-four years old, there was (as Hendra had noticed on the subway) a far more juvenile, as opposed to sophomoric, group reading the magazine for tits and dirty jokes. Going through the reader letters, Aaron noticed that with each month they seemed to be coming from younger and younger boys.

"That's who the core reader was becoming," Aaron says. "It was a great disappointment. Intellectually the bar was being lowered."

O'Rourke was spending as much time crunching numbers as he was guiding editorial, handling business that was of little concern to the rest of the staff. Whatever his personal tastes and desires, O'Rourke first and foremost saw the need to sell magazines and make money. In this area he received little help from other quarters. Kleinman was talented, but not good at coming in under budget. Covers were now being created to sell magazines, rather than for the precision and quality of parody. Nearly everyone thought O'Rourke was dictatorial and often nasty.

The perception among the editors and artists that they were kids housed on the fourth floor, constantly at war with the adult business folks, persisted. With Matty's absence and O'Rourke's management style, the tension was now firmly rooted in the creative end of the magazine.

O'Rourke's well-defined strength, beyond his own output, lay in his ability to get the magazine running in an orderly fashion and on budget. He worked on cleaning up its look and created a structure for delivering things on time.

"If he had a deadline, he met it," Mogel says. "He was tough on the contributors, but there wasn't a crisis every month the way there had been before."

His skills as an editor and manager were not as well developed. *National Lampoon* had been O'Rourke's only real job. He had no role models for running the ship aside from Henry and Doug, both of whom had been visionary and credited as geniuses. Neither was a particularly gifted editor or manager in any traditional sense, yet their reputations and abilities afforded them tremendous respect. The indefinable cohesion of their disparate styles created an open atmosphere of creative freedom and high standards. Both men also held power equal to Matty's and acted as a buffer for the writers and artists.

O'Rourke had no such credentials. He'd been ostracized by Kelly and Hendra, leaving him with few friends in editorial beyond Mann. Making matters worse, he was an admittedly bad editor, good at rewriting others' work but not capable of coaxing it from their pens. The result was that every piece that came in went through his blender and came out bearing certain hallmarks of his voice, negatively impacting the variety of styles that had originally given the magazine such freshness.

Beyond his editorial skills, O'Rourke's demeanor was difficult. While capable of greater warmth and generosity than Henry, he also flew into rages, screaming, breaking things, and punching his fist through office walls. It was from O'Rourke that Aaron learned the expression "go eat a bowl of suck." Aaron and others were walking on eggshells, fearing the next explosion.

Hendra and Kelly refused to work with O'Rourke, who was not at all disappointed by their decision. Each agreed to a severance package with Matty, but stayed on for at least a year to handle upcoming entertainment projects. The others, however, were not about to listen to O'Rourke.

"Once P.J. took over everything changed," Kreisman says. "There was no longer a place to congregate. People were miserable and now the guy who nobody was talking to was captain of the ship."

To demonstrate that change was afoot and achieve some solidarity with the editors, O'Rourke asked for a small budget to redecorate the offices. He had the common areas painted battleship gray, hoping the cool, placid color might calm things down a little and subliminally create a more disciplined environment.

For his own office, O'Rourke chose a motif that echoed the deck of a battleship, both befitting his personal tastes and signifying that he was in charge. Sussman's space was spare and modern. Mann took the greatest license, creating an environment that looked like the tent of a British colonial administrator in deepest war-torn Burma or some other exotic, far-flung destination. Complete with hammock, camouflage, and mosquito netting, with the lights frequently off, the office served as a dark haven from which the other employees could only see the burning red of its occupant's eyes.

Mann was probably O'Rourke's greatest ally. He completely mistrusted Hendra ("He was a film villain," Mann says. "You couldn't ask for a more conflicted, passion-ridden, Hogarthian monster") and admired O'Rourke's hardworking attitude, ethical boundaries, and contrarian political philosophy ("P.J. had a special gift for invective").

"One thing that P.J. did that Tony never did was work," Mann says. "P.J. had ethics, like a belief in personal property. This was something that never excessively troubled Tony."

O'Rourke and Mann bonded over their shared love for alcohol, fast cars, and reckless adventure. On one occasion the pair borrowed a truck from the editors of *Car and Driver*, intending to rescue the women of Long Island from an oncoming hurricane they'd heard about on the news. Driving against traffic and equipped with several quarts of whiskey, ropes, and ladders, they headed out to Islip, prepared for anything. When the hurricane turned out to be extraordinarily weak, the pair settled in at a Howard Johnson's restaurant for the evening, where they drank the booze and chatted up the waitresses.

Upon returning the vehicle, one *Car and Driver* editor told O'Rourke that Mann seemed "a little out of control." The moment would provide inspiration for Mann's greatest Lampoon creation, O. C. ("Out of Control") Ogilvie, in "The Adventures of O.C. and Stiggs," which chronicled the antics of two hell-raising, suburban teens who, on one occasion, steal a rare stamp collection from a hated neighbor and send him scatological postcards with the treasured stamps as postage.

And indeed, the editor was right. Mann was out of control. Frequently drunk at the office, he cared little about whom he offended. Before O'Rourke took over, Kelly and Hendra had approached Matty with the idea of running a full-page ad in the *New York Times* trumpeting a new, more mature *National Lampoon*. They were interrupted when Mann burst through the door, laid on Matty's desk, picked up the telephone, and dialed 911.

"I have a robbery to report," Mann told the operator.

Angry about some deduction from his paycheck, he said that a man named Matty Simmons, whom he had apprehended at 635 Madison, was the criminal and that he would subdue him until police arrived.

Enraged, Matty grabbed Mann, tossed him toward the hallway and into another office. Several minutes later, Matty announced solemnly, "Ted Mann no longer works at *National Lampoon*." Mann showed up the next day as if nothing happened and nobody asked him to leave.

If Matty had hoped to scare Mann, he did not succeed. Shortly thereafter, Mann met a bagpiper on the street, whom he hired to play "Hava Nagila" outside of Matty's office while the publisher was on the phone negotiating some aspect of the *Animal House* contract.

When Mann turned his surreal rage onto someone who seemed deserving, nothing was sweeter to the editors and staff. It was embarrassing and uncomfortable, though, when such behavior was foisted upon the unsuspecting public. As a dedicated smoker who lit up while in the hospital with a lung infection, Mann refused to put out his cigarettes in cabs and elevators. If a stranger objected, he would scream that the hapless interrupter was "a rat fucking, mother fucking son of a bitch." At the Lion's Head Tavern, a Manhattan bar frequented by the literati, he beat up another patron who failed to show the bartender proper deference. Less violent but equally distressing were his habits of berating French tourists for not speaking English, and purposefully bumping into blind people on the street and insisting that he was blind as well.

Writers and editors such as Weiner, Abelson, Kreisman, and Cluess admired Mann's attitude and ability to do what he pleased. He was completely unlike anybody else in the office. However, they were equally frightened that he might go off at any minute.

"He was like the Vietnam wacko in the office," Abelson says. "I liked him. You had to, or he might kill you."

Most of Mann's generosity and kindness were reserved for a street person he called "my bum" and to whom he would flip the occasional $100. Mann, Kelly says, had a tremendous fondness for the gutter and reprobates, thus his friends were all fringe characters with names like Squid and Weasel. The latter was a cocaine dealer, and henceforth the drug became known around the office as "weasel dust."

Doug appreciated Mann's outrageous behavior and spent significant time with him, touring late-1970s Manhattan nightlife at the Bells of Hell (owned by Malachy McCourt, brother of *Angela's Ashes* author Frank McCourt) and spending a bizarre evening at

J.P.'s, a secret bar that featured underground cement rooms where the famous, wealthy, and drug addicted went to snort cocaine. It was there that Doug surveyed the scene and began marching around with a Mars bar, calling in a singsong Germanic tone, "Eva! Eva! Come here, Liebchen! I have something for you!"

Around this time it became clear that Doug Kenney was using cocaine. He was not alone in this among his fellow writers, entertainment industry insiders, or the denizens of 1970s Manhattan. The drug, however, would, in large part, lead to his undoing.

* * *

Mann was not the only writer or editor determined to stick it to Matty or O'Rourke.

Kaminsky came across a satirical French magazine with a severely anticlerical bent. Within its pages he discovered a picture of the gates of heaven depicted as open legs with a particularly detailed and hairy vagina in the middle that housed a manger, three wise men, the Virgin Mary, and Jesus Christ.

The staff mocked the picture up as if it were going into the magazine and sent it to Matty for approval. Matty had lost RCA as an advertiser when the Vatican (which held considerable RCA stock) objected to the magazine's treatment of Catholics and was under endless pressure from religious groups all over the country, so the timing couldn't have been better.

As soon as the piece hit his in-box, the editors sat in their offices and waited. All at once, Matty's door banged open and the publisher began running down the hallways screaming, "What the fuck! What the fuck!"

* * *

The once-freewheeling editorial meetings became, in Weiner's words, "like college seminars with a strict teaching assistant." The tension had become nearly unbearable as O'Rourke's style seemed to leave little room for creativity.

"The atmosphere was oppressive and constrained," Weiner says. "You had permission to have ideas, but it's harder to have them under that atmosphere. If you're a bricklayer, and you know what your job is, that might be OK. But to have ideas, it makes a big difference."

The tenor of creative tension had devolved into tension without creativity. Where there once had been equal measures of anger, humor, and cutthroat competition, only anger remained.

By adopting the mantle of authority, O'Rourke, by definition, had become far less rebellious. This is not good for any humorist, and it caused a rebellion among those he managed. As they had done with Matty, the staff decided to let O'Rourke know precisely who was in charge.

A PBS station from Baltimore had arranged to film a day in the life of the *National Lampoon* with O'Rourke at the helm. A memo went out instructing the writers to attend an editorial meeting that would be filmed for the documentary.

Behind the scenes, word went out that it was time to have some fun with O'Rourke. Sitting at the head of the table, O'Rourke called the meeting to order, intending to demonstrate a typical, no-holds-barred, wacky editorial meeting at America's most irreverent magazine. As the cameras rolled, O'Rourke solicited theme ideas for upcoming issues. He was met with dead silence. Uncomfortable, he tried to prod them with a few suggestions, like sex and politics. Nobody bit. The only audible sound in the room was the whirring of the cameras filming the meeting. Suddenly, Sussman made a noise.

"Gerry?" O'Rourke said with a mix of hope and desperation, "Do you have something to say?"

"Nothing P.J." he replied. "Just clearing my throat."

The silence seemed to continue forever. The inmates had taken over the asylum.

* * *

The only things that appeared to be under O'Rourke's control were the budget and the production schedule. With a crew bent on mutiny, he kept his nose to the grindstone, but had a growing perception that there were other problems about which he could do absolutely nothing.

"In the wake of *Animal House* and *Saturday Night Live*, young, darkly comedic talent could go to Hollywood and make $100,000," O'Rourke says. "When the Lampoon started, young, darkly comedic talent could go to hell and be glad of the cheap rents."

National Lampoon humor had been created by young men who had nowhere else to go. Between 1970 and 1975, the magazine had been an island of sanity in Nixon's post–Summer of Love world. The stable of writers came from places that had seldom been mined: Catholics, the Ivy League, the upper classes, and Canada. They were men with adult skills and perceptions, but childish attitudes.

"We were standing in the flower garden with our noses pressed up against the dining room window, making faces at the grown-ups eating inside," O'Rourke says. "There would come a day for most of us when it would be time to go in the house, take our places, and have faces made at us in return."

That problem plagued not only the magazine's internal workings, but also its audience. The baby boom generation with which the magazine had so resonated was now sitting at the table. As Aaron had found, the new reader was of a considerably different sensibility and makeup. Bridging this gap was a monumental task that caused O'Rourke to wonder if he, Sussman, and the others might need to go inside and eat as well.

No matter how bright or funny they were, Kaminsky, Weiner, Abelson, Cluess, and Kreisman were not capable of operating at the same level as Kenney, O'Donoghue, Beard, and McConnachie. Rather than appearing out of nowhere, they had been influenced by *National Lampoon*. They were *National Lampoon* writers, not individual voices that came to the Lampoon. It was a small but significant difference.

In the coming year, O'Rourke would offset the situation by finding an original and talented voice in Chicago advertising executive John Hughes, with whom he collaborated on the magazine's Sunday Newspaper Parody. Hopes for survival, however, were directly pinned to *Animal House*.

* * *

Ever the gambler, Matty was banking on the success of *Animal House* to cure what ailed *National Lampoon*. A box office hit would not only refill the increasingly empty coffers, but also would give a massive boost to circulation and revitalize the brand.

Matty was right to believe in the film. It had come about through that most Lampoon-like process of organic growth, somehow discovering people like Landis who "got it" and could bring the magazine's humor to a wider audience while breaking new ground. Like the magazine, there had been no market research or clear plan, but the result was pristine and uncompromising. It had been an idea aimed, in part, at keeping Doug around, and yet it had found a life of its own. Landis's direction and the lack of attention from the studio made for a potent combination, and, at least in the short term, saved the *National Lampoon*.

* * *

Lucy Fisher, currently an executive with Francis Ford Coppola's American Zoetrope Studio, attended the first *Animal House* screening at the American Booksellers Association convention in Denver around Memorial Day 1978. Though it seemed clear throughout the screening that the audience loved the movie, almost no description could do justice to their reaction when it was over. Here was the riot that Tanen had predicted, but no African Americans were tearing out seats and destroying the theater; rather, the audience went insane as the credits rolled, standing on their chairs, applauding wildly, and screaming with abandon. It was more than a good, funny movie— *Animal House* had touched a nerve.

"It was a done deal immediately, you could just tell," Fisher says. "Doug was completely successful, yet again, in an even more difficult medium. He completely broke all of the Hollywood odds on his first try."

* * *

Animal House premiered at Manhattan's Astor Theater on July 28, 1978. Landis forgot his tickets and wound up late to the opening. Having held the lights for some time, Matty gave the go ahead to start the film. Arriving twenty to thirty minutes late, Landis had a tense screamfest in the lobby with Matty that devolved into physical threats. The pair made up at the end of the screening.

Kevin Bacon, still working as a Manhattan waiter, asked for the night off and found himself unable to get into the premiere or the after party at the Village Gate. Instead, he stood by the guard ropes, hoping to get the attention of cast members or others who might recognize him.

Around 635 Madison, hopes had not been high. The editors and other staffers wondered, "Who would go see a college comedy?" and some who'd read the script made dour predictions. Kreisman sat with the other editors at the premiere, after which they all panned the film.

"We were all jealous," he says.

At the Village Gate later that night, as bottles of champagne popped and everyone got drunk, stoned, or both, Mount avoided Tanen and other Universal executives who were still demanding that the Dexter Lake Club scene be removed before the film had a wide release. One executive threatened to punch Mount if the scene was not excised.

Knowing he had a hit on his hands that would catapult him into the big time, Matty seemed to be the happiest man in the room, save for Doug.

Friends who saw him that evening recall that the generally upbeat Doug was positively beaming. They'd never seen him happier.

* * *

Some critics dismissed or pigeonholed *Animal House* as the first "gross out" comedy, trading on sex, drugs, and collegiate antics. While true, this explains little of the film's success.

Mount described the depth of the film's appeal in a *Newsweek* article. "The humor is post-60s, post-acid, and politically closest to the Yippies. It's anti-establishment in every way. I like the anarchy."

Much as the *National Lampoon* magazine had done in print, *Animal House* was one of the first movies to take on, in an unflinchingly honest manner, American taboos on sex, masturbation, race, and other previously unspeakable topics.

The Dexter Lake Club scene was important, not only because it's memorable, but for the depth and honesty it applied to race in America. Upon entering the all-black club, Riegert's Boon can't wait to see Otis Day and the Knights. "He loves us!" Riegert says, before looking up at the musician and screaming, "Otis! My man!" inspiring a look of "Who the hell is this fucking white boy?" from the singer.

The Deltas and their dates, except for Boon, are terrified to be the only white people in the bar. And judging by Otis's reaction, they aren't exactly welcome. By setting the film in the early 1960s, Miller, Kenney, and Ramis were able to cloak the tense dance scene between the races as nostalgia, but even in 1978, few white men or women would feel comfortable in an all-black environment, nor would its denizens particularly roll out the welcome mat. What comes off as terrific comedy is also biting social commentary that takes no clear position other than to point out the absurdity of the situation. The audience intuitively understands both sides.

The moment is pure Doug. It is the same aesthetic ambivalence that he brought to "First Blowjob" and the Yearbook. It is America in a nutshell, both good and bad, presented in an open and non-judgmental manner, complex and never preachy, with a clear moral viewpoint.

Since the film's release, Landis has been approached time and again by people who believed deep in their hearts that they themselves were members of the Delta/*Animal House* on their college campuses. Nobody has ever claimed to be an Omega, not even the innumerable senators (including Sam Ervin), CEOs, and other men who clearly did not while away their college days drinking nonstop and trying to subvert authority.

Animal House works on so many levels. It is deeply political, with Wormer echoing Nixon and presenting class warfare between the outsider Deltas and well-heeled Omegas. Its worldview captures the American belief that at the bottom we're just a ragtag bunch of fun-loving individualists who hate the yoke of authority as much as the colonists hated the British crown. It is the same archetype of self-reliance and independence depicted in westerns—that the guys who break the rules (be they outlaws, nerds, drunks, Don Juans, psychopaths, or slobs) are who we want to be. Anarchy and mayhem is celebrated. Melding high and low humor, the writers allow Milton jokes to exist side by side with vomiting; a horse drops dead of a heart attack (and is removed from Wormer's office via chain saw); and Katy, the only sane character in the film (played by Karen Allen), offers to write a note for Boon, telling the Deltas that he is "too well to attend" a toga party. *Animal House* is many things, but it is not stupid. Beneath all of the "gross-out" humor (which would launch films such as *Porky's, There's Something About Mary,* and countless others), it is a smart and literate comedy that deftly blends satire, physical comedy, parody, high ideals, and bad taste without ever showing its seams.

With a $2.5 million budget, John Landis, Doug Kenney, and the rest had changed the direction of film comedy and touched off a youth movie revolution that earns hundreds of millions at the box office each year.

* * *

By October 1978, *Animal House* made $60 million at the box office. From the date of its July release, it maintained the top spot on *Variety*'s charts for two months, slipping for only a week and then returning to number one for several more. By Christmas, it had grossed $100 million, making it the most successful film comedy in Hollywood history, surpassing even *Blazing Saddles.* Within two years of its release (at $155 million), it became the eleventh highest grossing film of any kind. The film was such a phenomenon that *Newsweek* featured a toga-clad John Belushi on its October 23, 1978, cover below the headline "College Humor Comes Back."

For weeks, Matty ran around 635 Madison with *Variety* in his hands, expressing his pride in *Animal House.* The editors and staff believed that he was saying "Matty Simmons has done it again," taking credit for what Kenney, Miller, Ramis, and Landis had accomplished.

The financial impact was enormous. Within two years, proceeds from the film allowed Matty to pay off the debts incurred during the buyout. For 1979, pretax revenues exceeded $3 million, largely the result of *Animal House* profits and increased circulation due to the film. Though there was trouble back at the magazine, the film injected *National Lampoon* with much-needed life and momentum.

With plans to create an entertainment empire, Matty and his wife relocated to Beverly Hills, and *National Lampoon* attorney Julian Weber was named president of the company. Signing a development deal with Universal, Matty's future projects would include a never-produced film entitled *Jaws 3–People 0*, *Disco Beaver from Outer Space* for HBO, and *Delta House*, an ABC sitcom based on *Animal House*.

* * *

Around the time of *Animal House*'s release, Kreisman and Cluess were hired to write for a television special hosted by Alan King. Traveling back and forth from California, they were derided at the office as sellouts and generally looked down on by O'Rourke, Sussman, Kelly, Hendra, and the others.

While in New York, King invited the pair to watch a rough cut of the show. Seeing his name in the closing credits, Kreisman was aglow. Returning to the office on a high, he made the mistake of conveying his excitement to the other editors, who proceeded to give him endless shit.

Doug happened to be visiting that day. Hearing the treatment Kreisman was receiving, he pulled the writer into an empty room, where he confessed his own sense of glee at seeing his name on screen for the first time during the *Animal House* credits. Together the two men jumped up and down like schoolboys, overcome at realizing their show-business dreams.

Suddenly the door opened. It was Sussman. Immediately, Kreisman and Doug stopped smiling and began acting as if they were having a serious conversation. When Sussman left, they went back to jumping.

* * *

With the glow of success emanating from his pores, Douglas Clark Francis Kenney of Chagrin Falls, Ohio, headed for the dream factory of Hollywood, where he was now the most popular boy in town. As the man behind *National Lampoon*, much of the writing credit accrued to Doug. Nearly every studio pursued him, all wanting to cash in on a thirty-one-year-old who had struck gold in his first crack at filmmaking and in so doing had tapped the dormant youth market.

Signing a two-year production deal with Fox, Doug took an office on the studio lot and formed a production company with Harold Ramis, Alan Greisman, and Michael Shamberg (two young producers he'd met through his agent, John Ptak).

Shamberg was a college friend of Ramis's who'd worked as a Chicago crime reporter and documentary filmmaker before coming to Los Angeles and joining forces with Greisman on *Heartbeat*, a movie about Neal Cassady, Jack Kerouac, and the Beat Generation that starred Nick Nolte and Sissy Spacek.

Doug, Greisman, and Shamberg created Three Wheel Productions, which would be dedicated to making films written, developed, and possibly directed by Doug. In his first official act, Doug designed company stationery with a logo that depicted a sleazy agent type, dripping in jewelry and leaning on a Jaguar sports car, beneath which was emblazoned the motto See You in Court.

On the Fox lot, the threesome occupied offices across from Lawrence Kasdan and down the hall from both Mel Brooks and Barry Levinson. Doug assigned Mayer and Harvard friend John Leone to write a script about prep school and asked for a treatment from humorist Jules Feiffer. On his own, he began formulating a movie about Himalayan Zen Buddhists who could down airplanes with their minds.

Immediately, Doug injected tremendous enthusiasm and childlike energy into the enterprise. Ideas seemed to come nonstop, and he engaged with most creative people as if on a playground, once using sticks to simulate a sword fight with a screenwriter who was pitching a film about the Revolutionary War.

Shamberg found working with Doug similar to playing with a virtuoso musician. Like Thelonious Monk, John Coltrane, or Miles Davis, he worked in comedy riffs. Nearly all situations that entered Doug's consciousness were instantly refracted through a comedic lens and spit back out in his distinct rhythms. When the group prepared to make any kind of business deal, Doug would call out, "Round up the usual Jews!" It was, Shamberg thought, something like Tourette's syndrome, as the humor seemed to pour out every second of the day.

"He was completely in an alternate reality," Shamberg says. "He was disconnected from pragmatic reality, and intensely eager to succeed commercially."

Doug's instincts about material were pristine. He had an uncanny knack for sizing up writers and scripts, often without even reading them. He would simply say that somebody or their writing sucked and, almost always, he was right. In this he was completely confident and absolute in his belief that he always knew what was good and bad.

"Two prominent screenwriters sent us a script about something where there was a gun involved," Greisman recalls. "They got the description of the gun wrong. Doug said they were talentless."

He would do the same with Walker, giving her nutshell reviews of books and movies he'd neither read nor seen yet was able to sum up with clarity and insight that almost always proved to be dead on.

As a business partner, Doug was unpredictable. He cared little for, and resented, studio executives and those who made deals in Hollywood, often lighting a match and saying it was the work of Universal's special effects department.

"He didn't like grown-ups," Walker says. "Or those who were pretending to be grown-ups."

Though he had dreamed of Hollywood and the film business, there was no sense that Doug was thrilled to be there. Something about it seemed cheap and artificial to him, as if the Yearbook, with its idiotic and brutal teenage social order, had sprouted up on the Pacific. The rebellious nature that made him a brilliant writer, when commingled with his conflicted feelings about business and adult-hood, made for an often unpredictable partner who blew off all forms of authority. Once, in a meeting with Fox chief Alan Ladd Jr., Doug couldn't be stopped from endlessly quizzing the studio head about the company's hiring practices and whether they were discriminatory.

"And we weren't even high that day," Greisman recalls.

* * *

"The worst thing that ever happened to him was cocaine, and he knew it, too," Emily Prager said. "He was far too conscious of who he was; when you're as intelligent and perceptive as Doug, you can't do anything without knowing that you're doing it. It's almost a curse."

During the early 1970s, marijuana was the drug of choice in Hollywood. Anyone who was making pictures was smoking pot, which had taken precedence over the booze once swallowed in gallons by John Wayne, John Ford, Clark Gable, and other legends of Hollywood's golden age. And, much as marijuana had replaced alcohol, cocaine became the drug of choice during the late 1970s. It symbolized success and cost big money (which was never in short supply), while seeming to provide endless energy and an unerring sense of well-being. It would destroy the lives and careers of innumerable actors, directors, and producers. Scorsese was doing it. So was Dennis Hopper. It was openly snorted in offices across the Los Angeles basin.

Though he had used it frequently in New York, cocaine now took a central place in Doug Kenney's life in Los Angeles. There were always sugar bowls full of it wherever he went, and he indulged freely.

Whereas marijuana generally alters one's perceptions in a manner that can enhance creativity and, at the very least, provide a sense of calm and relaxation, cocaine has quite a different effect. As pleasurable as its initial effect may be, cocaine induces a substantial measure of paranoia and desperation, a belief that one can only be happy and function properly when he or she has access to more and more of it.

For Doug, the drug was poison. A fragile, gentle personality who saw things all too clearly, Doug would become increasingly unpredictable and sometimes cruel under its influence. Ultimately, it fractured his already conflicted personality into a million pieces. Yet somehow, cocaine—a drug that rarely enhances anyone's sense of humor—had no discernible impact on Doug's innate gifts. He remained focused on his work and very, very funny.

* * *

Doug and Kathryn Walker rented a home on Betty Lane in Coldwater Canyon. A dusty, moldy, one-floor place with a pool in the shade of eucalyptus trees, it became very much a bachelor pad for Doug, as Walker frequently was away working on location or the New York stage.

Decorated with books, a sofa, and, often, a gigantic bag of marijuana, the home became the center for a burgeoning Hollywood social scene that revolved around Doug's comedy friends such as Aykroyd, Belushi, Flaherty, and Ramis. Greisman, Shamberg, Ivers, Fisher, and others were also frequent guests, as Doug held massive parties where artists, college pals, and studio executives found themselves socializing with waitresses, valets, hitchhikers he had picked up, and whomever Doug had befriended that week.

"His life was one continuing, traveling party," Greisman says. "He was the kind of person who would befriend anyone."

* * *

With a multi-picture production deal at Universal, Matty was thrilled to be in Hollywood. Though his long marriage was beginning to crumble, the high stakes and payoffs of the movie business seemed to make his blood surge as it never had before. Unlike Doug, he had no ambivalence about authority or cynicism regarding the industry he was embracing. Matty went at it full bore—network television, cable, and movies.

Matty's first project was *Disco Beaver from Outer Space*, which is notable only for its title. Directed by Alice Playten's husband,

Joshua White, it's a series of sketches strung together by takes of a large costumed Beaver who roams New York City in an attempt to create havoc. Starring Durkee, Playten, Hendra, Elbling, Bumpass, Jamie Widdoes, and, strangely, British actress Lynn Redgrave, it went on to be the lowest-rated show in HBO history.

The film's content flies all over the place, ranging from pieces about a woman addicted to Perrier (then the rage) to Jeff Greenfield's game-show spoof, "The Breast Game," where the entire object is to get women to remove their shirts. Another Greenfield skit, about Ed Sullivan favorite Señor Wences (he of the talking hand), had originally called for the use of a fictitious name. Unfortunately, during production, the character was called Señor Wences. Seeing it by accident, Mrs. Wences was incensed by the filthy language and situations involved in the sketch and threatened legal action.

Of the show, Durkee says, "If there is one clear moment in a career when you look at your immediate circumstances and vow 'I will do better than this,' *Disco Beaver* was it for me."

*　*　*

Now living in Los Angeles, Cluess and Kreisman were called to meet Matty at his Universal offices. During the meeting, Matty asked the pair to write a sketch for *Disco Beaver*. Determined to create the most vulgar, reprehensible thing they could possibly write, Cluess and Kreisman devised a *Three's Company* spoof rife with lewd, unfunny sexual references, included a woman who pleasured herself with candles, and renamed the character's hangout (the Regal Beagle) the Split Beaver Café.

"It was basically a fuck you," Kreisman recalls. "Nobody would have touched the script with a ten-foot pole. We figured we'd never hear from Matty again."

Three weeks later, the writers received detailed notes from Matty's assistant, on Universal stationery, asking them to soften some of the language and perhaps find something more palatable than their constant reference to one female character as a slut.

"Matty took it seriously," Kreisman says. "I'm not sure he knew how to capitalize on *Animal House*."

* * *

In October, *Newsweek* interviewed O'Rourke for the Belushi cover story. His discussion of humor demonstrated a fierce divide between the politically liberal, young men who wrote for the magazine and their leader, signaling what he thought about the state of comedy.

"Almost all traditional humor has paid some homage to the serious," O'Rourke said. "It's a hallmark in our esthetic family that nothing is sacred or so important it shouldn't be made fun of. We never say, 'all kidding aside.' A lot of this is a backlash against the enormous seriousness of the 1960s, all the good vibes and piousness. It's a fair guess every one of the Lampoon editors was a member of the counter-culture back then, but look what happened; after all the folk songs and candlelit marches it didn't change a thing. You could argue that the world's a worse place now."

"I am not a fan of P.J.'s politics," Abelson says. "I was never comfortable with his version of countercounterculture humor. His attitude was that you could be just as funny making fun of gay rights. But he proved it. The man can make a sentence snap."

O'Rourke proved Abelson's statement true in the *National Lampoon Sunday Newspaper Parody*.

* * *

Billed as a sequel to the Yearbook, the Sunday Newspaper Parody was conceived by O'Rourke while he was snowed in during Christmas at a relative's home in Nebraska. Looking at the crappy Lincoln Sunday newspaper, O'Rourke believed that he'd located another uniquely American artifact that was the same in every midsized community around the country and begging to be parodied.

Now filling Doug's role of resident star, O'Rourke asked a new contributor, Chicago adman John Hughes, to assist him in creating the *Dacron Republican-Democrat*—"One of America's Newspapers."

O'Rourke had discovered Hughes's talent, and the two quickly became allies. When Matty wondered why they were using the Chicago-based writer, O'Rourke went to great lengths to defend Hughes.

When Matty seemed disinclined to credit Hughes for a piece of work, it was O'Rourke who went to bat for him.

Though not around the office, Hughes would call Betsy Aaron daily, reading her every single word that he was writing for the magazine. Quietly quirky, unassuming, and a generally pleasant fellow, Hughes was mistrusted by some editors simply because he was aligned with O'Rourke. His work, however, would be some of the most interesting and amusing to appear in the late 1970s *National Lampoon.*

Hughes was incredibly productive, a quality that had been in short supply. He could fill pages, and his work included "The Smart Set," which parodied gossip columns, as well as several articles per issue by mid-1978. Less angry and vicious than the early editors, Hughes's work echoed Garrison Keillor far more than it did Ed Bluestone or Michael O'Donoghue.

His best pieces, like Doug's, tapped into the mind of teenage American boys. In 1978, Hughes wrote "My Vagina" and "My Penis," which, in the dead-on voices of a pubescent boy and girl, tell of waking up with the wrong equipment attached between one's legs.

"It is so embarrassing to eat and talk with your mom and dad and brother with 'a thing' in your pants. Plus, it was hard to walk when it was stiff. But it was okay because by the time I sat down it was small, but then when it was small, it stuck to the skin of my leg and that just felt icky. The good thing about girls' 'privates' is that even though you get a 'visitor' every month, the stuff stays the same. . . . "

Before the decade was over he would write several funny, astute, and nostalgic pieces about family vacations that formed the basis for *National Lampoon*'s *Vacation* movie series, which helped keep the enterprise financially afloat and in the national consciousness during the 1980s.

* * *

Whatever his political agenda, O'Rourke showed himself to be an immensely capable humorist in the Sunday Newspaper Parody, which features such articles as "Negroes—The Problem That Won't Go Away," and a headline about the "Plan to Sell Soviet Jews."

The parody deftly captures the narrow-minded thinking that dominated small and midsized American towns in the years after Nixon and before Reagan. Beyond the local police's search for the "Powder Room Prowler," one headline focuses on the disappearance of two Dacron women in an Asian volcano, rather than the decimation of an entire nation, as the subhead reads: "Japan Destroyed" accompanied by a map of the Eastern Hemisphere showing "where Japan was formerly located."

A typical "man on the street" feature asks a wide cross section of Dacronians (postman, rocket scientist, steamfitter, housewife, phone repairman, and accountant), "How about all this that's going on in the Middle East?" He receives responses that range from "Can't make head or tail out of it," to "Oh, gosh, you'd have to ask my husband about that," and "It's a heck of a thing."

The parody is nearly as complete and precise as much of the Lampoon's early work, down to ads for Rosenberg's department store, which sells French Three-Legged Jeans and Colorful Japanese Paper Luggage, and includes an insert for the soon-to-be out-of-business grocery store Swillmart ("Where Quality Is a Slogan") that promises discounts on "perpetual lunch meat" and a Lady Swillmart "armpit dryer."

The "Sunday Week" magazine includes stories on Dacron's gay scene ("they don't really seem to be very happy at all") and the town's illegal aliens—both of them. It's a portrait of white American concerns that seem to be only slightly heightened and created with vicious accuracy.

With four printings, O'Rourke and Hughes's collaboration sold 350,000 copies and reaped over $1.5 million in revenue. Yet despite its success and the *Animal House* phenomenon, circulation remained in the neighborhood of 650,000 by year's end.

***

Doug Kenney's relationship to money had always been confusing and complex. Growing up in Chagrin Falls, he'd seen it as a tool in the social wars, as the thing that kept him from swimming with the leggy blond at the country club, stringing rackets in the tennis shop where his father had once been the pro instead. Coming from a family of skilled servants, the social stratosphere had been ingrained in Doug before birth. Unlike the child of a laborer, he was able to see up close what those "with" had, and its effects on those "without." He'd watched his father bristle under the burden of serving the wealthy, and created tales that portrayed Harry as some kind of everyman superhero who was far cooler than the rich guys to whom he taught tennis.

At Harvard, he traveled in all social classes, realizing that nobody was better than anyone else, regardless of their parents' social status. Yet he'd been enamored of the good life represented by Moss Hart and Kitty Carlisle's apartment, Khosla's Gatsby-like shirts, and Fishburn's tweed jackets. He had also seen, up close, Henry's silent but furious struggles against having grown up rich.

In Chagrin Falls, Cambridge, and Manhattan, he had witnessed the American dream firsthand. It was what his father had strived for and what Doug had achieved at such a young age. He had transformed himself from nerd to preppy to hippie and now to unassuming millionaire artiste. Yet inside his head was a continual battle between the perennial outsider, nose pressed against the country club window, and the Harvard-educated, brilliant, good-looking, wealthy insider. To lose that tension and give in to his newfound status would have been too much to bear and constituted a lifestyle decision that he was, by nature, completely incapable of making. In order to remain himself and produce the humor that was his lifeblood, he needed to be able to mock the house on the hill, even though he could now afford it ten times over. Instead, he bought it for his parents.

Thus began a string of fabled interactions with money that touched the lives of nearly everyone he met and has since become the subject of as much fascination as Henry's reasons for storming off in a rage.

While looking through a book on the shelf of Doug's Los Angeles home, Peter Ivers discovered a four-month-old, uncashed check for $186,000. When Ivers brought the check to Doug's attention, he responded with something like, "Oh, I was wondering what happened to that."

This story is typical and told by friend after friend. Checks found in books, sofas, and under the floor mats of his Porsche. Greisman recalls Doug calling him and asking his partner to look on the floor of his car for a $45,000 check that he'd misplaced several days earlier.

"Doug created hilarious chaos around himself," Greisman says.

At restaurants, it was always Doug who picked up the tab, quietly leaving 50 to 100 percent tips. Valets would frequently open their palms to find $100 bills, which Doug's friends often sought to retrieve.

"The money was just falling loose from his hands," Greisman says. "It was like he couldn't find the five, so, 'Oh fuck, take the hundred.' It wasn't showy. He just didn't know what to do with the money."

* * *

Doug and Kathryn Walker's relationship was serious and had the potential to become permanent. Yet ambivalence again became a substantial problem. Doug wanted a normal life with a wife, kids, and a nice stable home, yet he had never known anything like that in his thirty-one years. He'd only known the illusion.

With Walker, he was most himself, able to show his dark side as well as the perennially funny, charming demeanor that dominated his public persona. They would argue viciously, with Doug able to discern his mate's weaknesses and human failings, unafraid to point them out.

"He could be very mean," Walker says, "but it was enlightening. He could say the most insightful, painful things about you, things that nobody knew."

Walker, by her own admission, could be explosive, theatrical, and difficult. To her, Doug was often confounding and elliptical, opposing thoughts always coexisting in his mind. Ultimately, however, his calming, Zen quality prevailed. Doug was the only one who could ease her pain and bring her back down to earth.

Doug's childhood was a not infrequent topic of conversation. Having met his family, Walker believed that they had no idea who their son truly was and were mostly dismissive of his chosen career, success, and nontraditional lifestyle. To Walker, he was much like the protagonist of James Joyce's *Portrait of the Artist as a Young Man*, with a cold, emotionally violent family that could never embrace a sensitive genius in their midst.

And though he was now the financial, commercial, and artistic success he had spoken of becoming at Jim Rivaldo's apartment in 1969, when he was penniless and living off handouts, Doug Kenney was unfulfilled. In Los Angeles, where thousands came each year to pursue their dreams, he was a success and the center of a hip, smart, funny social circle that adored him. It was all that he'd ever dreamed. Yet it meant nothing. Somehow, it was ill-gotten and illegitimate.

Like his ex-wife, Alex, Walker asked Doug to see a psychiatrist. But after just a few sessions with a therapist he quit, again believing that he was whoring out his inner life in a commercial transaction. Instead, he coped as he always had.

During the next year or so, with Walker frequently away, his various personae would become increasingly diverse. Everyone loved him, yet he meant different things and became different versions of himself, depending on the group in which he was traveling. There were many lives and many circles—druggies, Harvard intellectuals, movie people, hippies, the rock 'n' roll nightlife, and home with Walker. Each distinct and separate from the other.

"He commuted through many lives and lifestyles simultaneously," says Lucy Fisher. "He could fit into all of them himself, but it was hard to have others who could traverse all of those things."

"I think he was miserable," says Michael Shamberg.

Soon he would meet Jon Peters, increasing the misery tenfold.

13

Pheasant Shake
for Mr. Kenney

    " Hollywood is a place where they'll pay you a thousand dollars for a kiss and fifty cents for your soul. **"**

—Marilyn Monroe

The following things happened in 1979: *Superman* led at the box office; John Mitchell and Patty Hearst were released from prison; the Shah left Iran; eight traders on Chicago's Options Exchange were arrested for cocaine distribution; via the efforts of Kurtis Blow and Grandmaster Flash, rap began to emerge; a poll showed that 99 percent of American homes had a television, up from 58 percent in 1974; Larry Bird's Indiana State team lost the NCAA basketball championship to Earvin "Magic" Johnson and Michigan State; Idi Amin was dethroned as dictator of Uganda (also foiled were his plans to grapple with a Japanese sumo wrestler in a match refereed by Muhammad

Ali); Saddam Hussein took over in Iraq; *Evita* opened on Broadway; Joe Walsh of the Eagles ran for president and Jello Biafra of the Dead Kennedys ran for mayor of San Francisco; and Iranian students took ninety American hostages at the U.S. embassy in Tehran. The crisis would last 444 days and destroy Jimmy Carter's presidency.

* * *

Delta House premiered on ABC in January 1979, and placed in the Nielsen top 10. Jamie "Hoover" Widdoes and Bruce "D-Day" McGill reprised their film roles. A then-unknown Michelle Pfeiffer took the role of "The Bombshell," an untouchable sorority girl. Zero Mostel's son Josh played Bluto's cousin, "Blotto." Chris Miller, who'd written the pilot, thought his script was reasonably funny and in keeping with the film's anarchic spirit. Much of the humor, however, was excised to maintain network standards. Miller soon saw that "the Omegas were in charge of the network." Airing at eight P.M. during prime time, it was on early enough that the kids weren't yet in bed. *Delta House* lasted only thirteen weeks before being canceled.

The essential problem with *Delta House* was that it could never be anything like the movie. The cast was different and of lesser capability, but moreover, there was no way that it was possible—or even allowable—to re-create the sex, booze, and brutally frank anti-authoritarian humor of Landis's film in the television medium. By 2000, it would have worked on HBO. In 2004, it might have worked on Fox. But in 1979, there was no chance.

Instead, though often funny, the show was a watered-down, safe-for-the-kids fraternity comedy that lacked the film's irreverence and spirit. It was utterly two-dimensional—where the movie had been larger than life.

* * *

In August 1979, a *St. Louis Post-Dispatch* reporter asked Matty Simmons if he was lucky.

"I don't think there's such a thing as being in the right place at the right time. I think that we all get our opportunities and some of us cash in on them and some of us don't. The proof is that except for *Delta House*, I've never had a major product that hasn't succeeded. I want to tell you that Universal pictures never thought that *Animal House* would be a hit. I said 'trust me' and they said, 'What the hell? It's a small budget. The guy does have the biggest humor magazine in the world. We'll trust him.' And they made $50 million. Now we're working on the sequel, which will start shooting in the fall."

"Why didn't *Delta House* get high ratings?" the reporter asked.

"They put us in the wrong time slot on the wrong night. I screamed and yelled and it didn't help. I mean everybody in the whole world knows that NL has enormous inroads with the 18–35 audience and the 18–35 audience is going to rock concerts and movies on a Saturday night. Very smart. But, that's how it is."

* * *

The failure of *Delta House* and the interview with Matty demonstrate the strengths and weaknesses that would, in part, prevent *National Lampoon* from becoming an entertainment empire.

On the plus side, Matty always had a firm belief in the talents of his employees. He might hassle them about budgets or scream that their work was too offensive, but ultimately he was a soft touch who believed in his boys. The instinct to generate projects on little more than a whim or an instinct was a tremendous asset, and the gumption to back such endeavors was invaluable.

The problem, however, came when Matty was left alone to make deals and generate projects of his own. The quality-control function suffered for the lack of creative talent like Beard, Kenney, O'Donoghue, Ramis, and others. The instinct to cash in on *Animal House* was completely appropriate. Yet the idea of doing a television show spun from the film—no matter how alluring or remunerative—was naive at best. Uncompromising, edgy, high-quality product had always been *National Lampoon*'s appeal. To water it down for prime-time display was asking for disaster and, when combined with the lesser quality of the magazine, damaged the *National Lampoon* brand. Matty seemed to be making deals where he could, but there just wasn't the product or creative instinct to back them up.

Despite the fact that he was a shrewd businessman, Matty, like many who came to Hollywood before him, was caught up in the deal-making process and his ability to get things going. The deals appeared more important than the product, which is logical in a more commodified business, but not in a high-stakes industry where he was selling an edgy humor product that blended scatology and violence with sophistication and wit. Many thought Matty believed that he—not the product—was the essential ingredient to making a successful movie deal. In 1979 Los Angeles, such a belief would not prove fatal, though it would place limits on the people interested in working with him.

At Universal, Mount recalls, Matty insisted on dealing with only Tanen, who did not hold Matty in high regard. Deluged with ideas from Matty, Tanen would have Mount call him to pass on the projects. These ideas included a sequel to *Animal House*.

"The process wasn't good," Mount says. "There was a huge disconnect."

* * *

Jon Peters's story could only happen in Hollywood. A California-bred seventh-grade dropout, Peters lost his father at age ten and wound up in juvenile hall. By sixteen, he'd conned his way into a job cutting hair in an L.A. beauty salon. Before he was twenty-eight, a combination of self-promotion, hustle, and ambition made Peters the hairdresser to the stars, with several successful salons that catered to Jack Nicholson, Warren Beatty, and, allegedly, Barbra Streisand. Streisand was instrumental in helping Peters realize his grandiose dreams, which far exceeded $100 haircuts and the famous clients who could afford them.

By the time he met Streisand in 1974, Peters was twice divorced and a womanizer of great repute. Having long boasted to anyone who would listen that the Brooklyn-bred singer was among his clients, he met one of her employees and offered to cut Streisand's hair for real and for free, which he soon did at her Beverly Hills mansion.

Before long, Peters became Streisand's personal hairdresser and wardrobe consultant on a movie project, transitioning into the role of Svengali-like lover. The two bought a large home in Malibu, and Peters, a volatile and controlling man, exerted great influence over Streisand's affairs and replaced her longtime manager Marty Ehrlichman.

In 1974, Peters came upon a script recasting *A Star Is Born* in a modern setting. Working with Warner Brothers, Streisand insisted that Peters be named producer. Before it was over, the pair would seriously suggest that Peters play the male lead. Though this request was never honored (Kris Kristofferson played the role of an aging rock star who witnesses the decline of his career as that of his lover, Streisand, soars), Peters left the haircutting business and became a producer.

The relationship between Streisand and Peters was tumultuous, with wild fighting and passionate reconciliation that rarely escaped public attention. On the set of *A Star Is Born*, Peters extended this behavior to the cast and crew, creating chaos and oftentimes an aura of violence. When Kristofferson and Streisand argued over a scene, Peters demanded an apology, with threats flying about a post-production fight.

"If I need any more shit from you," Kristofferson said, "I'll squeeze your head!"

Limited in his ability to assess scripts and often lacking the attention span to read them, Peters had several things working in his favor as he entered the film business. Adept at packaging and intuitively gifted at understanding the power of celebrity, sex, violence, and other broad-stroke concepts, he brought enthusiasm and determination to his projects. Yet his career, in large part, was founded on being the man who was always about to deliver Streisand for whatever project he pitched. In mid-1970s Hollywood, this was a significant credential.

Despite having star power in his corner, Peters was not an exceedingly popular man in the industry. According to one source, a crew member on one Streisand picture coldcocked the producer in a studio parking lot. When word of the incident spread, many in the business rewarded the crew member with more work than he could handle, at above-union rates, for the rest of his career.

That said, by 1978, Peters was making a name for himself, doing his own projects, and searching for new material. Upon the release of *Animal House*, he would be one of the many suitors to knock on Doug Kenney's door.

Mike Medavoy was one of five executives who resigned from United Artists in 1978 to form Orion Pictures, a joint venture with Warner Brothers. Orion would focus on providing financial and marketing support to filmmakers, providing stars (they had deals with John Travolta and Burt Reynolds), and staying out of their way on the creative end. In April 1978, Peters signed a three-year production deal with the company that grew out of a personal relationship with Medavoy via Orion's desire to sign Streisand.

* * *

Doug and Ramis met with Peters to pitch a couple of their film ideas. One was Doug's Buddhist film, parodying New Age religion and spirituality. The other was Ramis's dark satire about the recently litigated American Nazi Party march through the nearly all-Jewish suburb of Skokie, Illinois, that had made national news.

They took the ideas to Medavoy, who thought Doug's concept wouldn't work and couldn't imagine making Ramis's film.

Shortly thereafter, Medavoy received a call from Kenney and Ramis, this time pitching a raucous social comedy based in part on Brian Doyle-Murray's stories of caddying at an exclusive Chicago-area country club. Chase was set for the lead and Bill Murray was mentioned to play a smaller but memorable character. Medavoy was sold and *Caddyshack* was born.

* * *

Bill Murray and Brian Doyle-Murray grew up not far from the Winnetka, Illinois, Indian Hill Country Club, roughly twelve miles north of Chicago. Located near Kenilworth (the city's wealthiest and most restricted suburb, with no discernible Jewish or Catholic population), Indian Hill was one of the area's most exclusive clubs, reserved for well-to-do Protestants. Caddying at Indian Hill was a rite of passage for all manner of local Irish and Italian kids, like the Murrays.

Like his brothers before him, Brian Doyle-Murray had seen it all at Indian Hill. Old couples who took endless hours to complete a round. Reprobate caddy masters. Local kids trying to earn a few bucks when they weren't mowing lawns. It was a well-defined world forming a microcosm of American society, the "haves" and the "have nots" coexisting within defined boundaries. It was a concept with which Doug was endlessly fascinated.

Over the course of several months, Doug and Doyle-Murray shared their stories of working at Indian Hill and Kirtwood, with Doyle-Murray adding the tale of a pooplike Baby Ruth found floating in the pool at his Catholic high school. Working in bars and coffee shops around New York, the pair jotted ideas on napkins and eventually rented a Manhattan hotel room, where they worked on the script.

Doyle-Murray's efforts to teach Doug (who preferred tennis) to play golf were all for naught, as his overactive mind and perfection complex prevented him from embracing the calm necessary for mastery or even competence. A dedicated scorekeeper, Doug instead gravitated to a fascination with the various outfits and implements employed by golfers (ball markers, divot fixers, hats) and never perfected his long, loopy swing.

With Ramis's help, the pair drafted a gigantic script, not unlike what they'd done for *Animal House*. The collaboration was similar to the previous hit, with Doyle-Murray's stories, Doug's intuition, and Ramis's organization proving to be a strong combination.

By this time in his life, Doug no longer wanted to work alone. Though he'd written so many of his pieces in the wee hours by himself, he now believed in writing as a social experience. Having worked with O'Rourke, then Ramis and Miller, he drew energy from the process, as well as much-needed structure. Ramis, he would tell a friend, "makes me sit in a chair and write."

The writing of *Caddyshack* signaled a new divide in Doug's personality. Danny Noonan, the working-class Irish caddy who serves as the caddy/protagonist and hero of the story, was near and dear to Doug's heart—a kid from the wrong side of the tracks, smart, good-hearted, and stuck in a world of service to rich idiots. In many ways, Doug believed he was Danny Noonan.

Equally, however, Doug wrote the character of the wealthy WASP Zen master and ace golfer Ty Webb (played by Chase) as a reflection of who he wanted to be—cool, easy with women, devil-may-care, and filled with awkward grace. In the film, the unattainable, sexy WASP goddess Lacey Underall finds a large uncashed check in Webb's home. "Pretty pathetic, Ty," she says.

In some small way, both Stork from *Animal House* and Howard Lewis Havermeyer from the Yearbook began to recede into Doug's subconscious, either intentionally or through aversion. Something— likely a combination of guilt, Hollywood, cocaine, money, success, encroaching adulthood, and responsibility, as well as his big, complicated brain—was eating away at Doug Kenney as he tried on the new, improved persona of Ty Webb.

* * *

The son of the longtime head of MGM's costume department, Don MacDonald had been a child actor who appeared in Burt Lancaster's directorial debut, *The Kentuckian*, and grew up in the world of moviemaking. After UCLA film school, MacDonald interned at the American Film Institute and was recommended to Peters by well-regarded film editor Verna Fields.

Joining Peters as a story editor, MacDonald was given the choice of two projects—a Robby Benson vehicle named *Die Laughing* or *Caddyshack*. Having recently seen *Animal House*, he chose the latter. Peters, MacDonald believes, never actually saw the film, but was mostly interested in working with the hot and bankable new comedy writers the town was buzzing about.

Though Peters was charismatic and a schmoozer, MacDonald quickly saw that he was also a desperate, manipulative man who compulsively created divisions within a group as a means of asserting control.

"This is the situation that Doug came into," MacDonald says.

When it became clear that Ramis was intent on directing the film (something he'd never done before), Peters called a meeting at which he intended to demonstrate for MacDonald how to lowball a creative person. Offering a very basic, cheap directing deal, Peters was told to "fuck off" by Ramis's agent before a slightly richer contract was signed. When Ramis left the office, Peters turned to MacDonald.

"Let's get a list of directors who can replace him," Peters said. "He's kind of weak."

Around the same time, MacDonald was introduced to Doug, who smiled and said, "I'm Doug Kenney. And you're about to have the best time of your life."

In Doug, MacDonald saw not just a likable writer-turned-producer but a caustic man with a seething bitterness toward rich people and snobs. Doug told MacDonald that his vision for *Caddyshack* had been inspired in part by Lindsay Anderson's British boarding school class-warfare comedy *If* . . . .

As *Caddyshack* kicked into gear, MacDonald determined that his most important role on the film would be to protect Ramis and Doug from Peters, who clearly believed that both men were idiots he could manipulate and take advantage of.

* * *

Nineteen seventy-nine was not the optimal time for someone like Doug Kenney to join the film industry. The studio system had died over the course of the past twenty years, and took with it the genteel slavery that prevented actors from asserting creative control over their own projects, not to mention their careers. Despite its monopolistic nature, however, the studio system had been effective at creating some incomparable art.

During the late 1960s and early '70s, a group of young filmmakers (Scorcese, Coppola, and others) emerged, making unforgettable films and reshaping the dream factory far more realistically. They captured the spirit of their generation, a generation that knew that no one really talked like Cary Grant and that Spencer Tracy wasn't just an avuncular fella, but also a rip-roaring drunk.

Imperceptibly, however, by 1979 the business side of the industry had figured a way to reassert control. The directors—though important—were not the masters of the medium. Rather, the producers and dealmakers ran the town. It was everything that Doug Kenney hated—a world in which commerce trumped art.

* * *

Bill Murray demanded points from the profits of *Caddyshack*. Meeting with initial resistance from Peters and the studio, Doug fought for his friend and brought him on board—though the matter would not be officially resolved until filming was about to commence. With Chase also officially attached to the project, this left the key roles of Danny Noonan, snotty Bushwood Country Club president Judge Smales, and obnoxious millionaire Al Czervik to be cast.

Though Mickey Rourke was initially considered for the role of Noonan, Michael O'Keefe, who'd recently given a terrific performance as Robert Duvall's sensitive son in Orion's *The Great Santini*, landed the part.

Jason Robards was considered for Judge Smales, which would have been inspired casting, but *Mary Tyler Moore* veteran Ted Knight simply demanded the role. The idea of Don Rickles as Al Czervik was bandied about, but Doug and Ramis had seen Rodney Dangerfield on *The Tonight Show* and decided he could bring the coarse, hilarious outsider to life.

* * *

In the March 1979 Chance issue, O'Rourke wrote "How to Drive Fast on Drugs While Getting Your Wing-Wang Squeezed and Not Spill Your Drink," one of his best-known pieces and a reflection of where editorial was now headed.

A raucous paean to living fast, dying young, and leaving a twisted, mangled, smiling corpse, the article is part fantasy for the rebellious young man of 1979 who'd never listened to Bob Dylan or Lenny Bruce. Funny and well written, "How to Drive Fast . . ." embraces Doug's method to fit in jokes whenever and wherever possible, while moving at breakneck speed.

O'Rourke explains the importance of being inebriated while driving recklessly, so as to keep the body loose and relaxed (thus free of injury) when accidents—preferably caused intentionally by the driver—occur.

> O.K., now say you've been on a six-day drunk and you've just made a bet that you can back up all the way to Cleveland, plus you've got a buddy who's getting a blow job on the trunk lid. Well, let's face it—if that's the way you're going to act, sooner or later you'll have an accident. This much is true. But that doesn't mean that you should sit back and just let accidents happen to you. No, you have to go out and cause them yourself . . . it's a shame, but a lot of people have the wrong idea about accidents. For one thing they don't hurt nearly as much as you'd think. That's because you're in shock and can't feel pain, or, if you aren't in shock, you're dead, and that doesn't hurt at all so far as we know.

"How to Drive Fast . . ." also incorporates the attitude toward minorities and women that seemed to carry a different tone than what had been written during the early 1970s. For a female companion, O'Rourke's hallmarks of a crazy girl include "unusual shoes, white lipstick, extreme thinness, hair that's less than an inch long, or clothing made of chrome and leather. Stay away from girls who cry a lot or who look like they get pregnant easily or have careers." The benefit of driving in New York City, he writes, is that "it's real easy to scare old Jewish ladies in new Cadillacs," with the downside being that "Negroes actually do carry knives, not to mention Puerto Ricans."

"Women really became objects," Aaron says. "What Doug had written was really sweet and inclusive—anyone could relate to [his articles about sex and women]. Under P.J.'s rule—women were aliens, they were incomprehensible."

The magazine was still living by the sword, but to the leftist folks around the office, that sword was one they'd rather not wield.

* * *

Though *Caddyshack* was written by Hollywood's new golden boy, Orion still considered it a B picture with a budget of roughly $6 million. As it went into production, Kenney, Ramis, and Doyle-

Murray pushed for the film to be shot in the Midwest—preferably Chicago—but the studio, concerned about weather problems, insisted on Florida.

In October, the cast and crew took over Rolling Hills Golf Club in Davie, Florida, near Fort Lauderdale. The club was selected, among other reasons, for its lack of palm trees, which would allow the film to maintain the illusion of a midwestern location.

Legend has it that Ramis showed up on the first day of filming and put his eye on the wrong end of the camera. While this was actually untrue, the initial days of shooting were chaotic, to say the least.

Cinematographer Stevan Larner, most of whose experience was in television, had been hired by Kenney and Ramis in part because of his extensive knowledge of fine wines, which somehow struck Doug as a sign that he'd give the film a sophisticated look.

MacDonald, Peters, and executives in charge of production Rusty Lemorande and Mark Canton were all quite young and lacked extensive hands-on filmmaking experience. This was in keeping with the youth trend that struck Hollywood in the mid- and late 1970s, the era of the "baby mogul," of which Thom Mount, running Universal at the age of twenty-six, was typical. Because young people were flocking to the movies again and forming a substantial part of the audience, the thinking in Hollywood was that the people who understood their sensibilities and interests should be making the films.

"I had a job way beyond my years," Lemorande says. "It was an era of filmmaking where the executives were younger and younger and it was believed that youth knew everything."

Thus a lot of gifted creative people had been collected on the *Caddyshack* set, but there was no one to serve the role Cliff Coleman had filled for Landis. There was no master filmmaker who'd seen everything to guide Ramis through the process of making his first movie. With Orion's hands-off policy and Peters's relative inexperience, the shoot was destined for chaos. At the same time, however, the kind of film comedy that Kenney, Ramis, and the crew sought to create could only be made by young people, who often didn't know they were breaking rules and were sometimes better off because of it. It was in many ways, however, a jerry-rigged production.

On the first day, Ramis shot a scene where two caddies have a fight and a gumball machine is broken. Enormous attention was paid to how one kid would jump on another's back, and the sequence was filmed over and over. Nobody had the knowledge or experience to let Ramis know when to move on.

Ramis, however, was calm beyond belief, and took to the process naturally. He possessed an instinct for working with performers and knew when he'd gotten it right. Hard-working and open to ideas, Ramis was learning as he went along.

"He couldn't have been more professional," says Lemorande.

The same, however, could not be said for Rodney Dangerfield, who'd never appeared in a motion picture (beyond a bit part in 1971's *The Projectionist*) and with whom Knight would form something of a geriatric "odd couple" on the set.

"God bless Rodney," says O'Keefe. "But he didn't understand how to make a movie. Harold had to hold his hand through everything."

Dangerfield's first scene took place in the club pro shop, where he mocks a hat that Judge Smales is trying on, suggesting that anyone who buys it ought to "get a free bowl of soup." Scheduled to enter from another room, Dangerfield did nothing when Ramis called "Action." The director called to Dangerfield, asking if he was ready. "Sure," came the comic's reply. Again, Ramis called, "Action." Again, no Rodney.

"Rodney, when I call action, you need to come in and do the scene," Ramis explained.

"Do my bit?" Rodney asked.

"Yeah, do your bit," Ramis replied.

At the next call of "Action," Dangerfield again failed to appear. Ramis wound up telling Rodney to "do your bit" every time he needed the actor to appear in a scene. Later, during endless takes of a yacht club boat crash, Ramis stood on the dock explaining the scene to Dangerfield, who looked "as if he were learning quantum physics," according to O'Keefe.

By contrast, Knight was the consummate professional (having shot hundreds of *Mary Tyler Moore* episodes): always on time, always prepared, and genially going along with the on-set craziness. An exercise fanatic, he went to bed early and brought along a juicer to make special health drinks each morning.

"He was the only person who was free of liquor, coke, and pot on the movie," says Chevy Chase.

This included Dangerfield, who, despite bringing along his daughter to make sure that he took his heart medication, raised hell every evening with Doug, Chase, Murray, and the rest.

"We were absolutely out of control," says O'Keefe. "[Kenney and Ramis's] movie had just gone through the roof and they had carte blanche."

Though nobody wanted Orion to know about the on-set drug use, cocaine and other substances were rampant. Shooting in South Florida, the epicenter of cocaine distribution, eighty grams would routinely be brought in on Sunday and consumed by Wednesday. Many in the cast and crew, save Knight, were getting high all the time, and if they weren't indulging it was cause for suspicion. "I was twenty-four," O'Keefe says. "I thought it was the way you were supposed to live."

In 1979, Hollywood and white middle-class America were still in the honeymoon phase with cocaine. No one famous or notable had yet died of it, and cocaine was reputed to make you feel great, providing tremendous energy and stamina. Moreover, the drug was an accepted part of the creative atmosphere on the festive *Caddyshack* set, where work and play intermingled twenty-four hours a day. It was perceived as part of the creative process, feeding the end product rather than destroying it.

"If you compared the set to any musical group touring at the time, it was nothing," says Trevor Albert, an assistant on the film.

With everyone staying in rooms at the club, it was Albert's job to wake up the stars each day and ensure that they were present for the morning call after tearing up the course on golf carts all night.

"It was more difficult than waking up my roommates in college," Albert says.

Albert believed that he'd fallen into nirvana on the *Caddyshack* set, working hard with a group of people who were exactly the kind of anarchic, brilliant colleagues he'd hoped for in film school. Though Peters's economic strictures forced him to sleep in the production office, Albert was living a dream. So was Hamilton Mitchell, who played Motormouth, one of the more prominent caddies.

"There was always this thing where you can't believe that you're now actually next to one of the people behind *National Lampoon* and *Animal House*," Mitchell says. "Up until a week [before beginning the film], I had just been another kid fresh out of high school watching *SCTV* and reading *National Lampoon*."

Throughout the shoot, Doug took to his roles as producer and writer with unbridled energy. Though he was consuming massive amounts of cocaine, occasionally falling asleep on set, and annoyed by the intrusion of business and responsibility upon his art, he was determined to keep things loose, provide a good time for everyone, and make the best film comedy ever.

Doug befriended O'Keefe, Mitchell, and other young members of the cast. One evening in Mitchell's room, Doug left the bathroom door open and poured a gallon of water slowly into the toilet, pretending that he was taking the world's longest piss. Stepping back into the room, he mimed shitting various items, including a tennis ball and racket, for Mitchell's amusement. He also remained down to earth and accessible and refused to make ridiculous demands in a world where such things would be welcomed.

"The thing about Hollywood is that there's an id-pleasing factor," O'Keefe says. "Doug could have asked for pheasant under glass passed through a blender and shoved under his door and it would have been 'Here's your pheasant shake, Mr. Kenney.'"

He didn't.

Instead he consumed himself with details and improvisational writing sessions on set. Though spacey and stoned, he was passionate and excited. He improvised the line "Violence mars another beautiful day at Bushwood" for Mitchell's caddie fight scene, and worked intensely with Doyle-Murray and Ramis on rewrites during the shoot.

Perhaps more than anyone, Doug was obsessed with making everything look right. As Dangerfield shot a golf scene, Doug constantly queried Albert about the golfers playing ahead of Rodney. Could you see them? Were they colorful enough? Everything, he thought, could be different or better.

"He was on it every day," says O'Keefe. "He worked his ass off to make that movie happen."

Off the set, his behavior was more outrageous and unpredictable. Doug was committed to disrupting any formal or mundane scene, purposefully tripping and falling on his face in the dining room or putting a napkin over his head, with glasses on top, when he was bored with a dinner conversation. At a restaurant one evening, he uncharacteristically became belligerent with a maitre d' who wasn't giving his tables special treatment.

For MacDonald, Doug seemed to be conducting his longtime inner war, veering between being a man in love with all that life had to offer and being an embittered, angry idealist. Not infrequently, he would pretend to be a character named Little Johnny Heinous, a perfect man he'd invented who ironed his own clothes after fashioning them on a loom.

"The character did everything right. Nothing wrong," MacDonald says. "He was disgusting."

* * *

Everyone on the *Caddyshack* set was terrified of a possible explosion between Chevy Chase and Bill Murray. There seemed to be bad blood because Murray replaced Chase on *Saturday Night Live* and then confronted the newly minted movie star during his return to guest host the show. Yet when Murray arrived on the set, the two stars hugged like old friends, all their problems melting into the past. Though Murray had the smaller role, his performance as demented assistant groundskeeper Carl Spackler became the most memorable thing in the movie.

"My name was above the title," Chase says. "But it was Billy's film."

On set, Murray was demanding and intent on making sure people didn't look down on his character. He was temperamental and difficult to figure out. There was always a sense that he wasn't bound to the same behavioral norms that controlled everyone else. At one moment he was the Bill Murray that audiences know and love—charming, hilarious, spinning everything into comedy; other times, he would berate someone for interrupting the pickup basketball game he played on set with crew and extras.

"He was a force of nature," O'Keefe says. "He was a movie star when he came onto this planet."

Of all the parts in the film, Murray's, based in part on the Honker routine he'd developed at Second City, was the least well defined. Doug and Doyle-Murray left holes in the script that said things like "Carl cuts flowers," which they knew Murray would turn into classic moments. Of course, he did, improvising dialogue about a caddie who is about to win the Masters ("A Cinderella story. Out of nowhere. About to become Masters champion.")

"All of the insanity of the gopher being Viet Cong is Billy," O'Keefe says.

Once Murray was on set, it became clear that Doug and Doyle-Murray needed to write a scene for him and Chase. During lunch one day, the four men sat at a picnic table, playing with dialogue and concepts to be shot later that afternoon.

When the cameras were set up, Murray took the ideas from the meeting and winged it. He decorated the set for Carl's dingy apartment himself, pasting *Hustler* centerfolds on the wall and moving in a disgusting, torn couch. Chase, who is practicing golf at night, hits a ball into the greenskeeper's lair, and from there the two men improvised one of the film's most memorable scenes.

"I just reacted to whatever he did," Chase says. "I had no idea that Billy was going to go through the rap about being able to smoke the grass. Chinch bugs? I'd never heard of a chinch bug. The pond line. It all made sense. It took a lot to keep a straight face in that scene."

Playing a role written by Doug, Chase took tremendous inspiration and frequent direction from his friend. Doug would coach him on how he might interpret various scenes, such as when he is asked to move an English convertible off of the course by Judge Smales and gets in on the wrong side, amazed to find no wheel.

* * *

Midway through the shoot, Peters arrived for a visit, apparently intent on collecting negative opinions of the film's progress and the Kenney/Ramis team. Calling a meeting, Peters whisked the reluctant pair off the set to hear a litany of complaints about the amount of film that had been shot, the mounting expenses, and the pace of production.

"We need to work faster and do much better," he told them. "What do you think?"

There was silence. Peters looked at Doug.

"Well," Doug began slowly. "What I think is that if you come back here again, you'd better come back with a different attitude or not come back at all."

Peters shot a nervous glance at MacDonald, who averted his eyes.

"Hey, I'm just trying to help," Peters said. "Don't take it that way."

The damage, however, had been done. He'd underestimated Doug's brains and resilience, not to mention his aversion to any interference from the business side.

"[Peters] folded up like a little bully who'd been punched," MacDonald recalls.

The next day, Peters flew back to Los Angeles and didn't return.

A few weeks later the film wrapped, with everyone exhausted and ready to head for home. Though nobody else thought they were making a cult classic, Doug told his friends that *Caddyshack* would be a hit that would surely surpass *Animal House*.

* * *

In December 1979, Doug and Ramis returned to Los Angeles to begin editing *Caddyshack*. Each morning around nine o'clock, the pair arrived at Warners, where they smoked pot and went to work on the film. Editors William Carruth and his assistant Robert Barrere had lined the cutting-room doors with gaffer's tape so the pot smoke wouldn't give a contact high to everyone else in the building.

Neither Barrere nor Carruth had much experience putting together a big-time film, and Doug and Ramis were certainly taking their first shot. Much like on the film's set, there was no Papa Bear to lead them through the process.

Immediately, everyone could see that Ramis had elicited tremendous performances from Chase and Murray. The cinematography and look of the film, however, were in need of major work.

Doug, Barrere recalls, spent long nights in the editing room and a nearby office, doing coke and thinking about how to cut the film. It was clear that he wanted to outdo *Animal House* and felt a tremendous need to compete with his previous work. His relationship with Peters and Medavoy weighed on him equally. Unaccustomed to Hollywood politics, he seemed stressed and beaten down.

Though Medavoy made an upbeat phone call to Ramis lauding their progress, the suits at Orion were freaking out about the dailies. The cuts played very long; Murray's hilarious simulated masturbation scene, with the group of older women bending over to line up putts, seemed to go on forever.

All rough cuts are difficult to watch. They are always too long and include scenes that will never make it into the movie. Lighting has rarely been corrected, and the soundtracks haven't been synced up or even produced properly. The *Caddyshack* rough cut, which according to Barrere ran over four hours, went especially badly.

One thing that quickly became apparent was that Dangerfield's performance was both hilarious and thoroughly unprofessional. No one on the set had noticed that after Rodney uttered a line he completely turned off and stopped acting. As the other actors spoke, Dangerfield looked at them as if they were insane.

The rough cut created enormous tension between Peters and Doug. They both believed their careers were at stake. Peters thought the film sucked, which came through in his every action. Doug, though, was intent on protecting his project from the hands of a man he despised.

Yet it was clear to nearly everyone that there was need for a major behind-the-scenes repair job. A top film doctor was brought in to view the rough cut. His verdict wasn't pretty.

"This film's a mess," he said. "I can fix it, but you'll need to pay me $200,000 and give me total creative control."

Peters knew that they needed someone with the experience and ability to do a significant recut, but was equally aware that Orion would never pony up that kind of money for post-production work on a B picture with a budget of $6 million.

Lemorande suggested bringing in Academy Award–winning editor Ralph Winters (who had worked on Blake Edwards's *10* and *The Front Page*) to assess what they had. Over the course of one week, Winters looked at footage during the evenings and assembled notes on how the film could fit within the rhythms and conventions of traditional film comedy. He knew what worked and what didn't.

"He came in every night for a week and gave us notes and a lesson," Lemorande says. "Harold was ecstatic. He realized what he was making could actually be a fully realized film."

Kenney felt otherwise. Unhappy at ceding further control over the creative product, he felt he was giving greater authority to Peters and Orion.

Unable to handle the project himself because of other commitments, Winters recommended his friend David Breatherton, the son of a longtime Hollywood director and a man who'd edited many well-known films in a career that stretched back to 1955. Finding little narrative through line—save Danny Noonan's participation in the caddy tournament and his relationship with a club waitress—he sought an anchor on which to pin the film. That anchor would be a gopher.

* * *

It is hard to imagine that there could be so much uproar over something as simple as a mechanical gopher. After the rough cut, Peters, in his one great contribution to *Caddyshack*, asked Orion for $500,000 that would be used on special effects to enhance the film and the mechanical gopher that served as Murray's nemesis.

In addition, he asked that a master editor be brought in to recut the film. Orion complied.

Doug was horrified. He and Doyle-Murray had written a hilarious script about class warfare, cast with brilliant comedians and talented actors, only to be faced with Peters insisting at the last minute that it all be eclipsed for the sake of a puppet.

"That sent Doug over the top," Barrere recalls.

The ensuing weeks saw numerous battles between Doug and Peters, with the latter insisting, "I paid for that gopher and it's going to be in my picture."

With no choice but to acquiesce, Doug became completely disillusioned with the process, in stark contrast to his *Animal House* experience with Landis.

Kenney was now very much at a loss as to how he could participate in the end result of the film. Enraged, understanding little about editing, and feeling undercut by Peters, he was no longer a meaningful player in what would happen to *Caddyshack*.

Lemorande, spearheading much of the post-production enhancement work, recalls Kenney visiting his office, hands in pockets, to ask how things were going. No longer was he the charismatic master of ceremonies and genius of whom much of the crew was in awe. Instead, he seemed lost.

"I kept feeling more and more sorry for Doug," Lemorande says, "There was nothing for him to do."

As the final version of *Caddyshack* was taking form, Kenney called his Harvard friend Ollie Hallowell and spoke of being miserable in Los Angeles.

"No even knows who Evelyn Waugh is," he said.

As for *Caddyshack?* "God, Ollie," Doug said. "It's a piece of shit."

14

A Year with No Spring

66 Every act of rebellion expresses a nostalgia for
innocence. 99

—*Albert Camus*

The following things happened in 1980: Ronald Reagan trounced
Jimmy Carter in the presidential election; the hostages would
soon be set free; the Nixon era's forty-seven-year-old housewife from
Dayton was now nearly sixty. The grown-ups were victorious—it
would soon be "Morning in America."

* * *

"More than anything I'm an idea man. A concept man," Matty
Simmons told the *San Francisco Chronicle* for a February 1980 article, "A Happy Mogul Reviews His Empire." He explained that the

National Lampoon was "very healthy, [we're] very happy, [we're] very excited about the future." With the magazine nearing its tenth anniversary, Matty confessed that he wasn't "a riotously funny guy," yet the article credits him with dreaming up and writing both the Yearbook and *Animal House*.

Working from California, Matty split his organization into four divisions: the flagship magazine, books, *Heavy Metal*, and entertainment. With circulation still in the 600,000 to 700,000 range and an average reader age of twenty-four, the *National Lampoon* still contended with roughly $10 million in lawsuits each year.

Most of Matty's energies were focused on film deals, including a never-produced movie called *Kicks* and the company's next big project, *National Lampoon Goes to the Movies* (also known as *National Lampoon's Movie Madness*)—a collection of film and television parodies written by the staff.

Animal House 2 had gone through several scripts, including one written by Chris Miller and John Weidman, with the premise that the Deltas would gather in San Francisco during the Summer of Love for Pinto's wedding to a hippie chick.

Jaws 3–People 0, a film Matty had pitched to producer David Brown, was approved by Universal. The script was about a film company making a shark movie done in Lampoon-style parody. Bruce, the famous mechanical shark from *Jaws*, would costar with Bo Derek and Rodger Bumpass. With a script by John Hughes, the film was killed late in preproduction after Steven Spielberg stepped in and made Universal balk at the idea of mocking his blockbuster.

Meanwhile, the man whose screenplay had made these projects possible was having problems of his own in Hollywood.

* * *

No one was happy with the initial posters for *Caddyshack*. Peters hated the first sketches and assigned Ramis, Chase, and Doyle-Murray to come up with something marketable, clever, and involving the gopher. The three men sat on the floor of a production office like young kids, cutting and pasting promotional stills and other artifacts. Ramis suggested that they make several characters pop out of golf holes with Peters's beloved gopher hanging in the background like a gigantic invader, and within fifteen minutes they came up with something that appealed to everyone.

Shortly thereafter, Medavoy held a meeting at Orion, where he, Kenney, Peters, and several others intended to resolve some *Caddyshack*-related disputes.

Doug was extremely edgy. Frustrated at the editing process and the new importance of the gopher, he was keenly aware of the profound influence that Peters and Orion/Warners were having on his film. Disappointed that *Caddyshack* seemed to be such a low priority for the studio and strung out on cocaine and late nights, he was ready to explode.

At some point, Medavoy commented on either the poster or the marketing plan. Doug lost it and allegedly tossed off a nasty barb regarding Medavoy's personal life.

The mood became unbearably tense, and, before anyone knew what had happened, Doug Kenney attacked Mike Medavoy.

* * *

"The movie is as good as it is because of Harold and Doug, with very little contribution from me," Medavoy says. Medavoy is clear that Orion's policy was to let the moviemakers create their own film, with minimal involvement from the studio. He never visited the set. He knew nothing about the drug use in Davie, Florida. Warners was in charge of marketing the film, he says.

"The argument," he insists, "wasn't anything memorable."

In fact, he can barely recall anything physical having taken place.

* * *

In his book about filmmaking, Medavoy writes, "Doug Kenney was unstable. . . . A few months before the release of the film, Kenney and I nearly came to blows over the poster, which he hated. I didn't have control over the poster and—even if I did—it wasn't important enough to have a fistfight over. [Kenney] didn't feel the same way, so he jumped me outside of our bungalow and we literally ended up in a wrestling match on the sidewalk."

* * *

Though physical confrontation might seem odd in this case, it was a fact of life in Hollywood during the days of the studio system, when it wasn't uncommon for a director to loiter in a studio parking lot after hours, waiting for his producer to come around the corner so he could deliver an unexpected sucker punch. It was part of doing business.

That Doug Kenney resorted to physical violence, no matter how hazy the recollections, means something else entirely. Though he'd taken a swing at Ricardo Moreno at Harvard and was capable of erratic behavior, the male Hayley Mills wasn't accustomed to resolving situations with violence.

The intrusion of business in the form of Warners, Orion, Medavoy, and Peters upon his creative work was something to which Doug was highly unaccustomed. For many years, he'd been in charge, able to laugh off or good-naturedly ignore Matty's objections. In Hollywood he did not have that luxury.

First resorting to his wits, he attempted to devastate Medavoy by saying the worst thing he possibly could. When that failed, Doug became unhinged and lost all control.

"He bore [Medavoy] into the ground," Doyle-Murray told Ted Mann of the fight. In recalling the event, Doyle-Murray also said that Doug assaulted Peters and got him in a headlock.

Regardless of whether this event took place within Medavoy's office or outside the bungalow, one thing was clear: Hollywood and Doug Kenney were not mixing well.

"Everything came easy to Doug, or at least it appeared to," Kelly says. "He would write something overnight and it would be published and everybody would love it. It takes a long time to get a movie made. Hollywood was a very contraindicated place for Doug to go exercise his art. That particular way of communicating seemed unlike the kind of energy that Doug needed."

"Doug's relationship to the way in which he was funny changed when he went to L.A.," Weidman concurs. "The expectations were different. The arena was different. My friend was a very modest guy in an arena where modesty wasn't highly prized."

* * *

Doug and Kathryn Walker purchased a home at 2761 Outpost Drive in Hollywood, just above Sunset. Furniture was ordered. Walker was intent on making a home with Doug, perhaps the first that he would fully inhabit since childhood.

As the home was being readied, Doug spent considerable time with Chase. The two frequently indulged in cocaine (Doug now had a sugar bowl full of it at the home on Betty Lane and at a suite he frequently occupied at the Marmont) and raced their cars through the Hollywood Hills. Rumors spread that Doug would drive fast, late at night, with the lights off.

On a visit to Hollywood, Rick Meyerowitz had dinner with Doug, after which they visited the house on Outpost. Soon after their arrival, Doug lost his wallet (which he'd had when they entered) and the pair spent ten minutes searching the home. Ultimately, Meyerowitz located the wallet buried deep in a sofa.

"Doug," Meyerowitz said, "I don't know how you manage to get through the day."

Back at the Marmont, Doug asked Meyerowitz if he wanted to see what two thousand dollars' worth of cocaine looked like, then opened a drawer to reveal a pile of white powder.

"There was no plastic," Meyerowitz recalls. "My mother would have said, 'Use wax paper for the cocaine.' She would have done it for me. I thought the care was lacking. The attention to detail was lacking."

Doug, Meyerowitz thought, was like a child who'd never learned to take care of himself. Even in his drug use, he was at loose ends. He was immature, but at least he had intuitively understood how to be mature in his work. His life, however, was a mess.

"'Here I am. I've got all of this money. I can afford two thousand dollars' worth of coke,'" Meyerowitz thought Doug was saying. "'Here's my house; I don't know what the hell to do with it.'"

* * *

Like Jon Peters's career, Roy's Restaurant on Sunset Boulevard was something that could only happen in the Hollywood of the late 1970s. Founded by hustling record promoter and producer Roy Silver, who handled nearly every major rock band of the era (and orchestrated Tiny Tim's wedding to Miss Vicky on *The Tonight Show*), Roy's was housed in a small barnlike building that had once been part of a farm owned by Errol Flynn. Later converted to a restaurant and then leased by Silver in the mid-1970s, Roy's was the hip place du jour for the cool young drug-addled Hollywood of 1979.

Roy's menu included what the owner termed "Kosher Chinese" food, which was, according to Mount, "magnificently good." The restaurant offered only one dessert, which you got whether you ordered it or not—a frozen Snickers bar. On one side of the rectangle-shaped restaurant were several tables for four and large windows that looked out over Los Angeles. In the back were booths built to resemble separate Pullman cars—cabins that seated four to six, with a large drape that could be drawn around each table. This was, in many ways, the allure of Roy's.

In addition to being a restaurant, Roy's was an after-hours club (open until three or four A.M.) for people such as the Eagles, Mick Jagger, Neil Young, and Burt Reynolds; Hunter Thompson made it his Los Angeles headquarters. Roy himself catered to his clientele by providing instant access to cocaine for anyone who wanted it. If there wasn't enough available from the restaurant's private stock, Roy called a dealer who arrived in minutes. Even the dinner plates at Roy's were billed as perfect for using to snort lines. Everyone, it seemed, did coke openly at Roy's, and the restrooms were filled with young women who would do just about anything for a line.

"Cocaine was so prevalent," Mount says. "It wasn't just the fuel of choice. It was the requirement for getting through the day [in Hollywood]."

And when Doug Kenney was at his drug-addled height, it was Roy's to which he repaired most days, and evenings, to conduct business, unwind, and hang out. It was his de facto office and home.

* * *

Shortly before the release of *Caddyshack*, Doug and Ivers saw a screening of *Airplane!*, the Zucker Brothers parody of disaster films. Though he laughed, Doug was downcast and had the sense that he'd been trumped. Others were now doing what he had once done, and doing it well. Why the hell hadn't he come up with this idea? It was as if he sat in the theater and saw his preeminence pass before his eyes. It only increased the internal pressure for *Caddyshack* to be the greatest film comedy ever made.

Seeing him later that evening, Kelly immediately sensed Doug's depression and disillusionment. He saw the bowl of cocaine while visiting his home on Outpost. Though Doug always smoked dope and was a moderate drinker, Kelly had never suspected a substance abuse problem. Now he wasn't so sure. The one thing that he was certain about was that Doug was no longer the easygoing, happy, funny guy he'd always been around 635 Madison. The exterior remained, but it was showing cracks.

"I had this feeling that he was trapped. He'd never been trapped before. Everything he touched had turned to gold and all of a sudden he's a producer," Kelly says. "He had all of this brainpower and was this very soulful guy—everything in the world he was living in was totally bogus and nobody knew it better than him."

* * *

Shortly after Doug signed with Fox, his friend Lucy Fisher left the studio to take a position with Francis Ford Coppola at American Zoetrope, a studio dedicated to creative and unconventional projects driven by the talent, not the suits. Though happy for her, Doug was also jealous of both Fisher and her new boss. Zoetrope, he believed, was an atmosphere in which the artist had total control, and he envied Coppola's ownership of his own studio where hipper experimental projects could be created without interference. Fisher, he believed on some level, had abandoned him.

One evening in 1980, Doug Kenney got in his car and drove to Zoetrope, where he allegedly screamed at a security guard and demanded to be let in to see Coppola so that he could explain how a movie ought to be made.

* * *

"By 1980, it was clear that the magazine would have to change dramatically to prosper," O'Rourke says. "Everything else in America had changed since 1970. The bohemian/beatnik/hippie long march was over—compare and contrast the Reagan election to the Goldwater lack thereof. I started to think about redesign and relaunch. There wasn't much enthusiasm about this and there was no enthusiasm about spending the money it would cost."

O'Rourke called a two-day conference at Manhattan's St. Regis Hotel to plot the future of *National Lampoon*. With the staff, including John Hughes, in attendance, they discussed how to reinvent the magazine. There wasn't a single viable idea for restructuring or changing it in any material way.

* * *

In Los Angeles, Chris Miller and journalist David Standish were at work on a project that Doug was slated to direct. The pair—one suffering from a divorce and the other from dental surgery—had once decided to take a trip to Club Med as a means of recuperation. Finding the singles resort to be hilariously preposterous, they decided to write a film script set in a similar location. They would call it *Club Sandwich*.

Their original script called for all manner of wild doings, including a *Creature from the Black Lagoon*-like character who stalks around the resort. Doug loved it and committed Three Wheel to produce.

One morning, Doug arrived late for a nine-thirty *Club Sandwich* story conference. As the meeting began, it became clear that he couldn't keep his attention on the matter at hand. He paced around the room looking like a caged animal that'd been denied something he desperately needed.

After a short while, somebody called Doug away from the meeting. A few minutes later, he returned with a package of cocaine, which he laid out in a rail that stretched from his elbow to his fist. Ingesting it in one snort, he turned to Miller and Standish and offered the following advice: "Go with your own worst instincts."

"I thought, 'Holy Christ, this guy has gone over the top,'" Miller says. "His brain has got to be like some mirror that got broken into a thousand glittering shards; each one is very bright, but they're not connected anymore."

* * *

After divorcing Bobby London, Shary Flenniken moved to New York and accepted O'Rourke's offer of a staff position, which allowed her to witness the editorial fallout from pressure being applied by advertisers and the Christian Right.

"We were told not to criticize small cars and here we're running on cigarette and liquor ads," she says. "The reason we had a market for this material was because we were so out there and cutting edge, but the biggest enemy for advertising was the fact that we were so out there and cutting edge. Who are you going to write for, your advertisers or your market?"

There was never a decision made about that in any official capacity, due to Matty's simultaneously battling the religious right and imploring O'Rourke to lighten up on pressure groups and advertisers, while the editor in chief tried to keep the content relevant. By 1980, it was a constant and confusing battle that yielded editorial chaos.

That year, Flenniken, Mann, Tod Carroll (Mann's writing partner, best remembered for ordering a grilled cheese sandwich for lunch each and every day via a speed dial button on his phone), Sussman, Weiner, and other staffers were assigned to write *National Lampoon Goes to the Movies*.

The initial concept was a movie less than two hours long that parodied ten film and television genres. The project turned out to be a cocaine-fueled fiasco; nobody had a sense of structure or any idea how to write a screenplay. Writing sessions involved all manner of crazy suggestions, all embraced equally by the group. If one writer suggested that in one scene a limousine should feature a hot tub, it was put into the script.

No one, it seemed, had any sense of the proper length for each segment. In a world where ten parodies would fill 120 minutes of screen time, it stood to reason that each piece should run roughly twelve minutes. With one page of dialogue representing one minute of screen time, each segment needed to be twelve pages long. The scripts, however, were rambling and tangential, running far over their required length, and resulting in a film that would need to be seen on separate days, like *Nicholas Nickleby*.

Though mild by nature, Flenniken constantly had to remind the group that they would never be able to actually film the script they were writing. She was met with disapproval and frequently told not to worry. The result was a disaster.

"We cut stuff and boiled it down," Flenniken recalls. "It lost its purpose and just became a bunch of crazy crap."

According to Flenniken, a Rhode Island test screening of *National Lampoon Goes to the Movies* resulted in near violence, with audience members tearing up the seats to express their displeasure and shattered expectations. *National Lampoon Goes to the Movies* went straight to video in 1983.

Shortly after the test screening, Lampoon president Julian Weber took Flenniken out to lunch to tell her that she'd been right about the project.

"That's when I learned that being right doesn't mean shit," she says.

* * *

Caddyshack premiered at a Times Square movie theater in July 1980. Though the film got mixed reviews, the atmosphere that evening was positive. After the show, Peters ran around the theater telling everyone involved with the picture that it was a huge success.Doug, however, was despondent. Throughout the shoot, he'd been convinced they were making a great movie. Anything short of spectacular was bound to upset him. That night, one thing became clear—he hated *Caddyshack*.

"He was in a fugue state of unhappiness," Kelly recalls.

Doug's disillusionment was rooted in something far deeper than disappointment. He was not able to separate his work from his own self-worth and purpose. He couldn't be in the business just for the money. Humor defined his identity, and he utilized it to drown out the criticism that flashed like fireworks in his head—to make sense of them and give them meaning. Yet to fulfill his dreams, Doug had to deal with people he hated—such as Peters and Medavoy—who exercised control over the manner in which he lifted up well-manicured suburban lawns and showed the bodies buried beneath them. Perhaps the most American humorist since Mark Twain, he had run into the two national institutions that were most unlikely to support his vision—capitalism and Hollywood.

* * *

The day after the *Caddyshack* premiere, Warner Brothers arranged a press conference at Dangerfield's New York comedy club. MacDonald had spent the previous evening with Doug and Doyle-Murray in a room at the Essex House on Central Park South, where they drank Courvoisier and snorted cocaine.

Doug was not in his happy, host-of-the-party mood the night before the press conference. Instead, he was irritable, hypercritical, judgmental, and obnoxious. Exhausted, drunk, and high on coke, he complained about *Caddyshack*, its promotion, the graininess of the cinematography, and the condition of the greens at Rolling Hills. He could see none of the good in the film, only what had been done incorrectly. As he became more and more agitated, a couple in the next room banged on the wall, calling, "Shut up, we're trying to sleep."

Doug angrily hammered back and kept on yelling.

After five A.M., Doug and MacDonald went for a walk around Manhattan. As the sun rose, Doug talked about his future and the films he planned to make, including *Club Sandwich* (later changed to *Club Paradise*). Yet he frequently shifted back to his anger.

"He was such an out-of-control perfectionist that he became irrational," MacDonald recalls.

As rush-hour traffic crept into the city, Doug screamed at a mailman who wasn't doing his work with the appropriate vigor. He began a monologue about how to fix what was wrong with New York City. He seemed intent on confronting anyone who got in his way. MacDonald believed he was acting like a Bill Murray character that might just go off on you at any moment.

The pair made their way to 635 Madison, where Doug gained entrance, went up to the old radio offices, and tore a sign off the door. He explained all the ways in which the current administration was fucking up his magazine.

After walking for several hours, they arrived at Dangerfield's, which—though dirty and dingy by day—had been selected as the site for the press conference. Chase, Ramis, Doyle-Murray, and several others were seated on a dais. A publicist welcomed the group and the press took their seats among a smattering of fans the studio had recruited for the event. Harry and Stephanie Kenney were also in the audience.

The PR man opened by asking the audience if they'd enjoyed the film at the previous evening's premiere. "Wasn't it great?" Then he added kiddingly, "And who thought it sucked?"

From the back of the room, Doug burst into applause, "Yeah, it sucked!" He was taking over. "Didn't everyone think it was terrible?"

Nervously, the publicist said, "He's joking!"

Everyone began looking around the room. Doug's parents quickly got up from their seats. Stephanie gave her son a hug and Harry put his arm around Doug's shoulder. Together they guided him from the room.

Off to the side, someone suggested to Chase that Doug needed to go away and dry out for a while. Chase decided that he'd make that happen.

* * *

Doug told Walker that he wouldn't be traveling with her to New-foundland, where she was making a film. Rather, he and Chase were going to attend Vic Braden's tennis camp in Southern California and then possibly head for a vacation in Hawaii, where he was going to get off cocaine. Angered by the news, Walker doubted the transformation would occur.

For two weeks, Doug and Chase wore their tennis whites and learned the topspin approach to the game, playing up to eight hours a day and throwing themselves into the sport of Doug's youth. They shared a room and enjoyed each other's company immensely, with Chase, many believe, filling the role of the older brother who hadn't died, loving Doug as much as he needed.

In the morning, Doug would frequently look in the mirror and say, "Doug Kenney, you're the handsomest man in comedy." When Chase peered over his shoulder, Doug would amend the statement, "The second handsomest man in comedy."

"We were just like two gay guys," Chase says. "We had so much fun together. I emulated him and he emulated me."

But for all of the fun, Chase could see that Doug was becoming morosely cynical. Knowing that Doug wanted to become famous and score another hit movie, Chase believed that the desire for stardom combined with what renown he'd already achieved were causing it.

"For all people who become famous, there's something very depressing and frightening about it," Chase says. "You don't know what the hell it is. It's another world. Treating this kind of depressive part of you that says I don't deserve this. I'm not this good. I'll be found out some day."

At the end of tennis camp, after sequestering themselves from news about *Caddyshack*, the pair headed to Maui where they would spend a month relaxing and trying as best they could to free themselves from cocaine.

Chase and Doug checked into the Maui Hyatt Regency and took rooms across the hall from each other on the eighth floor. One evening, Chase called across the hall to Doug, asking him to come to his room. Then Chase screamed.

Finding the door open, Doug could only see a pair of empty cowboy boots positioned on an open balcony that overlooked the pool. Chase was hiding, playing a practical joke, wanting his friend to believe he'd jumped.

The pair spent their time on the island playing tennis, visiting the town of Lahaina, sailing, and going out to bars where Chase attracted women and onlookers who were shocked to find themselves in the presence of a movie star. Though they'd come to dry out, the effort didn't last long. Briefly curtailing their intake somewhat, they soon sent to the mainland for cocaine, which arrived, according to various sources, in the center of tennis balls and other packages.

Alan Greisman visited the pair and took long walks with Doug on the beach, where his partner talked endlessly about *Caddyshack*. Greisman got the distinct impression that Doug would have liked to stay away from Hollywood forever. Fisher, who was staying on Martha's Vineyard with Ivers and Mayer, called regularly with the film's daily grosses, hoping to cheer Doug up with news that the film wasn't doing badly. But nothing seemed to work.

After nearly a month, Walker arrived for a visit and Chase went back to Los Angeles. Always physically strong and able to tolerate colossal amounts of drugs and alcohol, Chase seemed no worse for wear. He was like a horse. Doug, by contrast, looked thin and exhausted, his sensitivity rising to the surface under the weight of his drug abuse. What Chase could handle, it seemed, Doug could not.

Anticipating Walker's arrival, Doug sent a limo, flowers, and champagne to greet her at the airport. Both were intent on having fun and wiping out the tension over his drug use and lifestyle.

"Whatever had happened in the past didn't matter," Walker said. "We felt we had arrived at a certain place."

The pair snorkeled, played in the pool, and walked on the beach. All the while they made plans for the future, including their new house in L.A.

Despite their best efforts, the reunion was not what they'd hoped. Whenever there was a sense of discomfort, Doug would start singing, "Having Fun Now!" to the theme from *Rocky*. Committed to each other and knowing it was nothing more than a vacation that failed to meet expectations, the pair agreed that Walker would go back to California, and leave Doug for a few days to have some alone time and scout locations for potential film projects. It was late August.

A few days after Kathryn left, she received a phone call from Doug, who sounded happy and told her that he'd be home in time for a Labor Day party they'd been planning. Shortly afterward, Doug called Chase, who thought his friend sounded more depressed and lonely than he'd ever heard him.

Doug told Chase that he'd fought with Walker, which was not out of the ordinary in their sometimes explosive relationship. Chase didn't take this to be a sign that the relationship was troubled. But the fight, combined with Chase's departure and the perceived failure of *Caddyshack*, seemed to be dragging Doug down.

"I just cheered him up a bit," Chase says. "I felt that some of it was due to his desire—and rightfully so—to be thought of as one of the great comedy writers and as an innovator, and wanting to become famous."

* * *

"We just kind of thought, 'Well, he's not ready to come back and deal with moving in with Kathryn and all of these things,'" Fisher says of herself, Ivers, and Mayer. "We heard he was missing and figured or hoped that he'd pulled another disappearing act. He'd already disappeared into our lives. We weren't even worried at first. Then it went on longer and it was scary."

When it became clear that Doug was missing, Walker was at home on Outpost. A large crowd of friends gathered, almost having a Kenney-style party as they waited for news.

* * *

Doug left Maui on August 26 and traveled to Kauai, where he checked into the Coco Palms Hotel that evening. Though reports show he occupied the room the night of the 26th, he did not return after the following evening.

Police discovered Doug's car parked at Hanapepe lookout and connected it to a missing person's report. A police and fire rescue team was dispatched to Hanapepe, where they discovered Doug's body wedged between some boulders at the base of the lookout thirty feet beneath a cliff. He was wearing a T-shirt and cutoff jeans. A pair of slippers and his eyeglasses were discovered at the top of the cliff. Officials looking into the death reasoned that Doug had removed his slippers to get better footing on the loose ground.

Over the telephone, Greisman identified Doug's body for police by describing how his eyeglasses folded outward.

"Except for the fact that he fell off the cliff, the rest is not clear," said Kauai Police captain Calvin Fujita. "Whether he was walking or looking over the rim is not clear."

The Kauai police fixed Doug's date of death as August 29, 1980, ruled it accidental, and closed the case six days later.

* * *

Greisman called Walker and Chase to tell them Doug was dead. The three set out for Kauai, with Doug's attorney, Joe Shapiro, to recover his body. They bought leis at a gift shop and took them to Hanapepe. As they tossed the flowers over the cliff, a rainbow appeared.

* * *

According to the evidence police could find, Douglas Clark Francis Kenney visited Hanapepe lookout early in the evening on August 28 or 29. Both days were lovely, with clear skies, cool ocean breezes, and moderate but warm temperatures. After parking his Jeep, he walked past a sign that clearly warned of danger ahead and a sheer drop. Either not noticing it—or deciding to take a risk—Doug walked past, through a small field loaded with brambles and toward the lookout.

The canyon below the lookout is not the type of place where one would necessarily choose to commit suicide. It looks like a Disney version of the Grand Canyon, one hundred feet down instead of a mile. The drop itself is not as sheer as advertised—dangerous, but not particularly precipitous, with landing places at thirty and fifty feet.

Whatever the case, on that beautiful Hawaiian day, Doug either fell or jumped to his death. Some theorize that he walked to the cliff's edge to better see the sunset, and the ground gave way. Had he viewed the rim of the overhang from below, Doug would have seen that it was comprised of loose brush and roots only two feet thick, but its instability was undetectable from above; these facts point to the event being an accident.

At *National Lampoon*, people joked that Doug had fallen while looking for a place to jump. Anne Beatts believes it was simply a case of the other shoe dropping, the first being Doug's note to Henry explaining his summer 1971 disappearance. This much is known: immediately before he died, Doug Kenney was addicted to cocaine, prone to strange behavior, and despondent over life in Hollywood and his most recent film. Therefore, according to some, it must have been a suicide.

Other rumors were circling that expatriate drug runners and locals often kidnapped wealthy tourists who were looking for drugs (a fitting description of Doug) and dumped their bodies in the canyon.

* * *

Investigators found several items in Doug's hotel room. A notebook contained random musings, some of which were humorous remarks about various friends, including one for Fisher that depicts a Star of David and a question mark, summarizing her confusion over the religion of her parents. Upon seeing Fisher, Doug frequently would scream, "Unchain the Jewess! She has found favor in the eyes of Caesar!"

Another note read, "These are some of the happiest days I've ever ignored." On the bathroom mirror, written in soap, were the words, "I love you."

For many, these two notes were the smoking gun.

Chase believes that the bathroom note was either for him or Walker, both of whom had discussed returning to Hawaii to visit Doug.

"We'd done that often—written each other messages. I don't know," Chase says, "but we did love each other."

Or perhaps, the "handsomest man in comedy" simply wrote it to himself as a reminder.

* * *

"All of us at the Lampoon had a habit of writing down any good line or concept that came to us," P. J. O'Rourke says, in explanation of the first note. "No matter how drunk or stoned or in the middle of making love. Henry had a clipboard of ideas, concepts, and lines that he crossed off when they were used."

* * *

"I still can't come up with a rational explanation for Doug's death," Greisman says. "The truth is that he could walk into my office tomorrow afternoon and it wouldn't surprise me a bit."

* * *

Rob Hoffman called the *National Lampoon* offices and told Julian Weber that Doug was dead. Weber located O'Rourke at a Manhattan restaurant where he was having dinner with friends. It was O'Rourke's job to tell Henry.

That evening, Henry was hosting a dinner party for several friends, including Chris Cerf. The phone rang during dinner. Henry left the dining room for a moment and returned. The party continued.

After the rest of his guests left, Henry pulled Cerf aside. "Doug died last night," he told him.

"I don't know anybody else who could have sat through that dinner," Cerf says. "It took him a day or two to react."

***

In Los Angeles, Michael Simmons was in his father's office when the news of Doug's death came over the telephone. Matty turned white as a sheet and did something that his son hadn't seen since the death of his father's brother. He cried.

***

Doug Kenney was not buried in Chagrin Falls, Ohio; Cambridge, Massachusetts; New York City; Los Angeles; or Hawaii. Instead, on September 8, 1980, he was laid to rest in Newtown, Connecticut, near the home that he'd purchased for his parents. It was not, in the words of O'Rourke, "one of those jolly funerals where everyone gets laid."

Instead, it was "a happening," according to Vern Weber, the Gilmour athletic director. Among the four hundred attendees were Bill Murray, Chevy Chase, Brian Doyle-Murray, Harold Ramis, Henry Beard, Michael O'Donoghue, singer Joni Mitchell, and Michael O'Keefe. Harry and Stephanie seemed overwhelmed with grief and surprised at the importance and popularity of their middle child.

The wake was a tense affair. Doug had been the first of their generation to die and was the linchpin for several groups in attendance. His Harvard friends appeared to keep to themselves. Some thought that they were looking down on the movie people, whom they believed had a hand in Doug's death. Lampoon writers and editors who hadn't spoken to one another in years were now in the same sad, uncomfortable room. Kelly thought it was not unlike the World War I Christmas truce.

At the buffet, O'Keefe stood eating shrimp and taking in the scene. Ramis approached, intent on breaking the tension. "How can you eat shrimp at a time like this?"

No one knew how to cope with the loss. Despite the jokes around the office that Doug had "fallen while looking for a place to jump," no one was laughing. O'Rourke was devastated and in shock.

O'Donoghue had driven to the event with Boaty Boatwright, a well-known talent agent who was friends with Doug and had dined with him at Manhattan's notorious club Plato's Retreat in the late 1970s. There, the pair laughed as naked men frolicked in a grotto-like pool and ate spareribs in the buff. *Saturday Night Live*'s Tom Davis and Emily Prager drove to Connecticut with O'Donoghue, arriving in a pink Chevy convertible with the top down. Boatwright was implored by The Presence to smoke her first joint in Doug's memory.

In addition to Prager, the other women from Doug's life were there: Judith Bruce, Alex Garcia-Mata, and, of course, Kathryn Walker. All were crushed, with Walker understandably barely able to function. Each was treated on some level as if they were the widow. With the exception of Alex, all had been witness either directly or via phone to Doug's unhappiness in Hollywood and his understanding that he had a problem with cocaine.

There was a requiem Mass at St. Rose Church in Newtown, where Bill Murray presented flowers to the Kenneys and was one of the few who knew the catechism by heart. Chris Hart, Chevy Chase, Mark Stumpf, Tim Mayer, Brian Doyle-Murray, Peter Ivers, and Harold Ramis acted as pallbearers. As they carried the casket from the church, Mayer motioned to Henry and asked him to help walk Doug to the hearse.

As the crowd left the church to head to the cemetery, Stephanie Kenney stayed behind for a moment, kneeling behind the casket. "I just want a moment alone with my son," she told one of Doug's friends. Earlier, at the funeral home, a devastated Harry walked the hallways nervously, frequently putting on his glasses to read and reread the messages on the huge number of floral arrangements. Asked where he was going after the funeral, Harry said, "I'm going home. I'm going to drink two fingers of good scotch and then I'm going to get in bed with my wife." In the space of eleven years, he and Stephanie had lost two of their three children.

Standing on a hillside overlooking a duck pond, Chase, Mayer, and Ivers eulogized their friend. Chase tried to be funny, but spoke through tears. Mayer spoke of Doug's friendship and achievements, ending with "Good show, Doug." Ivers took off his blazer and tied it around his waist before playing "Beautiful Dreamer" on his harmonica. Falling to his knees, he screamed.

After the funeral, O'Keefe got his guitar and went by himself to Doug's graveside where he sang to his friend.

Douglas Clark Francis Kenney left the entirety of his multimillion-dollar estate to his parents.

* * *

"I realized after leaving what a shitball editor I was," O'Rourke says. "People skills weren't in huge supply."

Shortly after Doug's funeral, O'Rourke gave notice at *National Lampoon*, and turned the magazine over to Sussman. Realizing that the magazine had been his only real employer and his home for more than ten years, he believed that life was too short to continue fighting the uphill battle facing the magazine he so loved.

More important, however, he came to realize that one of the reasons why he loved *National Lampoon* was that he had always associated it with a person whom he loved.

"I really loved Doug. But it was more than that. It's hard to frame this without retreating into cornball stuff, but there was a vitality there," O'Rourke says. "The idea of it stopping was like spring not coming."

* * *

His friends expected Doug Kenney to write the story of their generation. He never did so explicitly. But with his work at *National Lampoon* and in Hollywood, he chronicled the ethos of their lives, their better intentions, their shared sensibilities, and the world in which they grew up. In dying young, he, and so many others, mirrored the sad fallout of the largest generation in U.S. history, born to the group that defeated Hitler and won world peace—with both generations weaving together to form the essential fabric of the American Century. Though incomplete, Doug's work and the way he lived did tell that story, through a lens that was all his own.

The story he told was uncertain, capable of holding two opposing thoughts within each sentence. In that way, he was able to describe the confusion of growing up in what seemed the best of times, while also realizing that they might not be so great after all. But, he thought, they were the only times they would have.

Little is certain about Doug Kenney's death. Like the inner workings of his brain, the content of his humor, and the way he lived—it is shot through with ambivalence. Perhaps the best explanation is this: it was an accident that was no accident. Often reckless and given to taking chances, a stoned Doug took a risk, walking past danger signs into oblivion. He didn't want to die, but put himself in a position to do so. It seems the most fitting conclusion, though an uncertain one.

No matter the circumstances of his death or indicators that it was possibly a suicide, Doug Kenney was an optimist by nature. He was a man with plans for the future, possibly including the home, life, and family he longed for; film projects that might fulfill his creative soul; and a gentle but strong spirit that helped him rise from perceived failure and despondence—and back and forth from euphoria and brilliance—on a daily basis, as his mind took him to places both horrific and wonderful. There was, and always had been, too much hope inside of Doug Kenney for him to give up on the world he so loved to observe.

But he wouldn't have the chance to live out those hopes and dreams.

In the end, nearly everyone was left with the question "who was Doug Kenney?" The answer is not simple. He was Donleavy's hedonistic Sebastian Dangerfield; J. M. Barrie and Peter Pan; Stork, Howard Lewis Havermeyer, Danny Noonan, and Ty Webb; Doris Day, a Coke, and a hamburger; an idealist and a fallen Catholic; D. B. and Holden Caulfield; an optimist and a cynic; Faulkner's gentle, tortured, and poetic Quentin Compson; the all-American boy and the consummate nerd; Fitzgerald's midwestern observer Nick Carraway and the mysterious social climber Jay Gatsby; a hippie and a preppy; an insider and an outsider; a born aristocrat and a kid from the wrong side of the tracks, burdened by a desire to belong and a distrust of the very same; and a mature genius with the soul and outlook of a brilliant ten-year-old boy. He knew himself all too well, and as a result realized that he knew himself not at all. Mostly, however, he was a man who enjoyed the American experience of 1946 to 1980 like nobody's business, and wrote about it in a way that no one had before or has since.

He was, as Michael O'Donoghue said, "A big American jerk—in the best sense of the word."

Epilogue

66 We seem to be going through a period of nostalgia, and everyone seems to think yesterday was better than today. I don't think it
was, and I would advise you not to wait ten years before admitting
today was great. If you're hung up on nostalgia, pretend today is
yesterday and just go out and have one hell of a time. 99

—*Art Buchwald*

In 1983, *National Lampoon* produced John Hughes's scripted
Vacation, which was a gigantic box office success. By 1985, however, *National Lampoon* circulation dropped to 450,000, with the
company posting losses of $750,000. In December 1986, the maga-
zine's readership dropped again, this time to 300,000.

Over the next several years, *National Lampoon* produced films
and fended off hostile takeover attempts, including one from Tim
"Otter" Matheson of *Animal House* (who succeeded in taking
over the magazine for a time). *National Lampoon* ceased publication in 1994 and put out its last issue in 1998 while owned by J2
Communications.

In the late 1990s, Dan Laikin, an Indianapolis-based investor who made a considerable fortune in the Internet boom, began acquiring *National Lampoon* stock. After attempting to work with J2 at reenergizing the brand, which was subsisting solely on licensing agreements, he became frustrated by his efforts and acquired more stock—and engineered a hostile takeover in 2002.

Since that time, Laikin has reenvisioned *National Lampoon* as a multimedia comedy and college lifestyle enterprise—trading on its brand name in the comedy world. Today, *National Lampoon* is an integrated multimedia company active in feature films, book publishing, Internet humor, and live campus comedy events. The company owns a television network that reaches over six hundred campuses, produces both home video and motion pictures, and has reissued both the *National Lampoon 1964 High School Yearbook Parody* and the *National Lampoon Sunday Newspaper Parody*.

The new *National Lampoon* is currently developing several feature films, including *Totally Baked* and *Pledge This!*, starring Paris Hilton.

∗ ∗ ∗

After briefly and unhappily flirting with Hollywood screenwriting, **Henry Beard** embarked on a career writing straightforward parody. He is the bestselling author of such humor books as: *Sailing, Golfing, O. J.'s Legal Pad, Latin for All Occasions, Latin for Cats, Zen for Cats, French for Cats,* and *The Official Exceptions to the Rules of Golf.*

Still living with Gwynneth Cravens, Beard reportedly resides in the Hamptons, New York City, and California, where, it's said, he plays golf almost every day—but never keeps score.

He declined to be interviewed for this book.

∗ ∗ ∗

Michael O'Donoghue wrote and appeared in the first sketch ever aired on *Saturday Night Live*, in which he played a speech therapist who instructs John Belushi to say "I would like to feed your finger-tips to the wolverines. We are out of badgers."

At *Saturday Night Live*, O'Donoghue was responsible for many memorable sketches, including "Mr. Mike's Least Loved Bedtime Tales" and "The Little Engine That Died." In one sketch, O'Donoghue tells Garrett Morris's Uncle Remus, "There's no moral, Uncle Remus, just random acts of meaningless violence."

O'Donoghue won Emmys for the show in 1977 and 1978, then wrote and starred in the cult classic *Mr. Mike's Mondo Video* in 1979. He left *Saturday Night Live* but returned again in 1981 for a brief stint, during which he reportedly told actress Mary Gross that she ought to be selling shoes.

O'Donoghue also appeared in Woody Allen's film *Manhattan* and cowrote the screenplay for the Bill Murray Christmas film *Scrooged*.

In fall 1994, O'Donoghue awoke one morning and believed he was suffering from one of his frequent migraines. After taking some medication, he got into bed with his wife, Cheryl Hardwicke, and went back to sleep. Waking again, he screamed, "Oh my God!" Hardwicke says that O'Donoghue's eyes had turned red and "bolts of lightning" were visible behind his eyeballs.

Rushed to the hospital, O'Donoghue died that day of a cerebral hemorrhage.

For his wake, Hardwicke decorated their Manhattan apartment with CAT scans of O'Donoghue's damaged brain.

"It's very easy to make people laugh," O'Donoghue told one friend. "That's not the point. It's very difficult to make people think. Art is the cake. Comedy is the frosting. The trick is to get them to eat the cake."

O'Donoghue's story is chronicled in Dennis Perrin's book *Mr. Mike: The Life and Work of the Man Who Made Comedy Dangerous*.

* * *

After leaving *National Lampoon*, **P. J. O'Rourke** became the foremost conservative humorist in America. His 1987 book, *Repub-

lican Party Reptile, was a bestseller, espousing a Libertarian view of the world that mixed some of Doug's nostalgia for the days of Ike with a firm belief in the value of sex, drugs, fast cars, and weaponry. One of the most quoted humorists of the past twenty years, O'Rourke's essential sensibility is summed up in the following comment: "Personally, I believe a rocking hammock, a good cigar, and a tall gin-and-tonic is the best way to save the planet."

In the late 1980s, former *National Lampoon* writer **Chris Cluess** was on vacation in Hawaii. Sitting in a deck chair by the pool and reading one of O'Rourke's books, he heard a familiar voice behind him.

"Doesn't it piss you off that he's so fucking funny?"

It was his former colleague **Jeff Greenfield**.

O'Rourke has contributed to *Playboy*, *Rolling Stone* (where he served as international affairs correspondent), *Atlantic Monthly*, *Car and Driver*, and several other national publications. The author of *Bachelor Home Companion*, *Holidays in Hell*, *Modern Manners*, *Parliament of Whores*, *Give War a Chance*, *Eat the Rich*, and several other books, he is currently the H. L. Mencken Research Fellow at the Cato Institute and a regular on National Public Radio's game show, "Wait Wait . . . Don't Tell Me!"

Married for the second time, he has three young children and resides in Washington, D.C., and New Hampshire.

* * *

During the 1980s, **Matty Simmons** produced the films *Two Reelers*, *Class Reunion*, *Vacation*, *European Vacation*, *Class of '86*, and *Christmas Vacation*. After losing control of *National Lampoon*, he stayed in Hollywood and continued to work in the film industry, going on to produce *Vegas Vacation* and *Christmas Vacation 2*.

Remarried with a young daughter, he lives in Beverly Hills and works for Dan Laikin's *National Lampoon*, writing, developing, and producing film projects, while serving as director of *National Lampoon* Classics.

* * *

After working on the bestselling parody *Not the New York Times*, **Tony Hendra** appeared in several films, including *This Is Spïnal Tap*, in which he portrayed the band's unctuous, cricket-bat wielding manager, Ian Faith. He is also the author of *Going Too Far*, which is a history of baby-boom humor.

In 2004, Hendra wrote the confessional memoir *Father Joe: The Man Who Saved My Soul*, which received glowing reviews, but became the subject of controversy after Jessica Hendra, one of two daughters from his first marriage, contacted the *New York Times* and alleged that her father had molested her as a child.

Married for the second time, Tony Hendra lives in New York City with his wife and children.

* * *

Sean Kelly returned to *National Lampoon* for a stint in the mid-1980s. He has worked for *Saturday Night Live*, the BBC, and the children's shows *Shining Time Station* and *Between the Lions*. He also wrote and cowrote several books, including: *Not the Bible* (with Hendra), *The Book of Sequels* (with Henry Beard, Sarah Durkee, and Chris Cerf), *Boom Baby Moon*, *Saints Preserve Us!* and *How to Be Irish (Even If You Already Are)*.

Married for the third time and the father of six children, Kelly lives in Brooklyn with his wife and son.

* * *

Brian McConnachie is the only writer who has worked for comedy's holy trinity of the 1970s and '80s—*National Lampoon*, *Saturday Night Live*, and *SCTV*. He has written and produced comedy pieces for National Public Radio and appeared in the films *Strange Brew*, *Quick Change*, *Sleepless in Seattle*, and *Six Degrees of Separation*, as well as in Woody Allen's *Husbands and Wives*, *Bullets over Broadway*, *Deconstructing Harry*, *Celebrity*, *Small Time Crooks*, and *The Curse of the Jade Scorpion*.

McConnachie lives with his wife in a farmhouse in Garrison, New York. On the wall of his kitchen is a framed royalty check for one cent, drawn on a joint account for two major studios that produced one of those films.

* * *

At *Saturday Night Live*, **Anne Beatts** was responsible for the creation of two of Bill Murray and Gilda Radner's most memorable characters—the noogie-giving Todd and his erstwhile girlfriend, the nerdy Lisa Loopner.

In the 1980s, Beatts was creator and producer of the critically acclaimed high school sitcom *Square Pegs*, which starred Sarah Jessica Parker and was based on Beatts's experiences as a smart nerdy girl at a typical American high school. Despite a strong cult following, the show lasted only one season and was victimized by low ratings, egos, network infighting, and allegations of drug abuse.

Beatts went on to co-executive produce the NBC series *A Different World* and contributed to several other television shows. In addition to several books, she is the cocreator of the Tony-nominated Broadway musical *Leader of the Pack*.

Beatts lives in Los Angeles, where she teaches comedy writing at USC and improv at various venues.

University of Connecticut professor, author, and women's comedy expert Regina Barreca calls Beatts the "Jane Austen of women's humor."

* * *

Shortly after Doug Kenney's death, **Kathryn Walker** appeared in John Belushi and Dan Aykroyd's dark comedy *Neighbors*. Since that time she has continued to work in film and on stage, most recently narrating the PBS series *Colonial House*. Married from 1985 to 1995 to musician James Taylor, Walker is now divorced and lives in Santa Fe, New Mexico, New York City, and Connecticut.

* * *

A well-known figure on the Los Angeles underground music scene, **Peter Ivers** recorded several critically acclaimed albums and hosted a popular music show on local television. In 1983, he was bludgeoned to death in his Los Angeles apartment. Though the crime was never solved, many believed that a member of L.A.'s punk music underground was the culprit.

Tim Mayer wrote and directed several plays, including *My One and Only*, which ran on Broadway in 1983. Later collaborating on musical projects with Donald Fagan (of Steely Dan) and Peter Wolf (of J. Geils), he was diagnosed with liver cancer in 1987. He died on April 6, 1988, at his home in New York.

"All of them had started off as the brash young men—and the breakthrough new artist—and were all much more comfortable with that role than hitting your thirties and settling down. And each one wrestled with that in their own way," Fisher says of Ivers, Doug, and Mayer. "And [they] didn't find the language or terminology for themselves for what would be a graceful way to enter the next stage of their lives. In some ways—they were all flirting with being forever young."

* * *

In the immediate aftermath of his death and long thereafter, numerous subjects interviewed for this book told stories of being visited by Doug Kenney in their dreams. Harold Ramis recalled how a smiling Doug comes to him dressed in white but never says where he is. Gina Bourisseau, who dated Doug in Chagrin Falls, says that after reading about Doug's death, he appeared in her dreams, explaining that her son, who was having a difficult time, would be OK and would pursue an artistic career. He was and he did.

More than twenty years after Doug's death, Chevy Chase's wife asked him to accompany her on a visit to a psychic medium who worked from her small home in New York State. Reluctantly, Chase went along. A nonbeliever in such phenomena, he sat by as his wife tried to make contact with a deceased relative. Achieving no results, the woman asked Chase if there was anyone he wanted to contact. Chase mentioned that he had a deceased friend he often thought about.

"He's here," the psychic said, with her leg shaking under the table. She explained how the visitor said that he'd left his glasses on the cliff and that his death was both stupid and embarrassing. Chase had provided her with no information. It was clear that she didn't know, nor could she have known, anything about Doug and his death.

"He's very funny, isn't he?" she said.

Bibliography

Newspaper & Magazine Articles

1966
"Foftly, Foftly, Blowf the Gale." *Time*, November 11, 1966, p. 85.

1970
Casey, Phil. "National Lampoon Is on the Way." *Washington Post*, March 12, 1970, p. C7.

Kneeland, Douglas E. "Campuses Quiet but Not Content." *New York Times*, December 20, 1970, p. 1, 37.

"National Humor Magazine Makes Debut Tomorrow." *New York Times*, March 18, 1970.

"Postgraduate Humor." *Newsweek*, March 23, 1970.

1972
Bess, Donovan. "Lampooning America." *San Francisco Chronicle*, March 6, 1972, p. 4.

Donnelley, Tom. "Michael O'Donoghue and Other Stories." *Washington Post*, March 12, 1972, p. C1.

Frial, Frank J. "7 Dynamite Sticks Bring Bomb Squad to Magazine Office." *New York Times,* April 7, 1972.

Kennedy, Mopsy Strange. "Juvenile, Puerile, Sophomoric, Jejuene, Nutty and Funny." *New York Times Sunday Magazine*, December 10, 1972.

Pace, Eric. "New Special Interest Magazines Flourish." *New York Times*, December 17, 1972.

"Lampoon Revue Set for Village Gate." *New York Times*, December 21, 1972.

"Not So Funny." *Washington Post*, April 9, 1972, p. A6.

1973

Alterman, Lorraine. "Lemmings Is No Giggle." *New York Times*, September 9, 1973, p. 34, 37.

Brown, Les. "Two Radio Networks Turn to the Past." *New York Times*, October 30, 1973.

Gussow, Mel. "Lemmings Fails Early, Recovers Later." *New York Times*, January 26, 1973.

Kerr, Walter. "Less Sharp than Olsen & Johnson." *New York Times*, February 4, 1973.

Lax, Eric. "Why Do Young People Love Lemmings?" *New York Times*, May 27, 1973.

Metz, Robert. "Strong Growth but No Glamour." *New York Times*, February 16, 1973.

O'Connor, John J. "National Lampoon Takes to the Airwaves." *New York Times*, December 27, 1973.

Shenker, Israel. "Seven Long Faced Panelists at the New School Talk About 'Social Change Through Humor.'" *New York Times*, April 1, 1973.

Zito, Tom. "Oil on Troubled Waters." *Washington Post*, October 31, 1973, p. B1.

Zito, Tom. "Lending an Ear to Wacky, Zany Humor." *Washington Post*, November 17, 1973, p. C7.

"The Unkindest Cut." *Newsweek*, July 16, 1973, p. 60.

"Volkswagen Settles Suit Against National Lampoon." *New York Times*, October 30, 1973.

"Lampoon's Surrender." *Time*, November 12, 1973, p. 85.

"21st Century Says 1972 Profits Soared." *Wall Street Journal*, 1973.

1974

DeNeve, Rose. "National Lampoon: Art Directing the Humor Magazine." *Print Magazine*, July/August 1974.

Lingeman, Richard R. "This Side of Parodies." *New York Times*, February 24, 1974.

"Too Much Lampoon." *Washington Post*, April 3, 1974, p. B16.

"21st Century Says Operating Profits Rose Over 60% in 1973." *Wall Street Journal*, 1974.

1975
Business Week, "National Lampoon's Line into the Youth Market." November 3, 1975, p. 50.

Gussow, Mel. "Stage: A New Lampoon." *New York Times*, March 3, 1975.

New York Times, "Report of Rudd in Cuba Tied to Lampoon Hoax." November 22, 1975.

O'Connor, John J. "Sprightly Mix Brightens NBC's 'Saturday Night.'" *New York Times*, November 30, 1975.

Shales, Tom. "Marvelous Monsters." *Washington Post*, March 2, 1975, p. 4.

Washington Post, "1975 National Magazine Awards." April 17, 1975, p. B10.

Zito, Tom. "America's Good Days, Bad Days." *Washington Post*, September 20, 1975, p. E4.

1976
Dougherty, Phillip H. "Harvard v. National Lampoon." *New York Times*, March 9, 1976.

Englert, Brother Francis C.S.C. "Memories of Brother Ivo." *Gilmour Magazine*, Winter 1976/1977, pp. 4-7.

New York Times, "People." May 24, 1976.

Pierson, Frank. "My Battles with Barbra and Jon." *New West Magazine*, November 22, 1976, *New York*, November 15, 1976, pp. 49–60, www.barbra-archives.com/MagazineArchives/streisand_newwest_magazine.html.

Sloane, Leonard. "Lampoon Aiming at Marketers." *New York Times*, August 10, 1976.

Ward, Alex. "A Crass Chaotic Comedy Empire." *Washington Post*, February 5, 1976, p. H15.

1977
Dougherty, Phillip H. "Lampoon License Curbed." *New York Times*, March 24, 1977, p. D13.

Hiss, Tony, and Jeff Lewis. "The Mad Generation." *New York Times*, July 31, 1977, p. SM4.

McLellan, Joseph. "Laugh-a-Minute Lampoon." *Washington Post*, October 11, 1977, p. B4.

New York Times, "Blasphemy Complaint Against Magazine Denied." December 27, 1977.

1978

Ansen, David. "Gross Out." *Newsweek*, August 7, 1978.

Arnold, Gary. "Animal House: Bringing out the Beast." *Washington Post*, August 11, 1978, p. B1.

Arnold, Gary. "The Madcap World of John Landis." *Washington Post*, August 13, 1978, p. H1.

Carney, Thomas. "They Only Laughed When It Hurt," *New Times*, August 21, 1978, pp. 48–55.

Dougherty, Phillip H. "New Lampoon Parody." *New York Times*, May 9, 1978.

Maslin, Janet. "Screen: Animal House." *New York Times*, July 28, 1978, p. C7.

New York Times, "Paperbacks: New and Noteworthy." July 2, 1978, p. BR5.

New York Times, "5 New Shows Coming in '79 on ABC-TV." November 28, 1978, p. C10.

San Francisco Chronicle, "Tim Matheson: Peeling off the Labels." November 29, 1978, p. 56.

Schwartz, Tony. "The Good Humor Men." *Newsweek*, April 3, 1978, p. 70.

Schwartz, Tony. "College Humor Comes Back." *Newsweek*, October 23, 1978, pp. 88–97.

Shah, Diane K., with Ron Labrecque. "Toga! Toga! Toga!" *Newsweek*, October 2, 1978, pp. 76–77.

1979

Brown, Dennis. "Midas Touch of Lampooner." *St. Louis Post-Dispatch*, August 8, 1979.

Brown, Les. "ABC-TV Announces Fall Schedule." *New York Times*, April 24, 1979, p. C20.

———. "'Rocky' on CBS, Draws 3d Best Movie Audience." *New York Times*, February 7, 1979, p. C22.

Carter, Betsy. "The Mad Mondo of Mr. Mike." *Newsweek*, October 15, 1979, p. 118.

Dougherty, Phillip H. "Weber Is Named by 21st Century." *New York Times*, January 16, 1979, p. D15.

Graustark, Barbara. "Newsmakers." *Newsweek*, January 8, 1979, p. 45.

New York Times, "TV: Preview of ABC's Imitation of 'Animal House.'" January 18, 1979.

New York Times, "ABC-TV Tops Nielsen Ratings." January 24, 1979.

New York Times, "TV Ratings." April 11, 1979.

O'Connor, John J. "And Now, Back to the Bleak Weekly Program Scene." *New York Times*, March 11, 1979, p. D33.

Shales, Tom. "Bluto's Gone, but His Brother's Carrying On." *Washington Post*, January 18, 1979, p. B15.

Waters, Harry F., with Martin Kasindorf. "Send in the Clones." *Newsweek*, January 29, 1979, p. 85.

White, Timothy. "Is America Ready for Mr. Mike?" *Rolling Stone*, July 26, 1979.

1980

Newtown (CT) Bee. "Douglas Kenney Dies, Producer and Screenwriter." September 12, 1980.

New York Times, "Douglas Kenney, Founding Editor of National Lampoon Magazine." September 6, 1980, p. 26.

Stack, Peter. "A Happy Mogul Reviews His Empire." *San Francisco Chronicle*, February 7, 1980, p. 48.

San Francisco Chronicle, "Comedy Writer's Death an Accident." September 5, 1980, p. 50.

Washington Post, "Douglas Kenney of 'Animal House' Dies." September 5, 1980, p. B4.

1981

Anson, Robert Sam. "The Life and Death of a Comic Genius." *Esquire*, October 1981, pp. 37–46.

Boyer, Peter J. "UA's Lampoon Movie: Send in the Frowns." *Los Angeles Times*, October 26, 1981, Part VI, pp. 1, 4.

MacDougall, William L. "Movies' New Motto: Youth Will Be Served." *U.S. News & World Report*, June 15, 1981, p. 48.

———. "Corporate Earnings." *New York Times*. May 15, 1981, p. D13.

1983

Gelman, David. "Making Fun for Profit." *Newsweek*, April 25, 1983, pp. 64–70.

1985

Clarke, Gerald. "And Animal House Begat . . . Teenage Audiences Are Grossing Out on Gross-Outs." *Time*, Vol. 125 No. 15, April 15, 1985.

1986

Standish, David. "From Club Sandwich to Club Paradise." *Playboy*, July 1986, pp. 104, 126, 152–157.

1988

Blumenthal, John. "Playboy Interview: Chevy Chase." *Playboy*, June 1988, pp. 55–65, 162–165.

1990

Garry, Michael. "Can National Lampoon Be Funny Again?" *Folio*, February 1, 1990.

1991

Boyd, Robert. "Shary Flenniken Interview." *The Comics Journal*, November 1991, pp. 54–81.

1992

Heinricks, Geoff. "Pulling No Punches: Humor Magazines on Death Row." *Eye Weekly*, April 9, 1992, www.eye.net/issue/issue_4.9.92/news/med0409.htm.

Lambert, Craig. "Comic Sutra." *Harvard Magazine*, July/August 1992, pp. 24–40.

Preven, Joshua S. "The History of Humor at Harvard." *Harvard Magazine*, July/August 1992, p. 22.

1993

Lambert, Craig. "The Life of the Party." *Harvard Magazine*, September/ October 1993, pp. 36–45.

1994

Appelo, Tim. "John Huge." *Entertainment Weekly*, December 2, 1994.

1995

Sales, Nancy Jo. "The Original Smart-Alecky White Guy." *New York Magazine*, November 27, 1995, pp. 72–75.

1996

Rosenthal, Phil. "This Frat Reunion More than Chug-a-Lug Memories." *Los Angeles Daily News*, March 17, 1996.

2000

Heineman, Zachary, and Eliot J. Hodges. "Harvard Is Funny." *The Harvard Crimson*, February 10, 2000.

Stein, Ben. "I Didn't Even Know There Was a Dawson." *EOnline*, February 9, 2000, www.eonline.com/Gossip/Morton/Archive/2000/000209 .html.

2002

Hendra, Tony. "Morning in America." *Harper's*, June 2002, pp. 59–65.

2003

Cooke, Jon B. "The Comics of National Lampoon." *Comic Book Artist*, February 2003, Issue No. 24.

Hemel, Daniel J. "Legendary Humorist, Poonster Dies at 76." *The Harvard Crimson*, September 29, 2003, www.thecrimson.com/article .aspx?ref=349023.

Henderson, Evan. "Fraternity Ward: Old School, the Latest Comedy Spawned by *Animal House*." *Los Angeles Daily News*, February 18, 2003.

Mitchell, Elvis. "Revisiting Faber College (Toga, Toga, Toga!)." *New York Times*, August 25, 2003, Section E, p. 1.

Murray, Noel. "P. J. O'Rourke Interview." *Onion A.V. Club*, September 2, 2003, www.avclub.com/content/node/24198.

Pearson, Mike. "Delta: The House That Landis Built." *Rocky Mountain News*, August 23, 2003.

Rosenwald, Michael. "The Last Laugh." *Boston Globe Magazine*, February 21, 2003, http://graphics.boston.com:80/globe/magazine/3-11/featurestory1.shtml.

Thomas, George M., and R. D. Heldenfels. "Blame It on Animal House: 25 Years Ago It Forever Changed Comedy." *Knight Ridder/Tribune News Service*, August 25, 2003.

2004

Friend, Tad. "Comedy First: How Harold Ramis Changed Hollywood." *The New Yorker*, April 19 & 26, 2004, pp. 164–173.

Kleinfeld, N. R. "Daughter Says Father's Confessional Book Didn't Confess His Molestation of Her." *New York Times*, July 1, 2004.

Meyers, Kate. "King of Comedy: The Secret Life and Death of the Man Behind Golf's Greatest Movie." *Golf Digest*, May 2004, http://golfdigest.com/features/index.ssf?/features/gd200405kennedy.html.

2005

Tapper, Jake. "Go Ahead, Shoot the Dog." *New York Times*, July 3, 2005, Section 2, p. 1.

Books

Underground Comix

Rosenkranz, Patrick. *The Underground Commix Revolution—1963–1975*. Seattle: Fantagraphics Books, 2003.

Lampoon Personalities and General

Belushi, Judith Jacklin. *Samurai Widow*. New York: Caroll and Graf, 1991.

Hendra, Tony. *Father Joe: The Man Who Saved My Soul*. New York: Random House, 2004.

James, Darius. *That's Blaxploitatin: Roots of the Badassss 'Tude*. New York: St. Martin's, 1995.

Krassner, Paul. *Confessions of a Raving, Unconfined Nut: Misadventures in the Counter-Culture*. New York: Simon and Schuster, 1993.

McCall, Bruce. *Thin Ice: Coming of Age in Canada*. New York: Random House, 1998.

Murray, Bill (with George Peper). *Cinderella Story: My Life in Golf*. New York: Doubleday, 1999.

Schmidt, Paul (editor). *Running from America: The Poems and Plays of Timothy Mayer*. Santa Ana, CA: Seven Locks Press, 1992.

Trow, George W. S. *Within the Context of No Context*. New York: Little Brown, 1981.

Woodward, Bob. *Wired: The Short Life and Fast Times of John Belushi*. New York: Simon and Schuster, 1985.

National Lampoon

Hendra, Tony. *Going Too Far*. New York: Doubleday, 1987.

Perrin, Dennis. *Mr. Mike: The Life and Work of Michael O'Donoghue—The Man Who Made Comedy Dangerous*. New York: Avon Books, 1998.

Simmons, Matty. *If You Don't Buy This Book We'll Kill This Dog: Life, Laughs, Love and Death at National Lampoon*. Fort Lee, NJ: Barricade Books, 1994.

American Humor, Humorists and Humor Magazines

Altman, Billy. *Laughter's Gentle Soul: The Life of Robert Benchley*. New York: W.W. Norton, 1997.

Boskin, Joseph (editor). *The Humor Prism in 20th Century America*. Detroit: Wayne State University Press, 1997.

Dudden, Arthur Power (editor). *American Humor*. New York: Oxford University Press, 1987.

Gehring, Wes D. *"Mr. B." or Comforting Thoughts About the Bison: A Critical Biography of Robert Benchley*. Westport, CT: Greenwood Press, 1992.

Nachman, Gerald. *Seriously Funny: The Rebel Comedians of the 1950s and 1960s*. New York: Pantheon, 2003.

Nolan, Michael (editor). *American Humor*. San Diego: Greenhaven Press, 2001.

Reidelbach, Maria. *Completely Mad: A History of the Comic Book and Magazine*. New York: MJF Books, 1997.

Sloane, David E. E. (editor). *New Directions in American Humor.* Tuscaloosa, AL: University of Alabama Press, 1998.

Walker, Nancy (editor). *What's So Funny? Humor in American Culture.* Lanham, MD: SR Books, 1998.

Yaross Lee, Judith. *Defining New Yorker Humor.* Oxford, MS: University of Mississippi Press, 2000.

American Magazines

Abrahamson, David. *Magazine-Made America: The Cultural Transformation of the Postwar Periodical.* Cresskill, NJ: Hampton Press, 1996.

Peck, Abe. *Uncovering the 1960s: The Life and Times of the Underground Press.* New York: Pantheon, 1985.

The Baby Boom, Hippies, and Postwar America

Braunstein, Peter, and Michael William Boyle (editors). *Imagine Nation: The American Counterculture Revolution of the 1960s and 70s.* New York: Routledge, 2002.

Gitlin, Todd. *The Sixties: Years of Hope, Days of Rage.* New York: Bantam, 1987.

Halberstam, David. *The Fifties.* New York: Ballantine, 1994.

Marling, Karal Ann. *As Seen On TV—The Visual Culture of Everyday Life in the 1950s.* Cambridge, MA: Harvard University Press, 1994.

Miller, Timothy. *The Hippies and American Values.* Knoxville, TN: University of Tennessee Press, 1991.

Patterson, James T. *Grand Expectations: The United States, 1945–1974.* New York: Oxford University Press, 1996

Yenne, Bill. *Going Home to the Fifties.* San Francisco: Last Gasp of San Francisco, 2002.

The 1970s

Carroll, Peter N. *It Seemed Like Nothing Happened: America in the 1970s.* Piscataway, NJ: Rutgers University Press, 1990.

Frum, David. *How We Got Here—the Seventies: The Decade That Brought You Modern Life for Better or Worse.* New York: Basic Books, 2000.

Knobler, Peter, and Greg Mitchell. *Very Seventies: A Cultural History of the 1970s From the Pages of Crawdaddy*. New York: Simon and Schuster, 1995.

Rolling Stone Staff. *The Seventies: A Tumultuous Decade Reconsidered*. New York: Little Brown, 2000.

Schulman, Bruce J. *The Seventies: The Great Shift in American Culture, Society and Politics*. Cambridge, MA: Da Capo Press, 2002.

Hollywood & Television

Dick, Bernard F. *Engulfed: The Death of Paramount Pictures and the Birth of Corporate Hollywood*. Lexington: University Press of Kentucky, 2001.

Griffin, Nancy, and Masters, Kim. *Hit & Run: How Jon Peters and Peter Guber Took Sony for a Ride in Hollywood*. New York: Simon and Schuster, 1996.

Hill, Doug, and Jeff Weingrad. *Saturday Night: A Backstage History of Saturday Night Live*. New York: William Morrow and Co., 1989.

Medavoy, Mike, with Josh Young. *You're Only as Good as Your Next One*. New York: Atria, 2002.

Shales, Tom, and James A. Miller. *Live from New York: An Uncensored History of Saturday Night Live*. New York: Little Brown, 2002.

Miscellaneous Research

October 14, 2004, report on Doug Kenney's death, prepared by Brian S. Fujiuchi, Retired Chief of Kauai, Hawaii Police.

Peterson, Molly. "Present at the Creation: Making of the College-Themed Picture *Animal House*." *National Public Radio (Morning Edition)*, July 29, 2002, www.npr.org/programs/morning/features/patc/animal-house/.

January 17, 2005—Genealogical Research Report on Daniel "Harry" Kenney and Stephanie Kenney, including:

- Connecticut Marriage certificate, Daniel Kenney and Stella Karczewksa, 1936
- Birth record, Stefania Karczewski, Chicopee, MA, 1917
- 1930 U.S. Census, Daniel and Eleanor Kenney Household

Interview List

Kenney Family
Sandra Kenney, Margaretta Kenney Landry, and Frank Kenney.

Chagrin Falls
Bill Tienvieri, Scott Lax, Tom Luckay, Ginna Bourisseau, and Jim Vittek.

Gilmour Academy
Brother Robert LaVelle, Brother Alphonso Comeau, Jerry Murphy, John
    Mulligan, S. Roger Cox, Greg Nash, John Gale, Jim Schuerger, John
    Schubert, Peter D'Oreo, and Vern Weber.

Harvard
James "Ollie" Hallowell, Judith Bruce, Chris Cerf, Lucy Fisher, Mark
    Stumpf, Betsy Bruce, Walker Lewis, Jim Rivaldo, Christopher
    Hart, Anil Khosla, John Weidman, Governor William Weld, Donna
    Cusumano, Amy Carlson, Alex Garcia-Mata, Robert Hoffman, Conn
    Nugent, Dudley Fishburn, and Mark O'Donnell.

National Lampoon
Matty Simmons, Michael Simmons, Chris Miller, Jeff Greenfield, Sean
    Kelly, Peter Bramley, Bill Skurski, Stephanie Phelan, Michael Sullivan,
    Chris Miller, Sean Kelly, Rick Meyerowitz, B. K. Taylor, Bobby Lon-
    don, Shary Flenniken, Ed Subitzky, M. K. Brown, Louise Gikow, Betsy
    Aaron, Liza Lerner, Brian McConnachie, Anne Beatts, Tony Hendra,
    Janet Maslin, Tony Hendra, Ted Mann, P. J. O'Rourke, Michael Gross,
    Len Mogel, Bill Lippe, Gerry Taylor, Peter Kleinman, Terry Catchpole,
    Michel Choquette, Judy Jacklin Belushi Pisano, Mitch Markowitz, Stu
    Kreisman, Chris Cluess, Danny Abelson, Elaine Louie, Ellis Weiner,
    David Kaestle, Arnold Roth, Howard Jurofsky, Julian Weber, George
    Agoglia, Jr., Dr. Wendy Mogel, John Boni, Ed Bluestone, Peter Kamin-
    sky, Susan Devins, George W.S. Trow, Alan Rose, Ellen Taurins, Pedar
    Ness, Wayne McLoughlin, and Bruce Moody.

National Lampoon Stage Shows, Radio Show, and Albums
Emily Prager, Sarah Durkee, Gary Goodrow, Polly Bier McCall, Janis
    Hirsch, Eleanor Reissa, Dale Anglund, Paul Jacobs, Andrew Moses,

Rodger Bumpass, Alice Playten, Chevy Chase, Paul Shaffer, Stephen Collins, Rhonda Coullet, and Joshua White.

Movies & Television & Doug Kenney in L.A.

Joan Micklin Silver, Juliet Taylor, John Landis, Thom Mount, Harold Ramis, Michael Shamberg, Alan Greisman, Jon Ptak, David Standish, Hamilton Mitchell, Don MacDonald, Trevor Albert, Rusty Lemorande, Michael O'Keefe, Mike Medavoy, William Carruth, Robert Barrere, Vic Huetschy, Peter Elbling, Henry Jaglom, Laila Nabulsi, Kathryn Walker, and Ted Swanson.

Influence of National Lampoon

Dave Barry, Michael Beirut, Jeanine Basinger, Richard Roeper, Tim Harrod, Penn Jillette, Mark McKinney, Michael Gerber, Andy Borowitz, Kurt Andersen, and Regina Barreca.

Others

Boaty Boatwright, Kate Meyers, Robert Sam Anson, Holly Wertheimer, and Dennis Perrin.

Index